ENGLAND'S INSULAR IMAGINING

The Elizabethan Erasure of Scotland

LORNA HUTSON

University of Oxford

CAMBRIDGE UNIVERSITY PRESS

CAMBRIDGE
UNIVERSITY PRESS

Shaftesbury Road, Cambridge CB2 8EA, United Kingdom

One Liberty Plaza, 20th Floor, New York, NY 10006, USA

477 Williamstown Road, Port Melbourne, VIC 3207, Australia

314–321, 3rd Floor, Plot 3, Splendor Forum, Jasola District Centre,
New Delhi – 110025, India

103 Penang Road, #05–06/07, Visioncrest Commercial, Singapore 238467

Cambridge University Press is part of Cambridge University Press & Assessment,
a department of the University of Cambridge.

We share the University's mission to contribute to society through the pursuit of
education, learning and research at the highest international levels of excellence.

www.cambridge.org
Information on this title: www.cambridge.org/9781009253574

DOI: 10.1017/9781009253598

First published 2023

Printed in the United Kingdom by CPI Group Ltd, Croydon CR0 4YY

A catalogue record for this publication is available from the British Library.

Library of Congress Cataloging-in-Publication Data
NAMES: Hutson, Lorna, author.
TITLE: England's insular imagining : the Elizabethan erasure of Scotland / Lorna Hutson.
DESCRIPTION: Cambridge, United Kingdom ; New York, NY : Cambridge University Press,
2023. | Includes bibliographical references and index.
IDENTIFIERS: LCCN 2023024082 (print) | LCCN 2023024083 (ebook) | ISBN 9781009253574
(hardback) | ISBN 9781009253604 (paperback) | ISBN 9781009253598 (ebook)
SUBJECTS: LCSH: National characteristics, English, in literature. | English literature – Early
modern, 1500–1700 – History and criticism. | National characteristics, Scottish, in literature. |
Scottish literature – To 1700 – History and criticism. | England – In literature. | Scotland – In
literature. | Great Britain – History – Tudors, 1485–1603 – Historiography. | Scotland – History –
Mary Stuart, 1542–1567 – Historiography.
CLASSIFICATION: LCC PR408.N38 H87 2023 (print) | LCC PR408.N38 (ebook) |
DDC 820.9/35841–dc23/eng/20230623
LC record available at https://lccn.loc.gov/2023024082
LC ebook record available at https://lccn.loc.gov/2023024083

ISBN 978-1-009-25357-4 Hardback

Contents

List of Plates   *page* vi
List of Abbreviations   viii
Acknowledgements   x

   Introduction   1

1 Writing the Forgotten War I: Henry's War, 1542–1547   8

2 Writing the Forgotten War II: Somerset's War, 1547–1550   44

3 How England Became an Island: *The Faerie Queene*   69

4 Scotland *sui juris*? Scottish Literature and the Marian
   Constitutional Crisis, 1567–1573   116

5 On the Knees of the Body Politic: Scottish Succession
   and English Liberties, 1567–1608   154

6 Scotland Un-kingdomed: English History on Stage   188

7 Race-Making in the Invention of Britain: *The Masque
   of Blackness*   220

8 Divisions and Kingdoms: Oedipal Britain from *Gorboduc*
   to *King Lear*   245

   Coda: *Macbeth*. 'Alas, poor country'   279

Works Cited   294
Index   317

A plate section can be found between pages 148 and 149.

v

Plates

1.1 Queen Elizabeth I ('The Ditchley portrait') by Marcus   *page*
Gheeraerts the Younger. © National Portrait Gallery,
London.

1.2 'The Invasion of Scotland, September 23, 1545',
The Cecil Papers, vol.137. fol. 116. Reproduced with
permission of the Marquess of Salisbury, Hatfield House.

2.1 Allegorical Portrait of Sir John Luttrell, Eworth, Hans,
c.1520–after 1578. Reproduced with permission of the
Courtauld Institute.

3.1 Michael Drayton, *Poly-Olbion* (1613). The Bodleian
Libraries, University of Oxford, J-J Drayton d.35,
frontispiece.

3.2 William Lambarde's annotations to John Leland,
Cygnea Cantio, 1545. British Library, C.95.c.15, sig. E2 r.
Reproduced with permission of the British Library.

3.3 Laurence Nowell, map of Scotland, 1563. British
Library, MS Cotton Domitian A XVIII, fols. 98 v-99 r.
Reproduced with permission of the British Library.

3.4 Detail, Laurence Nowell, map of Scotland, 1563. British
Library, MS Cotton Domitian A XVIII, fols. 98 v-99 r.
Reproduced with permission of the British Library.

3.5 Nicolas de Nicolay, *Vray et exacte description hydrographique
des costes maritimes d'Escosse et des Iles Orchades, Hébrides,
avec partie d'Angleterre.* Paris, G. Beys, 1583. Bibliotheque
Nationale Français, ark:/12148/cb31016282 w.

3.6 John Dee, *General and Rare Memorials pertayning to the
Perfecte Arte of NAVIGATION* (1577). The Bodleian
Libraries, University of Oxford, Douce D subt. 30, titlepage.

3.7 Mercator map of Arctic region, showing northern tip of
Scotland, 1595. Bridgeman Images.

3.8 The Drowning of Britomartis (1547–9), probably by Jean Cousin the Elder (c.1490–1560). © The Metropolitan Museum of Art/Art Resource Scala, Florence.

3.9 'Britomartis Se Jetant à la Mer pour Echapper à Minos' (1547–8) engraving by Etienne Delaune, France. National Gallery of Art, Washington DC, Rosenwald Collection, 1964.8.609.

4.1 'M. Thomas Maitland died in italie 1572. And lived of yeiris 22', Maitland Folio, Pepys Library, Magdalen College, Cambridge, MS 2553, fol. 256. By permission of the Pepys Library, Magdalene College, Cambridge.

4.2 Lethington House, East Lothian (now known as 'Lennoxlove'), celebrated in Thomas Maitland's poem. Author's photograph.

4.3 Sir James Wilford (1515–50), siege of Haddington, 1547 after Hans Eworth. National Trust 135561, Coughton Court, Warwickshire. © National Trust Images.

5.1 Hardyng notes Edward the Confessor's homage from Malcolm III. *The Chronicle of John Hardyng* (London: Richard Grafton, 1543). The Bodleian Libraries, University of Oxford, 4° H 17 Art Seld, fol. 125 r.   166

5.2 Hardyng accuses James I of Scotland of wanting to 'embesele' (steal) his evidences of homage. *The Chronicle of John Hardyng* (London: Richard Grafton, 1543). The Bodleian Libraries, University of Oxford, 4° H 17 Art Seld, fol. 132 r.   167

5.3 Hardyng notes John's homage from William at Lincoln. *The Chronicle of John Hardyng* (London: Richard Grafton, 1543). The Bodleian Libraries, University of Oxford, 4° H 17 Art Seld, fol. 149 r.   168

5.4 'The proper nature of ye Scottishe', reader's annotation. *The Chronicle of John Hardyng* (London: Richard Grafton, 1543). The Bodleian Libraries, University of Oxford, 4° H 17 Art Seld, sig.§§2 v.   169

7.1 Ben Jonson underlining and noting the figures of 'Britannia' and 'Africa' with flowers and a manicule on his copy of Claudius Claudianus ed. T. Pulmann (Antwerp, 1585). The Bodleian Libraries, University of Oxford, 8° C 90 Art. Seld., p. 245.

Abbreviations

CSP, Domestic, James I	*Calendar of State Papers, Domestic Series, of the Reign of James I*, ed. Mary Anne Everett Green. 5 volumes. London: Longman, 1857–1872.
CSP, Foreign	*Calendar of State Papers Foreign: Elizabeth, Volume 10, 1572–1574*, ed. Allan James Crosby. London: HMSO, 1876.
CSP, Scotland, 1547–1603	*Calendar of the state papers relating to Scotland and Mary, Queen of Scots, 1547–1603*, eds. Joseph Bain, William Boyd, Annie Dunlop, and M.S. Giuseppi. 13 volumes in 14. Edinburgh: H.M.S.O, 1898–1969.
CSP, Venice	*Calendar of State Papers Relating To English Affairs in the Archives of Venice, Volume 7, 1558–1580*, ed. Rawdon Brown and G Cavendish Bentinck. London: HMSO, 1890.
CWBJ	Ben Jonson. *The Cambridge Edition of the Works of Ben Jonson*, eds. David Bevington, Martin Butler, and Ian Donaldson. 7 volumes. Cambridge: Cambridge University Press, 2012.
DOST	*A Dictionary of the Older Scottish Tongue*: https://dsl.ac.uk
ELR	*English Literary Renaissance*
HJ	*The Historical Journal*
HLQ	*Huntington Library Quarterly*
Holinshed	*Holinshed's Chronicles: England, Scotland, and Ireland*. 6 volumes. New York: AMS, 1976.
HP	*The Hamilton Papers*, ed. Joseph Bain. 2 volumes. Edinburgh: H.M. General Register House, 1890–92.
L&P, Henry VIII	*Letters and papers, foreign and domestic, of the reign of Henry VIII: preserved in the Public Record Office, the British Museum, and elsewhere in England*, eds. J.S. Brewer, James Gairdner and R.H. Brodie. 23 volumes in 35. London: Longman, 1826–1932.
Navy	*The Navy of Edward VI and Mary I*, eds. C.S. Knighton and David Loades. Farnham: Ashgate for the Navy Records Society, 2011.

ODNB	*The Oxford Dictionary of National Biography*
SC	*The Scottish Correspondence of Mary of Lorraine, 1543–1560*, ed. Annie Cameron. Edinburgh: Scottish History Society, 1927.
SHR	*The Scottish Historical Review*
Spenser Variorum	Edmund Spenser. *The Works of Edmund Spenser: A Variorum Edition*, ed. Edwin Greenlaw *et al.* 11 volumes. Baltimore, MD: Johns Hopkins University Press, 1932–1957.
SP	*Studies in Philology*
SQ	*Shakespeare Quarterly*
Statutes	*The Statutes of the Realm*, ed. Alexander Luders *et al.* 12 *volumes*. London: George Ayre and Andrew Strahan, 1810–1828.

Acknowledgements

My greatest debt is to the Leverhulme Trust, which awarded me a Major Research Fellowship for 2014–17 to begin work on a study of 'Shakespeare's Scotland'. I am immensely grateful to the supporters of my application and to the Leverhulme Trust for giving me the chance to embark on open-ended research which has led to new discoveries. As a result, this book is able to reconfigure some very influential ways of framing and understanding the rise of England's national consciousness in the sixteenth century. It shows that that newly vivid representations of England's island exceptionalism were in fact part of a strenuous imperial project supported by poets whose writings both furthered and skilfully veiled England's geopolitical ambitions with respect to Scotland. I hope the book will transform the questions scholars and students ask of England's relation to Scotland in the sixteenth century, and make people think about the legacy of that sixteenth-century history today. Literary studies are currently undervalued not just by governments, but even within institutions devoted to humanities research. This book, by contrast, reveals the creative and far-reaching power of literature and fiction in shaping economic and geopolitical reality. My hope is that by carrying through this characteristically humanist kind of enquiry I make what con- tribution I can to the case for the embattled academic humanities in general, and for literary studies in particular: for their necessity, and for their flourishing.

   I am grateful to special collections staff at the university libraries of St Andrews and Edinburgh, at the British Library and the Bodleian, as well as the college libraries of Christ Church College, Oxford, Merton College, Oxford and The Pepys Library, Magdalene College, Cambridge. Special thanks to the staff of the Bodleian for all the measures taken during the pandemic to enable research to continue. I have been exceptionally lucky in the talented research assistants who have helped me at different stages: Dr Anna Reynolds and Dr Emily Mayne early on; latterly Dr John-Mark

Philo and Daniel Haywood. I thank the Oxford English Faculty and Merton College for their indispensable research support.

Parts of this project at various stages of development have been presented to unsuspecting audiences on various occasions: at the University of Fribourg, Switzerland, and at University of California at Berkeley, in 2015; at St Andrews University, in 2017; at Victoria University of Wellington, in 2017; at Oxford University, the British Library and Barnard College, Columbia University, all in 2018; at Trinity Hall, Cambridge, in 2019; and at Universitat Autònoma de Barcelona, in 2022; thanks to Indira Ghose, Victoria Kahn, Kelsey Jackson-Williams, Sarah Ross, Ros Smith, Philip Schwyzer, Rachel Eisendrath, Subha Mukherji and Jordi Coral for invitations. Courtesy of Zoom, presentations were also made in 2020–1 at Zhejiang University, Beijing; at the Société Française Shakespeare; at the Shakespeare Institute, Stratford; at the University of California's Early Modern Studies Institute; and at the University of Reading's Inns of Court Seminar; with thanks to Hao Tianhu, Christine Sukic, Michael Dobson, Heather James and Jackie Watson. A final outing at St Andrews in valediction to Neil Rhodes in 2022 was a pleasure, thanks to Alex Davis.

Many friends, colleagues, former colleagues and scholarly acquaintances have listened, answered questions and read drafts. Kinch Hoekstra at Berkeley and Dale Hoak at William and Mary asked encouraging and formative questions at a very early stage. Sir John Baker generously shared his work on Magna Carta. Toshi Takamiya took the trouble to send me photographs of John Dee's annotations on his copy of Hardyng's *Chronicle*. John Hudson and Michael Brown answered my questions about medieval English law and Scottish history. Roger Mason, who has done so much to open up the field of early modern Scottish history, read and offered advice on several chapters; I am more grateful than I can say for his generosity and encouragement. Steven Reid let me see his highly original work in Scottish neo-Latin literature and gave helpful criticism. Mary Nyquist's ability to reveal the literary dimensions of foundational legal and political concepts has been an inspiration to me and her comments on drafts have been gratefully received. Vicky Kahn's critical intervention in an early draft talk was transformative. At Oxford, I want to thank Katherine Ibbett, Joe Moshenska and Katie Murphy for reading several chapter drafts and offering the most helpful, constructive and encouraging criticism along the way. I have greatly relished their individual intellectual styles and I value our reading group friendship. Bart Van Es was an insightful reader of the whole book at a late stage. I have also appreciated comments by John-Mark Philo and Daniel Haywood. It has been stimulating to be part of the research community associated with the Early Modern Literature Seminar and the Oxford Centre for Early Modern Studies and I have learned a lot from colleagues, graduate students and visiting speakers. Special thanks for conversations to Jake Arthur, Kate Allan, Colin Burrow, Nandini Das, Andrew Hadfield, Paulina Kewes, Claire Landis, Su Fang Ng, David Norbrook, Guilio Pertile, Emma Smith, Adam Smyth and Ros Smith.

At St Andrews my Head of Department, Gill Plain, was scrupulous in ensuring that my time was protected to work on the Leverhulme project. At Oxford, Ros Ballaster and Helen Small were warmly encouraging as Faculty Chair and Research Director respectively. I have been heartened by belief shown in the book by my editor at Cambridge University Press, Emily Hockley, and I have benefitted from a knowledgeable and responsive editorial and production team. Thanks to George Laver, Sarah Starkey, Subathra Manogaran and especially Charles Phillips. As always, my family have been a strength. The book was being finished in the last year of my father's life. I thank Robin, Nora and Steve, and my daughter Ellie and her partner, Henian, for affectionate support through this difficult, pandemic-affected time. No words can be adequate, however, to express my generosity for the patience, generosity and critical acumen of Linda Hardy, who read everything and offered formative criticisms at crucial moments and who also put up with endless book-related constraints on life in general. She is, like everyone else acknowledged here, in no way responsible for the resulting book, but to her it is dedicated with my love.

Introduction

The famous 'Ditchley' portrait of Elizabeth I (see Figure 1.1 in plate section), painted by Marcus Gheeraerts in 1592, has long been seen as marking a new departure in English national consciousness. For Roy Strong, the painting was the culmination of a growing interest in depicting the monarch next to a cartographic representation of her realm, set in the sea. Here, with the map of Oxfordshire at her feet, the map fringed like a rug by the south English coast, Elizabeth seemed to merge with the very island itself. Strong's comment captures the painting's achievement: 'in the "Ditchley" portrait Queen, crown and island become one. Elizabeth is England, woman and kingdom are interchangeable.'[1]

In the last twenty years, critics of English literature have talked more and more about the cultural production of space, about the artifice of carto-graphic representation. They note that the map spread under Elizabeth's dainty shoes derives from Christopher Saxton's officially commissioned atlas of the counties of England and Wales (1579). A revolution in geog-raphy, they say, was now enabling the English to imagine their nation through detailed cartographic representation, here captured in a painting. But there is a problem. *England is not an island.*

It seems so tedious, so pedantic to point this out. England-as-island is just a convention, isn't it? Without disparaging Scotland, it seems reason-able to assume that there was no need to register the northern nation's presence in what we might call the 'sceptred isle' conceit. So we are told that early modern writers referred to 'England' and 'Britain' indifferently, that there was an 'easy slippage' between effective synonyms for the nation and its historic past. In any case, we all know that James VI and I succeeded Elizabeth in 1603, fulfilling the indivisibility of monarch, island and nation that Gheeraerts here foreshadows so wonderfully.

---

[1] Roy Strong, *Gloriana: The Portraits of Queen Elizabeth I* (London: Thames and Hudson, 1987), 136.

But this account will not wash. Gheeraerts's painting antedates James's accession by ten years. It was painted when a Scottish succession was by no means certain, and when Scotland was a foreign and sovereign, albeit inferior, nation.[2] Yet the painting deters the gazer from imagining any land border. Indeed, the gazer might note by contrast the artfulness with which Gheeraerts has suggested the island of Britain's traditional triangular shape in the taper from Elizabeth's broad farthingale, through her be-ruffed neck and shoulders, to the narrow point of her head. Furthermore, we also know that the accession of James did not, in 1603, fulfil the promise of a single island nation. The English Parliament rejected union with Scotland, insisting on the separation of the two nations, each with its own allegiance to the king. In short, no easy slippage or adumbration of a future union with Scotland can explain Gheeraerts's frankly imperial vision here. There is nothing natural, empirical or 'unionist' about the insular fantasy into which the artist has brilliantly transformed the conceit of England as monarch and map.

This book, *England's Insular Imagining*, makes visible the poetic techniques by which Elizabethan poets, painters, lawyers, historiographers and cartographers created the strange conceptual space in which the idea of England-as-island could cohabit comfortably with the rejection, in 1603, of the Anglo-Scots union that would have secured a single island nation in reality. The vanishing of Scotland as a named nation from the great poetry and political writing of Elizabeth's reign is not an indication of that kingdom's actual insignificance in sixteenth-century English consciousness, but the effect, as I will show, of myriad acts of imagination which signal quite the opposite. The conscious project of English insular imagining was to make Scotland as nation inconceivable; to produce, by various means, a sense in which England stretched from shore to shore without diluting its identity by conquest or union with another *natio*, another sovereign people.

It is difficult, of course, to claim that indifference is an artistic effect and not an underlying sentiment. But there is good evidence that members of the sixteenth-century English governing class were far from indifferent to Scotland. They knew what the possession of Scotland would mean for England's geopolitical prospects in terms of coastline security and future empire. One piece of undeniable evidence for this is the attempt to conquer Scotland which England undertook between 1542 and 1550. The war was brutal, destructive and immensely costly for both nations: English

---

[2] Susan Doran and Paulina Kewes, eds., *Doubtful and Dangerous: The Question of Succession in Late Elizabethan England* (Manchester: Manchester University Press, 2014).

invasions killed more than ten thousand Scots, destroyed numerous abbeys, towns and villages and ruined the Scottish economy, while the cost of maintaining an English pale of fortresses emptied England's coffers and cost their Protector his life. Yet English literary criticism completely ignores this war. Indeed, such is the legacy of English insular imagining (which produces England as always merely defending the homeland) that modern literary critics and historians repeatedly reverse the war's facts. They write of 'defence of the Scottish border' as the motive for England's economically ruinous militarisation in the 1540s and of England's being 'threatened with . . . agitation from the Scots in the North', or of '1545. . . when the Scots were once again threatening England's northern border'.[3] These statements are astonishing reversals of the reality. In 1545 an English royal army marched, at Henry VIII's command, across the border and burnt Leith, Edinburgh and all the border towns, torching inhabitants as they slept. Given the British public's appetite for all things Tudor, one has to ask why this Tudor war of conquest remains so occluded.

The substitution of English insular imagining for the facts of the 1540s war does not just distort the literary criticism of 'early modern England'. It has shaped the terms of contemporary debates on devolution and union in the contemporary post-Brexit moment. In a recent piece in the *New Statesman*, Tom Holland sketches a history of England and Scotland as 'the two rival kingdoms of Albion' which were 'in many ways the mirror image of one another', with mythologies that were 'strikingly similar'.[4] What his account ignores is the goal that each of these nations, from the thirteenth to the sixteenth century, used its mythologies to pursue. English monarchs appropriate Geoffrey of Monmouth's legends of an island founded by the Trojan Brutus, the so-called 'matter of Britain', with its irresistible image of a sea-bounded insular unity, to pursue an *imperial* aim: they aimed for the conquest of Scotland and acquisition of an insular Anglo-British empire. The Scots, by contrast, developed fantastic legends of kings dating back to 330 BC in order to resist being conquered, to claim their own sovereignty over their part of the island and themselves. This is not, then, a rivalry in which the kingdoms 'mirror' one another, but in which the pretensions of one drive the reactions of the other. That Holland's account can seem even remotely plausible is a demonstration of the effectiveness of the Elizabethan rewriting of Galfridian legend that *England's Insular Imagining* seeks to trace.

---

[3] See below, Chapter 1.
[4] Tom Holland, 'How Alex Salmond's Alba Party reveals England's and Scotland's shared ideals', *New Statesman*, 3 May 2021.

After the failure of the attempt to conquer Scotland in the 1540s, England's poets, antiquarians and lawyers transmuted the Galfridian legends which justified Anglo-imperial British empire into new forms: allegorical epic, chorography, Oedipal tragedy and political theology. They thus produced a *trompe l'oeil* vision of England and Wales as the essence of Britain, with Scotland as an unnecessary supplement. In this vision, England's nationalism is fused with the idea of its peaceful inheritance of ancient Britishness, so it can be perceived as capacious and tolerant, while the very idea of Scotland's nationalism becomes inevitably excessive and partisan. At the same time, a Scottish desire for British union is perceived, in 1603, not as amicable but as predatory, while an English rejection of union is perceived as rightly respectful of local custom and the rights of the English 'constitution'.

England's Insular Imagining is concerned, as the title suggests, with imagination's power to body forth the forms of things unknown. Though it begins, in chapters 1 and 2, with war writing – the writing that justified the 1540s attempt to conquer Scotland – its chapters thereafter centre on major imaginative achievements of early modern English and Scottish literature and political thought: Edmund Spenser's *The Faerie Queene*, George Buchanan's *A Dialogue on the Law of Kingship among the Scots*, the poetry of Sir Richard Maitland, Edmund Plowden's theory of 'the King's Two Bodies', Shakespeare's English history plays, William Camden's *Britannia*, Jonson's *The Masque of Blackness*, Shakespeare's *King Lear* and *Macbeth*. The book shows that is through the dazzling achievements of the English literary imagination that we have come to accept as fact the unlikely idea that it was *because* Scotland was of no geopolitical value to England, *because* England was indifferent to Scotland's existence, that English politicians, historians and poets found it so easy to forget about Scotland's existence and think of England as the whole island of Britain.

And in case that sounds as though I am reducing the very greatest works of English literature to ideology, let me paraphrase the art historian, T. J. Clark, as he considers what distinguishes the brilliant, fantastical and unsettling 'Terrestrial Paradise' (c.1505–15) of Hieronymus Bosch from a painting on the same subject by Bosch's contemporary, Dieric Bouts. In noting the many similarities that suggest shared prototypes or even Bosch's citation of Bouts, Clark feels obliged to labour the obvious conclusion: the paintings are incomparable. While Bouts's work is a worthy exemplar of its cultural and artistic moment, Bosch's feels both strange and modern: alive with strange juxtapositions, suffused with irony, compassion and wit. He has felt obliged to labour this point, Clark says, because 'a majority of art historians are so anxious to see no difference between the one *Paradise* and the other'. Art historians are bound to want to place Bosch in a 'cultural' frame which 'inevitably shifts the attention away from the imagination, which has no history, to ideology, which has'. Ideology, he goes on, is 'the name we have for allowed, repeated legitimate imaginings – ways of picturing things that do not destabilise the world as it is, or don't do so too much'.[5] Yet Clark does not conclude from this that because the art historians' cultural and ideological framing of Bosch is inadequate, Bosch's work has therefore nothing to do with ideology or history. On the contrary, Clark says, 'ideology *needs* the imagination – including, occasionally, the kind of extremity of imagining we find in Bosch – to renew itself'. In other words, extremity of imagining, imagining of the kind we find in Bosch, but also Spenser, Shakespeare and even (in different ways) Jonson, can change the allowed, repeated imaginings that structure the world. As well as perpetually surprising us with vivid and sometimes disturbing experiences, these artists of imaginative extremity produce new ways of picturing things that become the reality for their own and later times, a set of images that future readers don't find destabilising, because their worlds (our worlds) have long been shaped by them. And great works achieve these two things simultaneously: they both ground a future reality and continually unsettle and renew the perceptions of future generations.

The usual objections to reading Shakespeare's imagined spaces – the ancient Britain of *King Lear*, say – in relation to what they might or might not seem to say about ways of picturing England and Scotland is to say that such ideological or topical readings are *reductive*. On reading *King Lear* in relation to James's accession and Anglo-Scots union, John Kerrigan has said that it would be 'fatuous' to claim that *Lear* 'could be *reduced to topicality*' (my italics).[6] From Clark's comments, however, we can see that this might be to frame the question the wrong way round. The question is not how some apparently sudden, merely empirical, merely topical 'event' (such as the accession to the English throne of a Scottish king) impinged on Shakespeare's imagination. The question is, rather, how Shakespeare's *Lear* brilliantly reimagines the ancient mythic materials of Anglo-imperialism that were everywhere in the literature of his upbringing. For the story of King Leir's 'division of the kingdom' derives from Geoffrey of

---

[5] T. J. Clark, 'Aboutness', *London Review of Books*, vol. 43, no. 1, 1 April 2021.
[6] John Kerrigan, *Archipelagic English: Literature, History and Politics, 1603–1707* (Oxford: Oxford University Press, 2008), 16.

Monmouth's *History of the Kings of Britain* (c.1137) with its legends of
Brutus, Leir, Gorboduc, Kymbeline and the great King Arthur. These
Galfridian materials had, since the thirteenth century and especially since
Edward I's invasions of Scotland (1296–1306), been continually deployed
to justify the argument that English kings were overlords of Scotland and
therefore had a right to invade it. Indeed, England's invasion of Scotland
under Henry VIII and Edward VI in the 1540s was explicitly justified by
recourse to Geoffrey's legends, albeit in somewhat updated form, and both
the legends and the war they justified filled the history books Shakespeare
read. Sixteenth-century debates about the veracity of legends of King
Arthur were thus not a mere 'battle of the books', as English critics have
thought, but were urgently geopolitical, deeply implicated in England's
Anglo-imperial claims.

Scholars of medieval English literature know all this very well. They
know that, at the end of the thirteenth and through the fourteenth to the
sixteenth centuries, Scottish historians responded to this Anglo-imperial
history with their own national story of origin in what R. James Goldstein
has called a 'war of historiography'.[7] The question that needs to be asked,
therefore, is: what happened to this 'war of historiography' over Scottish
nationhood in the second half of the sixteenth century, the reign of
Elizabeth I? It certainly had devastating material consequences in the
1540s, when conviction that Scotland was not a sovereign nation drove
England's diplomacy and made its conduct of the war especially brutal. But
it seems to fade from popular English consciousness between 1560 and
1603, although Elizabeth's leading statesmen and lawyers, as this book
shows, explicitly subscribe to Galfridian claims of English overlordship
of Scotland.

So what happened? As this book argues, the English belief that Scotland
was not a sovereign but merely a vassal nation does not simply disappear in
Elizabeth's reign. What happened, rather, accords with T. J. Clark's argument about ideology and the imagination. The medieval way of picturing
Anglo-Scots relations as those of overlordship and vassalage gradually
metamorphosed, with the help of the brilliant, disorderly, classicising
creativity of English poets, lawyers, cartographers and antiquaries, into
new epic, tragic and chorographic ways of imagining England's sovereign
insularity: depicted in Marinell's '*Rich strond*' in Spenser's Faery land, or
in Shakespeare's Henry V crossing of the channel to France, or as the

---

[7] R. James Goldstein, *The Matter of Scotland: Historical Narrative in Medieval Scotland* (Lincoln, NE:
University of Nebraska Press, 1993).

strangely unlocalised Britain divided by Shakespeare's Lear, or as the way in which, in Camden's *Britannia*, Picts suddenly become ethnic Britons, while Scots shrivel into mongrel interlopers. Thus, through all these powerful and sometimes extreme acts of imagination – which can themselves be untethered to history – Galfridian-derived stories of English overlordship morph into a new set of repeated mental visualisations of England's insularity, an insularity in which Scotland ceases to be named and occupies no conceivable space. *Lear*, a tragedy which specifies no geographical location at all except Dover (its imagined cliff epitomising, as John Kerrigan elsewhere says, the extreme verge of both life and land) not only can but should be read as an instance of the 'extremity of imagining' in which the ideology of Anglo-imperial insularity renews itself and becomes an irresistible image of human truth.[8] Such a reading is not reductive nor merely topical, but engages with the whole question of how tragedy imagines the relations of space, habitation and origin.

Insular Imagining is divided into chapters which identify and discuss Elizabethan England's great literary achievements as transformations of Galfridian British history. In doing so, these chapters offer original readings of major literary texts and produce new interpretations of key innovations in historiography, chorography and political thought, such as Plowden's doctrine of 'the King's Two Bodies', Camden's *Britannia* and Holinshed's *Chronicles*. The chapters range from exploring Faery land's offshore interests to contemplating the transatlantic race-making implications of turning tattooed Picts into painted Britons. Together, they reveal the myriad ways in which significant works of early modern English literature reshaped the materials of Galfridian British history so as to secure the imaginative identification of England as the whole island of Britain and thereby with British empire. Modern literary criticism's sense of the supreme unimportance of Scotland to the Tudors is itself testimony to the success of a rich creative effort to reduce this foreign kingdom to imaginative *non-nationhood* just as its ruling dynasty looked set to assume rule over England. This book is devoted to revealing with what complex, thoughtful and brilliant art that effort was undertaken and at what it costs us now to persist in the fiction of England's insularity, mistaking an artistic achievement for the natural 'way things were back then'.

---

[8] John Kerrigan, *Shakespeare's Originality* (Oxford: Oxford University Press, 2018), 68–9.

CHAPTER I

Writing the Forgotten War I: Henry's War, 1542–1547

I. Why It Matters to Remember the War

For almost a decade, from 1542 to 1550, England invaded, occupied and attempted to conquer Scotland. The attempt was finally unsuccessful, but invasive war was always legally and morally dubious, and these campaigns were designed to devastate: they were explicitly punitive, deliberately brutal. The report of the earl of Hertford (later Protector Somerset) to the English privy council on his 1545 border campaign itemises every one of the 287 Scottish monasteries, castles, market towns and villages 'brent, rased and cast downe' by his forces in that campaign; in 1544 the citizens of Dunbar, men, women and children, were suffocated and burnt as they slept.[1] At the Battle of Pinkie in 1547 between six and ten thousand Scots soldiers were slaughtered rather than (as would be usual) some being captured and made prisoners of war.[2] The economist S. G. Lythe long ago noted the devastation of Scotland's means of food production in the wake of Hertford's 1544 and 1545 campaigns, along with the plundering of Tayside and Fife during the occupations of Broughty Craig and Inchcolm in 1547–8.[3] From Dundee in November 1548, Sir John Brende wrote that there was like to be 'little doing' for the English forces that winter in Tayside and Fife, because 'The country is so wasted there is nothing to destroy.'[4] But as well as despoiling the means of material sustenance, soldiers attacked the country's spiritual infrastructure, smashing up the 'ydols' of traditional worship and 'stripp[ing] the Church of much of what

---

[1] 'Henry VIII: September 1545, 26-30', in *L&P, vol. 20, Part 2, 195–233*. For the citizens of Dunbar, see [John Brende] *The late expedition in Scotland, made by the King's Highness' army, under the conduct of the Right Honourable, the Earl of Hertford ... 1544* in *Tudor Tracts 1532–1588*, ed. A. F. Pollard (London: Constable, 1903), 45.

[2] Gervase Phillips, *The Anglo-Scots Wars, 1513–1550* (Woodbridge: Boydell, 1999), 199.

[3] S. G. Lythe, *The Economy of Scotland in Its European Setting 1550–1625* (London: Oliver and Boyd, 1960), 6.

[4] Brende to Sir John Mason, Nov. 29, 1548, *CSP Scot.*, I.337.

had made its piety live'.[5] The 'dissolution of the monasteries' is, to most of us, an episode in the well-known narrative of the formation of English exceptionalism. It has stirred richly expressed feelings about the ambiguous legacy of Henry VIII's Protestant Reformation, from William Empson's famous comments on Shakespeare's 'bare ruined choirs' to Eamon Duffy's evocatively titled *The Stripping of the Altars*.[6] The choirs of Scotland's magnificent abbeys and churches, by contrast, were stripped bare and brought to ruin by looting, killing and cannon-fire inflicted by English forces in 1544 and 1545. Even in Alec Ryrie's fine, witty analysis, this 'military iconoclasm' remains hard to assimilate to a meaningful narrative of Scottish Reformation.[7]

Yet this nine years' war was almost no less devastating for the English. By the summer of 1549, William Paget was writing to Protector Somerset, begging him to abandon his attempt to conquer Scotland: 'we are exhausted and worne to the bones with these eight yeres warres both of men money and all other thinges', he wrote.[8] In the same year, according to Sir Thomas Smith's *Discourse of the Commonweal of This Realm of England*, artificers and merchants were observing that England's cities, heretofore wealthy, had 'fallen into great desolation and poverty', that 'not only the good townes are sore decayed . . . but also in the country . . . there is a such a general dearth of all things'.[9] Exiled from court in the summer of 1549 precisely for having criticised Somerset's handling of the economy, Smith wrote the *Discourse* as his response: a brilliant analysis of the catastrophic effects of wartime currency debasement. 'For the furniture of his wars', wrote Smith, the king was continuing to import 'armor of all kind, artillery, anchors, cables, pitch, tar, iron, steel, handguns, gunpowder', squeezing his subjects to pay for it, though 'there is no treasure left within the realm'.[10] In political terms, the war's effects were, if possible, even

---

[5] Alec Ryrie, *The Origins of the Scottish Reformation* (Manchester: Manchester University Press, 2006), 78.

[6] William Empson, *Seven Types of Ambiguity* (London: Chatto and Windus, 1930), 2–3; Eamon Duffy, *The Stripping of the Altars: Traditional Religion in England* (New Haven, CT: Yale University Press, 1992).

[7] Ryrie, *Scottish Reformation*, 78.

[8] *The Letters of William, Lord Paget of Beaudesert, 1547–1563*, ed. Barrett L. Beer and Sybil M. Jack, Camden Miscellany, vol. XXV (London: Royal Historical Society, 1974), Letter 41, 77. See also Dale Hoak, *The King's Council in the Reign of Edward VI* (Cambridge: Cambridge University Press, 1976), 187–9.

[9] Sir Thomas Smith, *A Discourse of the Commonweal of This Realm of England*, ed. Mary Dewar (Charlottesville, VA: University of Virginia Press, 1969), 18.

[10] Smith, *Discourse*, 35–6; see Mary Dewar, 'The Authorship of the "Discourse of the Commonweal"', *Economic History Review*, new series, vol. 19, no. 2 (1966), 388–400.

worse. Franco-Scottish victory in 1550 brought about the very situation
that the war had been fought to prevent: Mary Stewart's marriage to Henri
II's son, the Dauphin François, gave the French Crown a claim to the
English throne, greatly exacerbating England's political isolation and
vulnerability at the accession of the Protestant Elizabeth in 1558.[11] Just
after the English defeat, in 1550, the English ambassador to France, Sir John
Mason, had to watch uncomfortably as Franco-Scots victory was cele-
brated in King Henri II's triumphal entry into Rouen. First, images of
the Scottish burghs freed from English occupation were paraded – '*Voilà
Dondy, Edimpton, Portugray*' ('Behold, Dundee, Haddington, Broughty
Craig') – and later on, as part of a magnificent spectacle on the river Seine,
Neptune appeared, offering Henri fair winds to conduct his navy up the
Thames, to conquer Albion and to become Henry IX of England.[12]

Ultimately, and more importantly, the harsh lessons of the failed
1540s war to conquer Scotland actually shaped the success of Elizabethan
England, economically, geopolitically and constitutionally. Sir Thomas
Smith and William Cecil, Lord Burghley, chief among the innovative
thinkers and political advisors of Elizabeth's reign, both began their
political careers as strategists and propagandists for Somerset's war in
Scotland.[13] They never abandoned their belief in the desirability of the
war's goal, which was the neutralising of Scotland's potential as an ally to
England's enemies by the creation of an Anglo-dominated 'Great Britain'.
However, they also fully absorbed and creatively transformed the harsh
lesson of the war's failure as the means to achieve that goal. Joan Thirsk
has shown how Smith's analysis of the war's economic effects laid
the ground for the astonishingly successful development of a consumer
society in Elizabethan England, through the encouragement of economic
projects.[14] Jane Dawson likewise demonstrated how central to William
Cecil's vision remained the need to achieve English control over the
unification, political and religious, of the British Isles, thus securing the

---

[11] See Stephen Alford, *The Early Elizabethan Polity: William Cecil and the British Succession Crisis, 1558–1569* (Cambridge: Cambridge University Press, 1998), 43–70.

[12] Margaret McGowan ed., *L'Entrée de Henri II à Rouen 1550* (Amsterdam: Theatrum Orbis Terrarum, 1973), 17–18, 27–28; Louis de Merval, *L'entrée de Henri II Roi de France a Rouen au mois d'octobre 1550* (Rouen: Henry Boissel, 1868), n.p., XIV, XVIII.

[13] See Dale Hoak, 'Sir William Cecil, Sir Thomas Smith and the Monarchical Republic of Tudor England', in *The Monarchical Republic of Tudor England*, ed. John F. McDiarmid (Aldershot: Ashgate, 2007), 37–54, 42.

[14] Joan Thirsk, *Economic Policy and Projects: The Development of a Consumer Society in Early Modern England* (Oxford: Clarendon Press, 1978), 24 and *passim*.

British coastline from the threat of foreign invasion.[15] And what we now think of as the Elizabethan period's most important innovation – a legally limited monarchy, famously described by Patrick Collinson as the 'monarchical republic of Queen Elizabeth I' – had its origins at least partly in William Cecil's and Thomas Smith's archival research on behalf of Somerset's vision of a united, Protestant Britain in the 'acephalous conditions' of Edward VI's minority.[16] Tasked to justify England's historic right to invade Scotland, Smith transformed the old feudal claim into a title based on England's legal and constitutional superiority within a new, godly 'British' imperium. 'If Smith's *De Republica Anglorum* had an intellectual antecedent', wrote Jonathan McMahon, it was the plan of Protector Somerset's war propaganda team 'for "De Republica Britannica"'.[17] Economically, politically and symbolically, then, what we think of as 'Elizabethan England' – a virgin queen ruling a peaceable and prosperous island nation, just beginning to be a maritime trading and colonial power – represents, at some level, the transmutation of the goals and lessons of England's war to conquer Scotland in the 1540s.

Yet few in early modern literary studies will recognise the account I have just given. I am not aware of a single general survey of Elizabethan literature that even mentions, let alone accords any formative importance to, England's attempt to conquer Scotland. And this is in spite of the last few decades' upsurge of interest in literary 'forms of nationhood' and in 'Archipelagic' or 'British' studies.[18] As far as any project of Anglo-Scots 'British' union is concerned, most literary scholars think that no such thing existed until a Scottish king, James I, provoked a clash with the English

---

[15] Jane E. A. Dawson, 'William Cecil and the British Dimension of Early Elizabethan Foreign Policy', *History*, vol. 74 (1989), 196–216.

[16] Hoak, 'Cecil and Smith', 41–2, 48, 51–4; Jonathan McMahon, 'The Humanism of Sir Thomas Smith'. Unpublished MA Thesis, College of William and Mary, 1999.

[17] McMahon, 'Humanism of Sir Thomas Smith', 30.

[18] See Richard Helgerson, *Forms of Nationhood: The Elizabethan Writing of England* (Chicago, IL: University of Chicago Press, 1992); Andrew Hadfield, *Literature, Politics and National Identity: Reformation to Renaissance* (Cambridge: Cambridge University Press, 1994); Claire McEachern, *The Poetics of English Nationhood: 1590–1612* (Cambridge: Cambridge University Press, 1996); Willy Maley, *Salvaging Spenser: Colonialism, Culture and Identity* (Basingstoke: Macmillan, 1997); David J. Baker, *Between Nations: Shakespeare, Spenser, Marvell and the Question of Britain* (Stanford, CA: Stanford University Press, 1997); Andrew Murphy, *But the Irish Sea Betwixt Us: Ireland, Colonialism and Renaissance Literature* (Lexington, KY: University Press of Kentucky, 1999); David J. Baker and Willy Maley, eds., *British Identities and English Renaissance Literature* (Cambridge: Cambridge University Press, 2002); Philip Schwyzer, *Literature, Nationalism and Memory in Early Modern England and Wales* (Cambridge: Cambridge University Press, 2004); Andrew Hadfield, *Shakespeare, Spenser and the Matter of Britain* (Basingstoke: Palgrave Macmillan, 2004); Cathy Shrank, *Writing the Nation in Reformation England: 1530–1580* (Oxford: Oxford University Press, 2004); Kerrigan, *Archipelagic English*.

House of Commons in his ill-advised attempt to force a union through against the will of Parliament.[19] This belief goes back to the 1950s, to David Harris Willson's influential and scathing biography of James, which plotted the union project within a Whiggish narrative of escalating tensions over the royal prerogative, narrowly held in check by the tactful Elizabeth, but pushed to breaking point by James I. As a foreign absolutist, James fatally underestimated (so this version goes) both the House of Commons and the English common law. Although Bruce Galloway's survey of the union debates of 1603–8 long ago discredited Willson's narrative (James did not press for rapid advances to union; he moved cautiously, listened to advice from all sides, and submitted proposals to parliaments in both kingdoms) it is still widely current among literary critics.[20] Its unspoken, unexamined ground is the assumption that, were it not for England's 'succession problem', Scotland as geopolitical entity, as separate, sovereign nation, would have remained a matter of complete indifference to the English. In other words, the usual story is predicated on the understanding of 'Great Britain' as the signifier of a Scottish monarch's desire, a fantasy of insular integrity in which England is decidedly *not implicated*. Thus, for example, Claire McEachern reads the conflict between the Commons and James I over the issue of 'Great Britain' as one of local, gentry resistance to a hegemonic imposition.[21] Martin Butler's extremely nuanced account of the politics of the Stuart masque identifies the terms 'Britain' and 'British' as descriptors of James's failure to understand the ancient constitution.[22] Likewise, it is often assumed that English projects of defining Britain and Britishness are not political *until* the Scottish accession. Angus Vine claims that William Camden's undertaking to solve the historical problem of Britain's origins in *Britannia* (1586) might have been read as 'a simple act of disinterested antiquarian enquiry' which only acquired 'a political charge' after the accession of James I, with his project for British union.[23] In the same vein, John Kerrigan refers to the frustrations of William Drummond's

---

[19] David Harris Willson, *King James VI and I* (London: Jonathan Cape, 1956, 1963).

[20] Bruce Galloway, *The Union of England and Scotland, 1603–1608* (Edinburgh: John Donald, 1986), 161–6. Alan Stewart, *The Cradle King: A Life of James VI and I* (London: Chatto and Windus, 2003) plots his Chapter 13 on David Willson's Chapter XIV, 'The Royal Prerogative', *James VI & I*, 243–70, presenting Anglo-Scots Union as James's private ambition, opposed by a public-spirited Commons.

[21] McEachern, *Poetics of English Nationhood*, 144.

[22] Martin Butler, *The Stuart Court Masque and Political Culture* (Cambridge: Cambridge University Press, 2008), 97.

[23] Angus Vine, 'Copiousness, Conjecture and Collaboration in William Camden's *Britannia*', *Renaissance Studies*, vol. 28, no. 2 (2014), 225–41, 228.

poetry writing in post-1603 Scotland as 'the *British* Problem', both anticipating the modern use of 'British' as a gesture of Scottish inclusion and marking that inclusion as problematic.[24]

As subsequent chapters of this book will show in much more detail, it would in fact be more accurate to think of English engagements with 'Britishness' and 'British history' – whether deriving or departing from Geoffrey of Monmouth's *History of the Kings of Britain* (c.1137) – as always already political. Moreover, these sixteenth-century English engagements with British history need to be understood as implicated in a geopolitical imperative to claim sovereignty over the whole island, as if recovering an ancient right. Alan MacColl has argued that 'the ideological dimensions of "the British history" as it was treated in the sixteenth century remain almost entirely unexplored'.[25] Standard early twentieth-century treatments by Edward Greenlaw, C. B. Millican and T. D. Kendrick depoliticised the Tudor argument over Geoffrey of Monmouth, treating it as a pedantic wrangle, a battle of the books.[26] Through the 1990s and 2000s, Roger Mason's and Philip Schwyzer's innovative work on the Scottish and Welsh dimensions of Tudor Galfridian history has revealed its importance for debates over national origins, while Gordon McMullan has shown us how stories from Geoffrey of Monmouth held an extraordinary sway over the early modern English stage.[27] Still missing from this picture, however, is any detailed literary analysis of the crucial early modern English transformations of Geoffrey's *Historia Regum Britanniae* in the so-called 'Edwardian moment' of British unionism during the 1542–50 wars.[28]

---

[24] Kerrigan, *Archipelagic English*, 141–68.

[25] Alan MacColl, 'The Construction of England as a Protestant "British" Nation in the Sixteenth Century', *Renaissance Studies*, vol. 18, no. 4 (2004), 582–608, 582.

[26] Edwin Greenlaw, *Studies in Spenser's Historical Allegory* (Baltimore, MA: Johns Hopkins, 1932); Charles Bowie Millican, *Spenser and the Table Round: A Study in the Contemporaneous Background for Spenser's Use of the Arthurian Legend* (Cambridge, MA: Harvard University Press, 1932); T. D. Kendrick, *British Antiquity* (London: Methuen and Co., 1950).

[27] See Roger A. Mason, 'The Scottish Reformation and Anglo-British Imperialism', in *Kingship and Commonweal: Political Thought in Renaissance and Reformation Scotland* (East Linton, Tuckwell Press, 1998), 242–71; Mason, 'Aspects of National Identity in Renaissance Scotland', in *Kingship and Commonweal*, 78–103; Mason, 'Scotland, Elizabethan England and the Idea of Britain', *Transactions of the Royal Historical Society*, vol. 14 (2004), 279–93; Schwyzer, *Literature, Nationalism*; Gordon McMullan, 'The Colonization of Early Britain on the Jacobean Stage', in *Reading the Medieval in Early Modern England*, ed. McMullan and David Matthews (Cambridge: Cambridge University Press, 2007), 119–42.

[28] The term 'Edwardian moment' was coined by Arthur Williamson, 'Scotland, Antichrist and the Invention of Great Britain', in *New Perspectives on the Politics and Culture of Early Modern Scotland*, ed. John Dwyer *et al.* (Edinburgh: John Donald, 1982). It is cited by Roger A. Mason, 'Scotching the Brut: Politics, History and National Myth in Sixteenth-Century Britain', in *Scotland and England, 1286–1815* (Edinburgh: John Donald Publishers, 1986), 60–85, 71, and by David Armitage, *The*

This was a moment when the English Crown committed itself to realising a providential opportunity for the military recovery of the British empire of ancient Galfridian legend.

It is, therefore, a matter of some importance to reinsert the nine years of England's attempted conquest of Scotland back into the story of the literary negotiation of English national identity within the years leading up to the accession of James VI and I. Attending to the violence and the cost of the war is also essential, for two distinct reasons. The first is that we need to counter the prevalence of the myth of England's indifference to Scotland's separate, independent nationhood. We need to understand the lengths to which England was prepared to go in order to realise the goal of 'Great Britain' and British empire by military force. The second is that literary critics need a better understanding of the stakes in the invocation of the terms 'Britain' and 'British', as well as of the image of England-as-island, in the literature and historiography of early modern England. This means that we need to acknowledge the key role that these terms and this image played in the literature of the 1540s war; specifically, in the official justifications of war emanating from the English press, which were designed to persuade English, Scots and European readerships of the legitimacy of invasion and English military aggression.

II.   A Brief Introduction to 'British History' in the 1540s

England's attempted conquest of Scotland in the 1540s may be seen as the last in more than four hundred years of military and discursive assertions of sovereignty grounded in what Rees Davies calls 'British pipedreams' – that is, 'the memories and dreams of an imperial Britain' in which historians from the twelfth to the fifteenth century continued to encourage their rulers.[29] If Aethelstan and Edgar, kings of tenth-century Wessex-England, had styled themselves rulers of Britain, memories of their achievements blended with dreams fostered by a Welsh history of the twelfth century, Geoffrey of Monmouth's *Historia Regum Britanniae* or *History of the Kings of Britain* (c.1137). Geoffrey's history told of the founding of an island kingdom of Britain by a wandering Trojan prince called Brutus, and of the kingdom's subsequent division, endless wars and climactic if ephemeral reunification as the centre of a vast transoceanic empire under the rule of King Arthur. In its

---

Ideological Origins of the British Empire (Cambridge: Cambridge University Press, 2000), 40. For a critique, see Ryrie, *Scottish Reformation*, 85 and 94, note 78.

[29] R. R. Davies, *The First English Empire: Power and Identity in the British Isles, 1093–1343* (Oxford: Oxford University Press, 2002), 9, 10.

moment of composition, as John Gillingham has shown, Geoffrey's *History*, though written for an Anglo-Norman audience, was shot through with prophetic hopes for the revival of Welsh kingship.[30] It was subsequently, however, adapted and repackaged as an English history. The sheer numbers of Brutan genealogies of Plantagenet kings that survive are evidence of how rapidly 'this vision of English regnal antiquity ... reached deep into the nervous system of English historical consciousness'.[31]

What infiltrated the later deep reaches of English historical conscious-ness, however, was not Geoffrey alone, but what we might call *the feudal-isation of Geoffrey*. By this I mean the use of Geoffrey's history to uphold the claim that Scotland, as a kingdom, had anciently been feudally subject to the king of England. Kingdoms could not, as Susan Reynolds observed, be held as fiefs, but a claim to feudal overlordship of the kingdom of Scotland was advanced by Edward I in response to the succession crisis following the death without heirs of Scotland's Alexander III in 1286.[32] In 1299, Pope Boniface VIII categorically denied that the realm of Scotland was 'feudally subject to ... the kings of the realm of England', reminding Edward that 'magnates of the kingdom' had been elected for its custody on Alexander's death.[33] Edward responded in 1301 with a famous letter which traced English overlordship back to Geoffrey's legend of Brutus's original division of the island kingdom of Britain between his sons, Locrine, Albanact and Camber. These sons were given the kingdoms of Loegres (England), Albany (Scotland) and Cambria (Wales), respectively. Edward, however, made two crucial additions to Geoffrey's narrative: first, Brutus had, he said, reserved the 'royal dignity' or overlordship of Britain to Locrine (*reservata Locrino seniori dignitate*). Second, after Albanact's slaughter by invading Huns, Albany, or Scotland, reverted back to Locrine (*sic Albania revertitur ad dicum Locrinum*).[34] The effect of these two minor adjustments

---

[30] John Gillingham, 'The Context and Purposes of Geoffrey of Monmouth's *History of the Kings of Britain*', *Anglo-Norman Studies*, vol. 13 (1990), 99–118.

[31] Dauvit Broun, *Scottish Independence and the Idea of Britain* (Edinburgh: Edinburgh University Press, 2007), 42.

[32] On his death, Alexander did have an heir: his three-year-old granddaughter, Margaret, daughter of Eric II of Norway and Margaret of Scotland. She, however, died in Orkney in 1290, on her way to Scotland to be crowned. On the question of fiefs, vassalage and kingdoms, see Susan Reynolds, *Fiefs and Vassals: The Medieval Evidence Reinterpreted* (Oxford: Oxford University Press, 1994), 391–3, and Reynolds, 'Fiefs and Vassals in Scotland: A View from Outside', *SHR*, vol. 82 (2003), 176–93.

[33] E. L. G. Stones, *Anglo-Scottish Relations, 1174–1328: Some Selected Documents* (Oxford: Oxford University Press, rev. ed., 1970), 162–7.

[34] Stones, *Anglo-Scottish Relations*, 192–219, 196–7; Mason, 'Scotching the Brut', 62; Goldstein, *Matter of Scotland*, 63–6; Emily Wingfield, *The Trojan Legend in Medieval Scottish Literature* (Cambridge: D. S. Brewer, 2014), 11.

on the subsequent political and affective power of Geoffrey's British history can scarcely be overstated. On the one hand, Brutus's establishment of Locrine as overlord of Albanact authorises a retrospective reconstruction of Anglo-Scots history as a continuous, unbroken relation of 'feudal' lordship and vassalage, in which the kingdom of Scotland is understood to be held as a fief of the English Crown. On the other, Edward's suggestion that Brutus reserved overall sovereignty for his firstborn introduced a powerful new affective potential into the legend. It implied that the island's division was *never intended*. 'Division of the kingdom' thus becomes a destructive aberration, the resonant original cause of the island's subsequent painful history of strife and warfare between peoples. By this means, too, Edward's addition redirects the prophetic energy that flowed so powerfully through Geoffrey's Welsh history (Diana's foretelling the destiny of Brutus; Merlin's prophesying Arthur's return; the voice telling Cadwalladr that the time is not yet) into imagining the future of Britain as an Anglo-imperial island.

These two modifications of Galfridian British history would have profound effects for Tudor war propaganda and its afterlife in Elizabethan English literature.[35] On the one hand, Edward's feudalisation of Brutus's division of the kingdom would, mediated by John Hardyng's chronicle and forged homages, become the model for the history of overlordship with which Henry VIII justified his brutal invasions of Scotland. Henry VIII's history, catchily entitled *A Declaration, conteyning the iust causes and consyderations of this present warre with the Scottis, wherin also appereth the trewe and right title, that the kinges most royall maiesty hath to the souerayntie of Scotland* (1542), became the widely cited backbone of the war's justification. On the other hand, Edward I's redirection of the Welsh prophetic strain of Geoffrey's text towards the restoration of an imagined *English* insular integrity would be joined, in the 1540s, with a new poetic, chorographic and military-strategic awareness of the need for England's jurisdiction to extend to the realm of Neptune – that is, for England to recover dominion over all the coasts of the island, securing it from foreign foes. This would be the theme of John Leland's antiquarian and poetic writings of the 1540s, and would govern the strategic aims of the war under Protector Somerset's leadership from 1547 to 1550.

---

[35] In a much-cited article of 1961, Sydney Anglo argued that the importance of 'British' symbolism for the Tudors had been exaggerated. Sydney Anglo, 'The *British History* in Early Tudor Propaganda', *Bulletin of the John Rylands Library*, vol. 44, no. 1 (1961), 17–48. What he defined as 'propaganda', however, excluded the texts of the 1540s war and did not extend to Elizabethan literature, thus obscuring the deep structural importance of 'British history' for the latter.

In a final, influential twist, Edward I's letter to Pope Boniface appropriated the structural and climatic centre of Geoffrey's Welsh history – Arthur's wearing of the royal crown at Caerleon in book IX – for proof of Edward's possession of Scotland.[36] Arthur, wrote Edward, citing Geoffrey, 'subjected to himself a rebellious Scotland' and 'destroyed almost the whole nation', installing one 'Augusel' as king, who afterwards bore the sword at the famous feast at Caerleon.[37] As the early sixteenth century brought the historicity of Brutus and Arthur under pressure from sceptical humanists, Arthur's fabled conquests and exploits were whittled back to a reliable kernel of credibility – this subjugation of Scotland. The entries for *Arthurus* and *Britannia* in the wartime (1545) edition of Sir Thomas Elyot's Dictionary thus expressed doubts about Britain's Trojan ancestry and the extent of Arthur's empire, but asserted that Arthur had indeed subdued Scotland.[38]

But what of Scotland's account of its own ancient regnal history? That a Scottish counter-mythology already existed as early as the thirteenth century can be seen from the response to Edward I given by the Scottish ambassadors at the Papal Curia in 1301.[39] The full-scale history of Scotland known as John of Fordun's *Chronicle of the Scottish Nation* has been dated c.1363–87, but Dauvit Broun has recently derived Fordun's account from an earlier narrative, possibly by Richard Vairement or 'Veremundus', *célé Dé* of St Andrews and chancellor of Queen Marie de Couci, active 1239–67.[40] Vairement seems to have synthesised a number of different elements – the lives of St Brendan and St Congal, Scottish and Pictish king lists, the mid-eleventh-century *Lebor Gabála Érenn* ('Book of the Takings of Ireland'), and aspects of Geoffrey of Monmouth's history – to produce the complex story of the Scots as a people emanating from Ireland, who then became the sole inhabitants of a kingdom – Scotland – which, even

---

[36] Scott Dempsey, 'The Evolution of Edward I's Historical Claim to Overlordship of Scotland, 1291-1301', in David Green and Chris Given-Wilson (ed.), *Fourteenth-Century England* no. 11 (Woodbridge: Boydell, 2019), 1–30. I owe this reference to Roger Mason.

[37] Stones, *Anglo-Scottish Relations*, 196–7.

[38] Kendrick, *British Antiquity*, 42–3. See the entries for 'Arthurus' and 'Britania', in *Bibliotheca Eliotae* (London: Thomas Berthelet, 1545). No such entries exist in *The dictionary of syr Thomas Eliot* (London: Berthelet, 1538).

[39] Mason, 'Scotching the Brut', 63; Goldstein, *Matter of Scotland*, 66–78; Wingfield, *Trojan Legend*, 12.

[40] Broun, *Scottish Independence*, 49, 215–34 and Dauvit Broun, *The Irish Identity of the Kingdom of the Scots in the Twelfth and Thirteenth Centuries* (Woodbridge: Boydell, 1999). Broun's 2007 account builds on the seminal research of Nicola Royan, 'Hector Boece and the question of Veremund', *Innes Review*, vol. 52, no. 1 (2001), 42–62. See also John and Winifred MacQueen, 'Introduction to Books I and II' to Walter Bower, *Scotichronicon*, ed. D. E. R. Watt, 9 vols (Aberdeen: Aberdeen University Press, 1987–98), I. xiii–xxxiii.

while shared with the Picts, a kindred people, had been primordially coherent as a regnal territory.[41] One aspect of this narrative, blending Irish and Galfridian sources, involved a wandering prince – a Greek, this time – called Gaythelos. Having married Scota, the daughter of the Egyptian pharaoh drowned in the Red Sea, Prince Gaythelos and his bride fled from Egypt to Spain. Finding themselves oppressed, the royal pair then sent their sons to discover uninhabited lands, where they could be free. Their descendants colonised first Ireland and then Scotland, taking the royal throne – stone of Scone – from one to the other. There were other elements: the arrival of Picts in Ireland, intermarriage and the settling of both peoples in Scotland, the Pictish foundation of the metropolitan church of St Andrews, as well as the ideology of Scoto-Pictish 'freedom' and independence from Roman and British rule.[42] But where the Galfridian British history remained imaginatively adaptable (however discredited *as* history) to sixteenth-century English geopolitical priorities, this synthetic history of Scottish origins, successively chronicled by Vairement, by John of Fordun, by Andrew of Wyntoun (c.1350–1425) and by Walter Bower (c.1385–1449) grew progressively less and less effective as mythic counterweight. In 1527 a new milestone was reached when the principal of King's College of Aberdeen, Hector Boece, published his *Scotorum Historia*, a fully fledged humanist transformation of Bower's chronicle material into Latin imitative of Cicero and Livy, reconciling the synthetic Scottish history with the recently rediscovered works of Tacitus.[43] R. James Goldstein has given a fine account of the 'war of historiography' out of which a Scottish national literature emerged in the fourteenth century to counter Edward I's Anglo-imperialism.[44] In the early sixteenth century, however, Boece's elegant Livyan infill of Scottish kingship back to the fourth century BC could not compete with the cartographic imaginative power that Geoffrey's ancient myth of Britain's insular unity was beginning to acquire. The idea of Britain as promised island, with Troynovant-London on the Thames, hinted prophetically at how a nation defended and encircled by the sea might expand into a great

[41] Broun, *Scottish Independence*, 240–6.
[42] *John of Fordun's Chronicle of the Scottish Nation*, ed. W. F. Skene, 2 vols (Edinburgh: 1872, facsimile reprint, Llanerch Publishers, 1993), 6–20, 25–9, 43–5, 71–2.
[43] Jack MacQueen, 'From Rome to Ruddiman: The Scoto-Latin Tradition', in *The Edinburgh History of Scottish Literature Vol. I: From Columba to the Union* eds. Thomas Owen Clancy and Murray Pittock (Edinburgh: Edinburgh University Press, 2007), 184–208, 188.
[44] Goldstein, *Matter of Scotland*, 57–132.

trading empire.[45] Over the course of the sixteenth century, a 'monarchical republican' vision of English legal and constitutional exceptionality would mesh with this neo-Galfridian insular imperialism, producing a vision of an England as stretching on all sides to the sea, an island trading nation-to-be.[46] Scottish origin stories could boast no comparable vision of recovery of a lost integrity or prophecy of riches to come. Boece followed Bower in telling a story of two interwoven peoples, the Picts and the Scots, sharing land divided by mountains, the Scots always joined by the ancient highway of the sea to royal ancestors and kin in Ireland.[47] Thus, though Scots histories were as rich in their way as Geoffrey's (if Geoffrey gives us *Lear*, Boece gives us *Macbeth*) their origin tales of Scots crossing and recrossing the Irish sea, or of Pictish kings honouring the relics of St Andrew, were weak counterpoints to a more resonant, pervasive and more easily Protestantised myth of England recovering Britain's *original island unity and religious purity*.[48]

The story of how English poets and lawyers transformed Galfridian myth in the later sixteenth and early seventeenth centuries will be the subject of later chapters. The rest of this chapter will analyse the foundational, dynamic and innovative part played by a Galfridian-derived myth of 'Great Britain' in justifying the invasion and laying waste of Scotland between 1542 and 1550. I am aware of the risk that literary critics who define their sphere of interest as 'early modern England' might switch off at this point, understandably reluctant to engage with Scottish materials that are 'not relevant' to English literature. But of course, my argument is that they *are* relevant, that this war is, in some sense, the unconscious of Elizabethan literature and the Elizabethan insular self-image. Let me, by

---

[45] See, for example, Mike Pincombe, 'Dream and Mystery in Sir Thomas Wyatt's "Tagus Farewell"', *Studia Neophilologica*, vol. 87, no. 1 (2015), 36–47. The relation of river poetry to empire will be discussed in Chapter 2.

[46] See Armitage, *Ideological Origins*, 24–60; Hoak, 'Cecil and Smith'; Arthur Williamson, 'The Edwardian Moment', in Williamson '*The Nation Epidemicall': Scotland and the Rise of Social Theory*, forthcoming.

[47] Hector Boece, *The History and Chronicles of Scotland written in Latin by Hector Boece, Canon of Aberdeen and Translated by John Bellenden, Archdean of Moray and Canon of Ross*, ed. Thomas Maitland, 2 volumes (Edinburgh: W. and C. Tait, 1821); See Alex Woolf, *From Pictland to Alba, 798–1070* (Edinburgh: Edinburgh University Press, 2007), 113–14, as well as Fordun, *Chronicle*, and Broun, *Scottish Independence*.

[48] Goldstein has written of the way in which Fordun's Gaythelos was made to speak for the ideals of freedom that marked Scottish resistance to Edward I's occupation, *Matter of Scotland*, 104–49. Sixteenth-century Protestantism complicated and fissured Scottish allegiances, however, while Geoffrey's myth of insular unity was imaginatively adaptable to John Foxe's idea of the Protestant English as 'elect nation'. See Arthur Williamson, *Scottish National Consciousness in the Age of James VI: The Apocalypse, the Union and the Shaping of Scotland's Public Culture* (Edinburgh: John Donald Publishers, 1979).

way of example, invoke one obvious 'English literature' payoff. Most of the war texts I will be discussing enjoyed a vigorous afterlife in the history book that all critics of Spenser and Shakespeare acknowledge to be rich source of inspiration: Raphael Holinshed's *Chronicles* (1577, 1587).

Holinshed's *Chronicles* were not only deeply indebted to historiography of the 1540s wars: they were the war's product. Raphael Holinshed took over what had originally been a plan conceived in the 1540s by the printer, Reyner or Reginald Wolfe, for a universal cosmography. As Philip Schwyzer explains, 'Reyner Wolfe had taken a leading role in the dissemination of the new ideology of British nationalism even before he became King's Printer in 1546.'[49] In support of the war, Wolfe printed, anonymously, John Brende's 1544 celebration of Hertford's brutal campaign, *The Late Expedition in Scotlande* (indeed, we know this text is by the soldier and humanist translator, John Brende, only because Holinshed cites it as a source).[50] Wolfe was also the publisher of a Latin version of Protector Somerset's wartime epistle to the Scottish nation, which, as we shall see, threatened the Scots with slaughter if they refused to embrace Anglo-imperial Britishness.[51] The poems of John Leland, in particular *Genethliacon* (1543) and *Cygnea Cantio* (1545), likewise issued from Wolfe's press. These poems were, as Schwyzer puts it, 'heavily imbued with Leland's distinctive vision of British antiquity reborn in the reign of Henry VIII'. Schwyzer makes admirably clear how Leland's poems shaped neo-Galfridian ideology: '[A]s if the island were already united under one imperial ruler', he says, 'Leland praised the future Edward VI as the darling of the British race, who would put down Scottish tumults.'[52] Within neo-Galfridianism nestled Geoffrey of Monmouth's own history, which was, of course, 'one of Holinshed's core texts', 'fundamental', for the early part of his history.[53] Holinshed also drew heavily on Edmund Hall's *Chronicle*, a history presented as an account of English intestine war (York against Lancaster) in the Galfridian tradition of lamenting the division of the kingdom.[54]

---

[49] Philip Schwyzer, 'Archipelagic History', in *The Oxford Handbook of Holinshed's Chronicles*, ed. Paulina Kewes, Ian W. Archer, Felicity Heal (Oxford: Oxford University Press, 2013), 594–607, 600.

[50] Henry Summerson, 'Sources, 1577', *Oxford Handbook of Holinshed*, 76: 'Among the sources he forgot to include in his main list he named "John Brend, who wrote the expedition into Scotland, 1544", thereby rescuing from anonymity the author of *The Late Expedicion into Scotlande, Made by the Kynges Highnys Armye, under the Conduit of the ... Erle of Hertforde* (1544).'

[51] Edward Seymour, *Epistola Exhortatoria ad Pacem* (London: Reginald Wolf, 1548). On Brende, see Harold Davis, 'John Brende: Soldier and Translator', *HLQ*, vol. 1, no. 4 (1938), 421–6.

[52] Schwyzer, 'Archipelagic', 600.   [53] Summerson, 'Sources', 62.

[54] Edward Hall, *Hall's Chronicle* (New York: AMS Press, 1965), 53: 'For while all was vnder one, no nacion durst either once inuade or attempte warre against the Briton.'

Hall's *Chronicle* was another wartime production, published posthumously in 1548 (at the height of the war) by Richard Grafton who, like Reyner Wolfe, was a printer wholeheartedly committed to the Protestant, Anglo-imperial agenda of the war. In 1543, Grafton had been responsible for publishing a special war-effort edition of John Hardyng's fifteenth-century *Chronicle* which, written to contextualise the author's forgeries of documents of English title to Scotland, made the case for invasive war. Hardyng's *Chronicle* was widely read: Edmund Hall drew on it, as did Holinshed and Spenser; John Dee annotated his copy.[55] William Harrison's 'An Historical Description of the Iland of Britaine', which prefaced Holinshed's *Chronicles*, made much use of Leland's British Anglo-imperial writings, as well as citing another key war text printed by Grafton, *An Epitome of the title that the Kynges Maiestie of Englande hath to the sovereigntie of Scotlande, continued vpon the auncient writers of both nacions from the beginning* (1548) in order to justify English sovereignty over the whole island.[56] Holinshed's *Chronicles*, in other words, were saturated, in every section, and across every period and national boundary, with the ideological justification of England's invasion of Scotland in the 1540s. Thus, although the ignominy of defeat in 1550 was, in some senses, forgotten, the war's self-justifying arguments for Scottish non-nationhood pervaded Elizabethan historiography, with important consequences for James's attempt at 'British' union in 1603.

What follows, then, sets these sources of Holinshed back amid the violence, the burning, shooting, raping and looting that their arguments were designed to justify in 1542–50. This chapter and the next tell a story of ideological and military transition, from the simple overlordship argument supporting Henry's high-handed but distracted campaign of punitive devastation, to Protector Somerset's more complex harnessing of the visionary potential of Geoffrey's island myth in the service of an amphibious military strategy and of a propaganda campaign which cast Scottish resistance to conquest as impeding God's provident plot for the invincible island of 'Great Britain'.

---

[55] John Dee's annotated copy of Grafton's edition of Hardyng is now owned by Toshiyuki Takamiya, Emeritus Professor, Keio University.

[56] *An Epitome of the title that the Kynges Maiestie of Englande hath to the sovereigntie of Scotlande* attributed to 'Nicholas Bodrugan, otherwise Adams' (London, 1548). Dale Hoak ascribes authorship to Sir Thomas Smith ('Cecil and Smith', 50–1). Although we know little about Bodrugan, alias Adams, other than that he was a young lawyer from Dartmouth (Hoak, 'Cecil and Smith', 50) the *Epitome* (1548) was a significant and influential piece of propaganda and will be referred to in subsequent chapters.

III.   'If we had minded the possession of Scotland': *Occupatio*, Distraction and Henry's Wars, 1542–1547

Among Cecil's papers at Hatfield House, as well as in the State Papers, there exists a detailed itinerary, like a tourist trail, of edifices that lined the banks of the river Tweed and its tributaries in the autumn of 1545 (see Figure 1.2 in plate section). The text is divided by waters and parishes, 'On the river of Twede', 'On the River of Tiviot' (Teviot), 'On the Water of Rowle' ('Rule'), 'On the Ryver of Jedde' and so forth. The buildings range from magnificent ancient monastic abbeys filled with treasures and manuscripts – Kelso, Melrose, Dryburgh, Jedburgh – to water mills, villages and 'spitals' (lepers' hospitals). At first glance, the text almost reads like one of John Leland's 'laborious journeys' along rivers and fenny waters in search of antiquities.[57] But no – there are those infrequent but dismaying past participles – 'raced and cast down', 'brent', 'raced', 'raced', 'raced'. And then, at the end of every section, a numerical sum. This is no gentle tourist meander round the border abbeys, but a meticulous casting of the accounts of a rampage. In the Hatfield House manuscript, the location is given to the left of a beautifully ruled vertical line, to the right of which is the list of places destroyed. Underneath, neatly centred, are the totals for each district, in roman numerals.

On the ryver of Twede.	First, the Abbey of *Kelso* raced and cast down; the Towne of *Kelso* brent; the Abbey of *Melrosse alias Mewrose, Darnyke, Gawtenside, Danyelton, Overton, Heildon, Newton* of *Heildon, Maxton, Lafeddon, Marton, Beamoundside, Loughflatte, Bateshele,* the Abbey of *Dryburghe,* the Town of *Dryburghe,* the Towre of *Dawcowe* raced, the Town of *Dawcowe, Rotherford, Stockstrother, Newtowne, Trowes, Makerston,* the *Manorhill, Charter-house, Lugton Lawe, Stotherike* Towre raced, *East Meredeane, West Meredeane, Flowres, Gallow Lawe, Broxe Lawe, Broxe Mylne,* the Water-mill of *Kelso.*
	Summa .xxxiij.

---

[57] John Leland, *The laboryouse Journey & Serche of Johan Lelande, for Englandes Antiquitees, geuen of hym as a newe yeares gyfte to kynge henry the viii. in the .xxxvii. yeare of his Reygne, with declaracyons enlarged: by Johan Bale* (London, 1549).

On the River of Tiviot.

The Freers [Friars] near *Kelso*, the Larde *Hog's* House, the Barnes of *Old Rockesborough, Rocksburgh* Towne, the Towre of *Rockesborough* raced, the Towre of *Ormeston* raced, the Towne of *Ormeston, Neyther Nesbett, Over Nesebet, Angeram Spittell, Bune Jedwourth*, the two Towre of *Bune Jedworth* raced, the Laird of *Bune Jedworth's* Dwelling house, *Over Angeram, Neyther Angeram, East Barnehill, Mynto Crag, Mynto* Towne and Place, *West Mynto*, the *Cragge* End, *Whitrick, Hessington, Bankehessington, Overhassington, Cotes, Esshebanke, Cavers, Bryeryardes, Denhome, Langton, Rowcastle, Newtowne, Whitchester-house, Tympinton.*

Summa .xxxvij.

On the Water of Rowle.

Rowle Spittel, Bedrowle, Rowlewood. The *Wolles, Crossebewghe, Donnerles, Fotton, Weast Leas.* Two *Walke Mylnes. Tromyhill, Dupligis.*

Summa .xij.

On the Ryver of Jedde.

The Abbey of *Jedworthe*, the Freers [Friars] there; the Towne of *Jedworthe, Hundylee, Bungate*, the *Bank End*, the *Neyther Mylnes, Houston, Over Craling*, the Wells, *Neyther Craling, Over Wodden, Neyther Wodden.*

Summa .xiij.

The list goes on, six pages in all, several more paragraphs of names, concluding with an overall total, and then numerical calculation of the destruction according to building-type (monastery, castle, town, mill, hospital):

> Summa totalis cciiij[xx] vij. In monasteries and fryres houses vij. In castelles, towres and pyles xvj. In merket towns v. In villages ccxliij. In mylles xiij. In spitelles and hospitalles iij.[58]

---

[58] Transcript of names from *A collection of state papers, relating to affairs in the reigns of King Henry VIII. King Edward VI. Queen Mary, and Queen Elizabeth*, ed. Samuel Haynes (London, 1740), 52.

A grand total of two hundred and eighty-seven places have been 'brent, raced, and cast downe' at the commandment of Edward Seymour, earl of Hertford, as part of the 'Invasion into the Realme of Scotland' between the 8th and the 23rd of September, 1545. The manuscript renders Hertford's stewardship of his charge to the privy council and the king. It applies the formulae of memoranda (neatly ruled lines, headings, items separated by commas, summed up in totals) to conjure their antithesis, obliteration: flames and cannon-shot tearing through roofs and walls, hovels and towers flattened, people terrorised and shot at close range, livestock plundered, the treasures of the abbeys violently desecrated and looted. Record-keeping obscures the annihilation it would represent.

This document's shocking clash of presentational styles, oscillating between affectionate chorography and military reconnaissance, or a sober casting of accounts and an orgy of iconoclasm, attests to the complexity of England's imperial project of conquering Scotland in these years. It adumbrates, per-haps, differences between Henry's ideological priorities and those of the earl of Hertford that were to emerge when, on Henry's death in 1547, Hertford took over the war as the duke of Somerset, Lord Protector of England. One's sense, for example, of an uncanny resemblance between this topography of oblivion in the Scottish borders and John Leland's contemporaneous memorialisation of the British antiquities which he tracked along the 'washes, lakes, meres, fenny waters' of Henry's dominions, is surely no accident.[59] Leland's deriv-ation of the traces of British histories of Brutus and Arthur from the Anglo-Welsh natural landscape was no nostalgic perambulation through monastic ruins. It was, rather, as Cathy Shrank has shown, an inventive Protestant humanist history, designed to enrich England's identification as 'Britain' by way of locating the mythic history of that claim in the writing of landscape. At the same time, as Shrank also notes, Leland's topographic description has affinities with the rise of cartography as a military resource.[60] Cartographic historian Peter Barber has noted that Henry VIII's reign was 'a watershed in the history of map consciousness and map use'.[61]

In the 1540s, a new humanist conception of the effective power of eloquence combines with a new appreciation of the uses of cartographic and hydrographic knowledge, as expressed in the concept of the 'plat'. This word 'plat' fused ideas of spatial mastery and future-oriented provision of material resources (such as military supply to an army in hostile territory)

[59] Leland, *Journey*, sig. D4v.   [60] Shrank, *Writing*, 86.
[61] Peter Barber, 'England I: Pageantry, Defence and Government: Maps at Court to 1550', in David Buisseret ed., *Monarchs, Ministers and Maps: The Emergence of Cartography as a Tool of Government in Early Modern Europe* (Chicago, IL: University of Chicago Press, 1992), 26–57, 27.

with ideas of rhetorical persuasion, which guarantee the commitment of human allegiance and assistance. Plats were, as I have elsewhere written, 'at once conceptual schemes for the better organization of means and resources and the discursive order or "emplotment" of their probable success'.[62] During the wars of the 1540s, letters show Hertford 'constantly evaluating and commissioning plats for the information of his master'.[63] One of these, indeed, was Hertford's 'plat' for the fortification of Kelso Abbey on this very 1545 campaign. Rejected by Henry and the privy council, the waste of this plat is implicitly marked as Kelso's prioritisation in Hertford's account of laying waste: 'On the *ryver of Twede* ... First, Abbey of *Kelso* raced and cast down'.

Thus, the perceptible clash of style and substance in this document may acknowledge, among other things, a tension between the somewhat haphazard and distracted nature of Henry's conduct of the war in 1542–7 and Hertford's sense of the provident accountability of iconoclasm itself. These two contrasting styles of military leadership of the war might be characterised as the mode (in Henry's case) of strategic *preoccupation* or *absence of mind*, while Hertford/Somerset conceived the war as a realisation of God's providential 'plat' for Britain. Henry VIII would keep contemporaries and modern historians guessing about his intentions in Scotland. For example, William Thomas's *Peregrine*, written in exoneration of Henry VIII after his death, describes a dinner party in Bologna at which his Italian hosts accuse Henry of having 'wasted ... no small parte of Scotlande with entent to subdue the hole without cause or reason'.[64] Protector Somerset, by contrast, would leave no one in any doubt of his 'entent' to unite the nations of Britain, he and his propaganda team providing endless iterations of causes, reasons and considerations for the army to proclaim as they burned and looted. Somerset, indeed, conflated rhetorical persuasion with military coercion in ways which would be ultimately self-defeating. His neo-Galfridian vision of an island empire of Great Britain, a mythical ancient unity recovered for godly and profitable future required the buy-in of the Scots in a way that Henry's mere assertion of sovereignty did not. Both, however, as we will see, licensed a contempt and brutality towards their addressees that contradicted their professed objectives of a peaceable dynastic union.

---

[62] Lorna Hutson, 'Fortunate Travelers: Reading for the Plot in Sixteenth-Century England', *Representations*, no. 41 (1993), 83–103, 87.

[63] Barber, 'England I', 40.

[64] 'will:thomas his peregrin', BL Cotton MS Vespasian D XVIII, fol. 48. See Ian C. Martin, 'The Manuscript and Editorial Tradition of William Thomas's *The Pilgrim* or *Il Pellegrino Inglese*', Unpublished PhD thesis, University of Toronto, 1999, 186.

In 1544–7, Henry failed, diplomatically and militarily, to achieve the betrothal of Mary Stewart (Mary Queen of Scots) to his son Edward. This was partly because he regarded efforts in Scotland as ancillary to more important conquests in France. It is also, however, because he really believed in his title to Scotland and overestimated the extent to which Protestant enthusiasm for union with the English might outweigh fears of English tyranny. Henry's *Declaration* is not a complex or especially per-suasive text and most historians let its titular description of its contents stand in for any analysis of the text itself. Its exceptional influence, however, obliges us to attend to it more closely. 'Virtually every single future English pronouncement accepted its case', not just for the duration of the war, but beyond, in the establishment of the constitutional relation between Scotland and England after James's accession.[65] Before we turn to the text itself, however, we need to look at the military activity that it justified.

It is tempting, as I have suggested, to imagine that, in the almost parodic form of Hertford's meticulously itemised invoice of violence in the bor-ders, one can detect a feeling of frustration at having to carry out Henry's scattershot orders without being able to build, militarily and in propaganda terms, on these successful raids. In the previous spring, of 1544, Hertford had received instructions from the king to capture Edinburgh Castle and its port of Leith and fortify them both. But plans suddenly changed. Henry, on the point of invading France, no longer wanted fortifications in Scotland. He now wished simply to 'devastate their countrey', preclud-ing the possibility of military aid from Scotland's allies, France and Denmark. 'His majesties pleasure', the privy council now told Hertford,

> is that ye shall forbeare to make the forsayde determined fortification either at Lythe or at the sayde mount, but only for this journey put all to fyre and swoorde, burne Edinborough towne, so rased and defaced when you have sacked and gotten what ye can out of it, as there may remayn forever a perpetuel memory of the vengeance of God lightened upon [them?] for their faulsehode and disloyailtye. – Do what ye can out of hande, and without long tarying, to beate down over throwe the castle, sack Holyrod house, and as many townes and villaiges about Edinborough as ye may conveniently, sacke Lythe and burne and subverte it and all the rest, putting man, woman and childe to fyre and sword without exception where any resistence shalbe made agaynst you, and this done, passe over to the Fyfeland and extende like extremityes and destructions in all townes and villaiges . . .

[65] Marcus Merriman, *The Rough Wooings: Mary Queen of Scots 1542–1551* (East Linton: Tuckwell Press, 2000), 267. I am indebted to Merriman's excellent account of the war.

not forgetting among all the rest so to spoyle and turne upset downe the Cardinalles town of S[t] Andrews, as thupper stone may be the nether, and not one stick stande by an other, sparing no creature alyve within the same . . . And yf ye see any likelyhode of winning the castle, gyve sum stout assay to the same . . . and destroye it pece meale . . . do nothing but such as ye see may easely be achieved.[66]

The instructions combine ludicrously unrealistic ambitions (to overthrow Edinburgh Castle and destroy St Andrews Castle 'pece meal') with a deprecating dismissiveness that must have irked: 'Do what ye can out of hande' (i.e. 'don't go to any extra trouble'); burn places 'as ye may conveniently' (i.e. 'don't go out of your way') and 'this done, passe over to the Fyfeland' (there was clearly no time to get over to Fife in Henry's new schedule). There is also, in the exuberance of the vision of the Cathedral and Castle of St Andrews turned so 'upset downe' that 'thupper stone may be the nether', a suggestion of the energy with which the Reformation, as Robert Scribner has argued, assimilated the *verkehrte Welt* or 'world upside-down' of carnival and radical Christianity.[67] Hertford, however, declared that he was grieved 'to see the King's treasure employed only in devastating two or three towns and a little country which would soon recover'.[68] But Henry's distraction by the greater prize of France did not preclude his sense of the importance of this expedition of admonitory devastation. Hertford was to 'put man, woman and childe to fyre and swoord without exception where any resistence shalbe made agaynst you'. This he most certainly was able to do.

As it turned out, Edinburgh Castle proved impregnable. The English were gunned down as they tried to approach by the only way possible – along the Royal Mile. Sir John Brende lamented 'the loss of divers of our men with the shot of the ordnance out of the said Castle', noting approvingly that Hertford determined not 'to waste and consume our munition about the siege thereof' but rather 'utterly to ruinate and destroy the said town with fire'.[69] Edinburgh sent out its provost, Adam Otterburn, to 'remonstrate against such unlooked for hostilities and propose an amicable adjustment of all differences'.[70] But the citizens could not possibly accept Hertford's terms, which were the immediate delivery of Scotland's infant queen into Henry VIII's custody. Hertford ordered his soldiers to 'put the

---

[66] *HP*, II.326.
[67] Robert Scribner, *Popular Culture and Popular Movements in Reformation Germany* (London: Hambledon, 1987).
[68] Merriman, *Rough Wooings*, 145.   [69] [Brende] *late expedition*, 43.
[70] Merriman, *Rough Wooings*, 145.

inhabitants to the sword' and then burn the town. 'Neither within the walls nor in the suburbs was any house left unburnt' Brende noted with satisfaction. The Abbey and Palace of Holyrood House were also destroyed; the army then 'burnt every stick' of Leith harbour, capturing ships and departing 'pestered' with booty, the spoils of Scotland's trade from France, Denmark and Flanders. On the way south, for good measure, they 'suffocated and burnt' the inhabitants of Dunbar as they slept.[71]

In 1545, John Leland flattered Henry by celebrating the Hertford's 1544 campaign as a great success. '*Scotti perfidiae graveis tulerunt / Poenas*', he wrote, 'The Scots paid heavy forfeits for their treachery' describing how 'Leith is prostrate, wholly reduced to sad ashes'.[72] Blatantly stretching the truth, Leland declared that Edinburgh Castle had been brought to ruin by fire and steel, and that this victory, along with Henry's capture of Boulogne, showed the favour of Neptune to the *British*.[73] But for Hertford, the frustration of neither being able to garrison nor to build on Leland's fervent propaganda, was to recur in the 1545 campaign on the borders. This time, as I have mentioned, he proposed to fortify the magnificent Romanesque Abbey of Kelso, a Tironensian establishment founded by David I in the twelfth century. For this Hertford had royal approval: Henry 'lyketh very well your nue platte', he was told. But once again, plans changed: Hertford was not to proceed with this fortification.[74] Frustrated, he utterly demolished the abbey. The monumental west tower still soars skyward amid the ruins of that assault in 1545, its dwarfing of all adjacent buildings a striking index of the grandeur and scale of what was destroyed that day.

In Hertford's army was a Protestant Highlander called John Elder, a fervent supporter of Henry VIII's Reformation, who wrote to William Paget, describing the operation with relish. Hertford's army marched towards the abbey, wrote Elder, with a discipline that Vegetius and Frontinus would have approved. When they met resistance from some monks and 'hackbuttiers' within (that is, soldiers with arquebusses or musket-like firearms), English forces drew up a cannon and fired it, while shooting into the windows so fiercely that none could peep out. Two hours' battery threw down the choir 'where such a noise was as I have seldom heard', wrote Elder, 'what of those that entered, and what of them that were within, calling and crying for mercy'. Hertford, he declared

---

[71] [Brende] *late expedition*, 45.
[72] John Leland, *Cygnea Cantio*. (London: 1545), sig. E2r-v. I have used the translation by Dana Sutton: https://philological.cal.bham.ac.uk/swansong/.
[73] Leland, *Cygnea Cantio*, sig. E2r-v.   [74] Merriman, *Rough Wooings*, 149–50.

impressively, had 'made all the abbeys upon the Twide tremble in a day'.[75]
Elder's conclusion of the letter with an itemisation of destruction in
Tweedside, Teviotdale and Jedburgh suggests that he may even have
provided the local knowledge for the fuller reckoning with which we
began.

So why was Scotland held to be deserving of such treatment by an
English royal army in 1544 and 1545? Leland referred to the Scots' *perfidia*,
their faithlessness. Likewise, Anthony Cope's 1544 translation of Livy on
Hannibal and Scipio encourages Henry VIII's military efforts against 'the
promisse breakers the double dealyne Scottes'.[76] Englishmen understandably thought the Scots perjured because they had, under their governor,
James Hamilton, the earl of Arran, broken the Treaty of Greenwich
(1 July 1543) according to which the country's queen, the infant Mary
Stewart, would be betrothed to Henry's toddler son. This might sound
a reasonable ground of war, but Henry had, in negotiating the Treaty of
Greenwich, stipulated conditions that it would be impossible for
a sovereign nation to accept. He did this because he regarded himself as
Scotland's true sovereign, and because he felt already aggrieved by perceived slights to his suzerainty on the part of Mary Stewart's late father,
James V, who was his sister's son. During the reign of James V, Henry had
hoped to persuade his young nephew to join him in breaking with Rome
and reaping all the consequent financial benefits of monastery dissolution.
He had probably felt quite confident in this strategy, for there were indeed
signs of growing numbers of Scots enthusiastic about the new Protestant
learning. Thomas Cromwell was told, in 1539, of Scots fleeing to England
daily for 'reading of the Scriptures in English'.[77] But James, though
tolerant, or even encouraging, of reformers, already controlled so much
of the Scottish Church's patronage and wealth that he had no financial
incentive to dissolve its monasteries.[78] Henry seems not to have informed
himself about Scotland enough to have understood this, so that what he
perceived as James's 'defiance' in receiving English Catholic refugees, and
in refusing to keep an appointment at York, stoked his anger. Henry then
sent a force into Scotland under the duke of Norfolk in 1542, and in
retaliation, James mustered an army which met the English on the Esk,
near the Solway Firth. The English won the field, known as Solway Moss,

---

[75] *L & P Henry VIII*, Vol. 20, part 2, 245–65.
[76] Anthony Cope, *The Historie of Two the moste noble Capitaines of the Worlde, Anniball and Scipio* (London: Berthelet, 1544), sig. A3r.
[77] *L&P Henry VIII*, Vol. 14, pt.1, 625. See Ryrie, *Scottish Reformation*, 32–3 and *passim*.
[78] Ryrie, *Scottish Reformation*, 37–52.

taking large numbers of Scottish noble prisoners, from whom they took pledges or hostages, on the assurance that these noblemen would, on their return to Scotland, advance Henry's cause. Shortly afterward, James V died (probably of cholera), leaving a daughter and heir who was a mere six days old. This, then, seemed to Henry a providential sign of the rightness of the time to recovery his ancient title to Scotland. He had already published his *Declaration*. He had all his 'assured' noblemen from Solway Moss ready to support him. It seemed as if Scotland was ready to embrace Protestantism and union with England. He had a son of perfect age to be betrothed to this infant female heir to the Scottish throne. The earl of Arran, Scotland's governor, though not the brightest nor most reliable of people, seemed encouraging. Nothing, it must have seemed to Henry, could stop him now. He could recover his ancient right in Scotland without any effort at all – he could even do so without paying much attention, while he concentrated on war with France.

But from the outset, Henry's assumption of his right to Scotland made the Scots uneasy about the marriage. Scottish ambassadors, arriving in London to negotiate the betrothal, conveyed the articles agreed by their Parliament, according to which, once the queen 'being of perfit aige & mareit in Ingland', Scotland should continue to 'evir haif and beir the Name of Scotland' with 'all the auld liberties, priuileges and fredomes . . . as it hes bene in all tymes bigane and salbe gidit & gouernit vnder ane gouernour borne of the realme selfe', with continuance of the College of Justice and other institutions.[79] Henry's aims, as Alec Ryrie has neatly summarised them, were quite different:

> Henry's hopes . . . were nakedly expansionist and imperialistic. The old English claim to feudal suzerainty over Scotland had been revived in 1542, and during 1543 Henry never allowed it to recede too far into the background. He wanted a marriage treaty, and one which would deliver the Queen of Scots into his own custody. He also wanted the title of Governor of Scotland for himself. He was ready, if necessary, to send an English army into Scotland to secure these objectives. And he did not want to make any guarantees regarding Scotland's laws and liberties, or regarding what might happen if either Prince Edward or Queen Mary died before the marriage could be solemnised. The marriage was, for Henry, a form of conquest, and his patience with the Scots was vanishingly short.[80]

---

[79] *The Acts of the Parliament of Scotland 1124–1707*, ed. Thomas Thomson, Cosmo Innes, Archibald Anderson. 12 volumes (Great Britain Record Commission, 1814–75), ii.412.
[80] Ryrie, *Scottish Reformation*, 59.

The negotiations quickly unravelled. The Scottish ambassadors wanted a clause in the treaty that would provide, in the event of Mary's death before the marriage, for the Scottish crown to go the next heir of blood, 'which', as Henry wrote to his ambassador in Scotland, Sir Ralph Sadler, 'should have implied a grant that there rested in us no right to that realm'.[81] But Sadler himself was writing back to Henry, explaining that the Scots would not concede his title; even Henry's 'assured' noblemen found English conditions for immediate custody of Mary unacceptable. One of these, Sir George Douglas, explained to Sadler why Henry's demands would not work. Take the long view, Douglas advised Sadler. If the betrothal goes ahead and Mary is permitted to reside in Scotland, brought up by nobles from both countries, over time, free intercourse between the countries would build amicable relations and trust. '[T]hat that is so wonne in tyme with love shall remayne for ever', said Douglas, but the English had 'often won with force, which hath engendred hatred'. To lay down such conditions as Henry wanted to impose so arbitrarily and immediately

> '. . . to bring the obedience of this realme to Englonde . . . is impossible to be don at this tyme, for', quod he, 'there is not so lytle a boy but he woll hurle stones ayenst it, the wyves woll com out with their distaffes and the comons unyversally woll rather dye in it; yee and many noble men and all the clergie fully ayenst it, so that this must nedes folowe of it'.[82]

But Henry was not prepared for a gradual approach. By the autumn of 1543 the treaty was dead, and by December Henry had declared war; in the spring of 1544 Hertford was sent north with an army of arquebusiers and heavy artillery to impart the necessary lesson in obedience.

What of Scottish Protestants, enthusiastic for the marriage? The highlander John Elder, already mentioned, seems to have been unusual in committing himself not only to Protestantism and Anglo-Scots union, but to the English monarchy's claims to suzerainty. In a letter to Henry VIII he offered his services and a 'plotte' or map of Scotland, which, he argued, was inhabited by wild Irish until 'Albanactus, Brutus second sonne', reduced it to civility.[83] He thus adapted the Galfridian story of Brutus and his sons to the Irish-Scots origin story, going so far as to blame the myth of the Egyptian Scota on the Catholic clergy. He held the Scottish clergy wholly responsible for obstructing union between England and Scotland, reserving his greatest

---

[81] *L&P Henry VIII*, VIII (i), 14 April, 1543, 402, p. 236.   [82] *HP*, I.477.
[83] John Elder, 'A Proposal for Uniting Scotland with England, Addressed to Henry VIII', *The Bannatyne Miscellany*. 3 volumes (Edinburgh: Ballantyne and Co., 1827–55), I.11.

loathing for Scotland's 'pestiferous' Cardinal David Beaton. Elder's was a rather extreme position, however. The poet David Lindsay, for example, did not subscribe to English suzerainty over Scotland. Yet, sympathetic to Protestantism, he shared Elder's opinion (as did many Scots) of Cardinal Beaton's venality. Lindsay's writings on this subject thus inadvertently supported the English propaganda which encouraged Scots to thank the cardinal for the havoc wrought on their country.

With brilliant, deadpan irony, Lindsay's *Tragedie of the Cardinall*, written after Beaton's assassination in 1547, allows the revenant cardinal to condemn himself out of his own mouth. The poem opens with the author, immersed in Boccaccio's stories of fallen princes, suddenly interrupted by the apparition of a wounded man, bleeding profusely over his crimson satin robes. This gruesome figure declares, blasphemously yet somehow with camp bravado, that there never was pain like to his 'passioun' and that he is quite sure Boccaccio would have loved to write it.[84] As he proceeds, with gusto, to narrate his own life story, cheerfully boasting of his brilliant career moves and his self-serving pro-French and pro-Rome diplomacy, the reader infers, in the poem's ironic undertow, all the corruption and misgovernment that will end in Scotland's sorry tragedy. 'Of all Scotland I had the governall,' Beaton's ghost brags, 'But my avyse concludit was no thyng.'[85] Appalled to find that a marriage with the heretic England had been contracted behind his back, the cardinal gleefully brags that it was through his 'pratyke and ingyne' that Arran was persuaded to dissolve the Treaty of Greenwich, causing England to respond with 'mortall weirs':

> I was the rute of all that gret myschief.
> The south countre [i.e. the Scottish borders] may saye it had bene gude
> That my noryce had smorde me in my cude . . .
>
> Had we with Ingland kepit our contrackis.
> Our nobyll men had levit in peace and rest,
> Our merchandis had not lost so mony packis,
> Our common peple had not bene opprest;
> On ather syde all wrangis had bene redrest.
> Bot Edinburgh, sen syne, Leith and Kyngorne   [Kinghorn]
> The day and hour may ban [curse] that I was borne.[86]

[84] The Tragedie of the Cardinall', in *Sir David Lyndsay: Selected Poems* ed. Janet Hadley Williams (Glasgow: The Association for Scottish Literary Studies, 2000), 112–27, 112.
[85] Lyndsay, *Cardinall*, 114.   [86] Lyndsay, *Cardinall*, 118–19.

Lindsay's poem was instantly recruited to the English cause, feeding into the writings of English Reformers, some of whom fought under Hertford/ Somerset against the Scots in 1547, confident in the godliness of their cause. The *Tragedie* was published in an Anglicised version as early as 1548 by the evangelical printer John Day, where it was joined to a prose account of the martyrdom of George Wishart. John Foxe quoted from this edition in his *Book of Martyrs* and it seems quite likely that it offered a model for *The Mirror for Magistrates*.[87] For all its wit, then, what Lindsay's poem chiefly reveals in the war context is the shrinking of a thinkable space of Scottish resistance to the violence legitimised by the argument of Henry's *Declaration*. It was hard to articulate Protestant sympathies and to express anger with Beaton's and Arran's self-serving failures of government, without endorsing the implication that these atrocities were justified as part of the English monarch's recovery of ancient title to Scotland.

In a striking illustration of this, Lindsay's vision of Lothian and the Borders cursing Beaton's wet-nurse had itself been precisely anticipated by the propaganda that accompanied the 1544 and 1545 campaigns. Henry and the English privy council had already instructed Hertford to be sure to lay the blame for his massacres at the door of Cardinal Beaton. A telling exchange in early 1544, however, reveals the contradictions of this strategy, foreshadowing the more complex propaganda message that Hertford would try to pursue when he took charge of the war. Henry had commanded Hertford when making 'rodes and burnings' to 'set bills on the chirch dores or other notabull plasis, purporting in the samme they might thank ther Cardinall therfor'.[88] Hertford, however, wanted to improve on this simple clerical scapegoating by composing a proclamation which explained and justified the legitimate 'causes' of the violence more fully and in such a way as might persuade or 'indeuse others to your majestes porpos'. In Hertford's media strategy, the whole project of Anglo-Scots union through the marriage was to be set out, stressing the mercy of Henry, who 'notwithstanding the just titulle and intrest that his highnis hath unt[o] this realme of Skotland' was nevertheless willing to negotiate with the Scots Parliament. The obstinate refusal of the Scots Parliament

[87] STC 15683. See Janet Hadley Williams, 'The Earliest Surviving Text of Lyndsay's *Tragedie of the Cardinall*: An English Edition of a Scottish Poem', in *Literature, Letters and the Canonical in Early Modern Scotland*, ed. Theo van Heijnsbergen and Nicola Royan (East Linton: Tuckwell Press, 2002). On the poem as possible model for the *Mirrour for Magistrates*, see Priscilla Bawcutt, 'Crossing the Border: Scottish Poetry and English Readers in the Sixteenth Century', in *The Rose and the Thistle: Essays on the Culture of Late Medieval and Renaissance Scotland*, ed. Sally Mapstone and Juliette Wood (East Linton: Tuckwell Press, 1998).
[88] *HP*, II.311.

to accept Henry's conditions for immediate custody of Queen Mary 'as her next kynsman . . . chef govrner and rewlar' would then be given as the cause of Henry's sending Hertford 'with his armi royall for to requiar and demand the deliveri of her saffli'. Henry and the English privy council responded to this suggestion with a tactful but firm negative. The publication of such a proclamation at Hertford's first entry into the country would be, they said, 'inexpedient' because it would make it difficult for Hertford to set about burning and despoiling Scotland, having just declared Henry chief governor of the Scotland's queen, and the country's protector.[89] Better simply to blame the cardinal than to provoke the question of why Henry was putting a torch to a realm which he was supposed to protect.

This dispute over the propaganda message reveals how much Hertford was invested in what I earlier described as reading for the 'plot' or 'plat'. As we will see in Chapter 2, Hertford's conduct of the war from 1547 was characterised by this future- and spatially- oriented strategic thinking, in which the objectives of mastering unfamiliar terrain and providing military supply were conflated and confounded with those of 'persuading' the Scots of the probability and justice of the English cause. Yet even Hertford's post-Henrician strategy built on the premise of Henry VIII's *Declaration*, which defined the Scots as 'rebels' to their English sovereign. To this extent, Hertford's strategy was itself divided. Its attempt to recruit Scottish support by means of a visionary rhetoric of fraternal British union – the plat of Great Britain, in which English and Scottish might collaborate as equals – was inherently in conflict with the tacit conviction that the Scots simply owed their allegiance and assistance to the English, and that any withholding, any resistance to invasion, was a punishable rebellion.

IV.   Henry VIII, War Criminal: Lamb's *Ane Resonyng*

To understand this clearly, we need to move in to get a closer look at Henry VIII's *Declaration*. Its model turns out to be quite venerable: it derives from Edward I's commissioning of historical proofs of Scottish homage from English monastic chronicles as published in the Great Roll of John of Caen (1297) in order to justify his invasion.[90] So effective was Henry's reprising of Edward's case that it persuaded the English Parliament to pass a Subsidy

---

[89] *HP*, II. 311–2, 314–5.
[90] See Goldstein, *Matter*, 59; E. L. G. Stones and Grant Simpson, *Edward I and the Throne of Scotland*, 2 vols. (Published for the University of Glasgow by Oxford University Press, 1978), I.49, 150, II.302–8.

Act to finance Hertford's expensive Scottish campaigns. The Subsidy Act's preamble referred to the perfectly legitimate King James V as 'the late pretensed King of Scottes, being but an Usurper of the Crowne and Realme of Scotland'. James's death, it added, was God's providing of 'a tyme apt and propyse for the recoverye of [Henry's] saide right and tytle to the saide Crowne and Realme of Scotland'.[91]

Henry's *Declaration* is split into two halves, both written in the first person, as if voicing the embodied sovereign authority of the King of England. In the first half, the king speaks in the persona of a caring but exasperated older kinsman, an uncle whose patience with his nephew's failures of respect has finally run out. The opening sentence is a master class in passive aggression, its declaration of war disguised as a regretful correction of former indulgence:

> BEYNG NOW ENforced to the warre, which we haue always hitherto so moch abhorred and fled, by our neighbour and Nephieu the kyng of Scottis, one, who, aboue all other, for our manyfold benefits towardis him hath most iust cause to loue vs, to honor vs, and to reioise in our quiet: we haue thought good to notify vnto the world his doings and behauiour in the prouocation of this war.[92]

The litany of James's 'doings and behauiour' that have provoked an armed response include James's failure to keep an appointment with Henry at York; his entertainment of Catholic 'rebels' from England; and his having 'vsurped' a small piece of border land 'of no great value' in spite of English commissioners having shown 'autentique' evidence of its belonging to England.[93]

It was, however, the second half of the treatise that exercised influence for decades, perhaps centuries, to come. The second half purported to be a redacted history of England's feudal tenure of Scotland, starting with Albanact's submission to his elder brother and overlord, Locrine, and ending with the homage performed by James I to Henry VI. Henry introduced it with a disclaimer, denying that he had ever sought to possess Scotland, in spite of his right to it: '*If we had minded the possession of Scotland*, and by the motion of war to atteyne the same, there was neuer kynge of this realme ... had more iuste title, more euident title, more certayn title, to any realme that he can clayme, than we haue to Scotland'.[94] This statement, at once absolute and disparaging, justifies the military

---

[91] 'An ACTE for the Subsidie of the Temporalitie', 34° and 35° Hen. VIII. c.27, *Statutes*, III. 938.

[92] Henry VIII, *A Declaration, conteyning the iust causes and consyderations of this present warre with the Scottis* (London: 1542) sig. A2r.

[93] Henry VIII, *Declaration*, sig. A4v.   [94] Henry VIII, *Declaration*, sig. B3v, *my italics*.

assertion of title, while disavowing motivation, interest and desire. It was to become a familiar formulation. William Thomas refuted the Italian accusation that Henry VIII had wasted Scotland unjustly with intent to possess it by arguing that the English king took up arms 'Not for the wealth of the Scottyshe domynion which in respect of Englande is of as good a comparison, as the barain mountaignes of Savoie unto the beaultie of the pleasannt Toscane, but for the uniforme quiett of their approved anncient contention.'[95] It is important to see that in these and other variants of the formulation, the denial of intent to possess exists in a productively uncertain relation with the assertion of title. Henry's conditional ('If we had minded the possession of Scotland') like Thomas's denial ('Not for the wealth of the Scottyshe domynion') disguises England's insular imperial ambition as restraint, while the military pursuit of that ambition is figured as a mere corrective to a title denied. William Thomas defines Henry's object as 'the quiett of *their* approved anncient contention', while Henry himself protests, 'We haue euer been always glad ... to omyt to demaunde our right ... than by demaundyng therof to be sene to moue war.'[96] War becomes the result of Scots resistance, literally *in spite of* commendable English restraint in pursuing possession. Denying any intention to possess because/in spite of already having possessive title is thus no ornamentally ambiguous figure; its ambiguity makes it a foundational trope of Tudor Anglo-imperialism with respect to Scotland. Even today, historians continue to assume that the question to ask is whether Henry was ever serious about possessing Scotland. This question obscures the truth that Henry's stance of disparagement and disavowal is a part of a claim of *always already* being in titular possession. This stance is highly adaptable to the political occasion. It can justify war; it can render a Scottish succession unthreatening; it can justify the refusal of reciprocal rights and common nationhood – and in time it did all these things.

The rest of the treatise's second half is narrated as a summary history of Anglo-Scots relations from the time of Brutus's division of Britain, listing twenty-two acts of homage performed by Scottish kings to their English 'overlords'. Ostensibly the fruits of Cuthbert Tunstall's research in the Durham archives, this is largely a fairly close translation of the entries in John of Caen's Great Roll, which compiled the monks' findings, in response to Edward I's instruction, of records of ancient Scottish homages.[97]

[95] Martin, 'Thomas's *The Pilgrim*', 266.   [96] Henry VIII, *Declaration*, sig. B4r.
[97] On Tunstall's research, see Merriman, *Rough Wooings*, 287. A similar collection of homages was made by Sir John Mason for Somerset and Edward VI in 1549; see BL Add MS 6128.

As E. L. G. Stones has written, Caen's entries follow the formula of recording a homage, dating it, and then giving a list of the chronicles where it may be found. The dates are 'clumsily done' and the records often misrepresent the homages as recorded by the chroniclers in question. Clauses explaining that the homage was for lands in England, and not for the realm of Scotland, are omitted.[98] The historical specificity of Anglo-Scots agreements in their political contexts disappears, as does any mention of treaties releasing Scottish kings from former obligations, such as the Quitclaim of Canterbury (1189) and the Treaty of Northampton (1328). In the *Declaration*'s version, moreover, Henry asserts that one after another of his 'progenitors' received homage from this or that Scottish king at such and such a date. The text thus designedly creates the impression of the king himself asserting an overlordship of Scotland as old as his own royal genealogy, a feudal inheritance lineally and uninterruptedly descended from his forebears. Yet, as hardly needs saying, no such inheritance of title existed. Assertions of sovereignty over Scotland made by early English kings were contingently military and political and were resisted as such.[99] But John of Caen's Roll, like Henry VIII's *Declaration*, produced history as a legal record of tenure *ab initio*, according to which the kingdom of Scotland had been held as a grant from England ever since Albanact first received it of Locrine.

Henry's history opens with a version of Geoffrey's Brutus legend which stresses his naming of 'Britayn' and determination to have his three sons govern 'the whole Isle within the Ocean sea' hierarchically, with the younger sons doing homage to Locrine. This primal overlordship legitimises Henry's declaration of war by setting it in a history of regular 'transgression' by Scots kings and 'chastisement' by their English superiors. We are to learn, 'howe for transgression against this superioritie, our predecessours haue chastised the kinges of Scottis, and some deposed, and put others in their places'.[100] The narrative then moves swiftly over the rest of Geoffrey ('passinge ouer . . . the victories of king Arthur') and proceeds to Caen's Great Roll. The *Declaration* follows Caen closely, for example, on Aethelstane: 'Athelstane . . . hauynge by battayle conquered Scotlande, he made one Constantine . . . to rule and gouerne the countray of Scotland vnder him, adding this princely woorde, That it was more honour to hym to make a kynge, than to be a kynge.'[101] This entry refers to Aethelstan's

---

[98] Stones and Simpson, *Edward I*, I.150–1. See Chapter 5.
[99] R. R. Davies, *Domination and Conquest* (Cambridge, Cambridge University Press, 1990), 103.
[100] Henry VIII, *Declaration*, sig. B4v-C1r.
[101] Stones and Simpson, *Edward I*, II.301; Henry VIII, *Declaration*, sig. C1v.

invasion of Scotland in 934, and Constantín's being forced to submit to him as '*subregulus*' to the '*rex et rector totius Britannia*', as well as to Aethelstan's 936 victory over Constantín and the Northumbrians at Brunaburgh or Dún Brunde.[102] An important victory for Aethelstan, wonderfully celebrated in the poem, *The Battle of Brunaburgh*, Brunaburgh by no means led to an enduring governorship of Alba by the kings of Wessex.[103] The *Declaration*'s contrary impression is merely the effect of sequential structure. Further examples of translations of Caen include the homage allegedly performed by Alexander III at his marriage to Henry III's sister in 1251, but no mention is made of the dispute about the homage in question.[104] For homages that post-date Edward I, Henry's *Declaration* is largely reliant on John Hardyng's forgeries, discussed in Chapter 5, below. The preamble to the Subsidy Act of 1543 expressed Parliament's satisfaction that 'divers and soondrye old auncient and autentique rolles patents, wrytings and recordes' had been 'maturelye redde and debated in this present parliament' to prove that Henry 'hath good juste tytle and interest to the Crowne and Realme of Scotlande'.[105]

The immediate and enduring consequences of Henry's *Declaration* – initially as justification for war, subsequently as a foundation of Anglo-Scots constitutional relations – were immense. The text's performance of Henry's royal *personae* (outraged uncle; disinterested possessor of Scottish sovereignty; patient sufferer of Scottish wrongs) coupled with the ostensibly referential clarity with which it set out proof of English title, would make refutation a daunting task. Yet the task was undertaken with qualified success in 1549 by a judge of the Scottish College of Justice, William Lamb.[106] Lamb's remarkable work takes the form of a fictional dialogue between an English and a Scottish merchant, who, as travelling companions on the road to Lyons from Rouen, debate the justice of the current war in Scotland. The text, *Ane Resonyng of ane Scottis and Inglis Merchand Betuix Rowand and Lionis*, comes to us unpublished (though apparently prepared for publication) and unfinished, with some rather gaping holes in the fictional structure. Nevertheless, the fiction's very conception is

[102] Woolf, *Pictland*, 168–75.
[103] When Aethelstan died in 939, Northumbria returned to Danish rule; Constantín went into religious retirement around 943, and the kingship of Alba (Scotland) passed to Malcolm or Mael Coluim, son of his cousin, Donald or Domnall. See Woolf, *Pictland*, 177.
[104] Henry VIII, *Declaration*, sig. C3r. Compare Caen in Stones and Simpson, *Edward I*, II.306. On the dispute, see Stones and Simpson, *Edward I*, I.151 and II.306
[105] *Statutes*, III.938.
[106] William Lamb, *Ane Resonyng of ane Scottis and Inglis Merchand Betuix Rowand and Lionis*, ed. Roderick J. Lyall (Aberdeen: Aberdeen University Press, 1985).

eloquent, for it throws into startling relief the artifice of the insular English perspective to which we are generally so habituated as to find it natural.

Discussions of Scots responses to Henrician and Edwardian war propaganda have tended to pay more attention to the Protestant 'unionist' arguments of John Elder and James Henrisoun (of whom more in Chapter 2), partly because they give evidence of a forward-looking pragmatic humanist interest in a united British commonwealth in what Arthur Williamson calls the 'Edwardian moment'.[107] Evidence of Scottish 'nationalism' tends to be written off, by implication, as anachronistic and irrelevant to the extent that, conformist in its Catholicism, it looks back towards the supranational authority of papacy. But Lamb's *Resonyng* looks not to Rome, but to European trade routes. However thinly sustained, its foundational fiction of travelling merchants is essential to its adumbration of an international legal perspective from which to articulate Scottish nationhood. This is not the supranational jurisdiction of the papal curia, but of *ius gentium*, an emergent space of adjudication between national jurisdictions that was, as Christopher Warren has shown, manifesting itself in the hybrid literary-legal forms of early modernity.[108] With striking power, the dialogue's opening locates the question of national feeling – national shame, national pride – within an international debate on the question of the justice or otherwise of the war. It opens with a Scottish merchant, travelling through France, asking an English-speaking stranger where he is heading, with a view to having company along the road. The Englishman immediately taunts him, is he not 'eschame' (ashamed) to be called a Scot these days? The Scot replies with surprise that he does not know why he should be 'eschamit' of his 'natioun'. Because, the Englishman mocks, his 'natioun' has been roundly humiliated and beaten in the present war. The Scot is unabashed: God may, he says, bring the Scots better expertise in warfare, but nothing can alter the fact that 'all vnaffectionat men', whether they be Scots, French or Dutch, think this present war is 'uniust'.[109] While God may adjudicate the contingencies of war, the salient question of the war's *justice* is to be debated between nations. And, by implication, national shame attaches not to those who lose a war, but to those who perpetrate war unjustly.

Lamb forgets to sustain this fiction of this commercial journey through France with any verisimilitude: the merchants arrive twice at Rouen and

---

[107] See above, note 28.

[108] Christopher N. Warren, *Literature and the Law of Nations, 1580–1680* (Oxford: Oxford University Press, 2015).

[109] Lamb, *Resonyng*, 3.

debating the second half of Henry's *Declaration* only gets them as far as Paris. In further, surreal twist, three illustrious Catholic victims of Henry's tyranny – Thomas More, John Fisher and Richard Reynolds of the Brigittine monastery of Syon – suddenly appear on the scene (speaking Latin) and agree (though dead) to judge the dispute. Nevertheless, the fictional setting of international trade is essential to Lamb's conception of a how a legal and moral challenge to English invasion should be mounted. Throughout the war, the English proceeded in international diplomacy as if Scotland *were not a nation*; the French, for example, negotiating peace with Henry in 1546 (the Treaty of Camp) wished to have the Scots signatories to the treaty, but Henry refused, saying Scotland was a wholly English concern.[110] Mary of Hungary, governor of the Netherlands, consistently insisted that the Dutch had no quarrel with the Scots. She deeply regretted Charles V's capitulation to war with the Scots at Henry VIII's request, as, later, did Charles himself. A six-year-long state of war between the Dutch and the Scots, which neither side wanted, cost the Netherlands dearly in lost Scots-Dutch trade.[111] Lamb's establishment of European trade routes as the setting for an Anglo-Scots debate on the justice of the war offers a startling shift of jurisdictional perspective from that of England's insular, genealogical fiction of continuous feudal tenure. It is, quite simply, a perspective in which Scotland is *assumed to be a nation*.

Attention to this international perspective surfaces throughout the dialogue, exposing the imperialist ambition veiled by Henry's rhetoric of disavowal. The English merchant solemnly rehearses Henry's grief at the disrespect shown to him by his Scottish nephew.[112] He repeats practically verbatim Henry VIII's complaints against James, including the missed York appointment, the harbouring of English Catholics and the retention of insignificant border lands. The Scot shrewdly counters by invoking the topics of circumstance (time and manner) to *infer Henry's intentions*. Henry's game, as we saw, was to make a virtue of denying intention to possess Scotland. Lamb's probable inferences expose the mendacity of Henry's game with dramatic or even novelistic effect: James's alleged 'contempt' in absenting himself from York emerges as a prudent avoidance of recruitment into the service of Henry's expansionist interests.[113]

As to James's harbouring of English Catholic 'rebels', these were, Lamb's Scotsman says, hardly dangerous political dissidents: five or six old mendicant friars who, having entered sanctuary, could not be legally

[110] Merriman, *Rough Wooings*, 196–7.   [111] Merriman, *Rough Wooings*, 187; see also 184–205.
[112] Henry VIII, *Declaration*, sig. A3r.   [113] Lamb, *Resonyng*, 45.

removed – here the Scot recognises jurisdictional plurality and the autonomy of ecclesiastical law (sanctuary in England had been abolished at the Reformation).[114] Finally, on the question of the border land alleged by Henry to have been usurped by the Scots, and of no great value, Lamb's Scottish merchant was openly scornful. When evidence is in doubt, there should always, in law, be two litigating parties and a judge, he insists: 'suld your kyng haue bene partie and also juge in his awin causs?', he asks. More importantly, even had the land been proved to have belonged to England, 'suld your kyng haue mouit so haistie crewell weir for ane thing of so sobir valour, quhilk als wes nocht challangit ij.ᶜ yeiris [two hundred years] befor that tyme?'. He cites a legal maxim, taken from Proverbs 18.1 in the Vulgate: 'He who seeks to abandon a friend, looks for opportunities.'[115] In fussing over some acres of the debateable lands that no one had cared to claim for the last two hundred years, Henry is clearly scraping the justificatory barrel for causes of international war. Indeed, this question of respecting jurisdictions (for the Anglo-Scots Marches had their own courts to decide such issues) epitomises Lamb's larger point about using the *Declaration* as a judicial decision about war. The justice of an invasive war cannot be decided within a country's own common law, but only within *ius gentium*, the law of nations. Can it be right, the Scot asks, that in a great, weighty and doubtful question of war between two 'potent realmes', one country's own national law should conclude and define the question?[116] As Henry respects neither spiritual nor border jurisdictions, so, argues Lamb, he wrongly imagines that an international legal question of the justice of war can be defined by English common law and decided by a court (Parliament) in London. This is a question we will return to in Chapter 6 on English history plays.

Lamb's *Resonyng* deftly exposed the absurdity of Henry's argument that James V had done him injuries enough to justify war. Arguing effectively against the *Declaration*'s second half was harder because its credibility relied on archival evidence, on the existence of documents and charters. Lamb, however, engaged in no Scottish counter-mythology. To the English merchant's querying his opinion of the 'probabilite' of the *Declaration*'s story of English 'superiorite from the first habitatioun of Albion' through the story of Brutus, Lamb's Scot replies that origins of peoples are so uncertain that 'vpone sic a ground ye may devyd this ile and beild sic probabilitie as ye lyk imagine'. To the rest of the historical

---

[114] Lamb, *Resonyng*, 47.   [115] Lamb, *Resonyng*, 47.   [116] Lamb, *Resonyng*, 19.

argument – the homages gathered by Cuthbert Tunstall from John of Caen's Great Roll and Hardyng forgeries – Lamb's response, as his editor, Roderick Lyall observes, was simple but inspired: to follow Polydore Virgil, 'scarcely a witness who can be charged by the English with pro-Scottish bias'.[117]

Lamb had, however, another trump card up his sleeve. As an active member of the Scottish government, he had access to the official archives ('oure Registre') and so was able to make good on a significant English omission. The *Declaration* made no mention of the so-called Treaty of Northampton (1328) by which the English Crown (in the minority of Edward III) renounced 'any right in the realm of Scotland which we our ancestors have sought in past times'. Lamb referred to this as a document under the Great Seal in which Edward II confessed that England 'neuer had sic a pretendit superiorite of Scotland'.[118] Amusingly enough, Cuthbert Tunstall seems to have turned up the 'renunciation of kinge Edward the seconde of the superioritye to the realme of scotlande' in his second round of research in the Durham palatinate archives in October 1547, warning Somerset that the Scots probably had a copy of this, and that it would certainly demolish the English case!119 (Both Lamb and Tunstall ascribe to Edward II a quitclaim in fact enacted by Edward III in his minority.)[120]

For all that it was unlikely to have had more than a handful of readers through the sixteenth century, Lamb's *resonyng* deserves our attention for what it says about Scottish national consciousness in the 1540s. Lamb's text reminds us how developed, relatively speaking, were the systems of government, administration, trade and legal learning that defined the Scots as a sovereign nation in the 1540s, *pace* English rhetoric to the contrary. We could go so far as to say that Lamb's text, surviving in the Cottonian collection, was suppressed. Its legal case was damaging to England, as wars of conquest were held to be unjust, *unless legitimate title could be proved*.[121] It is thus of the greatest possible significance that it remained unread, while Henry VIII's *Declaration* was so pervasively read and cited that 'the average Elizabethan saw the old assertions to suzerainty over Scotland as simple fact'.[122] The silencing of the Scottish case against the legality of the war

[117] Lamb, *Resonyng*, xxi.
[118] Alfred Hiatt, *The Making of Medieval Forgeries: False Documents in Fifteenth-Century England* (London: British Library, 2004), 109; Lamb, *Resonyng*, 163–4. See Stones, *Anglo-Scottish Relations*, 322–5.
[119] Merriman, *Rough Wooings*, 287.   [120] Stones, *Anglo-Scottish Relations*, 322–45.
[121] Lamb's *Resonyng* survives in a unique manuscript in the British Library, MS Cotton Caligula B.vii.
[122] Merriman, *Rough Wooings*, 267; Galloway, *Union 1603–1608*, 11.

contributes, as we will see in Chapter 3, to the flourishing of England's insular imagining in Elizabeth's reign. Before we move there, however, we need to learn about the phase of the war and its propaganda in which the makers of the Elizabethan regime – William Cecil and Thomas Smith – were most involved and active. This phase was ushered in with the death of Henry VIII in 1547 and the accession of his nine-year-old son, Edward VI. Edward VI's uncle, Edward Seymour, duke of Somerset, was now the Lord Protector of a realm which he was determined to expand, through the conquest of Scotland, into an empire of Great Britain.

CHAPTER 2

Writing the Forgotten War II: Somerset's War, 1547–1550

I. Metalepsis, Irony and Metaphor: Writing Somerset's War, 1547–1550

As the flames consumed his house on the south side of Edinburgh's High Street in May 1544, Scottish merchant James Henrisoun surmised, correctly, that the ensuing war would put paid to the trade with the Low Countries in which he had been so vigorously engaged.[1] As a secret Protestant, too, Henrisoun could see little future for himself in a native country prostrated by the superior might of a foe whose reformed ideas he shared. Days later, he was moving south with Somerset's army. From Newcastle, he wrote to his Protestant friend and fellow merchant, Francis Aikin, counselling him 'nocht to repair nor big [build] his hous for this yeir for we stand at ane evill poynt'. He was, he said, 'sary' [sorry] for what had and would happen to Scotland, but 'mekle mair trist and sorrowfull for the damnage to cum', as he prepared to enter Henry VIII's service to help advance the cause of a united, Protestant Britain.[2]

For two years, it seems, Henrisoun languished rather underemployed at the English court. Henry had little use for propagandists.[3] On the king's death in January 1547, however, Henrisoun's opportunity arrived. The Scots had been hoping, on the news of Henry VIII's death, that the peace with England brought about by the Treaty of Camp (1546) might be permanent. But that hope soon vanished. Scotland's ambassador, Adam Otterburn, wrote to the earl of Arran from London in the August of 1547, warning him of the imminence of another invasion: 'I saw afoir my eis', he wrote, 'the verray gret preparatioun of weir and actualie the gret hors the harness the hagbutaris and all gorgious reparrale set forwart towart our

---

[1] Marcus Merriman, 'James Henrisoun and "Great Britain": British Union and the Scottish Commonweal', *Scotland and England* ed. Mason, 85–112, 86–7 and notes.
[2] As reported by Adam Otterburn to Mary of Guise, 16th June 1544, *SC*, 93-4.
[3] Merriman, 'Henrisoun', 88.

realme.'[4] He must lose no time preparing for an English attack. Diplomatic efforts by himself and the French ambassador, Odet de Selve, had come to nothing, and for days, he said, he had been sending missives, 'declarand this army tobe set forwart be sey and land in the end of this moneth'.[5] Meanwhile, Henrisoun's pen had already been busy on the English behalf. His *Exhortation to the Scotts to conforme themselfes to the honorable, Expedient and godly Union betweene the two Realmes of Englande & Scotland* was published by Richard Grafton in July.[6] By the 27th of August, an English army, fifteen thousand strong, equipped with moveable field artillery and shadowed by a sizeable fleet ('a large cluster of bobbing, moveable gun platforms'), was on the move towards Edinburgh.[7] Marching with it were the men who would become the most prominent architects of the Elizabethan regime – William Cecil and Sir Thomas Smith – as well as humanist men of letters, such as William Patten, George Ferrars and Thomas Chaloner.[8]

Somerset's conduct of the war differed from Henry VIII's in three main ways. First, Somerset would have no more wasteful *chevauchées* or scorched-earth raids as ends in themselves. He meant to achieve a permanent conquest of the realm through the building of modern low-lying, thick-walled earth forts known as *traces italiennes*, which he would garrison with English troops, creating an English Pale.[9] From these garrisons, he made a novel use of light cavalry, or 'prickers', who periodically roamed the countryside about 'either offering protection to assured Scots, or persuading others of the wisdom of taking assurance by burning their houses down'.[10] Second, Somerset understood the extent to which the challenge to any English army invading Scotland would be logistical: it was enormously difficult, relying on overland transport from Newcastle, to keep an invading English army fed. Indeed, after the scorched-earth raids of 1545, the Scottish borders could scarcely feed themselves, let alone traversing armies. In 1542, the duke of Norfolk had had to abandon the capture of Edinburgh for lack of food. His army was forced to march from York to Berwick on empty stomachs and, even worse, without beer: wagons could not carry enough to victual them, and they had to turn back. But in 1544 Hertford hit on the solution: strategic use of the English

[4] *SC*, 192–3.   [5] *SC*, 194.
[6] James Harryson, *Exhortation to the Scotts to conforme themselves to the honourable expedient and godly union betwene the two realmes of England and Scotland* (London, 1547).
[7] Merriman, *Rough Wooings*, 233.   [8] See Hoak, 'Cecil and Smith', 43.
[9] Phillips, *Anglo-Scots Wars*, 178–81, 201–14, 224–53.   [10] Phillips, *Anglo-Scots Wars*, 180.

navy. As duke of Somerset, he 'would take full advantage of England's naval might, recognising the potential of amphibious operations'.[11]

Finally, all Somerset's military 'providence' or foresight and provision was thoroughly integrated into a communicative strategy of the kind we refer to as 'propaganda'. That word, however, hardly conveys the extent to which, in the case of Somerset and his writing team, rhetorical figures of thought, or tropes, informed a visionary military strategy, and vice versa. For some time now, historians and literary critics of Tudor England have appreciated the material contribution of rhetorical invention to 'plats' and policy-making. Historians have approached Cecil's political memoranda by way of his education in rhetorical *inventio*, while literary critics illustrate the practical, political application of Elizabethan rhetoric likewise.[12] One can, however, go further: what we think of as tropes and figures – part of *elocutio*, rather than *inventio* and *dispositio* – often have affinities with that part of *inventio* called 'artificial proof' (*probatio artificialis*). Of artificial proofs, 'argument' is the most important kind, the backbone of forensic pleading and political deliberation.[13] Two such tropes or 'arguments' dominate the structuring of Somerset's strategic conduct of the war as well as his print propaganda. One is metaphorical, involving a complex set of analogies between mutual affection, military security and the unity of sea-circled Britain. Somerset's determination to garrison, to create a fortified English Pale in Scotland, was part of a strategy to 'win the loyalty of the Scottish population within this Pale through a mixture of intimidation and persuasion' while at the same time overcoming the 'logistical problems that had always blighted English operations in Scotland' by 'the cooperation of a sympathetic population'.[14] This conception of Scottish loyalty and love as a potential resource is thematised in the very propaganda designed to secure it. In the *Epistle or exhortacion . . . to . . .*

[11] Phillips, *Anglo-Scots Wars*, 149, 159; S. Gunn, *Charles Brandon, Duke of Suffolk, c.1485–1545* (Oxford: Blackwell, 1988), 183–91.
[12] See, for example, Joel Altman, *The Tudor Play of Mind: Rhetorical Inquiry and the Development of Elizabethan Drama* (Berkeley, CA: University of California Press, 1978); Alford, *Elizabethan Polity*; Peter Mack, *Elizabethan Rhetoric: Theory and Practice* (Cambridge: Cambridge University Press, 2002).
[13] See, in general, Kathy Eden, 'Forensic Rhetoric and Humanist Education', in *The Oxford Handbook of English Law and Literature, 1500–1700* ed. Lorna Hutson (Oxford: Oxford University Press, 2017), 23–40. The overlap between *elocutio* and *inventio*, figures of ornament and argument, is illustrated by the fact that George Puttenham's example of *metalepsis* which Quintilian treats as an ornament in 8.6.8 of *Institutio Oratoria* trans. Donald Russell, 5 vols. (Cambridge, MA: Harvard University Press, 2001) is rather taken from Quintilian's treatment of arguments of forensic proof from 'causes' in 5.10; see note 145 below.
[14] Phillips, *Anglo-Scots Wars*, 178–9.

the inhabitauntes of the Realme of Scotlande (1548) (often ascribed to Sir Thomas Smith), Somerset exhorted the Scots to embrace peace and affection with England as the metaphorical 'garrison' of an insular, unified Britain, walled around by the sea. England and Scotland, he said, 'beyng made one by amitie, bee most hable to defende vs against all nacions . . . hauyng the sea for wall, the mutuall loue for garrison, and God for defence'.[15] The metaphor imitates John Leland's vision of a Britain 'snugly held within its maritime boundaries . . . buttressed against both incursion and deprivation', but in this new variant, peace between the English and the Scots is explicitly acknowledged and valued as the *military resource* that supplies and secures the island's sea-walled fortress.[16] 'Garrison' has etymological connections with treasure and supplies (perhaps through confusion with French '*garnison*'), facilitating the sense, in this passage, of affection between the nations as provisioning, or *providential* for the future of an island empire.[17] Such a conflation of the cultural resource of interracial amity and the military resource of fortification is both disturbing and absolutely fundamental to Somerset's military strategy, constituting the very logic of his belief in the value of propaganda to achieve God's purpose for England/Britain. I will discuss the complexities and inherent contradictions of this metaphor in the final section of this chapter, as part of an analysis of Somerset's establishing of garrisons on Inchcolm in the Firth of Forth and at Broughty Craig on the river Tay, from the winter of 1547 through to the Peace of Boulogne in 1550.

The second foundational trope is one which plays with temporal compression and causal elisions and reversals. Within *elocutio*, it is known as metalepsis, but as part of *inventio*, it is a variant kind of artificial proof known as an argument '*a causis*', from causes, in which the immediate cause is skipped over, for one further back.[18] The example the rhetorical handbooks

---

[15] STC 22268. *An Epistle or exhortacion, to unitie and peace, sent from the Lorde Protector . . . to the Nobilitie, Gentlemen, and Commons . . . of the Realme of Scotlande* (London: Richard Grafton, 1548), sig. C1r. The *Epistle* is reprinted in James A. H. Murray ed., *The Complaynt of Scotlande* (Early English Text Society, e.s. 1872), 237–46. Dale Hoak assigns authorship to Sir Thomas Smith, 'Cecil and Smith', 90.

[16] Shrank, *Writing*, 91.   [17] OED, 'garrison', n. †1.

[18] Quintilian, *Inst.*, 8.6.8: 'It is the nature of Metalepsis to be a sort of intermediate step between the term transferred <and the thing to which it is transferred>; it does not signify anything in itself, but provides the transition.' For Brian Cummings, metalepsis names the incessantly transitional activity characteristic of all figuration in language. He writes, 'The peculiar power of metalepsis in the Renaissance imagination is that It leaves certain steps in the exchange invisible . . . In this figure, we do not know how we got to where we are.' See 'Metalepsis: The Boundaries of Metaphor', in *Renaissance Figures of Speech*, ed. Sylvia Adamson, Gavin Alexander and Katrin Ettenhuber (Cambridge: Cambridge University Press, 2007), 217–33, 230. The nearness of temporal sequence to an effect of causality seems to be responsible for the power metalepsis to deceive; it enables

give is that of the opening of Euripides' *Medea*, where Medea's nurse curses the cutting of the pine wood on Mount Pelion to make ships for the Argonauts, the cause of Jason's meeting Medea and the ensuing tragedy. The figure is close to a vice or an abuse of rhetoric (pushing so far back to find an original cause that it almost reverses cause and effect).[19] It is also a staple of lamentation in times of war; Lindsay, as we saw, adapted it to imagine Lothian and the Borders cursing Beaton's wet-nurse. But it also legitimises aggression: just as Hertford's soldiers told the Scots that they had Cardinal Beaton to thank for their burnt houses, so, in Shakespeare's *Henry V*, Henry tells the citizens of Harfleur that themselves 'are *cause*' if their 'pure maidens fall into the hand / Of hot and forcing violation'.[20] Somerset's propaganda texts take this metaleptic habit of thought to extremes, with extraordinary temporal and causal effects. He repeatedly accuses the Scots in advance of a violence which, he says, will be caused by their hypothetical refusal to accept that the invading army comes to bring peace and friendship: '[H]ere wee protest and declare to you', ran the *Epistle*, 'not to conquer, but to haue in amitie, not to wynne by force, but to conciliate by loue ... Whiche, *if you refuse*, and driue vs to conquere, who is giltie of the blood-shed? Who is the occasion of the warre? Who maketh the battailes, the brenning of houses, and the deuastacion whiche shall followe?' (my italics).[21]

This metaleptic temporal compression and causal reversal is not just a trope functioning within a text: it structures both the violent conduct of the campaign on the ground, and its retrospective (and trivialising) construction as peaceable, restrained and even ironic. Although, inevitably, both the tropes I have identified are at work all through Somerset's campaign, it is analytically helpful to divide the war into two distinct phases, associating each with a specific trope. Metalepsis is the trope which governs the conduct and retrospective narration of the invasion of 1547 which led to the great English victory at Pinkie-Cleugh on 10 September 1547. I will discuss this first and conclude with what Somerset's garrisons in the Forth and Tay say about his metaphor of Britain as sea-walled garrison. In both these phases of the war, military action was anticipated and followed by print propaganda making use of the key tropes involved.

specious forensic argument. See Joel Altman, '"Preposterous Conclusions": Eros, Enargeia and the Composition of *Othello*', *Representations*, vol. 18 (1987), 129–57.

[19] Emphasising this quality of temporal and locational transition, or of leaving out intermediate steps, George Puttenham calls metalepsis 'the far-fet'. Puttenham's example of the nurse in Euripides' *Medea* is given by Quintilian, *Inst.*, 5.10.83, as specious forensic proof when the causes are sought too far back.

[20] Shakespeare, *Henry V*, ed. T. W. Craik (London: Routledge, 1995), 3.3.19–20 (my italics).

[21] *Epistle or exhortacion*, sig. A8r-v.

The first propaganda text of the Pinkie campaign was, as I have noted, John Henrisoun's *Exhortation to the Scotts* of July 1547. Henrisoun attacked the credibility of Scotland's origin stories, endorsing the Galfridian title set out by Henry VIII's *Declaration* and blaming the lamentations of Edinburgh, Lothian and Teviotdale on the resistance of their own 'devillish harts' to the liberation of Protestant union. He concluded with a vivid *prosopopeia* of a unified, Protestant Britain, urging the Scots not to 'divide' and destroy the plenty and security furnished by nature and God:

> Imagine you (I praye you) if Britayne coulde speake, mighte she not well saye thus: hath not the almighty prouidence seuered me from the reste of the worlde, with a large sea, to make me one Islande? ... Why then wil you diuide me in two?[22]

At the turn from July to August, in the very week when Adam Otterburn had been marvelling at Somerset's war preparations (horses, harness, guns and 'gorgeous reparrale' all 'set forwart' towards Scotland) Grafton printed a second piece of propaganda, Somerset's *Proclamation*, to be distributed by the army on their march towards Edinburgh. The *Proclamation*'s convoluted periods contain tightly packed subordinate clauses with the usual 'Godly considerations' for unity ('beyng bothe of one discent of blood, and one language, and by the main seas separated from all other') leading to a dramatic deixis: the announcement of the presence of the English army *here and now*, invaders inside the realm of Scotland:

> We, vpon the foresaied Godly considerations ... are now ... come into this realme: not as a enemie to the Quene or any of the realme, that mynd the perfeccion of this peace and the coniunccion in mariage of both Princes, but as a friend and conseruator of them ... and we are come in this maner, which pretendeth a force in apparence (but not in deede) onely to defende and maintein the honor of bothe the Princes and the realmes, and by fire and swoorde, to chastice such as wilbe rebelles to the same, ... Nor wee mynde by this coniunccion of marriage, to doo any more preiudice to this realme of Scotlande, then to the realme of Englande, but ... to vnite them togeders in one name, by the name of Britons ...[23]

A fascinating temporal/causal game is being played here. The *Proclamation* anticipates, as the occasion of its utterance, the encounter between the invader and invaded. Imagine it: the core of this invading army consists

---

[22] STC 12857. Harryson, *Exhortation*, sig. hır.

[23] STC 7811. Paraphrased in *The Warrender Papers*, ed. Annie I. Cameron (Edinburgh: Scottish History Society, 1931), 2 vols., I.17-18, no. XXVI.

of three battles of three and four thousand footmen each, led by the
Lord Protector himself, along with John Dudley, the earl of Warwick,
and Thomas, Lord Dacre. These three infantry battles (ten thousand
altogether) are followed by a mounted force of two thousand light horse
('prickers') and four thousand fully armoured heavy cavalry, including
Burgundian and Spanish mercenaries and two hundred Italian 'hackbutters on horseback', that is 'mounted firearm troops of the most modern
kind', led by the Spaniard Sir Pedro de Gamboa.[24] These state-of-the-art
armed forces are accompanied by fifteen pieces of 'great ordinance' and
victuals carried in nine hundred carts, along with fourteen hundred pioneers who, captained by Sir John Brende, are ready to dig the fortifications
to be devised by Sir Richard Lee, veteran engineer of Boulogne and earlier
Scottish campaigns.[25] It is this battlefield-ready, prepared-to-fortify host
that proclaims, at every single encounter on its march through Scotland,
that it 'pretendeth a force in apparence (but not in deede)' and that all this
force serves merely to 'chastise' those who oppose giving England the
custody of Scotland's queen. The metaleptic plot of causation has already
been laid, so that the army can be nothing other than 'a friend and
conseruator' of British unity and peace, no matter what it does to those
whom it deems to be against that unity and peace.

   We have a detailed contemporary account of precisely how Somerset's
army made use of this proclamation on its progress north from Berwick,
along the coast to Inveresk, the site of the Battle of Pinkie. This text,
William Patten's *The Expedition into Scotland*, was written up in
January 1547–8 from Patten's and William Cecil's notes from the field
and it appeared from Richard Grafton's press in June 1548. Patten's
evangelical fervour, typifying the 'strong sense of Protestant nationalism'
that seized England after Somerset's victory, is expressed throughout
his relation of the campaign in an idiom of desacralising carnivalesque
exuberance.[26] Robert Scribner suggests that the disruptive energies of
mockery and inversion helped Protestant reformers to combat the spiritual
danger of 'a world structured around the efficacious power of the Catholic
cult and ritual'.[27] Patten's mockery is frequently thus oriented. He laughs
to think of the eve of battle falling on a saint's day, appealing to 'JAMES of
the Sink-hole, saving your reverence' (Jacobus de Voraigne) for proof. He
discovers a bishop's battle-flag at Pinkie, bearing an image of the Catholic

[24] Phillips, *Anglo-Scots Wars*, 186.   [25] Phillips, *Anglo-Scots Wars*, 186.
[26] Scott C. Lucas, *A Mirror for Magistrates and the Politics of the English Reformation* (Amherst, MA:
     University of Massachusetts Press, 2009), 27.
[27] Scribner, *Popular Culture*, 97.

Church as a dishevelled woman kneeling before a crucifix, her right hand holding a church. This Patten turns into a homely image of the world-upside-down: 'a curst quean that would pluck her husband by the pate, except she had her will'.[28] Yet the pitiless laughter of carnival is, as has often been noted, more often directed against groups already ostracised than against the might of orthodoxy, and Patten is no exception here. He has a real gift for vivid base comparisons which render Scots soldiers and civilians comically animal or childlike. Scots soldiers, firing on the English, are said to come to battle as 'a good fellow . . . to a dicing board, very hastily thrusting'; before the battle they can be seen 'very busy pranking up and down'; their pike formation stood as thick and close as 'the skin of an angry hedgehog' and, as they flee, some, to escape the killing pursuit of the English, made a shift, with their helmets on, 'to shrink their heads into their shoulders, like a tortoise into its shell'.[29] The *Expedition* records the presence of Thomas Chaloner and George Ferrars at the battle; the former's merry translation of Erasmus's *The Praise of Folly* was published shortly after, in 1549, while Ferrars was a highly commended Lord of Misrule at the 1551–2 Christmas festivities at court. Patten narrates with some relish how he and Ferrars set light to some Scots who 'fondly' refused to emerge from the cave in which they were hiding.[30] Yet this idiom of boisterous and brutal desacralising – of what Joe Moshenksa has acutely called 'iconoclasm as child's play' – is clearly compatible with Patten's fervent idealisation of Somerset as the vehicle of God's purpose for the English nation.[31] Consider Patten's account of the gang rape of a heavily pregnant woman and her female kin in the East Lothian village of Longniddry on 7 September 1547:

> Here we found a gentlewoman, some said a Lady, the wife of one HUGH DOUGLAS. She was great with child, and, in a house of hers, there abode her good time of deliverance; and had with her, an ancient gentlewoman her mother, a midwife and a daughter: whose estate, the council understanding, my Lord's Grace and Lord Lieutenant took order, that all night, without danger or damage, she was well preserved. But soon after our departure in the morning, I heard that some of our northern prickers had visited her; not much for her profit, nor all for their honesty . . . Good people be they, but given much, as they say, to the spoil.[32]

---

[28] William Patten, *The Expedition into Scotland*, rept. in *Tudor Tracts*, 53–157, 99, 132.
[29] Patten, *Expedition*, 104, 105, 100, 112, 124–5.
[30] Patten, *Expedition*, 97. On Ferrars and Chaloner, see Lucas, *Mirror for Magistrates*.
[31] Joe Moshenksa, *Iconoclasm as Child's Play* (Stanford, CA: Stanford University Press, 2019); Patten, *Expedition*, 61.
[32] Patten, *Expedition*, 95.

Praising Somerset's exemplary conformity to the laws and disciplines of war, the anecdote simultaneously hints that this is excessive in the circumstances. The ironic undertow of 'a gentlewoman, some said a Lady' is unmistakeable. Licence to rape was an incentive to soldiers in siege warfare; hence the indulgent reprimand of these 'prickers' (the *double-entendre* is surely deliberate), the Yorkshire light horse, whose job was to intimidate the Scots into 'assuring'.[33] Innuendo obliges the reader to be complicit in what feels less like outrage at the conduct of the cavalry than a gentle correction of the Lord Protector's mistaken courtesy.

A similar light mockery, implicating the reader in the cheerful dismissal of its nastier unspoken depths, runs through Patten's many references to the uttering of Somerset's proclamation at various points throughout the campaign. On the army's arrival at Berwick, the proclamation was 'openly pronounced', as Patten reports, 'to the intent, the excuse of ignorance either of the cause of my Lord Grace's coming, or of his goodness to such of the Scots as should show themselves to favour the same coming, might be quite taken from them'.[34] Shortly afterwards, the army destroyed three castles, not one of which offered active resistance: first Dunglas, then Innerwick and Thornton. At each, anything but immediate surrender was construed as enmity, since, as Somerset said, 'it cannot be but ye must be witing ... of our Proclamation sent hither before and us and proclaimed also since'. Patten treats the taking of Dunglas (which was then undermined by Sir John Brende's pioneers, and blown up with explosives) as a cockaygnesque lark: 'sure', he says, 'it would have rued any good housewife's heart to have beholden the great unmerciful murder that our men made of the brood geese and good laying hens were slain there that day'.[35]

Patten's persistent, back-slapping jocularity reveals itself, perhaps surprisingly, as the perfect expressive vehicle for Somerset's metaleptic conception of the English as would-be friends to the perversely self-harming Scots. Strategies of trivialisation, as Moshenska has written, are not in themselves simple or trivial. Their complexity, however, is rarely recognised, since they function 'not only by denying power and complexity to that which they trivialize but by concealing their *own* power and complexity in the process'.[36] Testimony to the enduring power of Patten's trivialisation strategy is the fact that to this very day the war is ubiquitously known, even to serious military historians, by the joking

[33] Philips, *Anglo-Scots Wars*, 186.   [34] Patten, *Expedition*, 82.   [35] Patten, *Expedition*, 87.
[36] Moshenska, *Iconoclasm*, 20.

diminutive of 'the Rough Wooings'. That the phrase 'rough wooing' seems itself characteristic of Patten's indulgent, infantilising condescension is no accident. For although historians rightly attribute the phrase itself to Sir Walter Scott's *Tales of a Grandfather*, it turns out that Scott was reading Patten when he invented it from Patten's report of a Scottish riposte at Pinkie. The Scots, being 'merry men and feat jesters hardily' laugh at the splendid dress of the English army, joking that English were 'very gay, and came belike a-wooing'. This, says Patten, with an almost Erasmian irony, shows that they mistake *appearance* for *cause*:

> though they spake dryly more to taunt the sumpt [sumptuousness] of our show than to seem to know the cause of our coming; yet they said more truly than they would kindly consider. For indeed, even as they were ascertained by my Lord Grace's *Proclamation*, as well before our entry into their country, that the cause of our coming was nothing else but the performing of covenants ... about this marriage and not to make war, sure ... But what a marvellous unkind people were they, that where we came, as wooers come, not otherwise, but for good love and quiet, they to receive us with hatred and war? ... Yet since that we quit them their kindness, and departed so little in their debt; let us bear somewhat with them. Marry, I wot they were not all so well content with the payment. For the Earl HUNTLEY ... being asked of a man of Estate with us ... how he bare his affection toward the joining of the two Princes. In gude faith (quod he) I wade it sud gae furth, and haud well with the marriage, but I like not this wooing.[37]

Patten captures, in this serio-ludic form, the essence of Somerset's plot of divine causation: because they will not acknowledge the just, godly cause of this friendly English invasion (of which they were informed by the *Proclamation*), it is the Scots who are guilty of actively transforming the gentle wooing into a war. Somerset's *Proclamation* warned them to interpret the appearance of the army correctly: 'we are come in this maner, which pretendeth a force in apparence (but not in deede)'. The ironic point is that any Scot understanding the true *cause* of God's divine plan for Scotland – the perfection of 'Britain' by the marriage of Mary to Edward – would not have taunted the army's appearance of wooing, because it would have understood that, in a spiritual sense, the army really *did* come in a-wooing, seeking amity and a new, Protestant unity.

The enduring importance of Somerset's causal logic combined with Patten's iconoclastic mockery can be seen in the way in which the question

---

[37] Patten, *Expedition*, 76–7; see also STC 19476.5, Patten, *Expedicion*, sig. d2r-v; Sir Walter Scott, *Tales of a Grandfather* (London: Routledge, 1828), 147: 'even those who liked the proposed match with England best were, to use an expression of the time, disgusted with so rough a mode of wooing'.

of who was the aggressor in this English war of conquest keeps being forgotten today. It is surprising how often scholars specialising in the literature of this period assume that England was being threatened with invasion from Scotland. Joan Thirsk, for example, writes of 'defence of the Scottish border' as an English government preoccupation of the 1540s, while James Carley attributes the anti-Scottish sentiment of John Leland's *Cygnea Cantio* to England's being 'threatened with ... agitation from the Scots in the North' in the year 1545, a claim which Cathy Shrank repeats: '*Cygnea Cantio* was published in 1545... when the Scots were once again threatening England's northern border.'[38] Not history, but habit – 'once again threatening'; England is not imperial, that is to say, it just wants to keep safe. Yet 1545 was the year when, *once again*, Hertford was on the rampage, laying waste forever to abbeys, towns and villages in the Scottish borders. It is not clear why the war seems to be wrapped in such general oblivion, given the public's familiarity with almost every other aspect of the Tudors' activities, but a possible explanation might lie in the way in which Somerset's metaleptic plot of the war makes the Scots into the instigators of violence, while his own objective, his propaganda declares, is only *peace, peace, peace*: *An Epistle or Exhorcation, to vnitie & peace*; *Epistola exhortatoria ad pacem*; *A praier for victorie and peace*.[39]

In 1577 and 1587, Raphael Holinshed's account of the war juxtaposed Patten's vivid eyewitness detail with Somerset's *Epistle or Exhortation* printed in full 'that it maie appeare, that the duke of Summerset then protector, and others of the councell, did not without good ground and cause mainteine the warres against the Scots'.[40] Patten's witty disparagement, juxtaposed with Henry VIII's *occupatio* ('If we had minded the possession of Scotland') and Somerset's insistence on the justness of the English cause work together to produce, in Holinshed, an impression of the war that thoroughly obscures its Anglo-imperial aggression. Is it possible that Patten's trivialising style has affected the quality of modern historical attention to the war? Gervase Phillips has noted a tendency to disregard the Anglo-Scots wars as, militarily speaking, unworthy of notice.[41] Yet he shows how developments thought to be much later – the *trace italienne* fortress,

---

[38] Thirsk, *Economic Policy*, 34; James Carley, 'John Leland's *Cygnea Cantio*: A Neglected Tudor River Poem', *Humanistica Lovaniensia: Journal of Neo-Latin Studies*, vol. 32 (1983), 225–41, 232; Shrank, *Writing*, 95.

[39] *Epistola Exhortatoria*; STC 165035, *A Praier for Victorie and Peace* (London: Richard Jagge, 1548). This was a Latin translation of *An Epistle or Exhortation*, presented by Sir Thomas Smith to Charles V in the summer of 1548. *A praier for victorie and peace* was ordered to be recited weekly in every English parish church in 1548. See Hoak, 'Cecil and Smith'.

[40] *Holinshed*, III. 910–16.   [41] Phillips, *Anglo-Scots Wars*, Chapter 1.

innovative uses of pike and light cavalry – characterise these wars in the 1540s, and he stresses the modernity, competence and general operational effectiveness of both English and Scots, pike columns and gunners, at Pinkie.[42] He speculates as to whether that 'the disparity in casualties' at Pinkie has helped foster a view of Scottish incompetence in the battle, and has 'exaggerated the ease with which the English won the field'.[43]

Phillips' observations reflect interestingly on the influence of Patten's text. For the disparity in casualties seems to have been the effect, not of an egregious Scottish military failure (at Marignano in 1515, a Swiss pike column was likewise halted by cavalry and decimated by artillery fire), but of the English decision to massacre the Scots as they fled, rather than take prisoners, according to the laws of war. Patten tells us that pikes lay strewn 'like rushes in a chamber' as the pikemen fled from the English cavalry who killed them 'either in the head or in the neck, for our horsemen could not well reach them lower'.[44] For five miles along the sands of the Firth of Forth 'the dead bodies lay as thick as a man may note cattle grazing in a full replenished pasture. The river ran all red with blood.' Patten claimed that thirteen thousand Scots died that day; modern historians estimate a death toll of between six and ten thousand. International legal historian Theodor Meron gives Pinkie as his sole example of a battle in which indiscriminate slaughter rather than the taking of lucrative war prisoners was legally justified, due to the indistinguishability of noblemen from common soldiers and the doubts of their ransom value.[45] Meron takes at face value one of Patten's rather suspect list of excuses for the indiscriminate killing. 'I may well, perchance, confess that herein we used some sharpness,' Patten admits, but

> their armour among them so little differed, and their apparel so base and beggarly; where the Lurdain was, in a manner, all one with the Lord; and the Lound with the La[i]rde: all clad alike in jacks covered with white leather; doublets the same or of fustian; and most commonly, all white hosen . . . This vileness of port was the cause that so many of their great men and gentlemen were killed; and so few saved.[46]

Why were the Scots lords and lairds so difficult to distinguish from commoners? The reason seems not to have been poverty or sartorial

---

[42] Phillips, *Anglo-Scots Wars*, 65–75.   [43] Phillips, *Anglo-Scots Wars*, 199.
[44] Patten, *Expedition*, 124–5.
[45] Theodor Meron, *Henry's Wars and Shakespeare's Laws* (Oxford: Oxford University Press, 1993), 164. Meron cites Francis Grose, *Military Antiquities* (1786–8) who in turn cites Patten.
[46] Patten, *Expedition*, 126–7.

incompetence. Patten remarks on the nobles' tents, 'sumptuously beset, after their fashion' as well as marvelling at an inherent nobility in the naked corpses, for their 'their tallness of stature, cleanness of skin, bigness of bone'.[47] The decision of all, lords, lairds and commons, to dress in 'jacks' – lightweight body armour sewn within leather jackets – may have been taken, after the disaster of Flodden, to increase agility in pike warfare.[48] The lack of sumptuary legibility complained of by Patten does not, then, prove the slaughter at Pinkie justified according to early modern laws of war; the English knew that what took place was cruel and egregious.[49] Patten's bizarre attempt to combine the justifications of godly correction and sartorial tut-tutting is hardly convincing, but it stands as one of many examples of how the very *style* of the war's writing – Patten's sceptical mockery, Somerset's godly, high-minded professions of belief in peaceable union – has helped the fact of the war itself disappear from the cognisance of early modern scholars in literature departments.

But if sumptuary illegibility justified a failure to consider the Scots nobility worthy of ransom, the same could not be given as an excuse for the perfunctory treatment of one of Pinkie's few prisoners of war, George Gordon, earl of Huntly, whom Patten described as the best dressed and 'likest a gentleman of any of them that I could hear of or see'.[50] Sent to London immediately after his capture, Huntly was forced to consider terms of ransom for a year and a half, after which he simply fled his captors. His brother, Alexander Gordon, wrote angrily to his brother of the demeaning nature of the English refusal to come to terms. 'All christyn prenccis dispiccis this fasson off wyr,' he wrote,

> 'that is to slay nobill men efter thay be randeritt, and thay that ar presonerris will nocht put thame to ransome. Thocht the wysdome off Ingland be extemit greitt, thay gane nocht the rycht way to mak unuon off thyr twa realmis. Gyf thay thynk to hawe hartlynes, thay suld traist ws moir tendyrly'. ('All Christian princes despise this fashion of war, that is, to slay noblemen after they have surrendered, and not to ransom them that are prisoners. Though the wisdom of England be extremely great, they go not the right way to make a union of these two realms. If they think to have heartliness, they should trust us more tenderly.')[51]

[47] Patten, *Expedition*, 129.
[48] Phillips, *Anglo-Scots Wars*, 61.
[49] *The Ethics of War: Classic and Contemporary Readings*, eds. Gregory M. Reichberg, Henrik Syse and Endre Begby (Oxford: Blackwell, 2006), 231–438.
[50] Patten, *Expedition*, 128.   [51] *SC*, 213–14.

Gordon has here identified the contradiction in Somerset's metaphor of 'mutual love as garrison'. '[H]owever much he may have desired allies,' notes Phillips, 'Somerset could never bring himself to abandon the policy of coercion.'[52] Even James Henrisoun, Somerset's loyal propagandist, was finally disillusioned; he now asked Somerset, 'whether it were better to conquor hearts without charges, or burn and build forts at great charges, which will never conquor Scotland?'[53] Somerset's rhetoric of Anglo-Scots amity was finally incompatible with the Galfridian model of English sovereignty and Scots vassalage: he couldn't really bring himself to 'conquor hearts' or desire 'heartliness' from the Scots as a different but equal nation. Yet Huntly's detention was protracted to further a plan of closer union: the English and the Scots were to dissolve themselves into a single, British identity. Odet de Selve, the French ambassador in London, wrote to his master Henri II of the articles which had to be agreed before hostages would be received to allow Huntly to leave captivity. These stipulated the conclusion of the nuptials of Mary and Edward, and the delivery of the queen of Scots to Berwick for three years, during which time Edward VI would possess and hold 'all he had recently conquered' in Scotland. In addition, the Scots would, as a nation, renounce the pope, and finally, there would be, at the same time,

> a suppression and extinction as much of the name of Scotland and the Scots as of the name of England and the English, and the two peoples and the two realms shall be united and reduced into one empire which shall be forever called and named the empire of Great Britain and the prince and master of it the Emperor of Great Britain ('suppression et extinction tant du nom d'Escosse et d'escossoys que du nom d'Angleterre et d'angloys, et seront les deux peuples et les deux royaulmes unys et reduictz en ung empire quy sera dict et nommé tousjours l'empire de Grande Bretaigne et le prince dominateur d'icelluy empereur de la Grande Bretaigne').[54]

Here, unequivocally stated, was Somerset's and the privy council's project of British empire. But Edward VI never became the British emperor. Huntly gave his captors the slip. 'We suppose you have harde', wrote Somerset and the privy council to Sir John Luttrell in the winter of 1548, 'of the false and subtill departure of the Earle of Hontly who so mych did dissemble with us to favour the kyngis majesties providyngis with all his

---

[52] Phillips, *Anglo-Scots Wars*, 219.
[53] Phillips, *Anglo-Scots Wars*, 219.
[54] *Correspondance Politique de Odet de Selve Ambassadeur de France en Angleterre (1546–1549)*, ed. Germain Lefèvre-Pontalis (Paris: Félix Alcan, 1888), 268–70, my translation.

harte.' Trust none of these lying Scots, the letter went on, but 'kepe daily more suer and vigilant wache upon your pece'.[55] The great project of conquering Scotland was beginning to fall apart.

II.　The Sea as a Wall, Love as a Garrison: Amphibious Fantasies

Scotland, unlike Ireland, was never conquered and colonised; we are repeatedly told that the paradigm of post-colonial will not work for Scotland. Yet the fact is that conquest and colonisation were being attempted in Somerset's war. The previous section showed how propaganda that first metaleptically transferred the causes of war to the Scots and then veiled the war's brutal carnage as carnivalesque 'rough wooing' has trivialised the war to the point of oblivion in English literary criticism. This section will examine Somerset's amphibious and riverine strategies of conquest in the light of Lauren Benton's work on 'the importance of the role of rivers in efforts to establish European imperial claims' in the Americas.[56] It will unpack the violent contradiction at the heart of Somerset's propagandist metaphor of Britain as an Anglo-Scots island, having 'the sea for wall, the mutuall loue for garrison, and God for defence'.

After Pinkie, Somerset did not attempt to take Edinburgh, or Stirling, which would seem, to modern historians, a strange strategic error. Instead, he chose to set up garrisons in the broad estuaries of the Forth and the Tay, one on the island of Inchcolm, and the other at Broughty Craig, near Dundee. His Inchcolm and Broughty garrisons, Somerset seems to have thought, would establish English sovereignty by controlling the access to ports and preventing foreign merchandise and aid (French, Dutch, German, Norwegian), as well as ensuring an invincible English supply line by sea, and, at the same time, persuading the local populace – Dundonians and the people of Fife – to 'assure' and to provide further 'love' in the form of victuals and supplies. Where an assault on Edinburgh might quickly have become unsustainable, with the English army too long in the field, these estuary garrisons would, so the plan went, enable the safe victualling of troops by ship from Berwick and Newcastle and the opportune taking of prizes at sea and further inland – intercepting a French or Dutch vessel heading for Leith, perhaps, or going upriver from Dundee to 'suppress an abbey or two'.[57] Over the difficult winter of 1547–8, however,

---

[55] *SC*, 282–3.
[56] Lauren Benton, *A Search for Sovereignty: Law and Geography in European Empires, 1400–1900* (Cambridge: Cambridge University Press, 2010), 54.
[57] *Navy*, 45.

the incoherence of Somerset's metaphor of Britain as an island fortress was fully revealed in the fates of his two garrisons on the Forth and the Tay, the former captained by Sir John Luttrell, and the latter by Sir Andrew Dudley.

Luttrell and Dudley received their commissions immediately after Pinkie. A week after the battle, Luttrell (whom Patten had described as Castiglione's ideal courtier) was appointed captain of a garrison on the island of Inchcolm, in the Firth of Forth. Inchcolm or St Colm's (Columba's) Inch was a tiny island, but of ancient symbolic importance (it is mentioned in *Macbeth*), being the seat of an Augustinian abbey. It would seem a key stronghold, set before the narrowing of the Forth at Queensferry towards Leith, Edinburgh's port, but also looking out eastwards to the widening Firth and the English supply route from Berwick. Luttrell was, jokes Patten, 'elected Abbot' of this mock-monastic fort, having with him a 'Convent of a hundred hackbutters' (arquebusiers), fifty pioneers and two small pinnaces with seventy mariners 'to keep his waters'. Warming to his metaphor, Patten described Luttrell's orders to patrol the estuary as a kind of pastoral care for his marine diocese, 'row[ing] out abroad on a Visitation', accompanied by his 'Sumners'. In pre-Reformation England (and within Patten's own memory as a parish clerk) summoners were the officers who issued a summons to an offender to appear before an ecclesiastical judge. Summoning the Scots to face Luttrell's new jurisdiction, these officers are, Patten smirks,

> very open mouthed, and never talk but they are heard a mile off. So that ether for love of his blessings, or fear of his cursings, he is likely to be sovereign over most of his neighbours.[58]

A hated ecclesiastical discipline provides the perfect metaphor for the delegated imperial 'sovereignty' Patten imagines that Luttrell will establish over access to Leith and the whole Fife coast. Luttrell's summoners or spiritual agents are the guns peeking through his ship's portholes and, since their blessings and cursings make the same loud, death-dealing report, it matters not whether the local devotion they inspire is love or fear. Patten's inversion of spiritual soul-care replays, in a new key, the nasty ambiguity at the heart of the equation of love and supply in 'the sea for wall, the mutual love for garrison'.

The following day, Andrew Dudley, the earl of Warwick's brother, was dispatched to captain Broughty Craig, which, as Patten reported, 'standeth

---

[58] Patten, *Expedition*, 139.

in such sort at the mouth of the river Tay, that being gotten, both Dundee, Saint John's Town [Perth] and many towns else (the best of the country in those parts, set upon the Tay) shall become subject to this Hold or else be compelled to forgo their whole use of the river from having anything come inward or outward'.[59] The mouth of the river is imagined as the key to subduing and holding the richest towns of the interior, Perth and Dundee, by controlling access to them from the sea.

Where had this idea of a riverine English Pale come from? Under Henry VIII, Somerset, as earl of Hertford, had in his invasion of May 1544 been the first, as Phillips writes, 'to make more sophisticated use of the naval arm's offensive capability'. An armada of two hundred ships had sailed from Newcastle into the Firth of Forth that May:

> Although at the mercy of the weather, the mobility of an amphibious operation gave a striking advantage. Artillery and victuals did not have to be dragged over muddy roads or negotiate treacherous river fords . . . The army could strike from the sea almost at will, wrong-footing defenders, who would have to watch a whole coastline as well as the land.[60]

A contemporaneous manuscript entitled 'An abstract for Englishemen to knowe the realme of Scotland thorughe out' reveals the nature of Somerset's and his advisors' imagining of the advantages of this amphibious warfare as a strategy for conquering and holding the whole of Scotland. 'Note', it says, 'that the kinges navie maye lie in the River of Fourth savely whylest theost besegeth Edenborowe' ("while the host besieges Edinburgh")'. Access to Perth ('St John's town') up the river Tay from Dundee is clearly imagined: distances are given, and depths of the river around Perth ('the Water of Tay filleth it with water / yt is naviable and woole beare a shipp of xl tones and of the southside of St Johns towne ys a bridge ouer the Water of Tay'). The Tay is also said to give access to 'the contrie of Angus vnto Dund dee' so that 'thost nedeth litlie carrying for the navie may mere thost euery weke ons'. In other words, it is imagined that an army occupying Perth and Angus could be easily supplied by the English navy appearing once a week with supplies from Newcastle, Berwick and Holy Island. Around Aberdeen, likewise, 'the ~~sips~~ ships may vitayle thost'. Yet it is also imagined that the countryside along the banks of the Tay – Angus and Strathearn – will lie open and ripe for the

---

[59] Patten, *Expedition*, 141.
[60] Phillips, *Anglo-Scots Wars*, 161–2; see also *HP*, II.207; *L &P Henry VIII*, xix, 1.314.

harvesting by ships patrolling those waters, for here lie the 'best and moost plentefullest cuntries in all Scotland and full of good townes and the ships may vitayle thost euery weke ons by the See'.[61]

As Lauren Benton has argued, however, rivers were also symbolic of empire in the European imagination.[62] In 1539, before he rejected the pursuit of overseas empire, George Buchanan celebrated the arrival of Charles V in Bordeaux by summoning Europe's rivers, 'splendid with foreign spoils' – the Rhine, the Tiber, the Tagus, Ister or Danube – to the 'noble Garonne' (*genorose Garumna*).[63] Not coincidentally, the inauguration of English river-poetry and Anglo-imperial Galfridian chorography took place with John Leland's *Cygnea Cantio* which, as we have seen, celebrated Hertford's first amphibious assault on Edinburgh in May 1544 as proof of Neptune's support for Henry VIII's recovery of ancient British empire:

> The Scots paid heavy forfeits for their treachery. Leith lies prostrate, utterly reduced to sad ashes, and their threatening fleet has been made our prey. Then too, that castle which takes its famous name from maidens [Edinburgh], has been thrice stricken by steel and fire, suffering unadulterated defeat ... Neptune favors his British (*Neptunusque favet suis Britannis*).[64]

Indeed, *Cygnea Cantio* was presented to Henry VIII as Leland's 'swansong', a witty valediction to the Muses whom, he asserted, he was abandoning in order to pursue the study of British antiquity. The valediction was thus simultaneously a demonstration of the Muses' service to the project of British imperial recovery. The swan sang, not elegiacally but in celebration of the Thames, 'that foremost of all the rivers which water Britain'. Swansong as dying farewell morphed into swansong as the demonstration of literature's value to empire, revealing the secrets of British history from monuments along the riverbanks. Most striking, in the present context, was Leland's expression of Neptune's special regard for Britain through the celebration of Henry's revolutionary departure in the concept of sea-power, his standing navy.[65] As he swims along the river past Trenovantum's (London's) high walls, the swan feels seduced by the

[61] 'An abstract for Englishemen to knowe the realme of Scotland thorughe out', BL Cotton MS Vespasian D XVIII, item 20, fol. 135v.   [62] Benton, *Search for Sovereignty*, 54.

[63] George Buchanan, *George Buchanan: The Political Poetry*, ed. with translation and commentary by Paul J. McGinnis and Arthur H. Williamson (Edinburgh: Scottish Historical Society, 1995), 258–63, 259.

[64] Leland, *Cygnea Cantio*, sig. E2r-v tr. Sutton.   [65] *Navy*, xxviii–xxix.

invitation of 'Limodonus' (Limehouse) to make his way thither to see Henry's fleet:

> *Hoc sentire quidem videtur unda,*
> *Sic me flumine promovet secundo.*

> ('The waves seemed to sense this [our mutual desire]
> Thus the river swept me downstream.')[66]

The smell of the lime kilns assails his nostrils, he follows the bend of the river and suddenly sees the fleet before him. Leland's swan names all the ships, as well as the navy's treasurer in 1544, William Gonson, and the poet Thomas Wyatt, made a ship's captain and vice-admiral in 1542. The latter he claims to be '*Cultor Oceanitidum celebris: / Cultor Pieridum celebris ille*', 'As famed for devotion to the Oceanitides as to the Pierides [the Muses]'.[67] Whether or not true of Wyatt, this idea that a cultivation of poetry might be linked to the cultivation of England's power at sea was close to the heart of everything Leland wanted to say in his poem.

Cathy Shrank's reading of Leland's writings of 1544–5 sensitively reveals how his classicising of the English, Cornish and Welsh landscapes and coasts teaches his compatriots 'to reconceptualise their native land'. Yet in assuming that Leland's equation of 'English' with 'British' is simply an 'easy slippage', and that his preference for depicting 'his homeland as an island stronghold, ample, but also enclosed: "spacious Britain enclosed by the great Ocean"', Shrank surely underestimates the poetic power of this very reconceptualisation.[68] For the 'island stronghold' is not just *there*. Leland knows it must be *made by violence*, by the conquest of the Scots, reducing Edinburgh and Leith to ashes. The violent artifice of an island stronghold is more clearly exposed in Somerset's metaphor, where a disturbance is registered in the metaphorical equation of love and armaments. Somerset tells the Scots that the two peoples must be '*made* one by amitie', they must create spacious Britain enclosed by the great ocean, 'havyng the sea for wall', by their 'mutuall loue' which will 'garrison' them.[69] The island, then, in a final, bizarre incoherence, must be made safe and enclosed by being imperially invaded, its 'sea wall' breached and its interior penetrated by ships entering the mouths of its great rivers.

---

[66] Leland, *Cygnea Cantio*, sig. C2v.
[67] Leland, *Cygnea Cantio*, sig. C3r: '*Gunteri mea, filius nitela / Qui tot naumachiis Getas feroceis / Et Gallos domuit genus superbum*' ('My Gonson, shining son, who in so many sea-battles overcame the Geats and the French'). *Navy*, xxviii–xxix.
[68] Shrank, *Writing*, 83, 71, 84.   [69] *Epistle or exhortacion*, sig. C1r.

Yet it was not many months before this heady vision of a fluvial British imperial conquest of Scotland suffered shipwreck. An extraordinary portrait of Sir John Luttrell, painted in 1550 by Hans Eworth (see Figure 2.1 in plate section), gives vivid, if enigmatic, expression to what happened over the last two years of the war, from the time of Luttrell's captaincy of Inchcolm, in 1547, to his surrender of Broughty on 12 February 1550.[70] This painting, now in the Courtauld Gallery, was beautifully interpreted by Frances Yates in 1966, in a reading which grappled with the mystery of its arresting incoherence.[71] At the top right, an English ship, with a St George's flag, tilts into the waves, its mast lightning-struck, split and in flames, as tiny soldiers, their armour picked out in gleams of light, pile into a boat from the sinking vessel. Opposite, at the top left, an Olympian allegorical scene appears cloudily opalescent, enclosed in a kind of shell. This allegory is persuasively expounded by Yates as signifying the end of the Anglo-Scots war by the Peace of Boulogne, concluded between Edward VI and Henri II in 1550.[72] The figure of *Pax*, or Peace, in jeweled headband, a pearl in her ear and holding an olive branch in her right hand, reaches out with her left to caress Luttrell's incongruously belligerent upraised fist, as if the artist had not quite harmonised the subject's defiant pose with the rest of the composition. Behind Peace, on the right, Venus bridles an unruly horse, read by Yates as the symbol of *bellum*, war, while on the left, two female figures exchange money. Yates interprets this pair as the *Amicitia* part of the Boulogne Treaty of *Pax* and *Amicitia*, whereby France would pay 4,000 crowns to have England surrender Boulogne and give up all they had gained in Scotland.

Yet the painting's central subject seems to be less the fortunes of the war than Sir John Luttrell's retrospective *apologia* for himself. He rises, his nude torso luminously pale against the green turmoil, 'a naked man wading in an angry sea', as Yates says, raising a clenched fist 'into a world of allegory'. On his wrists, narrow bracelets spell out his integrity: On the right, '*Nec flexit lucrum 1550*', on the left, '*nec friget discrimen*': 'Neither swayed by love of gain nor deterred by danger'. At the lower left of the painting, a rock rises from the waters, inscribed with the words, 'MORE THEN THE ROCK AMYDYS THE RAGING SEAS / THE CONSTANT HEART NO DANGER DREDDYS NOR FEARYS. SIL. [Sir John Luttrell]'. Why

[70] Merriman, *Rough Wooings*, 346.
[71] Frances A. Yates, 'The Allegorical Portraits of Sir John Luttrell (1967)', in *Ideas and Ideals in the North European Renaissance*, vol. III of *Collected Essays*, ed. J. N. Hillgarth and J. B. Trapp (London: Routledge, 1984), 3–23.
[72] Yates, 'Allegorical Portraits', 8–9.

(as Yates and others have asked) did Luttrell choose to have his courage and truth portrayed in this eccentric, amphibious fashion? Luttrell's uncle, Captain Thomas Wyndham, who also served on the Forth and Tay as vice-admiral of the English fleet, was painted by Eworth as a much more conventional soldier-portrait, with plumed helmet and arquebusier visible from behind, his eyes impassively holding the viewer's gaze, thumbs matter-of-factly in belt, a tree and distant landscape as background.[73] In the Luttrell portrait, it seems, treacherous storms and political temptations to treachery ('*Nec flexit lucrum*') are identified in ways which recall Benton's analysis of New World rivers as the loci of Europe's imperial claims: 'the political dangers of distant riverine regions were set against their almost mythical promise', she writes, noting how the special hazards of river reconnaissance seemed to multiply opportunities for insubordination and betrayal.[74] Even the briefest of probing into Luttrell's experience as governor first of Inchcolm and then of Broughty Craig reveals the relevance of Benton's legal-geographical analysis to the English recovery of British empire in Scotland.

Soon after the excitement of the Pinkie victory and the setting up of Luttrell's and Dudley's garrisons at Inchcolm and Broughty Craig, the fantasies of abundant supply and control of mercantile sea traffic began to unravel. In late September, Admiral Clinton reported to Somerset that things were reasonably well begun for Dudley at the mouth of the Tay. The local population around Broughty and Dundee was, he thought, intimidated by the Scottish nobility and spiritual authorities, but once they saw that assurance to the English king would bring them

> refuge and succour if need be, there will a great number shortly come in, for already they desire assurance for their houses and goods ... and have promised to victual it [Broughty Castle] with fresh victuals privily as they may ... And since our coming here there hath been no resistance by sea nor land, for daily the people come and go peaceably to us, they have been gently used in the towns and villages hereabout unspoiled and unburned, according to your Grace's commandment.[75]

But this apparently sure foundation of loyalty and supply was more precarious than it seemed. The Scots 'desire assurance' – in other words, protection; meanwhile, they promise to victual the English 'privily'. Men from villages on the riverside, Clinton went on, 'have submitted themselves to the King's Majesty and have promised to victual the castle and fish for

---

[73] See Roy Strong, *Hans Eworth: A Tudor Artist and His Circle* (Leicester Museums and Art Gallery, 1966), plate 16.
[74] Benton, *Search for Sovereignty*, 41.   [75] *Navy*, 33.

them daily . . . *And if they will not do so*, Sir Andrew Dudley may beat them
down with ordinance or burn them when he will' (my italics; the *Calendar
of State Papers, Scotland* omits the punishment for refusing to victual).[76]
Nor was the rock on which Broughty Castle was said to stand as firm as
had been believed. '[W]hereas, wrote Clinton, "I understand that your
Grace was informed that the castle standeth upon a rock . . . the truth is . . .
the part towards the land . . . is nothing but pebble stone and sand . . . there
is none other ground but pebble stone which hath been cast up by the sea,
and a thin crust of sandy earth upon it."'[77] Judging that the castle could not
be immediately reinforced, Clinton left three large ships, rather than two
small pinnaces, to aid the castle 'should it be assailed before it be made
strong'. By these ships, he hoped, Dudley might be 'a great terror to the
country and a stay that nothing shall pass in and out of the River of Tay'.
Merchant vessels from Hamburg and the Netherlands lay upriver at
Dundee and Perth.[78] Already both the 'mutual love' and 'garrison' parts
of Somerset's sea-for-wall metaphor were looking doubtful.

Luttrell, meanwhile, had been left to manage Inchcolm and the Forth
with only two pinnaces, the *Saker* and the *Double Rose*. By November, he
was complaining to Somerset that the *Saker*, dispatched to Newcastle for
supplies, had simply vanished, while the *Double Rose* had been beaten off
by the Scots as it attempted to capture a French ship sailing past Inchcolm
into Leith harbour. Neither supply nor booty was forthcoming. Luttrell
remained confident, nevertheless, that he could 'keep the Firth against all
their power'. But this could only be done if 'I had one good ship here such as
your Grace hath appointed in the River of Tay unto Mr Dudley'.[79] Dudley
sent a ship, the *Bark Aucher*, to Luttrell, but Luttrell still felt inadequately
equipped to capture the prizes, vessels laden with wares, that sailed by his
little island. To Dudley's brother, the earl of Warwick, he wrote,

> Your Lordship's brother is merry at Broughty, and has made himself strong;
> and the country there have compounded with him for their fishing, and do
> bring him victuals daily. But I am matched with such stubborn neighbours
> that if I be a-cold they give me leave to blow my fingers; whose gentleness, as
> I may, I shall right well acquit, and the better whensoever it shall please the
> Council to appoint me wherewithal.[80]

Dudley was decidedly not merry at Broughty, however. As the winter of 1547
drew on, the French had arrived to strengthen Stirling and Edinburgh.[81]
There were troubling rumours that the earl of Argyll would appear with his

---

[76] *Navy*, 33, and see footnote.   [77] *Navy*, 31–2.   [78] *Navy*, 32.   [79] *Navy*, 35.   [80] *Navy*, 37.
[81] Merriman, *Rough Wooings*, 330–6.

Highlanders to recover Dundee for Mary of Guise. In early November, Dudley complained to Warwick of having only three months' victuals and nothing but rotten biscuits and sour beer, his men lying in the fort 'like swine, as wet as in the field' while the river was full of ships of divers countries.[82] By December, Dudley was begging for more men, victuals, armaments and a surgeon as well as 'a good preacher and good books, which would do more good than fire or sword'.[83] Broughty Castle could hardly withstand siege, 'being but rotten and sandy turf and s[h]ingle, falling down and ready to fall every day more', while all Scots noblemen from whom he had received assurance, said Dudley, were 'like to be overrun and destroyed'.[84] Wyndham was inclined to trust, not to preachers and texts, but to upriver reconnaissance for looting opportunities. If Somerset would send him the ships, mariners and guns, he promised, 'I will leave you neither town, nor village nor fisher-boat unburned from Fife Ness to Inchcolm' . . . I trust or it be long to suppress an abbey or two.'[85] As good as his word, he burned and looted Balmerino Abbey, a beautiful Cistercian nunnery on the Tay, on Christmas Day, bringing away 'the nuns and many gentlemen's daughters at school with them'.[86] When Argyll took Dundee back for the Scots and French in the spring, Dudley was devastated; he had warned Somerset in early January that Argyll was coming and begged for assistance: 'Dundee is fowlie lost for lack of help', was his bitter verdict.[87] Dudley begins, in his letters, to sound like a colonial settler defending his wild new country: in December, he writes indignantly refuting the accusation that any of his ships might have lost their tackle in his beautiful river of Tay. If only Somerset would think to invest properly in his garrisons, he would find the Tay as prosperous as the Thames itself:

> It is one of the goodliest rivers that ever I saw, and ships may ride as well as in the Thames, and better; and is one of the plentifulest for salmon, porpoise, seal, herrings and other kind of fish. And whoever informed your Grace that the ship[s] hath spent their tackle within the River of Tay, they made an untrue report unto your Grace, for there is none of them that spent or lost anything since they came within the River of Tay. I sent the *Bark Aucher* to Sir John Luttrell to help him . . . And at that time the *Bark Aucher* was with Sir John Luttrell at Incholm, and in the Firth there she spoiled and split her

---

[82] Dudley to Warwick, 30 Nov. 1547, *CSP Scot.*, 1.96.
[83] Dudley to Grey of Wilton, 20 Dec. 1547, *CSP Scot.*, 1.107.   [84] *Navy*, 48.   [85] *Navy*, 46.
[86] Wyndham to Somerset, 27 Dec. 1547, *CSP Scot*, 1.115; Dudley to Somerset 3 Jan. 1547–8, *CSP Scot.*, 1.119.
[87] Grey of Wilton to Somerset, 30 Jan., *CSP Scot*, 1.144, enclosure from Dudley. Dudley warns Somerset of Argyll on 3 Jan., *CSP Scot*, 1.119.

tackle, and not in the River of Tay ... The Earl of Argyll is come to St Johnston with a great company of Highland men ... to destroy Dundee ... Also, and it please your grace, I caused Mr Wyndham to go up alongst the River of Tay to burn an abbey ... and much corn, on Christmas day at night.[88]

Meanwhile Luttrell was being sternly advised by Somerset not to trust the servants of the former Abbot of Inchcolm; his requests for materials for fortification were refused: '[t]he tyme of the yere serueth not for buyldeng'.[89] By the spring, Dudley had been told to abandon Broughty and Luttrell been sent to govern it in his place; thereafter, as Somerset was plunged into troubles of his own in England, the correspondence shows an acceleration of suspicion and mistrust on all sides. Again and again, Luttrell's requests for munitions and victuals were met with the admonishment that he had been wasteful, that he did not take sufficient care.[90] In June, Lord Grey of Wilton warned him of possible assassination and admonished him to prepare for a sharp French siege.[91] A week later, the entire privy council warned Luttrell about his failure to support his lieutenants, to keep good discipline, to discharge his expensive German mercenaries, and to husband his resources of timber, coals and victuals. Similar admonishments went on for a year.[92] Luttrell, for his part, pleaded on behalf of the Scots supporting him, as well as lamenting that he lacked 'any kinde of thinge to clothe the powre soldyers here who bothe ar nakyd and barefote, neyther havinge fyar to keape them warme, nor wherewithall to dresse their meate'.[93] Anticipating the posture in his portrait, he protested to Somerset that he was neither provided with the means to hold Broughty safe, nor permitted to go home and pay his extreme debts:

> I have yn all thingis donn my dutye, I trust lyke a willinge subject, and shall do to the deathe. Butt I am ... consyderyd as tho yn my paynfull servys and good wyll I had attaynyd only for my rewarde your gracys utter yndignatione.[94]

By the summer of 1549, Somerset was preoccupied with rebellion, while Paget and Smith were both warning him that there was no income left to continue war in Scotland; it would not be dishonour, but wisdom, to yield up Haddington and Broughty, insisted Paget.[95] Negotiations began with the French, and Scotland was comprehended in the Treaty of Boulogne. The war was over; Somerset was succeeded as Protector by John Dudley,

---

[88] *Navy*, 49.   [89] *SC*, 215–16.   [90] *SC*, 236–7; 273–4.   [91] *SC*, 243–4.   [92] *SC*, 246–8; 304–6.
[93] *SC*, 273–8; 309–10.   [94] *SC*, 310.   [95] Merriman, *Rough Wooings*, 346.

who was made earl of Northumberland. Mary Queen of Scots was betrothed to Henri II's son, the dauphin.

At the start of this chapter, I justified its attention to the military events of the 1540s as essential to an understanding what was at stake in the English invocation of the terms 'Britain' and 'British' in the sixteenth century, as well as of the image of England-as-island in the literature and historiography of early modern England. Throughout the chapter, I have both sought to introduce readers to the enormous challenges, the violence and the destruction wrought by the conflict and, at the same time, to show how the writing of the war itself contributed to an unwarranted neglect of its very occurrence, not to mention of its historical importance and implications for the English rejection of British union in 1603. I have tried to show how tropes of *occupatio*, metaphor, metalepsis and irony variously contribute both to strategies of legitimation and to a subsequent sense that this was not a war of conquest but a justified retribution for treaties broken and title withheld. It seems appropriate to end with the image of Sir John Luttrell chose for himself, partaking as it does, implicitly, of the link between Neptune and empire, as expressed in Virgil's *Aeneid* and the Galfridian legend of Brutus. Luttrell as portrayed by Eworth is not, Yates insisted, 'a wader in the sea; he is a creature of the sea with an invisible fish's tail, a Triton, naked with the allegorical nakedness of a water divinity'.[96] I think that she is right, and that the shock of seeing this Triton striding through the sea away from a shipwreck is partly that of understanding the image's allusion to the epic poetry of empire as a demand that we acknowledge, rather than veil, the effort and violence involved in claiming that England has a right to be the whole island of Britain.

[96] Yates, 'Allegorical', 17.

CHAPTER 3

How England Became an Island:
The Faerie Queene

I. 'None of their Kings had attempted the conquest of Scotland'

In the last chapter, I showed how English war propaganda of the 1540s not only justified the nine years' war to conquer Scotland, but contributed to its being trivialised to the point of being forgotten altogether. As English war texts were reprinted or extensively cited in Holinshed's *Chronicles*, their dominant tropes persisted and throve on the ambiguity of Scotland's status in English eyes. If England had always had title – if, as Henry VIII said, the question was only whether an English king 'minded the possession of Scotland' enough to realise that title – then the question of conquest's necessity became curiously moot.[1] What if Scotland simply ceased to be a threat? Might one rewrite the past and imagine that English kings had never 'minded' its possession at all, because it was territorially worthless?

A short anecdote illustrates how this is, indeed, one of the consequences of the accession of James VI and I. In *A Treatise on the Union of the Kingdoms of Britain* (1604), Scottish jurist Sir Thomas Craig wrote approvingly of earlier English would-be conquerors of Scotland, including Henry VIII and Protector Somerset, on the grounds that they had understood that closer union (now on the point of being secured) would ensure future peace and prosperity for the island.[2] Astonishingly, as he reports, his account (which he took from English histories) was flatly denied by his English interlocutors at court, who scorned the idea that Scotland was significant enough *as territory* to have been the object of attempted conquest by any English king at any time at all since records began. 'There are many people in England,' Craig reported in amazement,

---

[1] Henry VIII, *Declaration*, sig. B3v.
[2] Thomas Craig, *De Unione Regnorum Britanniae Tractatus*, trans. and ed. Charles Sanford Terry (Edinburgh, Scottish History Society, 1909), 256–7.

so little informed upon their past history as to deny absolutely that any
English king ever thought of subduing Scotland by force of arms. Indeed,
I was told so by several persons of standing (in their own opinion) during my
recent visit to England, when I offered my congratulations that an ambition
so ardently pursued had been realised, and that Scotland, so often and so
variously menaced by force, had at length been united to England willingly
and without effusion of blood. They flatly contradicted me, and asseverated
that none of their kings had attempted the conquest of Scotland, though
they were quite confident that they would have succeeded had it been made.
One person actually added, that Scotland was of too little worth to tempt
the English to retain the country, even had she possessed herself of it; and
that Scotland owed her security solely to her cold climate, her poverty,
mountains and bogs.[3]

This is a fascinating anecdote. The denial of English imperial desire by
figuring Scotland's unworthiness – a country too cold, too poor and too
barren to have been the object of any such desire – performs a remarkably
creative feat of historical erasure. Here one consequence of the war –
poverty – is naturalised as part of a geography that simply repels imperial
desire. Scotland has been declared topographically insignificant. It has
begun, imaginatively speaking, to disappear.

By an odd twist, then, it was now not the Galfridian-derived history of
English overlordship, but *a denial of that history* that was undermining
Craig's case for British union. Not that Craig himself credited the existence
of Brutus, but he did see the value of a united island kingdom. In
enumerating the attempts of English kings to conquer Scotland, he was
not dispensing blame but rather trying to show that James VI and I's
project of British union was merely a peaceful version of what had always
been the English kings' obvious goal: the uniting of England and Scotland
to create (they said 'recover') a single island kingdom. King James, Craig
argued, was not *innovating* with the idea of 'Great Britain' but 'walking in
the footprints of his predecessors on the English throne, who were ever
animated by the ambition to unite the two kingdoms into one powerful
state'.[4] His difficulty was that he was trying, as Roger Mason explains, to
envision a union of equals, rather than an 'accessory' union, whereby one
territory was simply incorporated into another and ruled by its laws (as
Wales had been into the English state).[5] And the major problem with this,
Mason continues, was that 'the terminology of Britain itself militated

[3] Craig, *De Unione*, 242.   [4] Craig, *De Unione*, 258.
[5] Roger Mason, '1603: Multiple Monarchy and Scottish Succession', *History*, vol. 105 (2020), 402–21,
    403–4.

against' the idea of Scotland's agency or equality within a British union, bound up as that terminology was with the myths of Brutus's founding of Britain, and Arthur's reconquest as these fit into a neo-Galfridian pseudo-history of English overlordship and Scottish vassalage.[6] In this context, however, Craig's anecdote becomes even more fascinating. For his inter-locutors seemed themselves to eschew the old Galfridian chronicle form – the history of vassalage, rebellion and conquest, beginning with Brutus and Arthur. Their substitution of an assertion of Scotland's *geographical insignificance* for the old *historical* sequence of overlordship seems to mark a new departure. It is as if they have absorbed the shift – well documented by modern historians – of sixteenth-century English historiography away from assertions of the truth of Galfridian legends of origin and towards a more sceptical, spatially and materially oriented investigation of the monuments and remains of the English past in its landscape and ancient place names.[7]

II. 'British History' as Chorography: Critical Problems

Poetry is credited with being able to create new spaces and beings in the world: in Shakespeare's endlessly appealing formulation, to give local habitation to airy nothing. It might seem harsh to argue by contrast that poetry is also able to unmake local habitations that do exist in the world. And this argument would probably seem especially unjust levelled at so spacious a poetic habitation as Edmund Spenser's land of Faery. Yet this chapter will show how Spenser's *The Faerie Queene* makes Scotland unimaginable. In absorbing and transforming Galfridian British history into the ancient 'moniments' and prophetic destiny of Faery land, Spenser created an enchanted world expressive of inward moral struggle which simultaneously offered a vision of England's maritime imperial destiny.[8] Without crediting Thomas Craig's interlocutors necessarily as readers of Spenser, I want to show how Spenser's poem contributed to the shift in popular sensibility that they exemplify, in which the idea of a glorious Galfridian reconquest of the island was replaced by the idea of England *as*

---

[6] Mason, '1603: Multiple Monarchy', 411.

[7] As discussed, for example, by F. R. Levy, *Tudor Historical Thought* (San Marino, CA: Huntington Library, 1967), especially Chapter 4, 'Antiquarianism', 124–66.

[8] Spenser has Arthur begin to read 'An ancient booke, hight *Briton moniments*', in Book II, canto ix, stanza 59 of *The Faerie Queene*. References to *The Faerie Queene* ed. A. C. Hamilton (London: Longman, 1977) will henceforward appear in the text by book, canto and stanza.

always already an island nation, now girding itself to embrace its imperial maritime future.

At the centre of my argument will be a reading of the specific narrative strand of Spenser's Legend of Chasity in Book III, involving the entanglement of Britomart, Marinell and Florimell, which begins to be resolved at the great river wedding of Book IV, Canto xi. What, I will ask, has Spenser's conception of chastity to do with the amphibious regions inhabited by Marinell and his kin? Why is the sea-coast both Britomart's and Florimell's destination when the one is tormented by erotic feeling and the other by erotic pursuit (III.iv.6, III.vii.27)? What, more generally speaking, has *chastity* to do with *coastlines* and what has a procession of rivers towards an estuary to do with imagining England's sovereignty over Britain and its surrounding seas?

Before these questions can be explored, we need to consider, from the perspective of the literary imagining of Scotland, the impact of the English historiographical shift from chronicle to antiquarian chorography. Though not new to English literary criticism, the topic of English chorography needs to be reopened here because its Anglo-imperial and race-making dimensions have not been fully recognised. A fuller discussion of the latter will have to wait till Chapter 7, which will offer an extended analysis of the transformative effect of Camden's *Britannia* on the traditionally understood racial divisions of the British Isles. In this chapter we are concerned with the impact of English chorography – a kind of spatialising of British history – on the English imagining of Scotland and the Scots.

The shift begins with John Leland's introduction of a humanist antiquarian topography into England in the 1540s, followed in Elizabeth's reign by the work of Anglo-Saxonist and cartographer Laurence Nowell and his friend and pupil William Lambarde in the in 1560s and 70s, as well as by that of Humphrey Llwyd (1572), William Harrison (1577) and, of course, William Camden, whose *Britannia* (1586) was the *acme* of the genre.[9] John Dee's historical researches are also relevant here, as are their uses by Richard Hakluyt in his *Principal Navigations*.[10] In the work of these men, Galfridian history with its legends of Arthur and Brutus was not by

[9] Kendrick, *British Antiquity*, 34–133; Levy, *Tudor Historical Thought*, 129–58; James P. Carley, 'Harrison and Leland', *Oxford Handbook of Holinshed*, 187–202; Angus Vine, *In Defiance of Time: Antiquarian Writing in Early Modern England* (Oxford: Oxford University Press, 2010); Rebecca Brackmann, *The Elizabethan Invention of Anglo-Saxon England: Laurence Nowell, William Lambard and the Study of Old English* (Cambridge: D. S. Brewer, 2012).

[10] On John Dee, see below, 92–5. Richard Hakluyt included testimonies of Arthur's conquests in both the 1589 and 1598–1600 editions of *Principal Navigations*. See *The Hakluyt Handbook*, ed. D. B. Quinn (London: Hakluyt Society, 1974), 2 vols., II.354, 378.

any means forgotten, but it did gradually stop operating as a chronicle proving England's overlordship of Scotland and justifying conquest. Organised by topographical proximity rather than narrative sequence, antiquarian history strove to discover and interpret the material and textual remains of England and Wales as evidential forms that might enable a more plausible conjectural reconstruction of the British and Saxon past. What these antiquarians composed, then, were not narratives but etymological collections and spatialised descriptions, verbal and visual – chorographic and cartographic representations. They drew maps, compiled place-name lexicons, described topographies and traced the courses of rivers.

Chorography did not in itself fictionalise Galfridian British history. What it did, however, was to throw a new emphasis on thinking of historical work as the sceptical, yet patriotic, hermeneutic encounter with ancient texts and material remains in relation to specific sites and locations: a 'laboryouse Journey', a 'perambulation', or a description of the 'imagined course' of the 'ebs, flowings, and falles' of rivers.[11] Figures like Brutus and Arthur were not so much rejected as conjecturally reconstructed in the form of place-name etymologies and scattered remains. John Leland's *Assertio inclytissimi Arturi Regis Britanniae*, an antiquarian defence of Arthur, was intended in 1544 as a purging of fabulous elements to focus on the historicity of Arthur's conquests, especially that of Scotland. A poem concluding Leland's defence of Arthur praises Henry VIII as another Arthur 'who often vanquished the Caledonian Scots'.[12] But if Leland thus 'rescued Arthur', as C. S. Lewis famously declared, 'for Spenser and Milton', he also rendered the legend conjectural, fragmentary and relic-like – an Arthur of archaeological remains. Leland details with excitement, for example, the 'ringes, fragments of harnesse & brazen ornaments from Bridles' dug up by ploughmen in the fields near Padstow in Cornwall, to prove his 'coniecture' that this was the site of the river Camblan, where Arthur's last battle was reported to have taken place.[13] Later, during Elizabeth's reign, as Josephine

---

[11] Leland, *laboryouse Journey*; William Lambarde, *A Perambulation of Kent*; William Harrison, 'An Historical Description of the Iland of Britaine', in *Holinshed*, I.78.

[12] On the centrality of overlordship of Scotland to Leland's defence of Arthur, see James P. Carley, 'Arthur and the Antiquaries', *The Development and Dissemination of Arthur in Medieval Latin*, ed. Siân Echard (Cardiff: University of Wales Press, 2011), 150–78, especially 159–61. Carley translates Leland's poem at 161. Carley makes a case for Leland's authorship of Henry VIII's *Declaration*, though that text eschews Arthur as evidence.

[13] C. S. Lewis, *English Literature in the Sixteenth Century, Excluding Drama* (Oxford: Oxford University Press, 1954), 297; John Leland, *Assertio inclytissimi Arturij Regis Britanniae* (London, 1544), sig. F1r; *A Learned and True Assertion of . . . Arthure, King of great Brittaine* tr. Robert Robinson (London, 1582), sig. G1v.

Bennett long ago argued, 'antiquarians found a new use for the legend [of Arthur] as support to growing colonial and imperial ambitions'.[14] Key contributors here were William Lambarde, John Dee and Richard Hakluyt, bringing together antiquarian researches in Saxon law, history and geography. Arthur's conquests of the Scots remained an essential element, but no longer occupied the foreground of the research; rather, Arthurian evidence began, particularly in John Dee's writings and maps, to subtend larger claims for England's extensive maritime jurisdiction and became the precondition of arguments for pursuing an English overseas empire.[15] Though long known, Dee's uses of Arthurian history as imperial argument deserve renewed attention in the light of William Sherman's work on the way Dee's British historical reading informed his economic and political projects, and in the light of the relatively recently discovered (and now translated and edited) *Brytanici Imperii Limites* (1576–78), 'The Limits of the British Empire'.[16] The Arthurian basis for claiming England's overlordship of Scotland gained a new maritime importance, as Dee began to develop legal arguments for England's 'sea-sovereignty', or jurisdiction over coastal waters as far as Norway's shores. 'In terms of Elizabeth's sovereignty over the whole island, in terms of her claims in North America,' James P. Carley writes, 'Arthur was crucial to Dee's arguments.'[17]

We begin to see, then, that as British legendary materials ceased to be used to justify the invasion of Scotland, they begin to contribute figuratively towards a newly vivid vision of England as an island, a realm set in the sea. Over the course of Elizabeth's reign there develops the idea that England doesn't need to conquer or unite with Scotland in order to become 'the whole Isle within the Ocean sea' because it *already is that island*. So, for example, Edmund Spenser addresses Elizabeth in the proem to the *Faerie Queene* as 'Great Lady of the greatest Isle' (I.Proem, 4.3), while, in book II, Guyon, recalling Aeneas to Dido, tells Medina that she reminds him of that 'great and most glorious virgin Queene' who 'All Faery lond does peaceably sustene' while 'In widest Ocean she her throne does reare' (II.ii.40.2-5). In *The Araygnement of Paris* (1584) George Peele addresses Elizabeth as the nymph Eliza, whose realm, 'Elizium' is 'a

[14] Josephine Waters Bennett, *The Evolution of 'The Faerie Queene'* (Chicago, IL., University of Chicago Press, 1942), 70; see also Carley, 'Arthur', 163–5.
[15] John Dee, *Brytanici Imperii Limites*, BL MS Additional 59681. This MS has been valuably edited and translated as *The Limits of the British Empire [Brytanici Imperii Limites]*, eds. Ken Macmillan and Jennifer Abeles (Westport, Connecticut: Praeger, 2004). See below, 92–5.
[16] William H. Sherman, *John Dee: The Politics of Reading and Writing in the English Renaissance* (Amherst, MA: University of Massachusetts Press, 1995), 90–5, 148–200.
[17] Carley, 'Arthur', 164.

seconde Troie / Ycompast round with a commodious sea'.[18] Surely recollecting Peele, Shakespeare has John of Gaunt, in *Richard II* (c.1595) invoke 'this sceptred isle ... This precious stone, set in the silver sea, / which serves it in the office of a wall, / Or as a moat defensive to a house'.[19] As we saw in the Introduction, the famous 1592 'Ditchley' portrait of Elizabeth by Marcus Gheeraerts the Younger (see Figure 1.1 in plate section) exemplifies this trend. The painting's cartouche refers to 'This yle' in the 'boundless ocean'.[20]

Gheeraerts's design, as we saw, makes a bold imperial claim with respect to Scotland, but one that seems to have gone unnoticed in modern times. In the 1980s, Louis Montrose offered an important analysis of the way in which Elizabeth's virginal self-containment came to represent national strength and imperial ambition by being associated with England's *island status* in paintings such as the Armada and Ditchley portraits.[21] An increasing literary-critical interest in the social production of space and in the rhetoric of cartography enabled developments of Montrose's analysis, but there has been no questioning of what it meant to equate a virgin queen of England with the island of Britain, ignoring the fact of the island's other kingdom.[22] On the contrary, the findings of the so-called 'spatial turn' in literary criticism – whose emphasis has been on cartography's ability to abstract, measure, narrate and make space visually intelligible – simply deepen the mystery.[23] For, just as cartography seems to be developing more vivid and detailed ways of visualising the local habitations of

---

[18] George Peele, *The Araygnement of Paris* ed. R. Mark Benbow in *The Life and Works of George Peele*, gen. ed. Charles Taylor Prouty (New Haven, CT: Yale University Press, 1970), III.iii, V.i., TLN 1150–54.

[19] William Shakespeare, *Richard II*, ed. Charles R. Forker (London: Arden Shakespeare, 2002), II. i.40–8. It was Willy Maley who first brought the 'England as island' motif to critical attention, see, '"This Sceptred Isle": Shakespeare and the British Problem', in John Joughin ed., *Shakespeare and National Culture* (Manchester: Manchester University Press, 1997), 83–108.

[20] See introduction, 000.

[21] Louis Montrose, 'The Elizabethan Subject and the Spenserian Text', *Literary Theory/Renaissance Texts*, eds. Patricia Parker and David Quint (Baltimore, MD: Johns Hopkins University Press, 1986), 303–430, 312–15; see also Montrose, *The Subject of Elizabeth: Authority, Gender and Representation* (Chicago, IL: University of Chicago Press, 2006), 119–63; Helen Hackett, *Virgin Mother, Maiden Queen: Elizabeth I and the Cult of the Virgin Mary* (Basingstoke: Macmillan, 1995), 112–19.

[22] John Gillies, *Shakespeare and the Geography of Difference* (Cambridge: Cambridge University Press, 1994); Garrett Sullivan, *The Drama of Landscape: Land, Property, and Social Relations on the Early Modern Stage* (Stanford, CA: Stanford University Press, 1998); *Playing the Globe: Genre and Geography in English Renaissance Drama*, eds. John Gillies and Virginia Mason Vaughan (Madison, NJ: Fairleigh Dickinson Press, 1998); Bernhard Klein, *Maps and the Writing of Space in Early Modern England and Ireland* (Basingstoke: Macmillan, 2001).

[23] See Klein's excellent introduction, *Maps and the Writing of Space*, 1–11.

the English kingdom, the boundaries of England are rendered radically indistinct. We have no idea, in the Ditchley portrait, where England ends, but *it seems to be surrounded by sea*. Scotland has vanished.

Why have we overlooked this daring juxtaposition of detailed carto-graphic visualisation with a fantastical disregard for geography? One reason has been the tendency to associate cartography with the rise of English *national* consciousness and overseas empire, ignoring the imperial consciousness by which England sought sovereignty over the whole island. Most influential in this respect has been Richard Helgerson's magisterial *Forms of Nationhood* (1992), which ascribed to the rise of cartography and chorography the emergence of a spatial 'ideology of place and particularity' conceived in resistance to the temporality of the medieval chronicle, which legitimates the dynastic monarchy. Helgerson thus saw the Ditchley por-trait, where the queen's royal body obscures the land over which she reigns, developing into the frontispiece of Michael Drayton's *Poly-Olbion* (1612) (see Figure 3.1 in the plate section), where the implicitly 'antimonarchical' land consciousness of Christopher Saxton's mapping practices triumphs, and the land becomes monarch over herself: 'the monarch is now the land', he writes, 'the land as Saxton and his successors had been making it known'.[24] Helgerson's eloquent account has even influenced historians of early modern English geography. Lesley Cormack's study of the rise of geography at the English universities argues for a distinctly imperial motivation in all areas of geography except chorography. 'Geography,' she writes, 'provided a key to the imperialism that stressed the superiority of English people and customs and the knowability and controllability and inferiority of the wider world.'[25] Yet (citing Helgerson) she exempts chorography, which, she writes, 'supplied an alternative face of imperial thinking, giving English people a sense of identity, placement and purpose by encouraging them to distinguish themselves by their locale, whether that was England as a whole or a more local particularism'.[26]

A problematic aspect of Helgerson's influential account, however, is the assumption that the translation of the mythic 'British' history of Brutus and Arthur into chorography rather than official history – that is, into *local legends* and *curiosities* rather than *truth-claiming chronicle* – somehow renders it less ideologically effective as an imperial discourse. Noting the conquerors that flank the island of Britain in Drayton's

[24] Helgerson, *Forms of Nationhood*, 118.
[25] Lesley Cormack, *Charting an Empire: Geography at the English Universities, 1580–1620* (Chicago: Chicago University Press, 1997), 11.
[26] Cormack, *Charting an Empire*, 168 and n. 18.

frontispiece – Brutus, Julius Caesar, Hengist the Saxon and William the Norman – Helgerson argues that Drayton 'marginalises' their monar-chical claims, privileging the land itself, which he populates with natural deities, with river gods and nymphs, so that 'the rivers, hills and woods of England' themselves tell, in song, 'of the various dynasties that since Brut have ruled Britain'.[27] For Helgerson, such chorographic and carto-graphic forms of Anglo-British nationhood are celebrations of plurality and locality because they oppose 'absolutism', whether Elizabeth's or James's. Yet to be anti-absolutist is perfectly compatible with being imperial. The sixteenth-century English discourse of 'British empire' emerges, as Dale Hoak has argued, from the vision of the 'monarchical republic' conceived in writing and policy by men like Sir Thomas Smith and William Cecil, Lord Burghley.[28] Indeed, Lord Burghley's working 'atlas' of Britain, which comprised a set of proofs of Christopher Saxton's detailed county maps of England, together with an old printed map of Scotland, opens with Burghley's own handwritten notes on Brutus's conquest of Britain.[29]

For Helgerson, the antimonarchical features of chorography included its tendency to inscribe Britain's legendary narrative in the natural forms of the landscape, its revelling in a welter of ancient place names and its 'perambulatory' or fluvial organisation by order of topographical proximity.[30] Yet all these were definitive of rather than antithetical to the Anglo-imperial translation of the British history from truth-claiming chronicle to the animated past of the landscape itself. Chorography, cartography and the new genre of river poetry, especially as this last is incorporated into the legend of Chastity in Spenser's *The Faerie Queene*, are intimately interconnected in working to transform the older chronicle-based narrative discourse of England's claims to sovereignty over Scotland into a chorographic sense of the 'metamorphic indigeneity' of the much-conquered English, and the naturalness of their claim to the whole island and to jurisdiction over the surrounding seas.

III. Chastity and the Coasts of Faery Land

The marriage of the Thames and the Medway in Book IV, Canto xi is the section of Edmund Spenser's *The Faerie Queene* most obviously indebted to chorographical description. The Canto's sources have long been

---

[27] Helgerson, *Forms of Nationhood*, 140.   [28] Hoak, 'Cecil and Smith'.
[29] BL Royal MS 18 D III, f.2v.   [30] Helgerson, *Forms of Nationhood*, 143.

known: two are specimens of the new genre of English river poetry, John Leland's Latin *Cygnea Cantio* of 1545 and Camden's fragmentary *De Connubio Tamae et Isis*, while Spenser himself tells us the third. As early as 1580, Spenser wrote to Gabriel Harvey of the effect of chorography on his poetic imagination, explaining how he planned to write a poem on the marriage of the Thames which, he said, would 'describe all the Riuers throughout Englande, whyche came to this Wedding, and their righte names, and right passage, etc., ... wherein notwithstanding Master *Holinshed* hath much furthered and aduantaged me, who therein hath bestowed singular paines, in searching oute their first heades, and sourses'.[31] Though he names 'Master *Holinshed*', Spenser is actually here referring William Harrison's 'An Historical Description of the Iland of Britaine', which prefaced Holinshed's *Chronicles* in 1577 and 1587. Spenser critics agree that this projected *Epithalamion Thamesis* became the *Faerie Queene*'s marriage of the Thames and Medway, to which Spenser invites Neptune and all the sea gods, followed by the founders of nations, the rivers of the world and, finally, the rivers of England, Wales and Ireland.[32]

In the criticism of this canto, the accuracy of Spenser's knowledge of rivers has been thoroughly canvassed and its bearing on books III and IV, the legends of Chastity and Concord respectively, has been analysed in various ways as symbolic of cosmic harmony or cosmic *eros*, 'the continually changing organization of society', in Harry Berger's words, for example, being figured by 'the eternally recurrent flow-through of water'.[33] More recently, critics have pointed to disturbances in the procession's apparent triumphal order, particularly in relation to Spenser's inclusion of the Irish rivers with their 'hidden race' and 'saluage cuntries'.[34] Yet the registering of such disturbances still assumes a descriptive and referential relation between Spenser's chorographic poetry and the fluvial spaces

[31] *Spenser Variorum*, X.17.

[32] Harrison, 'Description', 1–220. On the composition of Harrison's 'Description', see Glyn Parry, 'William Harrison and Holinshed's *Chronicles*', *HJ*, vol. 27, no. 4 (1984), 789–810. On Spenser's debt to Harrison, see Charles Osgood, *Spenser's English Rivers* (New Haven, CT: Connecticut Academy of Arts and Sciences, 1920).

[33] See, for example, Thomas P. Roche, *The Kindly Flame: A Study of the Third and Fourth Books of Spenser's Faerie Queene* (Princeton, NJ: Princeton University Press, 1964), 167–84; Jack B. Oruch, 'Spenser, Camden, and the Poetic Marriage of Rivers', *SP*, vol. 64, no. 4 (1967), 606–24; Harry Berger, Jr., 'Two Spenserian Retrospects: The Antique Temple of Venus and the Primitive Marriage of Rivers', *Texas Studies in Literature and Language*, vol. 10, no. 1 (1968), 5–25, 15; Rachel E. Hile, 'The Limits of Concord in the Thames–Medway Marriage Canto of *The Faerie Queene*', *SP*, vol. 108, no. 1 (2011), 70–85.

[34] Andrew Hadfield, *Spenser's Irish Experience: Wilde fruit and Salvage Soyle* (Oxford: Clarendon Press, 1997), 144–5; Bart Van Es, *Spenser's Forms of History* (Oxford: Clarendon Press, 2002), 62–4.

of the British Isles. Critics notice what Spenser says about the Irish rivers because he names them. But omission – absence, occlusion – is also poetic choice. What does it mean that the rivers of Scotland – the Forth, Clyde and Tay – are nowhere mentioned and that Scotland itself only appears as a bloodstained 'limit' (IV.xi.36)? The answer might seem obvious: Spenser omits the Scottish rivers precisely because Scotland is a distinct kingdom and is not part of England. This is a possible interpretation, though it does not fit with the designation of Irish rivers as joining 'in neighbourhood of kingdome nere' (IV.xi.40), nor with the absence from the entire *Faerie Queene* of the name 'Scotland' when Ariosto, '*the* epic model in Spenser's circle', makes so much of *Scozie* as a romance location within *Bretagna*.[35] I am going to argue for a different interpretation, one that takes seriously Lauren Benton's arguments for the importance of rivers in the establishment of European imperial claims.[36] And my interpretation requires not only that we should examine the forms such Anglo-British imperial claims take in earlier English river writing, but that we should attend closely to the brilliance with which Spenser weaves his version of these claims into one of the stories begun in the legend of Chastity, a story finally resolved at the occasion of the Thames–Medway wedding. The story I mean begins with our first sight of Florimell and Britomart's subsequent wounding of Marinell. Or is it Britomart's wounding of Marinell and the subsequent flight of Florimell? Either way it is to that ambiguous sequence of events and its allegorical topography that I now turn.

Locations are not just where things happen in *The Faerie Queene*: the constitution of the moral allegory is itself partly topographical.[37] 'Deheubarth that now South Wales is hight' (III.ii.18), from deep in Malory's Arthurian Britain, is Britomart's childhood home and the place where her love-longing was first conceived by a stray glance in a magic mirror. We learn about it through a flashback which simultaneously associates *eros* – the desire for knowledge of a lover's body – with the exploration of uncharted lands and waters. Innuendo hovers over the repetition of the word 'parts', blending the idea of exploratory voyaging with dreams of bodily intimacy. When the Redcrosse knight asks Britomart what 'vncouth wind'

[35] Colin Burrow, *Epic Romance: Homer to Milton* (Oxford: Clarendon Press, 1993), 102; Ariosto, *Orlando Furioso*, trans. Barbara Reynolds (Harmondsworth: Penguin, 1975), 2 vols., vol I., for example: canto 4, stanzas 51–72; canto 5, canto 6, 1–16; canto 10, 91–115, canto 11, 1–53.

[36] Benton, *Search for Sovereignty*, 54.

[37] For a discussion of the complexities of allegory and space in Spenser, see Christopher Burlinson, *Allegory, Space and the Material World in the Writings of Edmund Spenser* (Cambridge: D. S. Brewer, 2006).

has brought her 'into those parts' (III.ii.4), she answers boldly (though with blushes like lightning bolts) that she seeks adventure 'by sea, by land' and so, she concludes, 'into *these parts* I came / Withouten compasse and withouten card' (III.ii.7, my italics). Already in Britomart's response uncharted seas seem to beckon with the words 'compasse' and 'card', for although a 'card' can be any kind of map, in this period the reference is most often nautical, as in 'sea-card' or 'mariner's card'.[38] In the ensuing small talk, Britomart endearingly attempts to cover up the inadvertent revelation of her interest in Artegall by disparaging his chivalry and, when Redcrosse graciously leaps to Artegall's defence, she begs him for a description of her beloved (III.ii.16). Redcrosse happily obliges '[a]nd him in euery part before her fashioned' (III.ii.16). This ekphrastic fashioning of Artegall 'in euery part' then beautifully and humorously introduces the analepsis by which we learn of Britomart's first eyeing of Artegall, as the next stanza confesses how little Britomart needed to hear Redcrosse's description: 'Yet him in euery part before she knew . . . Sith he whilom in Britaine she did vew / To her reuealed in a mirrhour plaine' (III.ii.17). We then hear the strange tale of how Britomart first saw her lover in this 'glassie globe' made by Merlin for her father, King Ryence, 'that neuer foes his kingdom might inuade' without his prior knowledge (III.ii.21). This sounds ominously as if Artegall is an invading enemy, but Merlin's prophecy reassures us that Britomart's passion for him will ultimately benefit rather than destroy her nation, uniting Briton and Saxon. And so, as we hear, it was thus that she made her way, instructed by Merlin, to Faery land and met Redcrosse from whom, having 'in each point her selfe informed' of Artegall, she took her leave. But the aftermath of Redcrosse's discourse arouses Britomart and makes her restless. She grows 'pensiue through that amorous discourse / By which the *Redcrosse* knight did earst display / Her louers shape and cheualrous aray'. Feeding her wound with 'self-pleasing thoughts', she is impelled to explore, to ride on 'without repose or rest, searching all lands and each remotest part . . . Till that to the sea-coast at length she her addrest' (III.iv.6).

　　Thus it is that the relation between Britomart's 'natiue soyle . . . the greater *Britaine*' and the 'remotest parts' of Faery land is conceived simultaneously from inside, as it were, as the threat of invasion and, moving outward, as expansive, erotic exploration of every 'part' to the land's very edge. Indeed, one could say that the flashback which explains the origin of Britomart's amorous passion instantiates a Faery land that, for the first time in Spenser's poem, has acquired a *coastline*. More than that, what

---

[38] See *OED*, 'card', n II†4.

stretches away from the coast is imagined as an adjacent realm, even an empire, with its own complex structures of governance, habitation and health arrangements. Not only are we constantly led to overhanging cliffs, roaring waves and sandy beaches strewn with shipwrecked spoils, we're even treated to the splendid marine architecture and modes of locomotion proper to Faery land's coastal waters. We enter submarine 'bowres' 'built of hollow billows, heaped hye ... And vaulted all within' (III.4.43). We watch as Nereids, the benevolent escorts of the sea, 'sheare' the 'brackish waues' in chariots drawn by teams of dolphins (III.4.31).[39] We learn that, in a submarine medical emergency, one can send for Tryphon, who 'of sea gods, the soueraine leach is hight' (III.iv.43). And we are aware, too, of a sense of amphibious habitations, of spaces that are ambiguously positioned between sea and land – Marinell's 'rich strond' as well as 'the margent of the fomy shore', an ambiguous, tidal region, too shallow to swim, where the water laps the 'stony ground' that might bruise the dolphins' tender fins (III.4.34).

The ostentatiously intricate narrative links which knit the ancient-British origins of Britomart's erotic passion to Florimell's endangered chastity repeatedly involve questions of propriety and jurisdiction over what we might call Faery land's 'offshore' interests – the submarine dominions ruled over by Neptune. Book III opens with Florimell appearing, without explanation, like a blazing star, hotly pursued by lust and violence. Guyon and Arthur immediately ride to her rescue; only Britomart steadfastly refuses the 'hope to win thereby / Most goodly meede, the fairest Dame aliue' (III.i.18). And it is precisely because Britomart refuses this 'goodly meede', the prize of Florimell, that we come to learn, through the conversation with Redcrosse, of her falling in love with the figure in the globe supposed to ward off invaders. The connection of erotic passion with ancient British national security is thus already evident, but the plot thickens when, as we have seen, a sexually aroused Britomart gallops to Faery land's seashore and pours out her tempestuous, visceral passion in a vow to Neptune, only to be interrupted in these maritime negotiations by an unknown knight who bars her passage, claiming he owns the beach she stands on, and all the riches that wash up on it (III.iv.14). Britomart immediately wounds this unknown knight – whom we then discover to be Marinell, a being of mixed mortal

---

[39] See Judith M. Barringer, *Divine Escorts: Nereids in Archaic and Classical Greek Art* (Ann Arbor, MI: University of Michigan Press, 1995).

and sea-god parentage – causing a diplomatic incident off the shores of Faery land, where his mother, Cymoent, lives. Cymoent is one of the daughters of Nereus – a Nereid, and so high-ranking in oceanic society (III.iv.19). In her grief, she is accompanied by her numerous sisters, all of whom command their own chariots and travel across Neptune's back to mourn with her, and to tend Marinell's wounds until the appearance of a Tryphon skilled in medicine. Meanwhile, Florimell continues to flee from Prince Arthur, whose shield and arms frighten her with their strangeness (III.iv.51). Losing her, Arthur sleeps fitfully on the ground that night, blending Florimell's image, in his waking dreams, with that of his elusive faerie queene (III.iv.54). The following morning, the weary Briton prince meets a dwarf from the Faery Court who declares that Florimell actually fled four days previously, on hearing that the sea nymph's son, Marinell, had been slain, for though she was 'belou'd of many a knight / Yet she loues none but one, that *Marinell* is hight' (III.v.8). Critics have puzzled over this chronologically preposterous revelation, since we have watched Britomart unhorse Marinell *after* having watched Arthur and Guyon disappear into the thick of the wood in pursuit of Florimell (III.i.19), so it is impossible that Florimell's flight should have been caused by the 'fame' that Marinell had been 'yslain' by a 'forreine foe' (III.v.9). Yet the very causal impossibility of this set of circumstances sets up suggestive spatial/structural parallels between the conceptions of chastity embodied by Britomart and Florimell. Britomart saw her lover in a mirror designed for her father 'that never foes his kingdom might inuade' (III.ii.21), while to Florimell and the Faery Court, it is Britomart, trespasser on Marinell's seashore, who is precisely that 'forreine foe' (III.v.9). The least we can conclude is, first, that Spenser's conception of chastity as embodied in Britomart and Florimell is bound up with questions of British national security and of legal propriety and jurisdiction over Faery land's amphibious regions and coastlines. Second, one effect of the dwarf's report of the news from the Faery Court is to involve the mystery of Florimell's identity with the preposterous revelation of her having fled for love of *Marinell*. The meaning of the much-desired Florimell's existence, in other words, now emanates in some way from the crisis precipitated by Britomart's challenge to Marinell's property claims in the space between land and sea. Finally, as it the occasion of the wedding of the Thames and the Medway in the house of Proteus that ultimately resolves this jurisdictional crisis and enables the marriage of Florimell and Marinell, Spenser's interest in rivers and coastlines seems to be more integral to his allegory of Chastity than we have previously thought.

IV. Mapping as Erasure: Scotland Vanishes From Its Own Map

Literary-critical accounts of the sources of Thames–Medway marriage tend to assume a purely literary genealogy. But the reading of English river poetry was bound up with antiquarian, chorographic and cartographic activity and hence, implicitly, with England's historical claims to sovereignty over all Britain and to all British coasts and seas. We need to look at how such poetry was read, annotated and used, especially by those close to men in government. In chapters 1 and 2 I discussed John Leland's *Cygnea Cantio* as a war poem, a celebration of the defeat of the Scots as well as a prophecy of England's recovery, under the favour of Neptune, of imperial rule over all Britain. In literary-critical studies Leland's work is hailed as 'a major literary achievement. . . a new kind of poem with a new vision of the landscape, its history and the present'.[40] How do these two elements – the poem's celebration of Anglo-British imperial conquest and its creation of new vision of history inscribed in the landscape – go together? Among the Elizabethan readers appreciative of both aspects were antiquarians – legal historians, Anglo-Saxonists, cartographers – who mined Leland's poem and its commentary in support of various projects establishing the antiquity and continuity of English laws, or the military conquest of Ireland, or the establishment of an English royal navy. The fictional premise of Leland's poem is that of the swan as poet, singing as he glides along England's mightiest river, the Thames, from Oxford to 'New Troy' or 'Trenovant', the ancient British name for London. The swan's song celebrates, as we saw in the previous chapter, victories against the Scots and the French while evoking the ancient glory of Britain by describing the cities and edifices that line the banks of the river.

If in his Arthurian researches, Leland tried to reassert Anglo-British title to Scotland by a humanist return *ad fontes*, to the archaeological evidence, his *Cygnea Cantio* innovates differently. Instead of narrating or excavating British history, this poem produces it as pleasing anecdotes linked to the viewing of ancient monuments along the riverbank. By turning history into a navigation through place and not time, Leland summons the past as numinous presence. He more or less invents, as Carley argues, the tourist appeal of place-name history.[41] And the illusion of visual pleasure – the sense of beauteous ancient edifices 'rising before our view' – is intimately associated with the pleasures of antiquarian etymology. Palaces and cities

[40] Wyman H. Herendeen, *From Landscape to Literature: The River and the Myth of Geography* (Pittsburgh: Dusquene University Press, 1986), 195.
[41] Carley, 'John Leland's *Cygnea Cantio*', 234–5.

along the banks of the Thames are given pseudo-ancient place names as 'Hydropolis' for 'Dorchester', 'Abbaduna' for Abingdon, 'Cavela' for 'Wallingford', 'Trenovantum' for London and so on.[42] Indeed, the poem comes with its own hefty scholarly apparatus. The swan's sightseeing voyage along the Thames, concluding with an enumeration of Henry's fleet and praise for his military victories, is followed by more than a hundred pages of prose commentary, including a fifteen-page (sig. C1 r-D4v) essay on evidence for the Trojan origin of the British people.[43]

Cygnea Cantio thus contributes to Leland's antiquarian project of recovering British history by inaugurating the identification of the beauty of the land with the prophetic truth of British antiquity. Philip Schwyzer observes that John Bale, Leland's editor, gives an account of Leland's antiquarian project that locates the aesthetic – the idea of beauty – not in England's architectural remains, but in the explication of toponyms, ancient place names. Bale, Schwyzer points out, appears unmoved by the contemporary landscape, but 'returns eagerly to the aesthetic' the moment he thinks about Leland's etymologies. 'for the syngular bewtye of Englande', says Bale, 'he [that is, Leland] calleth agayne to lyvely memory, the auncyent names of cyties, townes, castelles, hylles, havens, ryvers, and suche lyke, which have bene longe buryed in oblivion' (E7v-D8 r). 'If we take Bale at his word', Schwyzer comments, it appears that nothing that is to be seen in England, no building, hill, or haven, ranks as a thing of beauty. Beauty resides only in their long-disused names.[44] But the reason for that is that etymologies are the storehouses of British antiquity. So the swan poet, in *Cygnea Cantio*, 'tell[s] many things about the Thames, drawn from the secret storehouses of antiquity' (*multaque ex penetralibus antiquitatis de Tamesi referentem*).[45] And just after the passage quoted by Schwyzer, Bale turns to that very poem: 'In this kinde of writing, haue Lelande plenteously done in his part *in Commentarium Cyngnea cantionis.*'[46]

We might think that, after the failure of the 1540s war to conquer Scotland, Leland's poem would lose its credibility. On the contrary: the poem acquired a new relevance, in the 1560s, for scholars supporting what Jane Dawson has called William Cecil's 'British policy'.[47] Dawson puts it thus:

> With a unified British Isles, both the doors into England would be closed to foreign invaders and any subsequent threat could first be faced upon the seas

[42] Leland, *Cygnea Cantio*, sigs. B2r, B3r, B3v, C1r; Carley, 'John Leland's *Cygnea Cantio*', 234–5.
[43] Brackmann, *Elizabethan Invention.*   [44] Schwyzer, *Literature, Nationalism*, 66.
[45] Leland, *Cygnea Cantio*, sig. A3r.   [46] Leland, *laboryouse Journey*, sig. D8r.
[47] Alford, *Elizabethan Polity.*

surrounding the islands of Britain . . . with the land border completely safe, the main burden of defence would fall upon a revitalised royal navy.[48]

This strategic focus on the seas surrounding Britain and on the building up of a navy required a stepping up of detailed, cartographic knowledge of ports, havens, rivers and estuaries. Cecil, in other words, needed maps. Ever since the 1540s war, Cecil had understood the value of maps; his 'cartographic thinking' has been much commented on.[49] But his carto-graphic thinking, like his 'British policy' in general, had its legal-historical dimensions. A memorandum written by Cecil in 1559 shows that he believed that there were documents to prove that '[t]he Crowne of england hath . . . a iust and vnfeyned title . . . vnto the superiority of Scotland' and we have already seen how he prefaced his 'atlas' of Saxton's maps with dates from the legendary history of Brutus.[50]

In the 1560s, moreover, Cecil's chief cartographer – the man who made him military maps and notes for the conquest of Ireland – was Laurence Nowell (1530–c.1570), distinguished antiquary and founder of Anglo-Saxon studies.[51] Galfridian history had figured the Saxons as pagan invaders and enemies of the British, but any serious history of the continuity of English law before and after the Norman Conquest would need resources for the study of Old English or Anglo-Saxon. Rebecca Brackmann has shown how Nowell set about producing these resources, gathering vocabulary, including place names. For these, it seems, he found Leland's work especially useful, because, unlike sources from the Anglo-Saxon period itself, it 'set out to present England as a unified entity'.[52]

So it is here, in William Cecil's household, that we find John Leland's *Cygnea Cantio*, being read, annotated and mined for of Old English place names and British history by Laurence Nowell and his friend and pupil, the legal antiquary and chorographer, William Lambarde. Both Lambarde and Nowell had copies of *Cygnea Cantio*; Nowell transcribed into his copy the index to Leland's *Genethliacon*, probably from Lambarde's copy.[53] From their annotated copies, now in the British Library, one can see how they, like Bale, appreciated the beauty of the landscape as that of 'long-disused

[48] Dawson, 'British Dimension', 197.
[49] Dawson, 'British Dimension'; R. A. Skelton and J. Summerson, *A Description of Maps and Architectural Drawings in the Collection Made by William Cecil, First Baron Burghley, Now at Hatfield House* (Oxford: Roxburghe Club, 1971); Peter Barber, 'England II: Monarchs, Ministers and Maps, 1550–1625', in Buisseret ed., *Monarchs, Ministers and Maps*, 57–99.
[50] BL Cotton Caligula B. X, fol. 33v-34r.
[51] Retha M. Warnicke, 'Laurence Nowell, (1530–1570)', *ODNB*, 2008.
[52] Brackmann, *Elizabethan Invention*, 22.   [53] Brackmann, *Elizabethan Invention*, 110.

names'. In Fig. 3.2 (see plate section), reading the passage glorying in the destruction of Leith and Edinburgh, we see Lambarde gloss '*Litha*' as 'Leyth' and '*Castrum / Cui nomen celebre inditum à puellis*' ('the Castle famously named for maidens') as 'Edinburgh'.

Robin Flower argued that Nowell's and Lambarde's shared annotations of *Cygnea Cantio.* should be read 'in connexion with Nowell's cartographical work' for William Cecil.[54] Though Cecil was later to choose Christopher Saxton over Nowell for his survey of England, he found Nowell's maps indispensable through the 1560s. He was said to have carried 'always about him' the so-called 'Burghley-Nowell atlas' (BL Additional MS 62540) with its maps of England and Ireland 'with the costs [coasts] adioyning'.[55] A map drawn for Cecil in another of Nowell's notebooks of maps, which appears on fols. 98v–99 r of British Library MS Cotton Domitian xviii (see Figure 3.3 in plate section) is, in this context, extremely intriguing. It is, quite clearly, a map of Scotland, oriented so that the west coast and the Hebrides are at the top of the page. And it occurs in a notebook that combines, as Rebecca Brackmann has described, an interrelated sequence of historical chronicles, strategic military intelligence and original maps of Ireland, Scotland and southern England, all the work of Nowell.[56] The Scotland map is strategically positioned just after passages of notes on how Ireland might be reformed and conquered, preceding further descriptions of Irish clerical power, earldoms, battalions and so forth. Oddly, Brackmann refers to this map as being of 'the Hebrides'. Yet it is not: it is unequivocally a map of the whole of Scotland, with the sea-coasts rendered with an accuracy unprecedented in English mapping.[57] Brackmann's misnomer tacitly registers the fact that nowhere on the map does 'Scotland', the name of the kingdom, appear. Nowhere is there any sign of sovereign nationhood, such as a cartouche with the lion rampant. In this sense, although the map reveals Scotland, it simultaneously makes the country *disappear* (since critics don't appear to recognise it), by folding it into England – literally, by its position in the notebook, into England's imperial designs on Ireland and over all Britain.

---

[54] Robin Flower, 'Laurence Nowell and the Discovery of England in Tudor Times', *Proceedings of the British Academy*, vol. 21 (1935), 45–73, 59; see also Levy, *Tudor Historical Thought*, 136.

[55] BL Additional MS 62540; Barber, 'England II'; Sarah Tyacke and John Huddy, *Christopher Saxton and Tudor Map-Making* (London: The British Library, 1980), 10; Peter Barber, 'The Minister Puts His Mind on the Map', *British Museum Society Bulletin* vol. 43 (1983), 18–19.

[56] Brackmann, *Elizabethan Invention*, 162–3.   [57] Brackmann, *Elizabethan Invention*, 162.

Nowell's map is designed to supply cartographic information to support the English where they were most at risk of French invasion. The stretch of sea which joined Ireland and Scotland was, as Jane Dawson writes,

> even more vulnerable than the land border. Only twenty miles separated Ulster from the Scottish coast and there were no English defences on the Irish side. Antrim itself had been taken over by the MacDonnells – the Southern branch of the Scottish clan Donald, who were also masters of Kintyre.[58]

But it is not just because Cecil's interest in Scotland is purely strategic that the map is not named or represented as a kingdom. In tiny writing at the tip of the Dornoch Firth, in Ross, Nowell has written 'Hitherto King Edward 1st first subdued Scotland', marking the northernmost point of Edward I's conquest of Scotland in the campaign of 1303 (see Figure 3.4 in plate section).[59] Scotland is thus marked and mapped as *conquered English territory*, Robert the Bruce's victory at Bannockburn in Edward II's reign notwithstanding.

The value of marking Scotland in this covert and unostentatious way as a territory conquered by Edward I becomes evident when we consider the most significant and surprising feature of the map in terms of the history of the cartography of Scotland. It is, according to map historian D. G. Moir 'altogether a remarkable map . . . in the detail of *coastline*' (my italics).[60] The story of how Nowell might have managed to obtain such rare and valuable knowledge comes to light with the publication, in 1583, of a quarto book with a folded folio hydrographic map of Scotland (see Figure 3.5 in plate section) by the French cosmographer, Nicolas de Nicolay, entitled *La Navigation du Roy D'Escosse Jacques Cinquiesme du nom, autour de son Royaume, & Isles Hebrides Orchades, soubz la conduicte d'Alexandre Lyndsay excellent Pilote Escossois. Recueillée et redigée en forme de description Hydrographique, & representée en carte marine* ('The Navigation of the King of Scotland, James the Fifth of that name, around his Kingdom and the Hebridean and Orcadian Isles under the conduct of Alexander Lyndsay, the Excellent Scottish Pilot. Gathered and redacted into a Hydrographic description and represented as a sea chart'). Nicolay drew his map (which itself was 'a great advance in the cartography of Scotland') from a 'rutter' – that is, a set of sailing directions used by a pilot in coastal navigation (French, *routier*; Portguese *portolan*) written in Scots by the

---

[58] Dawson, 'Cecil and the British Dimension', 202.
[59] See Michael Prestwich, *Edward I* (New Haven, CT: Yale University Press, 1997), 498–9, 488.
[60] D. G. Moir, *The Early Maps of Scotland to 1850* (Edinburgh: Royal Scottish Geographical Society, 1973), 16–17.

pilot Alexander Lyndsay, about whom little else is known.[61] In his dedica-
tion to the Cardinal of Lorraine, Nicolay explained that he obtained
a manuscript of the Scottish rutter when he was at the court of Henry
VIII in 1546, at the height of Henry's war against Scotland, from Admiral
and later duke of Northumberland, John Dudley. Realising how valuable
such detailed knowledge of the Scottish coast would be to his master, the
King of France, Nicolay had the Scots text translated into French with
the aid of 'Maitre Jehan Ferrier' (Giovanni Ferrerio, Abbot of Kinloss),
presenting it to Henri II, who immediately sent it to Sieur Leon Strozzi, the
Prior of Capua and general of the French galleys, who promptly sailed,
with sixteen of his galleys, to St Andrews and laid siege to the castle,
winning St Andrews back for Regent Arran, Mary of Guise and Catholic
Scotland.[62] In other words, the secret knowledge of the rutter, once in
French hands, furthered the Catholic Franco-Scots cause in the war,
disadvantaging the English and their Scottish Protestant adherents.

D. G. Moir hypothesises that Nowell must have drawn his map using
one of the manuscripts of Lyndsay's rutter circulating among the English
and French in 1546.[63] When in *The Faerie Queene* Britomart, complaining
to Neptune, deploys the well-worn trope of the lover as storm-tossed vessel
seeking a harbour, she develops, with a suggestive precision, the kinds
of hazards that a rutter like Lyndsay's was designed to protect against. Her
feeble vessel will, she says 'be wrackt / On the rough rocks, or sandy
shallowes' since her 'lewd Pilot', Love, sails 'without starres gainst tide
and wind' (III.iv.9). In the northern waters of the British Isles (unlike the
Mediterranean), the rutter, giving times of high water, distances, locations
of harbours, whirlpools etc., was indispensable for the coastal pilot,
'moving from one headland to the next, keeping in mind the effect of
tidal streams on the risk of shoals and hidden rocks'.[64] The knowledge of
the Scottish coast which Lyndsay conveyed in his rutter first enabled, in
1540, James V's circumnavigatory assertion of sovereignty over the isles and
all of Scotland, sailing in the *Salamander* (one of the 'goodly ships' which,

[61] Moir, *Early Maps*, 20.
[62] Nicolas de Nicolay, *La Navigation dv Roy D'Escosse Iaqves Cinqviesme* (Paris, 1583) Sig. aii^v; Moir,
Early Maps, 20; A. B. Taylor, *Alexander Lindsay: A Rutter of the Scottish Seas Circa 1540* (London:
National Maritime Museum, 1980), 30–1. On the siege of St Andrews Castle, see Merriman, *Rough
Wooings*, 227–9. Odet de Selve also mentions the rutter, writing to Henri II, 23 May 1547, 'Sire, je
vous envoye quelques cartes et ung livre de la navigation d'Escosse que j'ay eues d'ung painctre
françoys' ('Sire, I am sending you some maps and a book of the navigation of Scotland, which I had
from a French painter'), *Correspondance Politique*, 145. The 'French painter' is Nicolas de Nicolay.
On Giovanni Ferrerio, see Nicola Royan, *ODNB* (2004).
[63] Moir, *Early Maps*, 17.   [64] Taylor, *Lindsay: Rutter*, 5.

as John Brende tells us, was seized by the English from Leith in 1544).[65] In Nicolay's French translation, Lyndsay's knowledge facilitates the French taking of St Andrews in 1546 and then, translated into cartographic form in Nowell's map of c.1563, it serves Cecil's policy for an integrated Anglo-Britain by enabling him to visualise threats of invasion, not unlike Merlin's 'glassie globe' protecting Ryence's 'greater *Britaine*' (III.ii.12, 7). While Scotland's coastal topography becomes visible and instrumental in the protection of Britain's coastal integrity or chastity, all historical place names and signs of her sovereignty are erased, and she becomes part of the 'singular bewty of England' expressed in the accompanying maps of southern England which Nowell has filled with reconstructed Anglo-Saxon place names in insular miniscule.

V. Limits of Sea-Sovereignty: Rivers and Nations

Nowell's map of the Scottish coastline, like Merlin's globe for King Ryence, simultaneously promises an expansionist maritime future and points to threats of foreign invasion; the prevention of the latter and assurance of the former being dependent, in Spenser, on Britomart's negotiations with Neptune over the perils of love and chastity, and in Nowell, on the suppression of any acknowledgement of Scotland's historic and present sovereignty. But mapping the Scottish coastline while denying Scottish sovereignty was not simply, for English policy-makers, a matter of national security. For in the 1570s, Elizabeth and her ministers began to be seriously interested in the compilation of historical, legal and cartographic proofs of England's ancient claims to lands in Europe, the polar regions and the Americas. The seas around Britain, in other words, had become newly significant in legal-geographical terms. For, as Lauren Benton writes, 'the high seas were not a lawless zone, but a legal space constructed by interimperial tensions'.[66] The English state needed legal pretexts or justifications for their confrontations with the Spanish and Portuguese in their imperial territories.[67]

The texts and maps designed to advance such claims focused, as William Sherman has written, 'not on the centres of state power, but on the boundaries or limits'.[68] Scotland, along with the Hebrides and the Orkney and Shetland islands valuably extended England's limits, if one believed in dubious Galfridian and neo-Galfridian histories of ancient conquest. John Dee's claims for English sea-sovereignty rested, as Sherman explains, on

---

[65] *Tudor Tracts,* 44.   [66] Benton, *Search for Sovereignty,* 34.   [67] Dee, *Limits,* 13.
[68] Sherman, *Politics,* 194.

a distinction between Limits Absolute and Limits Respective. If a body of water was bounded on either side by the same monarch's dominions, that monarch had absolute rights over that ocean; if, on the other hand, two or more monarchs' territories bordered the sea, each would have 'respective' jurisdictional limits, perhaps up to a hundred miles offshore, or midway between the realms.[69] The English conquests of Scotland alleged in all the familiar sources (Geoffrey of Monmouth, Edward I's 1301 letter to Pope Boniface VIII, John Hardyng's fifteenth century *Chronicle*, Henry VIII's 1542 *Declaration*) thus assumed a new importance not in respect of ruling Scotland, but simply as the ground of these more valuable maritime limit claims. If Scotland counted as an English possession, the fact that its coastline faced towards Norway in the east, the Americas in the west and Iceland in the north, gave Dee ammunition for arguing both respective and absolute British limits over those seas and lands. So we see, for example, that Dee's annotations in his copies of Geoffrey of Monmouth and John Hardyng's *Chronicle* tend to note outer limits of ancient British conquests – that Brennius ruled '*ad Cathenesiam*', 'as far as Caithness', or that Arviragus conquered '*Orcades & [^com^]prouinciales insulas*' (Dee here inserts the 'com'), 'the Orkneys and adjacent islands', or that Arthur commanded armies from '*sex insulis, videlicet Hyberniae, Islandiae, Gelandiae Orcadum Norwegiae atque Daciae*' ('the six islands of Ireland, Iceland, Gotland, the Orkneys, Norway and Denmark').[70] That Lord Burghley finally felt unconvinced by Dee's 'Geographical Reformation' of Europe and the Atlantic did not mean he and other government figures did not attend carefully to Dee's legal and cartographic representations. Indeed, Burghley made a summary of Dee's *Britanni Imperii Limites* and kept a map of the Northeast Passage in Dee's hand in his copy of Ortelius's *Theatrum Orbis Terrarum*.[71]

Dee's arguments turned on familiar civil law analogies between coastal and fluvial land-water boundaries, analogies which take an erotic and

[69] Sherman, *Politics*, 195, citing T. W. Fulton, *The Sovereignty of the Sea: An Historical Account of the Claims of England to the Dominion of the British Seas* (Edinburgh and London: Blackwood, 1911), chs. 1 and 3.

[70] Dee's copy of Geoffrey of Monmouth, *Britanni[a]e vtriusq[ue] regu[m] et principum origo & gesta* (1517) is in Christ Church, Oxford, W.b5, 12, fols. XVIIr, XXXIr, LXXXr. Dee's copy of John Hardyng, *Chronicle* (London: Richard Grafton, 1543) is in the possession of Professor Toshi Takamiya, who kindly sent me photographs of Dee's marginal annotations. Relevant pages are fol. Iiiir and fol. xliiiiv.

[71] William H. Sherman, 'Putting British Seas on the Map: John Dee's Imperial Cartography', *Cartographica*, vol. 35, nos. 3-4 (1998), 1–10, 3, 4–6; Carley, 'Arthur', 166. For a more sceptical account of Dee's influence, see Glyn Parry, 'John Dee and the Elizabethan British Empire in Its European Context', *HJ*, vol. 49, no. 3 (2006), 643–75.

racialised turn in contemporary river poetry and chorography in Camden, Harrison and Spenser. For if islands, like virginity, require defending against those who would invade and violate, thalassocracy, or sea-empire, must be associated with a more aggressive, confrontational erotics of exploration and conquest in to 'remotest parts', involving new ways of imagining tributaries, rivers and estuaries as both mapping the nation's historic interior and celebrating its openness to the salt tides of an imperial future. As we shall see in the final section, Spenser figures these antithetical and complementary features of island empire as the contrast between the proactive chastity of Britomart and Florimell's perpetual flight, each of which involves a crisis at the limit of land and sea.

In this section, however, I want to consider the contradictions and tensions, for the representation of Scotland and its people, of this translation of the neo-Galfridian myth of Scottish vassalage into legal and cartographic proofs of the outer limits of England's sea-sovereignty. In Dee's plats of British empire, as in Harrison's chorographical description of the island of Britain, Scotland figures simultaneously as foreign and vassal, as predator and proof of English jurisdiction over Britain's coasts. That such incoherence goes unnoticed by modern readers testifies to the success of strenuous English engagements with and denials of the Scots' own self-definition as an ancient sovereign *natio* (nation or people) of Britain. Spenser is not unaware of these engagements, being a close reader of Harrison (and very likely, of Dee) and, in *A View of the Present State of Ireland*, an ethnographer of the Scottish people, drastically rewriting a chorography of Scotland by the great humanist George Buchanan.

In *The Faerie Queene*, the question of which 'nations' or peoples have a legitimate claim to be British or English bears a complex relation to the imagined time of the poem's action. As many critics have observed, the narrative present in which we explore the moral topography of Spenser's Faery land brilliantly conflates the young manhood of Arthur (on the verge of succeeding Uther to recover Britain from the Saxons, Picts and Scots) with the present, opportune moment of Gloriana's imperial reign. This is the time that Richard McCabe has described as 'The Arthurian Moment' in which Arthur, embodying unwritten or excised pages of Book II's *Briton moniments*, fills the poem with promise in the form of moral preparation for the immediate, Elizabethan present.[72] Critics also observe that Arthur's famous purging of 'the Saxon menace' is subsumed by Merlin's prophecy

---

[72] Richard McCabe, *The Pillars of Eternity: Time and Providence in* The Faerie Queene (Dublin: Irish Academic Press, 1989), 81, 103.

of 'an eventual union of Saxon and Briton' to produce a celebration of the mixed British-Saxon heritage of England and Wales under Elizabeth ('Thenceforth eternall vnion shall be made / Betweene the nations different afore', III.iii.49).[73] No such subsumption and union, however, could ever join the 'nations different' of the Scots with the British-Saxons. Yet, as Gloriana's claims to oceanic empire depend on ruling the whole island, this produces a conceptual problem that is both temporal and spatial: where is Scotland, where are the Scots, in the 'Arthurian moment' of Spenser's Britain/Faery land? This section will explore dimensions of this problem by looking first at how an English claim to sovereignty over Scotland grounds John Dee's oceanic 'Brytish Impire'. It will then consider analogies between coastal and riparian geographies and their racial figurations in William Harrison's 'An Historical Description of the Iland of Britaine'. Harrison's racial history of Britain anticipates Spenser's own ethnographic history of the Scots as this is explicitly expressed in his *A View of the Present State of Ireland* and implicitly and figuratively in the river poetry of *The Faerie Queene*. Harrison's treatment of rivers and nations in his 'Description' thus prepares us for the chapter's final section, a reading of the Britomart-Florimell-Marinell allegory and the marriage of the Thames and Medway.

Let us first consider the place of Scotland in John Dee's work for policy-makers. Scotland's disavowed centrality to John Dee's vision of England as centre of a maritime empire emerges clearly in three interrelated texts. These are the *General and Rare Memorials pertayning to the Perfect Arte of NAVIGATION* (printed 1577), the *Brytanici Imperii Limites* ('The Limits of the British Empire') – manuscript texts and maps presented to the queen in 1580, and the *THALATTOKRATIA BRETTANIKI*, a manuscript composed for Sir Edward Dyer in 1597, which revisited the *Brytanici Imperii Limites*, describing itself as 'a . . . Miscellany on the Sea-Jurisdiction of the British Empire'.[74] The first of these, the *General and Rare Memorials* was a plea for the establishment of a royal navy to patrol the British coastline for the purposes of national security. In this treatise, Scotland figured both as enemy to Britain and British dominion. He writes, Dee says, 'That . . . neither *France, Denmark, Scotland, Spaine,* nor any other Cuntry, can haue . . . liberty, for Inuasion' but he also argues that a 'Brytish Impire' will 'come to pas, through the Royalty and Souerainty of the Seas adicent,

[73] McCabe, *Pillars*, 108–9.
[74] John Dee, *General and Rare Memorials pertayning to the Perfect Arte of NAVIGATION* (London, John Day, 1577); Dee, *Limits*; Sherman, *Politics*, 183, 193.

or enuironing this Monarchy of England, Ireland and (by right) Scotland and the Orknayes allso'.[75] Dee, as Sherman says of phrases like this, struggles with 'the appropriate *tense* of the imperial outlook': he claims Scotland is 'by right' part of the monarchy of England, but this is still something he hopes will 'come to pass' and meanwhile, the Scots are foreigners to be distrusted.[76] Thus, answering the objections to the victualling of this navy at the public expense, Dee is careful to specify that victuals will only be bestowed on Englishmen and not 'on FORREYNER, SCOT, FRENCH, FLEMISH, DANE or SPANIARD etc.'[77] If 'Scot' is a foreigner, but 'Scotland' 'by right' part of England, the Scot has the not-so-rare distinction of being a foreigner without a country.

Dee says he presented his 'work of Imperium Brytanicum' to the queen in 1580; the beautiful fair copy of the *Brytannici Imperii Limites* in the British Library was made in 1593.[78] Both King Arthur and Scotland feature centrally in the evidence Dee lays out to prove that Queen Elizabeth has a just title to 'sondrie forrein regions and countris', especially around the Arctic, which would enable routes to Cathay and further exploration in the Americas. The most 'vpartiall searchers of ancient moniments' agree, he wrote, that Arthur, succeeding his father, defeated and expelled the Saxons, 'the *Picts* and *Scots* beinge vtterlie subdued'.[79] Thereafter he cites, at some length, the usual suspects: Geoffrey of Monmouth himself; Edward I's 1301 letter to Boniface VIII; Henry VIII's *Declaration* of 1542. He seems, oddly, to think he has clinched the matter by further citing Hector Boece's *Scotorum Historia* (*History of the Scots*, 1527) and John Mair's *Historia Maioris Britannia* (*History of Greater Britain*, 1527) despite their evidently sceptical rehearsal of Geoffrey's claims with reference to Arthur's conquest. 'Why', Dee asks of John Mair, 'did he leve it recorded in his owne booke' if 'he know certenly that it were fals?' But his reasons for including Mair's text become clear: Mair's very epithets, as he explains to the queen, further confirm the evidence for her title to 'Friseland' (Iceland) and beyond.[80]

Dee apologised to the queen for the tedious detail with which he presented the evidence for her title to Scotland, since she, of all people, must be very familiar with Edward I's Great Cause and Henry VIII's *Declaration*. But he was, he says, impelled to spell it all out because of the urgency of the moment, the eschatological fullness of the present *time*. It was of vital importance that title to Scotland be 'remembred, revived, and dulie regarded and declared *in these days*' (my italics) for Elizabeth was,

---

[75] Dee, *Memorials*, 3, 6.   [76] Sherman, *Politics*, 151.   [77] Dee, *Memorials*, 31.
[78] Sherman, *Politics*, 182–3; BL Add. MS. 59681.   [79] Dee, *Limits*, 53.   [80] Dee, *Limits*, 66.

of all British monarchs ever, the one best placed by 'iustice, habilitie, and acceptable opportunety' to 'recover, enlarge, mayntayne and enjoy your British Imperiall Dominions, far and nere'. But the place of this 'opportunity' (Scotland) was also the place 'where most danger is (your Majestie omyttinge the oportunetie yet remanyng), lest your owne vassalls be to your royall and Imperiall state most damageable'.[81] Here the *Limites* connects clearly with the titlepage of the *Generall and Rare Memorials*, where 'Opportunity' or *Occasio/Kairos*, is figured as a woman standing on Britain's shore, backed by a royal navy, her lock of hair ready to be grasped by the queen in her ship of state (see Figure 3.6 in plate section). And in Dee's words here, as in *Memorials*, the value of title to Scotland is in direct tension with the 'damage' threatened by the Scottish *natio*: the queen is urged to declare her title 'lest your owne vassalls be to your royall and Imperiall state most damageable'. Having completed this 'zealous digression', Dee proposes to conclude

> with matter very rare and excellent (as I esteem it) for your *Brytish Impier* (and that breiflie and evidentlie), confirming by Kinge *Arthur* his incomparable actes and forayne conquests cheiflie. The halfe of whose marveillous prowess and true gestes is not in these dayes any where in your Majesties British *Monarchie* knowne, had or hard of: *Velut Temporis filia docebit veritas*.[82]

What follows are fascinating and esoteric accounts, from Gerard Mercator and others, of conquests of Arthur as far as a North Pole centred on a whirlpool, into which four 'indrawing seas' empty themselves, flowing around a magnetic rock.[83] Mercator's revised map of this region shows the northern tip of Scotland and the Orkneys at the southernmost edge (see Figure 3.7 in plate section), visually corroborating Dee's sense of Scotland's importance for England's 'British' claims in these Polar regions. Is it fanciful to compare this 'zealous/jealous' digression' to Elizabeth with the 'gealousy' of erotic conquest that urges Guyon and Arthur to follow Florimell at the beginning of the legend of Chastity (III.i.18)? Dee's longing for Time's daughter, Truth, to reveal at length the deeds of Arthur's prowess is likewise suggestive of the erotic longing Spenser evokes so skilfully in Arthur's tedious night of vexatious dreams, as he waits for the 'long expected light' of day, of which Truth is the daughter, for 'he her first did breed' (III.iv.59–60).

---

[81] Dee, *Limits*, 82.   [82] Dee, *Limits*, 82–3.
[83] E. G. R. Taylor, 'A Letter Dated 1577 from Mercator to John Dee', *Imago Mundi*, vol. 13, no. 1 (1956), 56–68; Sherman, 'British Seas'.

Finally, Dee's *THALATTOKRIA BRETTANIKI*, written for Sir Edward Dyer in 1597, is a fascinating revisitation of the arguments of the *Memorials* and the *Limites* in the form of an imagined circumnavigation of the British Isles, 'delineating in every direction what he considers to be the "British Seas"', even renaming the *Mare Germanicum* (the North Sea) as *Mare Britannicum*.[84] Scotland, as Sherman observes,

> took on a special importance for Dee . . . not only because of its potential to unite the kingdom of Great Britain but because of its position opposite 'that famous, and very Ancient *Platonicall* or *Salonicall* Atlantis'. Having in his earlier writings claimed the queen's title to North America, Dee's claim to Scotland would result in another case of Limits Absolute.[85]

Sherman goes to on show how Dee, citing many precedents of homage done by Scottish kings to Elizabeth's progenitors, proposed that Elizabeth re-enact, with James VI, the scene of James I's homage to Henry VI at Windsor in 1423.[86]

Dee was politically naïve about the advisability of England's government insisting out loud on its alleged sovereignty over Scotland. Burghley knew better, though was no less convinced than Dee as to the legitimacy of England's Scottish title.[87] But Dee's views were not unusual. His way of imagining Scotland as reduced to the value of its coastline, taking no interest in its interior topography or history and regarding its people as a foreign threat, was standard. We find a similar view authoritatively prefacing Holinshed's *Chronicles*, in 'An Historical Description of the Iland of Britaine' by William Harrison (1577 and 1587). This was the text that Spenser told Harvey had 'much furthered and advantaged' him in his project of an *Epithalamion Thamesis*, showing the marriage of the Thames and describing 'all the Riuers throughout England'.[88]

Harrison was not, of course, assembling legal and cartographic proofs to persuade the queen to claim her empire overseas. He was doing something arguably more influential: he was helping, in Jacques Rancière's terms, to establish the 'distribution of the sensible', the determination of 'what is seen and what can be said about it' around which politics revolves.[89] Prefacing the chronicles of England, Scotland and Ireland, Harrison's description of the island of Britain was designed to contain and determine what could be seen and said about the histories and chorographies of

---

[84] Sherman, *Politics*, 195.   [85] Sherman, *Politics*, 196.   [86] Sherman, *Politics*, 196–7.
[87] Dawson, 'British Dimension', 207.   [88] Spenser, *Prose*, 17.
[89] Jacques Rancière, *The Politics of Aesthetics*, trans. Gabriel Rockhill (London: Bloomsbury, 2004), 8–9.

individual nations that followed. Dee's sense of an England on the cusp of
recovering British empire finds its chorographical equivalent in Harrison's
description of the island in two main respects: first, in the order and
selection of chapters and second, in the use of the first person singular
and plural to establish the national community of readers who shared the
imagined voyage around the island's coasts and then into its interior. An
early chapter – Chapter 4 – defines the national community by describing
'What sundrie nations haue dwelled in Albion'. Then Chapter 10, 'Of such
Ilands as are to be seen on the coasts of Britaine', takes the reader on an
imagined circumnavigation of the coastline of all Britain – England and
Scotland and the islands. The author describes 'making mine entrance at
Thames mouth, and directing this imagined course by the south part of the
Iland into the west' and then proceeding north up the west coast, around
the Orkneys, and joyfully 'home againe: & although not by the Thames
mouth into my natiue citie (which taketh his name from Troie), yet into
the English dominion, where good intertainment is much more frank and
copious'.[90] This circumnavigation of the island beginning and ending with
a mention of the city of the mythic Brutus then introduces seven further
chapters on the interior topography of England and Wales by way of these
nation's navigable rivers. These are, for example, Chapter 11 'Of riuers,
and first of the Thames, and such riuers as fall into it', Chapter 13, 'The
description of the Sauerne, and such waters as discharge themselues into
the same'. The chapters thus chart England's waterways both in relation to
the three arterial and mythic rivers of Thames, Severn and Humber,
moving from the interior to the sea, concluding with a description of
English ports and harbours. These, then, exhibit 'singular paines' for which
Spenser was so grateful, in 'searching oute' the rivers' 'first heades, and
sourses: and also in tracing, and dogging oute all their Course, til they fal
into the Sea'.[91] We can also see, however, that the juxtaposition of these
two kinds of navigation – the circumnavigation of Britain followed by
the complex tracing of the fluvial hinterlands of England and Wales –
establishes a kind of analogical relation between the sea-coast and the
riverbank. This analogy was well known in civil law as part of an argument
being advanced in the 1560s and 1570s by men like John Dee and the lawyer
Thomas Digges, to the effect that the English Crown might have both
property in and jurisdiction over the seas around all of Britain. As in
'Riuers and fressh shores or banks called *Ripe*, the Lords of the soyle
adioyninge hould a propretye', argued Digges, 'So in the great salt riuer

---

[90] Harrison, 'Description', 53, 77.   [91] Spenser, *Prose*, 17.

I meane the sea enuironinge the whole Ilande, and in the salt shores thereof, the great and cheefe lorde of the whole soyle the Kinge himself only must haue interest and propertye'.[92] And Dee concurred: 'it is not vnreasonable, to deme Seas betwene diuers next Kingdoms, to be in like and Analogicall Condition, in respect of King and King: As fresh water Riuers, are, in Respect of of Priuate Subiects.'[93] If the Ocean is imagined as a great river, Harrison's imaginary circumnavigation of Britain figuratively establishes the English Crown's interest and property in the banks of this river, the island's coastline, while also recalling Leland's swan's Anglo-imperial river journey, setting forth from and returning to the place where the Thames meets the sea. As he moves northwards, Harrison tellingly refers to 'the north coast of this Ile now called Scotland', marking the nation's name as an innovation while reducing the nation itself to a mere coast.[94]

It is easy to see the appeal, for Spenser, of the prose of Harrison's chapters on rivers, for Harrison writes with a most endearing immediacy, addressing his patron, lamenting his want of information, celebrating 'fat and sweet salmons' and exclaiming over the 'infinit number of swans dailie' on the Thames, digressing over a spot of sightseeing and repeatedly recalling himself to the task in hand: 'but to go forward with my description of the Ouse, which being past Oxford goeth to Iflie, Kennington'.[95] In these fluvial chapters Harrison employs a first person plural which, as Andrew McRae argues, turns his readers into voyaging companions: 'the text is punctuated with personal pronouns and active verbs: "we rowed", "we come unto", "we sailed on", and so forth.'[96] Chorography, as Bart Van Es has pointed out, addresses us immediately, in the 'now' of our lives, producing a direct, emotional connection with the past, as we imagine and animate it from our reading of the land's ancient names and local legends.[97] No small part of Harrison's stylistic appeal, then, is the emotive sense of local affinity, the reader's sense that the land viewed from the riverbank is 'ours'. Yet this first-person plural and the sense of propriety that goes with it have been carefully circumscribed by the previously mentioned Chapter 4 on the 'sundrie nations' which have 'dwelled' in Albion which describes the succession of nations that have invaded and

---

[92] Stuart A. Moore, *A History of the Foreshore and the Law Relating Thereto* (London: 1888), 191.
[93] Dee, *Memorials*, 21.   [94] Harrison, 'Description', 63.
[95] Harrison, 'Description', 80, 82, 84–5.
[96] Andrew McRae, 'Fluvial Nation: Rivers, Mobility and Poetry in Early Modern England', *ELR* vol. 38, no. 3 (2008), 506–34, 511.
[97] Van Es, *Forms of History*, 55–6.

conquered Britain. Harrison's Chapter 4 shows why Helgerson's reading of
Drayton's frontispiece (discussed above) is so misleading. The four conquerors depicted by Drayton – Brutus, Caesar, the Saxon Hengist and
William the Norman – are not 'marginalised': they signify the indigeneity
and propriety of the English and Welsh as a people. For Harrison achieves
what we might call a narrative of 'metamorphic indigeneity' in which
a sequence of different invading peoples (British – Romans – Saxons –
Danes – Normans) each become, in turn, the indigenous victim of a new
oppressor, until at last, the six-times conquered English, identified as 'us'
and 'we', are confirmed in their propriety over 'Our Iland'. Thus, at first,
when the Saxons arrive, we are told that 'these new comlings [the Saxons]
began to molest the homelings' [the Britons].[98] Later, however, when the
Normans conquered the Saxons, Harrison laments, 'it was lesse reproche to
be counted a slaue then an Englishman, or a drudge in anie filthie businesse
then a Britaine', The reader is invited to identify with both 'Britons' and
'English', 'Saxon comlings' who become 'British homelings' – who become,
in fact, 'us'.[99] The Scots, by contrast, are presented as radically out of this
sequence of incomer to indigene. They are volatile infestation, a kind of
vermin always proximate, always lurking, from which 'a portion of the land'
can't be 'cleansed'. In a move familiar to literary critics from Spenser's *View
of the Present State of Ireland*, the Scots are identified with 'Scythians' who
come from the 'Hyperborean' regions behind the north wind:[100]

> How and when the Scots, a people mixed of Scithian and Spanish blood,
> should arriue here out of Ireland, & when the Picts should come vnto us out
> of Samartia, or from further toward the north & the Scithian Hyperboreans,
> as yet it is vncerteine ... I iudge them to haue stolne in hither within the
> space of 100. yeares before Christ ... so the Scots did often aduenture hither
> to rob and steale out of Ireland ... after the which they so planted
> themselves in these parts, that vnto our time that portion of the land cannot
> be cleansed of them.[101]

Once again, the 'our' in 'our time' excludes 'them', the peoples being
described, while the vantage point of place is also seen from the imagined
English 'we' of Harrison's readership. The land of which 'a portion' needs
ethnic cleansing is also, thereby, implicitly, 'ours' – that is, belonging to the
English. Drawing on Gildas, perhaps via Humphrey Llwyd who refers to
the Picts coming from the north 'in their little leathern boats ("*suis*

[98] Harrison, 'Description', 11.   [99] Harrison, 'Description', 13.
[100] Edmund Spenser, *A View of the Present State of Ireland* in *Spenser Variorum*, X. 82.
[101] Harrison, 'Description', 10.

coreaceis")', Harrison says it was the habit of the Scythian Scots 'commonly to steal ouer into Britaine in leather skewes'.[102] Harrison's seems to be the Oxford English Dictionary's only instance of this transferred, nautical sense of 'skew', a word whose primary sense was a begging bowl: the semantic associations he wants are clearly those of disreputable, homeless vagrancy. The mental picture of Scotland that emerges from Harrisons's description of the island of Britain, then, is very similar to that which emerges from Dee's 'Geographical Reformation'. Scotland has been reduced from a kingdom to a thin 'north coast', a place without a hinterland and without rivers or other topographical features; infested rather than inhabited by a pilfering race that can make no claim to ancient status within the island of Britain. Indeed, Harrison's conclusion in Chapter 22, 'After what manner the souereigntie of this Ile dooth remaine to the princes of Lhoegres or Kings of England' turns out to be a redaction of the *Epitome of the title that the Kinges Maiestie of Englande, hath to the soueraigntie of Scotlande* of 1548.[103] As in Dee, all these pseudo-historical proofs of Scotland's vassal status with respect to England have become, as it were, inscribed in the land, naturalised as geography and chorography.

On the other hand, there might seem to be little new to say about Spenser's reading of Harrison's racial analysis. As Richard McCabe pithily summed it up, citing Harrison: '[n]either the "Picts" nor the "Scots" are to be accounted "natural Britons" but "barbarous interlopers" of "Scithian" origin – and "the Scots and the Irish are all one people"'.[104] Since the 1990s, there have been a number of excellent analyses of Spenser's derivation of the Scots-Irish from the ancient Scythians and of the comparative ethnology that 'proves' this racial identification by alleging their barbarity.[105] But if the effects of Spenser's race-making ethnography on English attitudes to the Irish have been thoroughly analysed, no attention has been paid to this ethnography's effect on the English imagining of Scotland and the Scots. Yet Spenser's achievement demands analysis, too.[106]

---

[102]   Harrison, 'Description', 10.
[103]   Compare Harrison, 'Description', 196–214 and Bodrugan (alias Adams), *Epitome.*
[104]   Richard McCabe, *Spenser's Monstrous Regiment: Elizabethan Ireland and the Poetics of Difference* (Oxford: Oxford University Press, 2002), 143.
[105]   See for example, Patricia Coughlan, '"Some secret scourge which shall by her come into England": Ireland and Incivility in Spenser', *Spenser and Ireland: An Interdisciplinary Perspective* ed. Patricia Coughlan (Cork: Cork University Press, 1989), 46–74; Andrew Hadfield, 'Briton and Scythian: Tudor Representations of Irish Origins', *Irish Historical Studies* (1993), vol. 28, 390–408; McCabe, *Monstrous Regiment*, 142–64.
[106]   See Lorna Hutson, '"beinge an Irishe Scott or Pict by nacion": Spenser's rewriting of Buchanan', forthcoming.

VI.   Erotics of Empire: The Plight of Florimell

Quite a lot has, by now, been said about coastlines, British sea-
sovereignty, rivers and questions of race, but little about erotics or
the relation of these geopolitical and imperial questions to an allegory
of Chastity. Yet we know that when Spenser was first reading
Harrison's chorography of English rivers around 1580, he was thinking
of an erotic poem, an *Epithalamion Thamesis*.[107] So what is the connection between rivers, *eros* and empire? Literary criticism seems to
have overlooked the tendency of early modern English river poetry to
give erotic expression to Anglo-British imperial themes of past and
future conquest and maritime expansion. One of Leland's early poems
from his time as a student in Paris anticipates this cluster of associations, promising to regale a seductive, sparkling French river with
a song of British history. The poet imagines swimming naked in the
Seine as being embraced by a beautiful, playful nymph, whose acquies-
cent naked body is the water itself. 'Your shining water', he writes, in
J. P. Carley's translation,

> Is altogether shining to my wishes.
> Show yourself always such for me, O Seine,
> And the British Muse (*Musa Britannia*) will sing your divinity.[108]

William Camden's *De Connubio Tamae et Isis* is clearly and explicitly
erotic – it celebrates the connubial mingling of the rivers Isis and Tame to
make the Thames – but its imperial theme is elusively presented, appearing in fragments dispersed across his chorographical description of the
counties of England, at appropriate locations to complement the perambulatory movement of the text. New fragments were added with new
editions of the *Britannia,* and each was presented as a kind of found
object, its authorship coyly disavowed by Camden himself.[109] The rivers'
imperial bower of connubial bliss does not appear in the Oxfordshire
section of *Britannia* until the 1607 edition, so Spenser may never have
seen it. Here, breaking into poetry, Camden imagines a space of sexual
consummation – the marriage chamber of the two rivers, Isis and Thame,
mingling to form the great and powerful *Thamesis* – decked with the

---

[107] *Spenser Variorum*, X. 17.
[108] James P. Carley, 'John Leland in Paris: The Evidence of His Poetry', *SP*, vol. 83, no. 1 (1986), 1–50,
48–9.
[109] See Oruch, 'Marriage of Rivers', 608.

spoils of subject realms, including Scotland. Basil Kennet (1674–1715) produced a lively translation from the 1695 edition of *Britannia*:

> On this the Virgins in vast numbers pile
> Proud spoils and trophies of the conqu'ring Isle;
> What Bundwic, Gurmund, Brennus, Brute brought home,
> From Greece, from Gaul, from Ireland, and from Rome:
> What mighty Arthur from the Saxons won,
> What Edward from the Scots, and from the French his son.[110]

For all that his Brutus and Arthur clearly inhabit the playful space of fiction, there's something slightly disturbing about the way in which Camden the judicious scholar and antiquary gives way, in this passage, to the rapturous association of violent conquest and nuptial embrace.

Spenser may never have read the description of Isis and Tame's imperial marriage bed, but in the 1586 edition of *Britannia* he will have read the charming description of Tame hurrying down the Chilterns, kindled with love, ambitious to put her name before that of her spouse, hardly deigning to notice her own banks but taking time to salute Dorchester as she rushes by. As she flows towards Isis, resplendently beautiful, robed in green, crowned with ears of corn, the two rivers join in embraces and kisses and descend to the *thalamum*, nuptial-bed, while Faith and Concord speak the vows.[111] Concord, of course, is the virtue ostensibly allegorised in Book IV of *The Faerie Queene*, the Book in which the marriage of the Thames and Medway occurs. But the eroticism of Spenser's river marriage in *The Faerie Queene* is very different from Camden's, not least because (as critics often point out) in Spenser the rivers never actually embrace, kiss and mix their waters. It is an easy metaphor, says Gordon Braden, to say that Thame and Isis marry to make Thamesis, but 'in simple geographical fact' the same cannot be said about the Thames and Medway, since one of the Medway's mouths empties into the North Sea and the other into the Thames estuary.[112]

From Braden's argument, critics conclude that there is a sceptical disturbance, something uneasy, in Spenser's conception of the Thames–Medway marriage. But the rivers' union in the sea, creating an estuary, is the point. Markers of imperial settlements in the Atlantic region were, as

---

[110] George Burke Johnston, 'Poems by William Camden: With Notes and Translations from the Latin', *SP*, vol. 72 no. 5 (1975), iii–xii, 1–143.

[111] William Camden, *Britannia* (London: Ralph Newberry, 1587), 239.

[112] Gordon Braden, 'riverrun: An Epic Catalogue in "The Faerie Queene"', *ELR*, vol. 5, no. 1 (1975), 25–48, 37–8.

Laura Benton writes, 'most often placed in estuaries, or at the joining of two rivers near the sea, precisely in order to indicate the intention to travel and settle vast, unbounded riverine regions'.[113] Though the recovery of an Anglo-British empire through the British Isles did not involve exploration and settlement, the symbolism of making an English legal claim to the whole island was the same. The meaning of the Thames–Medway marriage thus draws on the analogical relation of seas to rivers in legal arguments establishing sea-sovereignty. And this is why it is plotted as the resolution of the jurisdictional conflict arising from Marinell's denial of Britomart's right to contract with Neptune along the margin of land and sea. The wedding canto begins with Florimell, captive to love and in the dungeon, 'wall'd . . . with waues' of Proteus house, where 'it fortun'd' that the bride-ale feast for the spousals of Thames and Medway should be held (IV.xi.3, 8–9). The marriage, then, concludes a story begun in the legend of Chastity, involving the relation of chastity to coastal integrity and national security.

At least since C. S. Lewis's celebration of marital love over the courtly, adulterous version in the *Allegory of Love* (1936) scholars have assumed that Spenser's primary aim in the legend of Chastity corresponds to Lewis's. Lewis, as Harry Berger put it, had 'insight that Spenser was his predecessor in sketching the history and demise of courtly love'.[114] In the C. S. Lewis reading, inflected by mid-twentieth-century assumptions of what constitutes a 'normal' and 'healthy' heterosexual compatibility, the central, salient contrast of the legend of Chastity is thus between the figures of Amoret and Britomart. Busyrane's perverted *amour courtois* enchantment of Amoret figures 'an objectification of Amoret's fear of sexual love in marriage', while Britomart's varied encounters with forms of lust and domination educates us all in the virtues of companionate marriage, providing, to cite Berger again, 'a "natural" basis for the institution of monogamy, though it does not preclude the continual threat of breakdown between lovers unprepared to navigate the perilous course of a sustained intimate relationship'.[115] Yet Britomart herself proves a somewhat resistant figure within this influential reading. Colin Burrow mocks Lewis's description of Britomart as 'married chastity': 'She only "is" married chastity if you forget that she was once a young girl overwhelmed with passion for a man she sees in a mirror, that she complains for Artegall and violently

[113] Benton, *Search for Sovereignty*, 53–7, 57.

[114] Harry Berger, Jr., *Revisionary Play: Studies in the Spenserian Dynamics* (Berkeley, CA: University of California Press, 1988), 91.

[115] Roche, *Kindly Flame*, 77; Berger, *Revisionary Play*, 98, 98, 105, 107, 111, 116.

wounds Marinell after doing so.'[116] And Berger himself worries that Britomart is '*too* fierce and aggressive' and that the passion she conceives for Artegall and complains about to Neptune is, in fact, indistinguishable from lust. Spenser, Berger writes, 'distinguishes between noble and base love, but at the same time in the cantos surrounding this distinction he describes Britomart's "sacred fire" for Artegall in terms which make it identical to the elemental affections "that move in brutish minds"'.[117]

Berger's worry about the animality of Britomart's love registers the exceptionally visceral terms in which her passion is initially expressed. Her nurse, Glauce, speaks of the 'huge *Aetn*' of deepe engulfed griefe' erupting in the girl's body (III.ii.32), while Britomart herself describes the image in the mirror as a baited hook which has fixed itself within her 'bleeding bowels', so that her 'entrails flow with poysonous gore' (III.ii.39). At the sea, too, she complains of a 'stormy strife' in her 'troubled bowels' (III.iv.8). Not much to choose, then, between Britomart's bowels and those of the witch's son later in Book III, whose 'brutish love' for Florimell 'his bowels brent, / And shortly grew into outrageous fire' (III.vii.16). This is no accident: if Spenser has made it hard for us to distinguish Britomart's sacred fire from the churl's 'outrageous fire', this is because he wants us to feel the fearful danger and transgression of Britomart's passion. Not that she might commit rape, but that her love might open her father's kingdom to violation. And this is a danger which has something to do with the sea. Britomart's erotic impulse to ride as far as Neptune's 'sea-coast' (III.iv.8) led, as we have seen, to a calamitous confrontation with a knight who claimed the shoreline as his property. Indeed, if we read Britomart's wounding of Marinell as the *cause* of Florimell's flight, as Spenser teases us to do, it is not hard to see Britomart and Florimell (rather than Britomart and Amoret) as the pair key to Spenser's conception of chastity as an imperial virtue, expressing antithetical but complementary aspects of its identity as both expansive, outward-looking maritime power and insular integrity and security.

This seems more likely when we consider that Spenser derived both Florimell and Britomart from an erotic epyllion, dubiously attributed to Virgil, called *Ciris*.[118] The pseudo-Virgilian *Ciris* involves stories of two women's erotic entanglements with the enemy of the Attic sea-kingdom of Megara. Megara, ruled by King Nisus, was being besieged by the brilliant

[116] Colin Burrow, 'C. S. Lewis and *Allegory of Love*', *Essays in Criticism* vol. 53, no. 3 (2003), 284–94.
[117] Berger, *Revisionary Play*, 107, 98.
[118] *Spenser Variorum,* III. 334–5; 'Ciris', in *Virgil*, 2 vols., trans. H. R. Fairclough, rev. G. P. Goold (Cambridge, MA: Harvard University Press, 2000), II, 442–83.

and handsome Minos, legendary king of Crete and said by Thucydides (in a claim cited by John Dee) to be the first thalassocrat, or ruler over a sea-kingdom. He expelled piracy and established colonial provinces across Hellas, or Greece.[119] Minos is thus an ambivalent figure in the pseudo-Virgilian poem, which is lyrical in its introduction of the sea-girt kingdom of Megara, lying 'between Attic hills and Theseus' gleaming shores, smiling from afar with their purple shells'.[120] The Fates have assured the safety of Megara from coastal invasion, as long as the red lock of hair on Nisus's head remains untouched. But Nisus's daughter, Scylla, experiences such a raging and insatiable lust for the city's dazzling foe, Minos, that she is impelled to betray her father, for which she is transformed into the sea-hawk (*ciris*) of the title. There can be no doubt that Spenser meant the suggestion of Scylla's betrayal of father and kingdom to hover around Britomart's uncontrollable passion for the stranger imaged in her father's glassy globe. The stanzas in which Britomart confesses the cause of her turmoil to her nurse, Glauce, are closely imitative of Virgil's Scylla's speech to her nurse, Carme. Each nurse takes a sleepless, shivering girl into her arms, guesses that the malady is love, laments the monstrous forms that love can take and performs a magic rite to help her charge achieve her desire (III.ii.30–3, 40–2, 49–52).[121] Like a sinister shadow behind the convulsed Britomart stands the frenzied Scylla, concealing the knife with which she will enter her father's bedchamber and cut the hair that will betray the kingdom. More than that: in Virgil's poem, Scylla's nurse Carme cries out in horror on hearing Scylla name Minos as the object of her love. For it was Minos's attempted rape that drove Carme's own daughter, Britomartis, to her death when she threw herself into the nets of fishermen in the sea.[122] So in elaborating the relation between Britomart and Florimell, Spenser has performed something like a chiastic reversal of the Virgilian epyllion: just as Britomart feels Scylla's passion for one who may be the Welsh-British kingdom's foe or the founder of a bigger, better British sea-empire (Artegall-Minos), so Florimell, like Virgil's Britomartis, has to flee from certain unspecified dangers inherent in such imperial desire. We see that

[119] Thucydides, *The Peloponnesian War: The Complete Hobbes Translation*, trans. Thomas Hobbes, ed. David Grene (Chicago, IL: University of Chicago Press, 1989): 'For Minos was the most ancient of all that by report we know to have built a navy.' Cited by Dee, *Memorials*, 4. See further, Kinch Hoekstra, 'Thucydides and the Bellicose Beginnings of Modern Political Theory', in Katherine Harloe and Neville Morley, eds., *Thucydides and the Modern World: Reception, Reinterpretation and Influence from the Renaissance to the* Present (Cambridge: Cambridge University Press, 2012), 25–54.
[120] 'Ciris', II.450–1.   [121] 'Ciris', *Virgil*, II.460–3, ll. 220–56, 470-3, ll. 369–85.
[122] Ciris', *Virgil*, II.464–7, ll. 285–309.

Florimell flies just as fast from Arthur as from the wicked forester, she 'no lesse the knight feard, then the villein rude', significantly 'dismayd' by Arthur's shield and arms (III.iv.50, 51). The ambiguity of Minos (kingdom's invading foe, or prescient founder of sea-empire?) is translated, in Spenser's poem, first into Britomart's apprehension of the hazards of navigating her chastity safely through tempests, piloted by love, and then into Florimell's desperate attempt to escape the witch's monstrous hyena by riding '[t]o reach the sea . . . to drowne herselfe' (III.vii.26), instead of which she lands in the boat of a fisherman who slept 'the whiles his nets were drying on the sand':

> Into the same she leapt, and with the ore
> Did thrust the shallop from the floting strand
> So safetie found at sea, which she found not at land.   (III.vii.27)

If we look at Spenser's legend of Chastity from the point of view of the relation between Britomart and Florimell, rather than that between Britomart and Amoret, the twentieth-century critical assumption that female chastity involves some kind of 'balance' between 'extremes' of virginal purity and sexual passion disappears and what we have in its place is the realisation that geopolitically speaking, chastity involves *contradictory imperatives*: on the one hand, the dynastic expansiveness of matrimony, progeny, alliance and trade; on the other, integrity and security from foreign invasion. And the fact that both Britomart and Florimell are impelled towards the seashore by contrary yet related responses to the hazards of sexual love suggests that the resolution to the problem of chastity's geopolitical contradictions is going to involve the resolving of a problem of propriety and jurisdiction – of who owns and adjudicates – the dangerous yet profitable spaces along the coast, where the sea washes over and reveals the land, wrecking ships, bringing spoils and launching imperial ventures.

Where Britomart complained to Neptune that Love, her 'lewd Pilot' (III.iv.9), was going to steer her boat into the rocks and shallows, Florimell rather more responsibly took charge of the skiff in which she unexpectedly landed, grabbing the oar to push it away from the shore. But just as the legendary Britomartis found no safety in falling into fishermen's nets, neither does Florimell in the fisherman's boat. She leaves onshore her girdle – that circumscriptive symbol of male propriety in the female body – along with her Scythian simulacrum, the false Florimel (made of snow 'of *Riphoean* hills' in Scythia, III.viii.6), where they immediately become the objects of intense chivalric competition. This competition is,

as the narrator observes, an irrelevant distraction from the source of the real
danger which, if they only knew it, involved Florimell's being *at sea*:

> But if thou then, Sir *Satyran*, didst weete
> Or thou, Sir *Peridure*, her sorie state,
> How soone would yee assemble many a fleete,
> To fetch from sea, that ye at land lost late   (III.viii.28)

This wry apostrophe occurs in the middle of the emergency, as the fisherman awakes and is excited by lecherous desire for the beauteous Florimell
into near rape, tarnishing her garments with the lowly stuff of his trade as
he advances to defile her body. He throws her down roughly or 'Beastly',
'ne car'd to spill / Her garments gay with scales of fish, that all did fill'
(III.viii.26).

The banal detail of fish-stains on Florimell's garments seems odd. Why
does Spenser introduce it? The legend of Britomartis was known, in
sixteenth-century European art, to have a special and positive association
with fishermen and their nets. A tapestry by Jean Cousin the Elder now in
the Metropolitan Museum in New York (see Figure 3.8 in plate section)
shows Britomartis in the sea, the goddess Diana in the foreground and
Minos in the middle distance, both looking on, horrified, as Britomartis
struggles in the waves which curl about her body, the woven threads
skilfully revealing her submerged limbs. Behind, we see her being lifted
by the fishermen, a lifeless corpse, naked flesh showing through their nets.
The legend above explains Britomart as Chastity's martyr, praising her
preference for death over Minos's outrage, and tells us that, to sanctify her
death, Phoebe/Diana invented fishermen's '*retz et filez*', 'nets and toils', so
that hers is a '*saint mort*', a sacred death, which has brought into the world
'*chose tant estimée*', so worthy a thing as the fisherman's net.

Spenser might have known of a version of Cousin's depiction in the
work of the French Protestant engraver, Étienne Delaune (see Figure 3.9 in
plate section), who made engravings for English noblemen. But if he did,
he transposed its positive view of virginity's blessing on the fisherman's
trade into part of his larger allegory of endangered Chastity as a failure to
control navigational knowledge of the coastline. Like Britomart's metaphorical 'lewd Pilot', the lusty fisherman neglects the steering of his boat;
in an innuendo-laden rebuke, Florimell begs him to 'guide the cock-boat
well' while he leeringly quips back that 'the boat his way could wisely tell'
(III.viii.24). When Proteus hears Florimell's cries of distress and comes
upon the rape scene, his indignation is aroused both by her degradation
and by the vessel's aimless path, the latter seeming to allegorise the former.

He steers his chariot of stately *phocae*, or seals, to 'that Fishers wandring bote / That went at will, withouten carde or sayle / And therein saw that yrksome sight, which smote / Deepe indignation and compassion frayle / Into his hart attonce' (III.viii.31).

When John Dee set out his case for a 'Pety Navy Royall' establishing a 'Brytish Impire' by controlling British seas, he imagined its role in securing the island from invasion as a patrolling of foreign fishermen, intent on charting the secrets of the country's coastline. These foreign fishermen, he claimed,

> by colour and pretence of coming about their feat of fishing, doo subtilly and secretly vse Sowndings, and Serchings, of our Channells, Deeps, Showles, Banks, or Bars, along the Sea Coasts, and in our Hauen Mowthes allso, ... And ... are become (allmost) perfecter in them then the most parte of our Maisters, Loadmen, or Pylots.[123]

Spenser's lecherous fisherman offers similar 'shamefull wrongs' to Florimell, whose safety and honour will, as it turns out, involve an adjudication of propriety in the relation of land and sea along the coast of Faery land.

The resolution of the plight of Florimell, so beautiful, so beloved and so perpetually at risk, is deferred until the very end of Book IV. Although 'the Shepheard of the Seas' (III.viii.30), Proteus, rescues her from the fisherman's wandering hands and boat, Florimell's reward for rejecting Proteus's own equally lascivious advances is to be flung deep into a rocky dungeon which was 'wall'd with waues, which rag'd and roared' (IV.xi.3). In an extraordinary twist, however, we learn that the 'brideale feast' of the Thames and Medway, to which all the world's rivers are invited, 'should for the Gods in *Proteus* house be made', right next to the strange sea walls incarcerating the beautiful prisoner, Florimell (IV.xi.9). All the river gods, '[a]swell which in the mightie Ocean trade, / As that in riuers swim, or brookes do wade' (IV.xi.9), have been invited by Proteus to banquet at his residence, but no thought has been taken for those with an intolerance of immortal food. The half-mortal Marinell, having recovered from the wound dealt him by Britomart's blow, has been brought along to the feast by his solicitous mother, Cymoent. Being half-mortal, Marinell 'might not', as Spenser tells us 'with immortal food be fed' (IV.xii.4), so we hear how he skipped the banquet and 'walkte abrode, and round about did rome / To view the building of that vncouth place' (IV.xii.4). From under the overhang of a cliff he hears a voice piteously complaining. It is, of

---

[123] Dee, *Memorials*, 7.

course, the imprisoned Florimell, who loves him. Listening to the harrowing sound of her cries, he finds his heart touched with love and remorse,
wishing it in his power 'her for to redresse' (IV.xii.12). For several lines he
revolves ideas for how to 'enlarge' Florimell from her prison: should he
make a formal request for her release to Proteus? Fetch her out by force of
arms? Steal her away? But all his plans founder on her sea-girt inaccessibil-
ity (IV.xii.14–16). The party over, he lingers, loath 'that his departure
thence should be so short / And leaue his loue in that sea-walled fort'
(IV.xii.18). We could think of Florimell's prison, 'sea-walled' as it is, as
islandness itself – or, to put it another way, the universally desired Florimell
('for none alive but ioy'd in *Florimell* IV.ii.23) might herself be the
honeyed flowery future of an imperial island kingdom whose chaste integrity and seaward commerce have been rendered secure. Florimell's enlarge-
ment, then, might be not so much a matter of breaking out of a confined
space as of transforming the meaning of that space: sea and land must wed,
the sea's restrictive walls must become the sea's loving embrace, the relation
between land and sea be jurisdictionally transformed. The Thames–
Medway marriage thus redefines the relation between the country's interior and its coasts by means of the navigable estuary, as Leland's swan swims
out to see the English fleet 'where the salt waves drink the inflowing seas'.

Camden's ingenious poem of river marriage was, as we saw, an
aetiology – the story of the origin of the Thames, or 'Thamesis' from the
union of Tame and Isis, and from this critics have drawn the inference that
the failure of the Thames and Medway to mingle their waters in one river
constitutes a kind of critical disturbance, jarring with 'the prevailing theme
of concord'.[124] But if my reading is correct, Spenser's imagining of the
wooing of the 'proud nymph' Medway (IV.xi.8) by the river Thames is
quite deliberately not the story of a river's origin. Rather, the courtship
prophesies the seaward turn that will make a nation into an empire. For the
Thames and the Medway meet to form a vast estuary: where they meet is
both river and sea. Their marriage signifies a legally and navigationally
defined relationship of land and sea that will be key to the British coastline's integrity and England's overseas imperial expansion and trade.
Where Camden's Tame and Isis enjoy their connubial embraces under
hymeneal torches raised in Oxfordshire, Spenser's rivers mingle their
waters in the salt inflow of the sea where, as we read 'the Sea Nymphs
marched all' (IV.xi.48).

---

[124] Van Es, *Spenser's Forms of History*, 60.

The connubial mingling of the rivers to create the estuary links back both to Britomart's expression of sexual longing by the sea, and the wandering of Florimell's boat, 'withouten carde or sayle' (III.viii.31), while she fought off the lustful fisherman. But where these scenes associate the bounds of land and sea with threats of violation, the Thames–Medway marriage, recognising Marinell's right to Florimell, marks the jurisdictional transformation of England's relation to the seas surrounding Britain through the establishment of English coastal sovereignty. The Medway's bridesmaids are, after all, those marching Nereids and the Medway begins, in this period, to be used as the headquarters of England's fleet. As the bride Medway approaches her groom, the Thames, we might detect, as well as the shimmer of water, the glitter of the sun on gunmetal, for Medway's vesture, 'of unknowen geare'.

> seemed like siluer, sprinkled here and there
> With glittering spangs, that did like starres appeare,
> And wau'd vpon, like water Chamelot
> To hide the metall, which yet euerywhere
> Bewrayed itself   (IV.xi.45)

At the heart of Dee's advocacy for a royal navy was, as we have seen, the question of whether the English Crown had propriety and jurisdiction over the seas surrounding the British Isles, including Ireland and Scotland. As the landowner owns the bank of the river, but not its water, so, Dee argued from civil law, the English Crown might claim the seashore and seas to the midpoint between its shores and those of another kingdom. Spenser, as someone deeply involved in 'the fine print of *wreccum maris*, flotsam and jetsam, prize goods, waif, and replevin' in Admiralty cases on Irish shores, would have been aware both that the Crown was increasingly advancing its prerogative claims with respect to wreck and to salt-water tidelands and would know that these were contestable and controversial.[125] With respect to crown property, it seems that claims that royal prerogative gave the monarch property in the foreshores of the kingdom had never been pursued before the mid-sixteenth century, but from the time of Philip and Mary onward, commissions of enquiry began to be very active in hunting out such lands and claiming them for the Crown.[126] In 1568, as we have seen, Thomas Digges even wrote a treatise claiming to prove 'the Queen's Interest in Lands left by the Sea and the Salt Shores thereof' where

---

[125] See Andrew Zurcher, *Spenser's Legal Language: Law and Poetry in Early Modern England* (Cambridge: D. S. Brewer, 2007), 110–15, quotation at 110.
[126] Moore, *Foreshore*, 169.

he used the analogy of private ownership of the banks of a river to prove that the monarch of a country could claim the ownership of lands at the margin of the sea.[127] It was on the strength of Digges's civil law analogy between the riverbank and the ocean strand that Dee founded his notion of a 'Brytish Impire', with a royal navy patrolling a shore belonging to the Crown. In 1575, however, just before Dee's text was published, the great lawyer Edmund Plowden had argued, in *Sir John Constable's Case*, that however much the Crown might have *jurisdiction* over the coastal waters around the kingdom, it had no *property* in the tidal zone – that is, the land covered in water at high tide and revealed as land when the tide was out. Constable was charged with claiming a shipwreck taken between the low-water mark and the greensward of his manor at Holderness which, it was argued, belonged to the Crown by right of its property in the seashore. Though Plowden conceded the civil law analogy of sea and riverbank and defined the queen's jurisdiction as extending either to the midpoint of a sea adjoining another realm or across the entire breadth of the sea, he distinguished this from a property in the underwater land, or the tidal zone. '[A]lthough the Queen has jurisdiction in the sea adjoining her realm,' he argued,

> still she has not a property in it, nor in the land under the sea, for it is common to all men ... Then as to the property of the place between the greensward and the low-water mark, this belongs, as seems to me, to him who has the greensward adjoining ... if a man have land adjoining to the sea upon which the sea is accustomed to flow and re-flow, when the water overflows it any man may fish there, but when the water is gone away he shall have the land left dry, and may in this bring trespass.[128]

The case was adjudged for Constable, who got to keep his wreck, though he disclaimed the royal fish.[129] Plowden's argument thus produced a viable compromise, by which the subject had *property* in the foreshore and lands washed by the tides and the Crown had *jurisdiction over the sea*. Thus lords like Marinell could claim all the 'rich aray / Of pearls and precious stones' along 'the strond' (III.iv.18) without coming into conflict with Briton Princes, like Britomart, in their negotiations with imperial Neptune.

The plight of Florimell's chastity, endangered by the confrontation of Britomart and Marinell over the '*Rich strond*' (III.iv.20), seems to belong to something like this distinction between the subject's property and the Crown's jurisdiction. Hardly surprising, then, that Florimell's release is

---

[127] Moore, *Foreshore*, 180–210.   [128] Moore, *Foreshore*, 230.   [129] Moore, *Foreshore*, 233.

not brought about by Marinell heroically storming the prison and carrying her off, but by his mother's canny legal complaint to Neptune. As Andrew Zurcher shows, the case cleverly built by Cymoent turns on description of Florimell as a 'waift' (legally, a piece of lost and unclaimed property) which belongs to Neptune 'by high prerogative' since he is 'the seas Sole Soueraine' and in which, therefore Proteus's claim to 'propertie' is illegal (IV.xii.31, 30). We know from the story of Marinell's upbringing that his mother had long ago ensured him a right to 'wreck' (goods cast onshore from a ship, or a right to unclaimed flotsam) when his grandfather, Nereus, commanded the waves

> Out of their hollow bosom forth to throw
> All the huge threasure, which the sea below
> Had in his greedie gulfe deuoured deepe,
> And him enriched with the ouerthrow
> And wrecks of many wretches   (III.iv.22)

Marinell's right to wreck thus feels as if it is in some tension with a sovereign prerogative over waif on the seas, as well as with Proteus's claim of property in the latter. Zurcher suggests that 'Marinell's coastal proximity to Proteus's dominion has enriched him immeasurably, and yet in social and economic terms, Marinell is frigid and isolationist'.[130] The resolution of the case involves Neptune's warrant, sealed under the authentic seal of the sea gods,

> Commanding Proteus straight t'enlarge the mayd
> Which wandring on his seas imperiall
> He lately took, and sithence kept in thrall   (IV.xii.32)

Proteus reads the warrant and though 'grieued to restore the pledge, he did possess / Yet durst he not the warrant to withstand' (IV.xii.32), so he delivers Florimell to the Nereid Cymoent for her half-mortal son and lord of the seashore, Marinell. The restoration of Florimell to Marinell thus also resolves Marinell's original conflict with Britomart, since it achieves an accommodation of his property in the riches of the foreshore with an imperial jurisdiction of Faery land's coasts and seas.

Yet there is a mystery about Marinell's mother. Zurcher notes parenthetically in his reading that Spenser changes her name, referring to her as *Cymodoce* during this episode.[131] The name-change first appears when she is catalogued, in epic fashion, among the 'Sea Nymphs ... Whom of their

---

[130] Zurcher, *Spenser's Legal Language*, 109.   [131] Zurcher, *Spenser's Legal Language*, 103 n.32.

sire *Nereides* men call' (IV.xi.48) who follow the Medway with her hand-maids and page boys. Cymodoce seems more important than all the other Nereids, because among the fifty whom Spenser lists for four stanzas, she is the only one whose epithets take up two whole lines:

> And she, that with her least word canst assuage
> The surging seas, when they do sorest rage,
> *Cymodoce*   (IV.xi.50)

This, the most eloquent of the Nereids who rule the tides and surges, is, Spenser leaves us in no doubt, Marinell's mother:

> And there amongst the rest, the mother was
> Of lucklesse *Marinell Cymodoce*   (IV.xi.53)

And again, filing into Proteus's house for the banquet:

> Amongst the rest, was faire *Cymodoce*,
> The mother of vnlucky *Marinell*   (IV.xii.3)

This apparently insignificant detail, changing the name of a Nereid, has momentous implications. The Nereids – splendidly beautiful daughters of the wise and eloquent Nereus – played a specific role in Greek literature as the protectors of travellers over dangerous seas, riding the waves on the backs of various sea-creatures, most often dolphins. Classicists have also argued that in Hesiod's naming of the Nereids there is evidence of a connection between the skills of navigation and those of distributive justice (the latter identified with the art of speaking well).[132] Spenser, following Hesiod, links Cymodoce's ability to calm the open seas with her excellent wit.[133] Furthermore, in Book 9 of Virgil's *Aeneid*, Aeneas's ships, threatened by an enemy, are turned into sea nymphs, dipping into the water like dolphins and resurfacing, in womanly form, to swim away. Later, in Book X, this erstwhile naval power, now in sea-nymph form, swim towards Aeneas to warn him of the enemy. The nymph who addresses Aeneas is the cleverest, who is called *Cymodoce*:

> From among them Cymodocea, most skilled in speech (*doctissima*) follow-ing behind, grasps the stern with her right hand, and lifts her back above the waters, while with her left hand, she rows under the silent waves[134]

---

[132] See Barringer, *Divine Escorts*; also Jeremy McInerney, 'Nereids, Colonies and the Origins of *Isegoria*', in *Free Speech in Classical Antiquity*, eds. Ineke Sluiter and Ralph Rosen (Leiden: Brill, 2004), 21–40.
[133] *Spenser Variorum*, IV.274.
[134] *Aeneid*, X.225–7 in *Virgil*, II.188–9, translation slightly altered.

In renaming Marinell's mother 'Cymodoce' Spenser invokes the essential pairing of navigational skills with the skills of legal argument that plays so prominent a role in the legal geographies of oceanic empire. And in this particular story, it is Cymodoce's wit that resolves the crisis of the coast-line's chaste, jurisdictional integrity and the subject's right to property on the foreshore, joining the no-longer-endangered Florimell with the no-longer-isolationist Marinell.

As the delightful pageant of the world's rivers – the Nile, Ister, Scamander, Tigris and Euphrates, Rhone, Ganges and Amazon (IV. xi.20–1) – files into the house of Proteus to honour the long-awaited spousals of the Thames and Medway, the Thames and his tributaries are accompanied by 'neighbour floods which water all the English soil throughout' (IV.xi.30). These are the 'stately Severne' and 'storming Humber' as well as the Tamar, Plim, Dart, Avon, Stoure, Mole, Cam and many others (IV.xi.30–4). Irish rivers mark another kingdom: 'Ne thence the Irish Riuers absent were / Sith no less famous than the rest they be / And join in neighbourhood of kingdom nere' (IV.xi.40). But the Scottish rivers – the Forth, Clyde and Tay – are absent. Scotland is unmentioned, but for 'Twede the limit betwixt Logris land / And Albany' and Eden 'often staind with bloud of many a band / Of Scots and English both' (IV.xi.36). In the *Briton moniments* read by Arthur in Alma's castle in Book II, the familiar Galfridian story is told of the island's division between Locrine, Albanact and Camber, except that Spenser turns the invasion of Humber and the Huns into a flood:

> But *Albanact* had all the Northrene part,
> Which of himself *Albania* he did call . . .
>
> Vntill a nation straung, with visage swart,
> And courage fierce, that all men did affray,
> Which through the world then swarmd in euery part,
> And ouerflow'd all countries farre away
> Like *Noyes* great flood, with their importune sway
> This land inuaded with like violence
> And did themselues through all the North display   (II.x.14-15)

This inundation, this invasion of a strange, dark-faced nation swarming over the north of Britain becomes in the pageant of rivers, nothing other than the advent of the 'Scythians', whom Spenser equates with the Irish and the Scots. This becomes evident, when, in stanza 37 of the river pageant, we are told that Humber – the river named for the leader of this invasion, who killed Albanact – is 'a Scythian king', the murderer of several British knights, now rivers in Yorkshire (IV.xi.37). So while Spenser's identification of the Irish with Scythians does not preclude the presence of Irish rivers at the wedding, his reimagining of the tripartite division of Britain as a Scythian inundation licenses him to ignore the rivers that water all the soil of Scotland – and therefore Scot*land* – altogether. Rivers signify sovereignty. In the cartouche of George Lily's 1546 map *Britanniae Insulae quae nunc Angliae et Scotiae Regna continent . . . nova Descriptio* we find 'England is divided as if into three regions by three vast rivers: Thames, Severn, Humber; Scotland likewise into three: Clyde, Forth, Tay.'[135] The omission of Scotland's rivers is Spenser's powerful and effective artistic choice, an erasure of local habitation and name.

Spenserians cite Coleridge's words about Faery land as 'mental space' and the 'true absence of all particular space and time in the Faery Queene' in order to refute them with good arguments about the social production of space and the referentiality of space in *The Faerie Queene*. But I am not aware of any critic noticing that Coleridge's words about the absence of spatial particularity are themselves contradicted on the following page by his words about the power of spatial referentiality – of *national names*. 'There is a great magic in national names', he enthuses, 'No one of our poets has touched this string more exquisitely than Spenser; especially in his chronicle of the British Kings (B.II, c.10), and the marriage of the Thames with the Medway (B.IV, c.11). In both of which passages the mere names constitute half the pleasure we receive.'[136] Christopher Burlinson, refuting Coleridge's words about 'mental space', wants us to think about the ways in which *The Faerie Queene* 'seems to reach out into the spaces and locations of the sixteenth-century world – Ireland, England, Europe and beyond'.[137] Though he is right to insist on referentiality, one can also see a problem here: Spenser's poem has defined for Burlinson the 'spaces and locations of the sixteenth-century world' to which reference seems possible and salient. Burlinson's not mentioning Scotland – though a significant place in Spenser's sixteenth-century world – is itself a response to the art with which Spenser's *The Faerie Queene* has dealt with Scotland's immensely problematic existence by rendering it unimaginable. It was not necessary or usual to make Scotland invisible in a poem about enchanted knights in a chivalric Britain. Indeed, Spenser's

---

[135] My translation. On George Lily's important map, see Edward Lynam, *The Map of the British Isles of 1546* (Jenkintown, PA: George H. Beans Library, 1934) and Moir, *Early Maps*, 10–12.
[136] *Coleridge's Miscellaneous Criticism* ed. Thomas Middleton Raynor (London: Constable, 1936), 36–8.
[137] Burlinson, *Allegory, Space*, 24.

chief and brilliant precursor, Ariosto, filled *Orlando Furioso* with adventures set in *Scozie* as much as in *Inghilterra.*

The Faerie Queene is, among many other things, a poetic solvent of the contradictory logic of Elizabethan Anglo-British-imperialism, a logic which requires both the jurisdictional integration of the British coastline and the exclusion of Scotland's 'neighbourhood of kingdom nere' as an emotive, historical presence. It thus predicates the mental space of English national imagining on (again among other things) the topographical and historical impossibility of the kingdom of Scotland. This English literary achievement helps to explain the historical amnesia of Thomas Craig's interlocutors in 1603 and our own today.

CHAPTER 4

Scotland sui juris? *Scottish Literature and the Marian Constitutional Crisis, 1567–1573*

I.   George Buchanan and the Maitlands of Lethington

George Buchanan's *De iure regni apud Scotos Dialogus* ('A Dialogue on the Law of Kingship among the Scots') opens with fears about what other people think. Not what other people think about him, but about his people (*gens*), or his nation (*natio*). Benedict Anderson famously defined nations as political communities that could only ever be imaginary because 'the members of even the smallest nation will never know most of their fellow-members'.[1] In Buchanan's dialogue, however, the catalyst for imagining the nation as a political community is speculation about what others outside it are saying about it. What are those others, outside Scotland, thinking about the action Scots have taken or are about to take? The act that had already brought shame to Scotland was the mysterious murder of the queen's husband, Henry Lord Darnley, on 9 February 1567. The action imagined as not yet having happened was perhaps even more shameful to contemplate: that of a people deposing their monarch. For Buchanan's *De iure*, famous in the history of political thought as the first modern revolutionary theory of the sovereignty of the people, was originally drafted in 1567, in time for the meeting of the Scots Parliament in December that ratified the deposition of Mary Queen of Scots.[2] The text, which goes on to provide a theoretical justification for this unprecedented action, takes shape as a Socratic dialogue between two real-life friends and fellow-poets, George Buchanan himself and a younger man called Thomas Maitland. Buchanan seems to have got to know Thomas while the latter was a student in Paris in 1566.[3] Thomas, who until recently has been better

---

[1] Benedict Anderson, *Imagined Communities* (London: Verso, 1983), 15.

[2] Roger Mason, 'Introduction', George Buchanan, *A Dialogue on the Law of Kingship among the Scots: A Critical Edition and Translation of George Buchanan's De Iure Regni Apud Scotos Dialogus*, eds. Roger A. Mason and Martin S. Smith (Aldershot: Ashgate, 2004), xxvii.

[3] Steven J. Reid, 'Classical Reception and Erotic Latin Poetry in Sixteenth-Century Scotland: The Case of Thomas Maitland (ca.1548–1572)', in *The Impact of Latin Culture on Medieval and Early*

known as Buchanan's fictional interlocutor than as a poet in his own right, seems to have had, as we shall see, quite a complex relationship to the opinions ascribed to him by Buchanan in the *De iure*.[4] For the moment, however, I want to focus on the emotions in play in Buchanan's imagining of the dialogue between these friends and fellow poets.

Buchanan sets the scene of his dialogue with theatrical immediacy: In his own persona, he questions his youthful friend Thomas (imagined as having just arrived from France) about French responses to recent troubles in Scotland. This fictional Thomas is distressed. He confesses that he can't, for all his tough humanist education, conceal the sensitivity (*mollities*, tenderness or effeminacy) of his feelings when he hears the French expressing disgust at the foulness of his nation (*De iure*, 6–7). He now fears that, with the imminent deposition of the queen following the murder of the king, Scotland's barbarity will seem unparalleled in the eyes of other nations. Other nations will despise a realm that honours neither rights, customs, laws, nor respect for authority, nor the reverence due to the lawful magistrate (*Ius, mos, leges, respectus imperii, reverentia legitimi magistratus*) nor has compassion for the weakness of the female sex and the innocence of youth (*neque sexus imbecillitas nec aetatis innocentia*).[5] It is as a cure for that fear of national shame that Buchanan undertakes to prove the right of the Scots to rid themselves of tyrants. '*At ego te facile hoc timore nostramque gentem falso crimine liberabo*', Buchanan replies, 'But I shall easily rid you of this fear and clear our nation of this spurious charge'.[6] The arguments of the *De iure* begin to unfold as a kind of therapy, a recovery of national self-esteem.

This chapter will unpack the implications of the apparently small detail of Buchanan's choosing to begin his defence of revolution with this scene of chagrin at national shame. In what follows I will try to tease out, from a comparison of the writings of George Buchanan with those of the Maitland family – Thomas's father, brothers and sister, the Maitlands of Lethington in Lothian – two distinct versions of Scottish national consciousness, each with a different reaction to the Marian crisis and a

---

Modern Scottish Writing, eds. Alessandra Petrina and Ian Johnson (Kalzamazoo, MI: Western Michigan University, 2018), 3–39.

[4] Thomas Maitland's poetry is gradually gaining recognition, largely thanks to Steven Reid's scholarly labours of translating, editing and criticism. On Maitland's complex relation to Buchanan's ideas, see Steven J. Reid, 'A Disciple of Buchanan in the Marian Civil War: Thomas Maitland's "The Consecration of James VI, King of Scots" (Jacobi VI, Scotorum Regis Inauguratio)', in Reid (ed.), *Re-thinking the Renaissance and Reformation in Scotland: Essays in Honour of Roger A. Mason* (Boydell: St Andrews Studies in Scottish History, 2023). See also note 36.

[5] Buchanan, *De iure*, 6–7.   [6] Buchanan, *De iure*, 6–7.

different vision for Scotland's political future. Before embarking on this
comparison, however, I will set out a brief introduction to the constitutional crisis and ensuing wars of 1567–73 to orient early modernists whose
familiarity with the period comes from the study of English literature. To
them this Scottish history will be largely unknown (as it was to me).

The deposition of Mary Queen of Scots followed by her flight into
England in 1568 are events not usually seen in terms of a constitutional
crisis for Scotland. Nor are they seen as contributing to a transformation in
the writing of Scottish national identity. For most people and in most
scholarly writing, Mary Queen of Scots is figured as the great danger
threatening Elizabethan England and shaping of English national identity.
She is Spenser's Duessa, the Whore of Babylon, an important catalyst of
the anti-Catholicism that became so central to the formation of English
nationalism.[7] Yet Mary's flight from Scotland led, in Scotland itself, to a
devastating period of what has been called 'civil' war from 1567 to 1573. The
warring parties were, on the one hand, those who favoured Mary's restoration to the Scottish throne (the 'queen's party') and, on the other, the
'king's party', her opponents. The king's party, first known as 'the
Confederate Lords' and led by Mary's illegitimate half-brother, James
Stewart, earl of Moray, had imprisoned Mary and forced her deposition
and flight for safety. This party favoured a regency in Scotland till Mary's
son, James, should come of age. Baby James, crowned at the age of one, was
thus obliged, symbolically, to lead forces opposing his mother. Most
historians, as Claire Webb writes, have 'tended to follow Mary to
England' rather than attend to this war in Scotland, and what scholarship
there has been on the war has tended to treat it entirely as an internal,
Scottish affair.[8] English financial and military involvement was, however,
the *sine qua non* of the victory of the king's party in 1573. As Clare Webb
and Katherine Thompson have argued, the king's party and the earl of
Moray had limited support in Scotland, while, in the queen's party, the

---

[7] Anne McLaren, 'Gender, Religion and Early Modern Nationalism: Elizabeth I, Mary Queen of Scots
and the Genesis of English Anti-Catholicism', *The American Historical Review* (2002) vol. 107, no. 3,
739–67. On Mary and Spenser, see, for example, Richard McCabe, 'The Masks of Duessa: Mary
Queen of Scots and James VI', *ELR*, vol. 17, no. 2 (1987), 224–42.

[8] Claire Webb, 'The "Gude Regent"? A Diplomatic Perspective upon the Earl of Moray, Mary,
Queen of Scots and the Scottish Regency, 1567–1570'. Unpublished PhD University of St Andrews,
2008, 6–7. Gordon Donaldson, *All the Queen's Men: Power and Politics in Mary Stuart's Scotland*
(London: Batsford Academic, 1983); I. B. Cowan, 'The Marian Civil War, 1567–1573', *Scotland at
War AD 79–1918*, ed. Norman Macdougall (Edinburgh, Donald: 1991), 95–113; Katherine P.
Thompson, 'All Things to All Men: Mary Queen of Scots and the Scottish Civil Wars 1568–73',
Journal of the Sydney Society for Scottish History, vol. 9 (2001), 1–74.

chief nobles of the realm, the earls of Huntly and Argyll and the Hamiltons, had a large following among the landed classes.[9] The earl of Moray, however, had enjoyed English military support and correspondence with William Cecil since 1559, when he had first led a rebellion against Mary's mother, the regent Mary of Guise. This culminated, thanks to English backing and the death of Mary of Guise, in the Scottish Reformation. England had also protected Moray after he was 'put to the horn' (outlawed) for leading the rebellion known as the 'Chaseabout Raid' against his half-sister, the Queen of Scots, in 1565.[10] And just as there is clear evidence for regarding the management of Mary's arrival in England as a triumph of William Cecil's Anglo-imperial 'British policy' (successfully establishing an English-compliant Moray regime in Scotland) so the brutal English military invasion and suppression of the queen's party after Regent Moray's assassination in 1570 may be seen as consolidating English influence in Scotland to the point of dominance, realising by force the overlordship that Cecil quietly believed was England's ancient right.[11] The rebellion of the Northern Earls in England in 1569 gave the English government the excuse it needed in 1570 to launch a series of invasions of Scotland led by the Earl of Sussex and Lord Hunsdon (who later became the patron of Shakespeare's company, the Lord Chamberlain's Men). These invasions, ostensibly justified by the pursuit of fugitive Northern rebels, were in fact a devastating series of military assaults upon supporters of the queen's party, eventually forcing Huntly, Argyll and the Hamiltons to withdraw from the Marian cause, thus assuring the regency of the English-backed Earl of Lennox, father of the murdered Henry Darnley.[12]

The trial of Mary Queen of Scots in England qualifies as a constitutional crisis for Scotland in that it divided opinion among the governing classes to the point of setting them at war with one another. Some of Mary's noble and gentry subjects (the latter known in Scotland as 'lairds'), led by the earl of Moray, were content to permit a foreign jurisdiction to decide the legality of the queen's deposition, an issue quickly displaced by Moray's evidence that Mary was guilty of murder. An equally considerable party among the governing classes, however, saw this 'voluntarie submitting' to

---

[9] Webb, '"Gude Regent"?'; Thompson, 'All Things'.

[10] Webb, '"Gude Regent"?', 5, 17. For the English encouragement of Moray's rebellion against Mary, see Gordon Donaldson, *The First Trial of Mary Queen of Scots* (London: Batsford, 1969), 83.

[11] On the success of Cecil's 'British policy' in the management of the Marian crisis, see Alford, *Elizabethan Polity*, 120–208; on England's military suppression of the Marian party in Scotland in 1570, see Ronald Pollitt, 'The Defeat of the Northern Rebellion and the Shaping of Anglo-Scottish Relations', *SHR*, vol. 64 (1985), 64, 1–21.

[12] Pollitt, 'Northern Rebellion'.

the jurisdiction of England as (in their own words) 'an infringing of the liberties of Scotland, and a derogating from the honor of the croune'.[13] Though there were more evangelical Protestants in the king's party and the Catholic minority tended to be in the queen's party, the division was not, as has sometimes been assumed, primarily along confessional lines. Writing of Scottish affairs to Heinrich Bullinger in 1569, Edmund Grindal reported that the parties' 'disagreement was not respecting matters of religion; for each party, even when the dispute was at its highest, professed the gospel'.[14] Mary's supporters, in other words, were largely Protestants and their support was a constitutional rather than confessional matter.

Mary's trial also bears analysis as a crisis of Scottish national identity because of the way in which the rights being claimed by the Crown of England over that of Scotland harked back to those claimed by Edward I in 1291, a period which became a crucible for the forging of a literature of Scottish regal and national autonomy. The Scottish Wars of Independence had been fought and the epics of Barbour's *Bruce* (c.1375) and Blind Harry's *Wallace* (c.1470s) written as acts of resistance to the consequences of Edward I's assertion of overlordship. In 1291, Edward I had insisted that in order to judge the Scottish succession, he must be acknowledged overlord of Scotland; he later drew on Galfridian British history to justify his claims.[15] It is abundantly clear from Stephen Alford's detailed study of Cecil's memoranda on Scottish affairs for the decade 1559–69 that Edward's claims of overlordship were never far from Cecil's mind in his justification of Elizabeth's jurisdiction over Mary and oversight of a compliant Scottish regency in her stead. English relations with Scotland rested on what Alford calls 'competing traditions'. The more recent was 'an amity reinforced by Protestant religion, and … profound similarities in culture and language', but the older was

> a theory of English superiority over Scotland which, politically, could be traced back to the 'Great Cause' of Edward I and culturally to the myth of Brutus, established by Norman-Welsh clerics like Gerald of Wales and Geoffrey of Monmouth and promoted by Ranulph Higden in the

---

[13] John Maxwell Herries, *Historical Memoirs of the Reign of Mary, Queen of Scots and a Portion of the Reign of King James VI*, ed. R. Pitcairn (Edinburgh: Abbotsford Club, no. 6, 1836), 106.

[14] Bishop Grindal to H. Bullinger, 13 Aug. 1569, in *The Zurich Letters*, ed. H. Robinson (Cambridge: Parker Society, 1845), 322–3. The most detailed breakdown of allegiances is in Donaldson, *Queen's Men*.

[15] Goldstein, *Matter of Scotland*, 33–4.

fourteenth century, William Caxton in the late fifteenth, and Richard Grafton in the 1560s.[16]

Finally, as a crisis in the *writing* of Scottish national identity, or as a crisis in that identity's literary formation, Mary's trial fascinatingly polarises two important expressions of sixteenth-century Scottish literary genius and sensibility, each with its own political vision for the nation. On the one hand, George Buchanan, commissioned by Moray and the English government, produced brilliant deliberative and forensic accounts respectively of the Scots' right to depose tyrants and of the murderous guilt that defined Mary Queen of Scots.[17] Buchanan also, as Tricia McElroy has vividly shown, participated in a sophisticated literary and propagandistic fiction of popular discontent with Mary, in which he and the poet Robert Sempill and printer Robert Lekpreuik produced, with the support of Moray and the English government, a full-blown literary fabrication of an anti-tyrannical, anti-Marian 'Scottis Natioun'.[18] On the other hand, the poet and jurist Sir Richard Maitland of Lethington (1496–1586) led his family in collecting older Scots vernacular poetry and composing lyrics on current events from Mary of Guise's regency in the late 1550s to the beginning of James VI's personal reign in the early 1580s. The Maitland family's manuscript books known as the 'Maitland Folio' (MF) and the 'Maitland Quarto' (MQ) give us insight into these years from a perspective which

---

[16] Alford, *Elizabethan Polity*, 44–5.

[17] Buchanan, *De iure*; *De Maria Scotorum Regina, totaque eius contra Regem coniuratione … tragica plane Historia* (STC 3978); *Ane Detectioun of the duinges of Marie Quene of Scottes, touchand the murder of hir husband, and hir conspiracie, adulterie, and pretensed mariage with the Erle Bothwell. And ane defence of the trew Lordis, maintaineris of the Kingis graces actioun and authoritie* (London: John Day, 1571). The compositional and publishing history of Buchanan's *Detectioun* is complex. Buchanan seems to have drafted the narrative in 1568 for presentation to the English quasi-judicial investigation of Mary's deposition at York in October 1568; see Donaldson, *First Trial*, 83. His Latin *De Maria Scotorum Regina … Historia* was then published by John Day in 1571, along with an *Actio* by Thomas Wilson. It was simultaneously translated into pseudo-Scots by Wilson and published by Day as the *Detectioun*, ascribed to Buchanan ('G.B.'). See James Emerson Phillips, *Images of a Queen: Mary Stuart in Sixteenth-Century Literature* (Berkeley, CA: University of California Press, 1964), 62 and notes, 253. Henceforward Buchanan's Latin text will be referred to in the body of the text as *Detectio* and the pseudo-Scots as *Detectioun*. Both will thus be ascribed to Buchanan, but it should be borne in mind that these texts are English-sponsored, partly English-authored and printed by an English press.

[18] See Tricia A. McElroy, 'Imagining the "Scottis Natioun": Populism and Propaganda in Scottish Satirical Broadsides', *Texas Studies in Literature and Language*, vol. 49, no. 4 (2007), 319–39; see also McElroy, *Executing Mary Queen of Scots: Strategies of Representation in Early Modern Scotland*. Unpublished D. Phil. Thesis, University of Oxford, 2004; McElroy, 'A "Quarrell sett out in metre": Towards a New Edition of Scottish Reformation Satirical Literature', *Studies in Scottish Literature*, vol. 39, no. 1 (2013), 22–30; McElroy, 'The Uses of Genre and Gender in "The Dialogue of the Twa Wyfeis"', in *Premodern Scotland: Literature and Governance*, eds. Joanna Martin and Emily Wingfield (Oxford: Oxford University Press, 2017), 199–210.

registers, as Buchanan does not, the difficulties of maintaining the integrity of Scottish nationhood amid the oscillations of French- and English-backed divisions among the governing classes.[19]

Buchanan's writings and the writings of the Maitlands thus offer sharply contrasting literary fabrications of the Scottish people and the Scottish nation in the 1560s and 70s. The contrasts are multiple: where Buchanan writes in Latin first for political and judicial audiences and then for translation and print distribution by the English government, the Maitlands mainly write in Scots, and their writings circulate in manuscript in what Sebastiaan Verweij has called 'various familial satellite-courtly networks' which link to homes in regional settings, such as the Maitland home of Lethington in Lothian.[20] Buchanan draws with consummate skill on the techniques of classical forensic rhetoric to produce the convincing and scandalous reality effects that have shaped this period's history and determined the questions that historians still ask.[21] (I use the term 'reality effects' here for the techniques of narration and description producing a vividness and credibility known to humanist poets as *enargeia* or *evidentia*.)[22] Buchanan even produces a fiction of a politicised Scottish *vulgus* or 'pepill' whose bearing of witness to Mary's tyranny essentially justifies deposition.[23]

The Maitlands, uninterested in such techniques and drawing rather on the varied lyric forms and genres of Scots poetry from the previous century, convey a contrasting sense of national identity as a developing aesthetic and critical practice and a commitment to conviviality and good governance, especially in the sphere of judicial administration. As a retrospective collection of lyrics on (among other things) political events since 1558, the Maitland Quarto foregrounds the devastating material impact of the

[19] See *The Maitland Quarto: A New Edition of Cambridge, Magdalene College Pepys Library MS 1408* ed. Joanna M. Martin (Scottish Text Society, fifth series, no.13, 2015); *The Maitland Folio Manuscript*, ed. W. A. Craigie, 2 volumes (Edinburgh: W. Blackwood and sons for the Scottish Text Society, 1919–27).

[20] Sebastiaan Verweij, *The Literary Culture of Early Modern Scotland: Manuscript Production and Transmission, 1560–1625* (Oxford: Oxford University Press, 2016), 105.

[21] McElroy, *Executing Mary*, likens Buchanan's *Detectioun* to his tragic drama. Rosalind Smith, 'Reading Mary Stuart's Casket Sonnets: Reception, Authorship and Early Modern Women's Writing', *Parergon*, vol. 29, no. 2 (2012), 149–73, and Cathy Shrank, 'Manuscript, Authenticity and "Evident Proofs" Against the Scottish Queen', in *Tudor Manuscripts, 1485–1603*, ed. A. S. G. Edwards (London: British Library, 2010), 198–217, both discuss the forensic-dramatic effects of Buchanan's text.

[22] See Lorna Hutson, *The Invention of Suspicion* (Oxford: Oxford University Press, 2007); Hutson, *Circumstantial Shakespeare* (Oxford: Oxford University Press, 2015); Kathy Eden, *Poetic and Legal Fiction in the Aristotelian Tradition* (Princeton, NJ: Princeton University Press, 1986).

[23] McElroy, *Executing Mary*, 122.

wars on the common people.[24] 'I trow wes neuer harde nor sein / In Scotland greter miserie' begins one, while another declares, '[i]t is the caus of our calamitie / Amang yow lordis the inimitie / That ar devydit now in parties twa'. Poems lament the effects of war on the 'commounis of this countrye' who 'Can na thing keip in their possessioun / Qhairof that thay may mak ane lyfe'.[25] They omit any account of the scandal of Darnley's death or Mary's trial, explicitly opposing the uses of printed poetry as a rumour machine 'to gar the peopill euill opinioun tak' (MQ 55.5).

Buchanan and the Maitlands had many other connections. As we have already seen, Buchanan was a friend and literary mentor in Paris to Sir Richard's youngest son, the neo-Latin poet, Thomas, and fictionalised him as his interlocutor in *De iure*. Buchanan also composed satires on the 'chameleon' quality of Sir Richard's eldest son, William Maitland of Lethington, secretary of state.[26] William, a talented politician, was initially the most energetic, eloquent and effective proponent of the Anglo-Scots amity which he believed offered the best future for the Scottish polity. Originally Moray's most trusted negotiator with Cecil and Elizabeth, William Maitland was at the centre of events that led to the deposition of Mary and the crowning of James.[27] By 1569, however, he was disillusioned with England's management of Scotland: 'it breaks my hart', he wrote, 'to see us at this point that Englishmen may give us sik law as they will'.[28] He regretted his part in James's coronation, describing it as an improvisation, a 'clocke [cloak] of some new authority' to legitimise the revolutionary turn things were taking after the defeat of the earl of Bothwell and the queen at Carberry Hill on 15 June 1567. But he had been wrong, he admitted, for James 'can neuer justlie be king as long as his mother liues'.[29] From 1569 William was a tireless supporter of Mary's restoration. He died, perhaps by

---

[24] See Joanna Martin, 'The Maitland Quarto Manuscript and the Literary Culture of the Reign of James VI', in *James VI and I, Literature and Scotland* ed. David J. Parkinson (Leuven: Peeters, 2013), 65–81.

[25] *Maitland Quarto* ed. Martin, poem 30, lines 3–4, poem 25, lines 12–13; poem 21, lines 2–4. Further references will appear in the text as MQ, with poem number and lines.

[26] See 'Chamaelon', in *Vernacular Writings of George Buchanan*, ed. P. Hume Brown (Edinburgh, 1892), 37–53; Mark Loughlin, '"The Dialogue of the Twa Wyfeis": Maitland, Machiavelli and the Propaganda of the Scottish Civil War', in *The Renaissance in Scotland: Studies in Literature, Religion, History and Culture offered to John Durkan*, ed. A. A. MacDonald (Leiden: E. J. Brill, 1994), 226–45; McElroy, 'Uses of Genre and Gender'.

[27] Mark Loughlin, 'The Career of Maitland of Lethington, c.1526–1573', Unpublished PhD Thesis University of Edinburgh, 1991, excellently reconstructs Maitland's political activities.

[28] Loughlin, 'Career', 332.

[29] Richard Bannatyne, *Memorials of Transactions in Scotland, 1569–72* ed. R. Pitcairn (Edinburgh, 1836), 127.

suicide, after the taking of Edinburgh Castle by English forces in 1573 and 'realistic hopes of Mary's restitution died with him'.[30]

What can the juxtaposition of Buchanan's writings with those of the Maitland family tell us about Scottish national imagining in this period? From the mid-thirteenth to the mid-sixteenth century, as Roger Mason sums it up, Scottish national identity was expressed, above all, as ancient sovereign autonomy: 'the Scots had developed an understanding of their own unique past which was perfectly capable both of countering the imperial pretensions of British history and of articulating a powerful sense of their own collective identity'.[31] According to historians of Scottish national consciousness from the mid-sixteenth century on, however, the historical task of countering the imperial pretensions of Galfridian British history disappears with Protestantism. The Scottish Reformation first stimulates 'British unionism and a pan-European perspective on the papal antichrist'.[32] Buchanan then produces a new account of Scottish national identity in the *Rerum Scoticarum Historia* (1582) when he applies his resistance theory to Hector Boece's account of an ancient Scottish regnal line going back to Fergus I in 330 BC. Buchanan 'transformed the story of the Fergusian foundation of the Scottish monarchy into an ideology of popular or at least aristocratic sovereignty'.[33] In doing so, he also transformed the idea of ancient Scottish liberty from a counter-Galfridian claim (defying English claims of overlordship with ancient sovereign independence) into an internal constitutional right – the rights of the Scots to elect kings and depose tyrants. Yet, as Stephen Alford's work shows, the trial of Mary for which Buchanan was commissioned to write was conceived by the English themselves as the exercise of Edward I's ancient Galfridian right. As Cecil noted in 1568, preparing for the trial, 'it belongeth of very right to the Crown of england to gyve ordre to dissensions moved for the Crown of scotland'. 'This,' comments Alford, 'was written as a statement of fact and justification and not as a point for debate.'[34] Reading Buchanan alongside the Maitlands helps us understand the role played by the Buchananite shaming of Mary in the veiling of a more consequential constitutional shame – complicity in permitting the English Crown to judge 'dissentions moved for the Crown of scotland', that is, disputes over legal right to the Scottish succession.

[30] Mark Loughlin, 'Maitland, William of Lethington', *ODNB*, 2004.
[31] Mason, 'Aspects of National Identity', 84.
[32] Colin Kidd, *Subverting Scotland's Past* (Cambridge: Cambridge University Press, 1993), 21. Kidd draws on Williamson, *Scottish National Consciousness*.
[33] Kidd, *Subverting*, 25.   [34] Alford, *Elizabethan Polity*, 163–4.

II.   The Genius of Caledonia: Thomas Maitland's 'Lethington House' (1567)

I opened this chapter by introducing Sir Richard Maitland's youngest son, the poet Thomas Maitland, through his becoming a fictional persona in George Buchanan's *Dialogue on the Law of Kingship among the Scots*. In the history of political thought, Thomas has long been no more than the 'the easily bullied figure of Maitland', eventually persuaded by Buchanan's arguments for the rights of the Scots to depose tyrants.[35] Thanks to Glasgow University's excellent online edition of a selection of the *Delitiae Poetarum Scotorum* (1637) and to Steven Reid's and David McOmish's edition of Neo-Latin poems on James VI, however, modern readers now have more direct access to Thomas Maitland's political ideas through his printed poems, with translations by Steven Reid.[36] Reid's recent work has also valuably illuminated Thomas's relation to his mentor both in terms of poetic practice and political thought.[37] Had Thomas not died in his twenties, in Italy, of quartan fever, this remarkable poet might not have disappeared so thoroughly from the historical record. A touching poem to Charles XI's physician, Louis Duret, hoping he might cure him, and a note scribbled between two poems in the family book, the Maitland Folio – bear witness to this untimely illness and death, 'M. Thomas Maitland died in italie 1572. And lived of yeiris 22', it says (see Figure 4.1 in plate section).[38] Thomas was, in his way, as talented as his brother politicians (William was secretary to Mary of Guise and to Mary Queen of Scots, and John secretary to James VI).[39] He and George Buchanan seem to have met in Paris. Reid describes the 'hardcore humanism' – the emulative composing of erotic and obscene elegiac poetry in imitation of Ovid,

---

[35] Quentin Skinner, *The Foundations of Modern Political Thought*, 2 vols. (Cambridge: Cambridge University Press, 1978), II. 340.

[36] University of Glasgow Bridging the Continental Divide, 'Neo-Latin and Its Cultural Role in Jacobean Scotland, as Seen in the *Delitiae Poetarum Scotorum* (1637)': www.dps.gla.ac.uk. Thomas Maitland, 'The Consecration of James VI, King of Scots', in *Corona Borealis: Scottish Neo-Latin Poets on King James VI and His Reign, 1566–1603*, eds. Steven J. Reid and David McOmish (Glasgow: The Association for Scottish Literary Studies, 2020), 70–95.

[37] Reid, 'Classical Reception', 3–39; Reid 'A Disciple'.

[38] William S. McKechnie, 'Thomas Maitland', *SHR*, vol. 4, no. 15 (1907), 274–93. For Maitland's poem to Duret, 'Elegia III: Ad Ludovicum Duretur', see University of Glasgow Bridging the Continental Divide, 'Neo-Latin and Its Cultural Role in Jacobean Scotland, as Seen in the *Delitiae Poetarum Scotorum* (1637)': www.dps.gla.ac.uk. For the note, see Maitland Folio, Pepys Library, Magdalen College, Cambridge, MS 2553, 256. McKechnie, 275 n.5, supposes '22 years' a mistake for '27 years'.

[39] See Loughlin, 'Career of Maitland'; Maurice Lee, Jr., *John Maitland of Thirlestane and the Foundation of the Stuart Despotism in Scotland* (Princeton, NJ: Princeton University Press, 1959).

Catullus and Tibullus – that occupied both poets.[40] On returning to
Scotland in 1567, Thomas seems at first to have supported, as did his
brother William and his mentor Buchanan, the revolutionary action
against Mary. His striking poem 'The Consecration of James VI, King of
Scots' (*Jacobi VI, Scotorum Regis Inauguratio*) carefully refrains from
attacking the queen but rejoices in the defeat of Bothwell and celebrates
the Scots – both senate and common people – as ever ready to seize the
sceptre from a tyrannical ruler.[41] Reid's carefully nuanced analysis of the
poem shows how Thomas crafts a poetic account of Mary's ceding of rule
to her son which fits with the fiction of voluntary abdication presented in
the instruments that the Queen was forced to sign in 1567, while reserving
his vilification of tyranny (in language consonant with Buchanan's *De iure*)
for the figure of Bothwell. Assuming it was composed in 1567, Reid argues
that the poem shows Thomas actively developing Buchanan's ideas:

> the poem provides important corroborative evidence for the development of
> Buchanan's *De Iure Regni*. Given its close synergy with Maitland's descrip-
> tion of the 'tyrannical' qualities of Bothwell's character and the resulting
> punishments due to him, and with Maitland's account of the nature of good
> kingship and of tyranny, we can further assume that Buchanan was actively
> discussing these ideas with Maitland close to or at the time of the
> coronation.[42]

By 1569, however, Thomas had decisively distanced himself from
Buchanan and from the revolutionary justification of Mary's deposition.
He defected, along with his brothers William and John, to the queen's
party. Both William and Thomas worked tirelessly till their deaths towards
achieving the queen's restoration. Arrested and imprisoned in Stirling in
1570, Thomas set out for Aberdeen as soon as he was liberated, to join an
expedition for Flanders to beg the duke of Alva for resources to strengthen
Dumbarton and Edinburgh castles, still being held by the queen's party.
Further writings from 1570 testify to Thomas's conviction that the only just
course for Scotland now lay in the restoration of the legitimate monarch,
Mary Stewart. A satirical prose pasquinade attributed to Thomas purports
to reveal a secret conference among the earl of Moray's supporters in
which, each speaking in the style of his ideology, they betray their collective
venality. So, for example, John Knox, with pious gestures and 'a stuir

---

[40] Reid, 'Classical Reception', 3–39, 8.
[41] Thomas Maitland, 'Consecration', *Corona Borealis*, 70–95, especially lines 25–31, 343–6. See Reid, 'A
    Disciple'.
[42] Reid, 'A Disciple'.

[harsh] and brocken voice', 'luiking up to the heaving [heaven]' and praising God, recommends that to establish a true religion, it would be better if Moray took the crown, 'ffor when this bairne, whom we call now King, shall come to age, dois ony man think he will lieve all royal insolence ... borne of sic parentis?'[43] 'Your grace hes persavit', this fictional Knox goes on, feeding Moray's ambition,

> how my blast of the trumpet against the regiment of weimen, is approved of all the godlie. I haue written in lyk manner, and hes it ready for printing, a bouke, whairin I prove by sufficient reasones, that birth hes no power to promote, nor bastardry to exclude men from government.[44]

From this time, too, survives a letter in Latin believed to be by Thomas, addressed to Elizabeth in support of Mary's restoration.[45] As Thomas set sail for Flanders, he wrote a now-lost letter to Queen Mary in which, according to Father Thomas Innes, 'he protests to her Majesty, that his being brought interlocutor into that dialogue to say whatever Buchanan thought proper to his purpose was wholly Buchanan's own invention'.[46] In the summer of 1571 bullion did reach the queen's party (including William) in Edinburgh Castle, but Thomas himself died between Genoa and Rome in 1572.[47]

We can't, of course, know what made Thomas change his mind about the revolution. I am interested, however, in teasing out cross currents in post-Reformation Scottish national imagining, elements not entirely subsumed, as they are in modern accounts, by Buchanan's anti-Marian British unionism and his transformation of ancient Scottish liberty into anti-tyranny. I want to ask what happens, in the period 1567–73, to the double movement Roger Mason identifies in the Scots understanding of their past: the traditional inseparability of Scottish collective identity from the need to counter British imperial history's denials of Scottish nationhood. Coming from a family so immersed (as Buchanan was not) in a vernacular tradition of Scottish poetry, Thomas Maitland complicates the post-Reformation

---

[43] Thomas Maitland, attrib., 'An account of a Pretended Conference held by the Regent, Earl of Murray, with the Lord Lindsay and others. January MDLXX' in *The Bannatyne Miscellany*, 3 volumes (Edinburgh, 1827), I.40, 42.

[44] Maitland, 'Conference', 43.

[45] 'Thomae Metalani ad serinissimam principem Elizabetham Anglorum Reginam Epistola', Edinburgh University Library, MS De.4.22. This work is currently being translated by John-Mark Philo.

[46] Thomas Innes, *A Critical Essay on the Ancient Inhabitants of the Northern Part of Britain or Scotland* [1729] (Edinburgh, 1885), 204. See Mason, 'Introduction', *De iure*, xxvii, n.57.

[47] McKechnie, 'Thomas Maitland', 282–88.

story of Protestant Scotland's enthusiastic British unionism. Even in his
'Consecration of James VI', celebrating the revolutionary defeat of
Bothwell at Carberry Hill and coronation of the infant James at Stirling,
Maitland has none of Buchanan's pro-British insular imagining.
Buchanan's *Genethliacon* or 'birth-poem' for James reworks Galfridian
prophecy to identify Britain's renewal with the birth of this little boy. As
he bids the boy grow and thrive, Buchanan exhorts the island Britannia to
rise out of tempests that are simultaneously the seas that beat around her
and her long history of internicene war:

> And you, Britannia, so often battered by foreign storms, so often lacerated
> by your own blade, lift up your head in happiness, bind your hair with the
> peace-bearing olive wreath.[48]

Buchanan was hardly alone in seeing James' birth as foretelling British
union. Elizabeth had been angered by even more extravagant prophecies in
Patrick Adamson's birth-poem for James. The earl of Bedford, her emis-
sary sent to protest Adamson's poem, found himself, at James's baptism at
Stirling, in the midst of a festivity as magnificent as those arranged by
Catherine de Medici for her son, the young king Charles IX of France, in
1563–5. These fêtes, triumphs and masques staged across France in the two
years after a truce in the war of religion both demonstrated the power of the
Valois monarchy and emphasised its role as bringers of peace to a divided
nation. 'Reconciliation of her Protestant nobles, the elevation of the status
of the monarchy and conspicuous display' were all part of Mary's design at
Stirling as they had been for the Valois in France, and, as at the fêtes of
Catherine de Medici, a prophecy of Merlin was adapted to make a specific
political point – at Stirling, Merlin's prophecy implied that the infant
James was the ruler who would unite Britain. In Michael Lynch's summary, 'Bedford, who had been instructed to complain about the claims
made in Adamson's poem, which was a thinly disguised tract of Anglo
Scots union on Stewart terms, found the celebrations awash in images
anticipating the fulfilment of Merlin's prophecy.'[49] But Thomas Maitland
has no such vision. His 'Consecration' rather glories in telling the baby
James what a rich and beautiful country he has for a kingdom (mountains
swollen with tawny gold, veins of sky-blue silver … fertile fields full of
cattle and corn), and what a brave people, conquerors of the Picts,

---

[48] Buchanan, 'A birth-poem for James VI, King of Scots', *Corona*, 6–15, lines 5–6. See also Buchanan,
      Political Poetry, 154–5.
[49] *Corona*, 22–37; Michael Lynch, 'Queen Mary's Triumph: The Baptismal Celebrations at Stirling in
      December 1566', *SHR*, vol. 69, no. 187 (1990), 1–21, 7–13.

Cimbrians and Saxons, are set under him.[50] Thomas's is not a vision of British union, but of Scotland's sovereign flourishing as a separate country within the island. It is a version of Scottish national consciousness that finds little place in modern critical accounts.

Teasing out these distinctions in Scottish national imagining in the aftermath of Mary's deposition in 1567 enables a Scottish constitutional crisis to emerge into visibility alongside the much better-known English history of Mary as part of England's succession crisis. In the next section, I will come back to the importance of Buchanan's beginning *De iure* with the question of Scottish national shame, but first I want to enlarge a little on the poetic culture of the Maitland household and what the family's commitment to the preservation and reworking of Scottish vernacular poetry might have meant in the context of the Marian crisis. I am not so interested in forms of political allegiance as in conceptualisations of Scotland as a nation. A remarkable poem written by Thomas in celebration of the family home on his return to Scotland in 1567 sets the scene by identifying the Maitland home itself and by implication the family's poetic genius or spirit, with the nation's ability to flourish in defiance of English imperial claims.

Thomas Maitland's *Domus Ledingtona* (Lethington House) combines an extravagant classicising fancy with an intensity of familial and national feeling. The poet returning home describes self-mockingly how, like a lover from a Roman elegy, he presses his lips fervently against Lethington's doorposts, worshipping the incense burning in the lamps at the doorway and greeting the *lares*, or household gods.[51] He offers exuberant praise to the massive, lofty edifice and the cultured conviviality within it. Defiant in its ponderous weight and its heavenward aspiration, Lethington's exterior enrages the god of winds with its impervious solidity (see Figure 4.2 in plate section). But inside its hall is open and welcoming (*aula patet populo*), its splendid furniture (*pretiosa supellex*) dazzling to the eye, its walls hung with tapestries to rival the work of Arachne, its ceilings perhaps painted in characteristic Scottish fashion, certainly decorated '*aurea ... variis simulacra figuris*', with gilded images of various colours and forms. It is a space of entertainment, its dances and games '*exhilarant ... animos*', enlivening the festive spirits of dinner guests sprawled on couches (*epulis onerare toros*, ll. 91–113).[52]

---

[50] 'Consecration', *Corona*, lines 177–220, pp. 82–85.

[51] University of Glasgow Bridging the Continental Divide, 'Neo-Latin and Its Cultural Role in Jacobean Scotland, as Seen in the *Delitiae Poetarum Scotorum* (1637)': www.dps.gla.ac.uk. Lines 15–19. Further line references in text.

[52] For the tradition of decorative ceiling painting, see Michael Bath's wonderful *Renaissance Decorative Painting in Scotland* (Edinburgh: National Museums of Scotland, 2003).

Essential to Thomas's double conception of the house is the idea of Lethington's *genius*, both in the architectural sense of the wonder of its foundation and endurance as a defensive structure (*ingenio artificis*, l.21) and in the sense of the *domini praestantis honore* (l.21) the honour of its *dominus* or lord, Sir Richard.[53] The quotidian heroism of the house's exterior genius is expressed as its resilience to the Scottish weather. First it withstands the four winds released by the furious Aeolus; these batter the walls through the seasons of the year with wild storms and thudding hail, soaking rain and, finally, soft spring breezes from the west. Then begins the tower's summer shielding against the firebrands of Phoebus, its comic triumph expressed in the windows' spitting back the sun's flames in brilliant reflection, while the sun god in turn caresses (*demulcet*) the roof with a balmy evening warmth (ll.38–69).

But this mock battle is immediately followed by a more sombre episode from the nation's and family's recent history. During the attempted English conquest of Scotland in the 1540s, as I explained in Chapter 1, Scottish nobility and lairds who refused to 'assure', or swear loyalty to the English king, risked having their houses 'herriet' (ravaged) and burnt, and their families harmed by English soldiers.[54] It was extremely hard to resist the pressure to assure. Sir Richard's grandson later wrote that 'most pairt of the Gentlemen of Louthian, Mers and Teviotdaill did assure, bot my grandfather would not assure, albeit the English did possess Hadington and Lauder'. Sir Richard 'thairfore did leiue al that tyme with verie great difficulties having a wyffe, manie children, and a great family'.[55] One of these difficulties must have been the conflagration which Lethington house narrowly escaped during the English occupation of Haddington in 1548–9. Once again it is the house's genius – tutelary guardian of the sacred temple (*sacram aedem*, l.70) – that is invoked as its saviour.

Lethington lies about a mile south of Haddington, in the area described by Marcus Merriman as 'Scotland's most devastated cockpit of war'.[56] The incident the poem commemorates probably took place in Thomas's toddlerhood, in September 1549. In the spring and early summer of 1548, Haddington had been fortified and was being held by the invading English

[53] David G. Orr, 'Roman Domestic Religion: The Evidence of Household Shrines', *Aufsteig und Niedergang der römischen Welt*, ed. Wolfgang Haase (Berlin: De Gruyter, 1978), 1559–91, 1558.
[54] See Chapter 2, p.45.
[55] *Maitland's Narrative of the Principal Acts of the Regency*, ed. W. S. Fitch (Ipswich: 1833), n.p., sig. B1v; see also M. H. Merriman, 'The Assured Scots: Scottish Collaborators with England during the Rough Wooings', *SHR*, vol. 47, no. 143 (1968), 10–34.
[56] Merriman, *Rough Wooings*, 359.

forces under the command of Sir James Wilford, whose portrait, with an inset image of the besieged town, now hangs at Coughton Court, Warwickshire (see Figure 4.3 in plate section).[57] The town was thought to be of great strategic importance for Somerset's conquest. 'I trust to rejoice your grace,' wrote Thomas Palmer to Somerset on 30 June 1548, 'kepyng Haddyngton ye wyne Skotland.'[58] However, in July thousands of French and Scots cavalry and arquebusiers came, with cannon, to lift the English siege of the town. They were joined by the earl of Argyll's Highlanders, whom the French marvelled at as '*sauuages*', being '*nuz fors que de leurs chemises taintes, & de certaines couuertures legeres faites de laine, de plusiers couleurs*'[59] (naked but for their painted shirts and certain light mantles made of wool in diverse colours). The English held out bravely and with great suffering.

Meanwhile, the town was slowly devastated in the ensuing crossfire of artillery and cannon, 'not one whole house' left standing, as Ulpian Fullwell later reported.[60] A mile away, the Maitlands' house of Lethington played its part as the military headquarters of Argyll's Highland forces (sleeping, perhaps, in their diversely coloured woollen mantles). The *Diurnall of Occurents* describes how, on 14 September 1549, the surrendering English fired the town and the Maitland home: 'the Inglishmen past out of Haddingtoun and brunt it and Leidingtoun [Lethington] ... for the pest and hungar was rycht evill amangis tham'.[61] This must be the occasion of the miracle described by Thomas when 'the Saxon enemy' (*Saxonidae ... hosti*) heaped torches of fire and set explosives around Lethington, but, wondrous to tell (*dictu mirabile*), the tower was not engulfed in flame, but somehow held the site of the fire (*locum flammae*) in the midst of the bronze roof, as if spilling from split *viscera*, or entrails (ll.70–80). In this moment, as elsewhere in the poem, the tower's defensive exterior and interior genius seem to fuse: the roof's cupping and containing of the flames converts violent destruction into an image of the hearth. And as the hearth in Roman literature is the place

---

[57] National Trust 135561. The National Trust's website mistakenly describes Sir James Wilford as the 'heroic defender of Haddington in Kent'. No such place exists. In a classic example of English insular imagining, the NTS has invented Wilford as defending England from invasion: www.nationaltrustcollections.org.uk/object/135561.

[58] *CSP Scot*, vol. 1, item 269, p. 133.

[59] Jean de Beaugué, *L'Histoire de la Guerre D'Escosse* (Paris, 1556), fol. 22v.

[60] Ulpian Fulwell, 'The History of the winning of Hadington in Skotland', *The Flower of Fame*, sig. P3r.

[61] *A Diurnall of Remarkable Occurents that have passed within the country of Scotland* (Edinburgh, 1833), 48.

over which the *di penates* or gods of the household stand watch, this image proposes that the house is cunningly subverting the national objectives of the enemy invasion itself, the attempt to overcome '*patrium, et patrios ... populare penates*' (the nation, and the people's *penates* or national spirits, l.74). No wonder, then, that the poet asks if this house is to be thought not the work of man (*opus humanum*), but rather 'made by the hands of Gods, when ancient deities inhabited Caledonian lands?' (*an manibus fabricata Deorum / Prisca Caledonias colerent cum Numina terras*? ll.22–4).

Thomas's praise of Lethington brilliantly reworks a traditional conception of the Scottish nation as thriving in defiance of hostility. The tower itself, enclosing a civilised culture while withstanding the assaults of the elements, figures the nation's resistance to English attempts at conquest while asserting the distinctive collective identity of its inhabitants. In this sense, the poem's praise of Lethington's rich and sociable interior implies another kind of nation-making: the inhabitants' collection and composition of Scots poetry.

Modern scholarship has reason to be grateful to what C. S. Lewis called 'the praiseworthy taste' of the Maitlands for compiling a collection of older Scots poetry.[62] The Maitland Folio (MF) is a heterogenous assemblage mixing family lore with poetry transcription compiled over many years and involving layers of scribal additions.[63] As such it is quite distinct from the MQ, which is, rather, a commemorative anthology of writing by the Maitlands and their affinity.[64] The poetry of the MQ was transcribed in a fair copy by Marie Maitland in 1586, the year of Sir Richard Maitland and his wife's death. It has a distinctly retrospective and analytical cast, looking back through the family's poetry over changes of regime and a great diversity of events and topics: Henri II's winning of Calais in 1558, Mary Stewart's marriage to the dauphin in the same year, war made by the Lords of the Congregation against Mary of Guise in 1559, Mary Stewart's arrival in Scotland in 1561, 'this cruell ciuill weir' (MQ18) – wars of the king's and queen's parties – oppression of the country by thieves (MQ2, 18, 58), losses suffered by the Maitlands (MQ14, 20), the use of poetry in the propaganda campaign against Mary (MQ 43, 55), later English propaganda against the Scots after the Northern Rising (MQ61). Poetic forms and metres are

[62] Lewis, *Sixteenth Century*, 69.
[63] Julia Boffey, 'The Maitland Folio Manuscript as a Verse Anthology', in *William Dunbar, 'The Nobill Poyet': Essays in Honour of Priscilla Bawcutt*, ed. Sally Mapstone (East Linton: Tuckwell, 2001), 40–50.
[64] Martin & McClune, 'Maitland Folio and Quarto' Manuscripts in Context', 237–63. See also Martin, 'Introduction', *Maitland Quarto*, 1–40.

diverse. Lamenting the wars between the Lords of the Congregation and Mary of Guise's French allies takes the jaunty form of a New Year's carol: 'I can not sing for the vexatioun / Of Frenchemen and the Congregatioun / That hes made trowbill in this natioun, / And monye bair bigging [ruined building]' (MQ 8). Popular festive forms are repurposed to convey the ghastliness of war: 'I saw na gysaris all this yeir / But kirkmen clad lyik men of weir' (in Scotland 'gysaris' are holiday mummers and masquers, here nightmarishly metamorphosed into a militarised clergy, MQ5). Political poems mingle with satirical and admonitory poems and love lyrics, such as Alexander Montgomerie's to Margaret, describing how the stars descended 'Vpon hir shoulders, twinkling euerie one', 'lyik diamontis, with cristall perlis mixit', or MQ 49, a love poem addressed by one woman to another, credibly attributed to Marie Maitland (MQ 49).[65] A final sequence of four interlaced 'Spenserian' sonnets entitled 'Visiouns' commend John Maitland, by then Secretary to James VI, and feature the nine muses rejoicing in his release from prison, happier than Ovid in Pontus. These poems bear a fascinating relation, as Sebastiaan Verweij has shown, to earlier versions among the manuscripts of William Fowler, which actively intercede for John's release from prison. '[O]n his back', prophesies Polhymnia, 'sall leane this common wealth' (MQ 94).[66] But this was a hard-won achievement. During the civil war period commemorated in the MQ, all three of Sir Richard's sons were imprisoned by the king's party, the Maitland property of Blyth was attacked by English forces, their home of Lethington forfeited, and both Thomas and William died. 'Ane Consolatore Ballad' to Sir Richard (MQ 46, l.125) observes that he is left, like his ancestor '[b]ot burdalane', the Scots expression for having an only child.

The MF, by contrast, is the messier book on which the Maitlands drew when composing poetry and in which many of Sir Richard's poems are first collected. It is an incalculably valuable resource of fifteenth-century Scots poetry, both canonical (fifty-six of William Dunbar's eighty-three extant poems) and anonymous, from fabliaux such as *The Freiris of Berwick* to poems of popular festivity such as *Peblis to the Play* and *Christis Kirk on the Grene*, whose somersaulting rhythms enact the

---

[65] Evelyn S. Newlyn, 'A Methodology for Reading Against the Culture: Anonymous, Women Poets and the Maitland Quarto Manuscript (c.1586)', in *Women and the Feminine in Medieval and Early Modern Scottish Writing*, eds. Sarah M. Dunnigan, C. Marie Harker and Evelyn S. Newlyn (Palgrave: 2004), 89–103; Jane Farnsworth, 'Voicing Female Desire in "Poem XLIX"', *Studies in English Literature* vol. 36, no. 1 (1996), 57–72.
[66] Verweij, *Literary Culture*, 101–6.

midsummer celebrations they narrate.[67] Within this richly diverse collection are two historical poems in octosyllabic couplets which give a
flavour of an older tradition of Scottish national consciousness. One of
these, an extract from Andrew of Wynton's *Original Chronicle* (c.1420),
recalls an incident in 1391 when the English mock the Scots for being able
to bring no more than 'fyve hundred speiris' to help the French against
John of Gaunt. The duke of Orléans responds defiantly, observing that
while the English are a 'michtie natioun / Excelland in presumptioun'
who suppress with 'segnory' all adjacent lands, yet they have not been
able to conquer 'the few folk of Scotland'.[68] Following Wyntoun a
popular poem known as 'The Ring of the Roy Robert' tells how Henry
IV of England demanded that Robert III of Scotland should come 'in
loundoun for to mak homage / Eftir the richt of brutus king' (10–11).
King Robert responds with an epistle styling himself, through God's
might, as 'King of Scotland and ylis richt / That inebbis in the occeane
see', but refusing the title of king to Henry IV, allowing him only the
style of duke of Lancaster (24–30). The rest of the epistle refutes Henry's
Galfridian claims. The 'barnis of auld brutus' ('the children of Brutus')
have many times 'halelie conqueist bene' ('been wholly conquered') by
the Romans, the Saxons and the Danes, while Scotland, Robert declares,
'euir yit hes bene fre / Sen scota of egipt tuike the see' (57–65).[69]

Here we have, perhaps, a clue to Buchanan's astute decision to make an
entry into his revolutionary resistance theory by way of a therapeutic
purging of the fear of national shame. For these extracts from older Scots
poetry in the Maitland archives reveal the part that shame plays in the
double task of Scottish national imagining as the assertion of collective
identity through resistance to denials of the realm's viability. In the
Wyntoun extract, the English are 'schamit' and 'spak na mair' while
Robert III received 'na ... answer' to his refusal to perform homage to
Henry IV. Buchanan's acute intuition of the extent to which Scottish
national imagining was bound up in the repudiation of humiliating denials
of Scotland's existence *as a realm* – whether slurs of vassalage, taunts of

[67] On Dunbar in the MF, see A. A. MacDonald, 'Sir Richard Maitland and William Dunbar', *William Dunbar*, 134–49, 135; on *Peblis* and *Christis Kirk*, see Lewis, *Sixteenth Century*, 105–6; Christopher Whyte, 'Bakhtin at Christ's Kirk: Carnival and the Scottish Renaissance', *Studies in Scottish Literature* (1993), vol. 28, no.1, 178–203.

[68] Maitland Folio, ed. Craigie, 125–7. See Joanna Martin, 'The Border, England and the English in Some Older Scots Lyric and Occasional Poems', in *The Anglo-Scottish Border and the Shaping of Identity, 1300-1600*, eds. Mark P. Bruce and Katherine H. Terrell (New York, NY: Palgrave Macmillan, 2010), 87–102, 95–6.

[69] Maitland Folio, ed. Craigie, 127–30. See Martin, 'The Border', 95–6.

diminutive forces or barbarity of manners – offered him the opportunity of characterising his resistance theory as a kind of therapy, a cure for such debilitating fears. '*At ego te facile hoc timore nostramque gentem falso crimine liberabo*', he replies to Thomas, 'But I shall easily rid you of this fear and free our nation (*nostrum gentem*) from this false accusation of crime' (*De iure*, 6–9). But Buchanan's cure is predicated on locating the amorphous guilt for the first foul deed of Darnley's murder – which Thomas Maitland said touched the whole nation, since it was unknown who authorised it – in the queen herself. Deposing her would thus become, not a further proof of Scots barbarity, but the expulsion of the shame of the first. Buchanan proposes this argument in the form of a dilemma: if the other nations find atrocity in the murder of a king, they can hardly condemn as further atrocity the punishment of the person responsible: 'For if they [the French] detest the cruelty of the first crime so much, how can they reasonably criticise the severity used in avenging it?', asks Buchanan, 'Or if they are angry at the queen being deposed, they must necessarily approve the earlier deed' (*De iure*, 6–9).

III.   'not subject to forane iurisdictionn'? Disavowals of the *Detectioun*

Buchanan's ingenious transformation of Scotland's shame into the portrait of a tyrant queen cunningly elides the murky uncertainty surrounding the authorship of the first atrocity, the murder of Henry Stewart, Lord Darnley. And in so doing, it implies the predication of the arguments of *De iure* on its more obviously shame-exposing companion text, the *Maria Scotorum Regina … tragica plane Historia*, more commonly known as the *Detectio*.[70] Jenny Wormald's much-cited characterisation of Buchanan's *Detectio* as 'copy for the *Sun* in the style of the *Times*' gets at the text's discomfiting prurience, but misses its skilful adaptation of classical forensic rhetoric, with its circumstances of time, place, motive and opportunity, to produce a narrative full of vivid (in Latin, *evidens*) reality-effects.[71] McElroy's sharp and compelling reading identifies the play of various genres in the text – tragedy, melodrama, low comedy – drawn together by the figure of a queen

---

[70] See Phillips, *Images*, 62 and notes, 253. I will cite Buchanan's Latin text by the title of *Detectio*, but from John Day's 1571 edition, STC 3978, and the 'Scots' text by the title of *Detectioun*, also printed by John Day, 1571, STC 3981.

[71] Jenny Wormald, *Mary Queen of Scots* (London, 1988), 14. On vividness as *evidentia* see note 22, above. Cf. Buchanan, *Detectioun*, 'The maner and circumstances of the dede', sig. B3r; 'the rest that follow are euident argumentes' (*manifesta sunt argumenta*), sig. C3r.

whose energetic, bustling deceitfulness is reminiscent of the theatrical tyrant or Vice. Contradictions between 'Mary's duplicity and her laughably obvious schemes' are, as McElroy astutely notes, resolved by the essential role Buchanan gives to the *vulgus* or the 'commoun pepill' who 'discover her tyranny and become the benchmark for her condemnation'.[72] Even more vivid and persuasive than its fiction of Scotland's guilty queen then, is the *Detectio*'s fiction of a Scottish nation, from lowest to highest, united in being undeceived and unintimidated by corrupt majesty. As the queen tries to stir up mutual suspicions among her nobles ('if at any time she espied the suspicions of the one against the other to languish, by and by ... she whetted tham on againe'), the common people detect, in her neglect of Darnley, her true motives. '[T]he pepils suspicioun' increases as they witness 'the unchast companying of the Quene with Bothwell' (C2 r-v) until 'quhen euery man was out of dout, quho did the murder ... the mair they kept their own names vndisclosit, so much the peoples grudge restraynit, brake out mair openly' (*quanto magis ipsi sua nomina supprimere conabantur, tanto magis vulgi dolor inhibitus erumpebat*).[73]

Buchanan's *Detectio* began life a little later than *De iure*, with Elizabeth's demand that Moray come to York prepared 'to clear the ground of the cause that made the subjects of Scotland rase wars against their monarch'.[74] Moray's defence against charges of treason, in other words, depended on setting out proof before the English commissioners that the Scottish queen had murdered her husband. Within days of Mary's arrival in England in May 1568 Cecil wrote one of his many memoranda on the management of the situation, resurrecting previously used arguments from Galfridian history on the right of English monarchs, as overlords of Scotland, to 'hear and decide any controversy for the crown of Scotland'.[75] From the perspective of Moray and his followers, who had taken the initiative in contacting the English government, the imperative to prove a watertight case against Mary was now an urgent matter of political survival.[76] Moray acted immediately, instructing Buchanan to prepare a case against Mary. The result was, ultimately, the *Detectio*, later to be translated by Thomas Wilson into a pseudo-Scots easily legible to English readers yet bearing the signs of Scottish authenticity; Wilson also added an '*Actio*', or speech for

[72] McElroy, *Executing Mary*, 130.
[73] Buchanan, *Detectioun*, sig. A3r, sig. C2r, E1v; *Detectio*, pp. 2, 12, 22.
[74] Herries, *Historical Memoirs*, 106.
[75] 'Thynges to be considered upon the Scottish Quene coming into England', *CSP Scot, II*, item 679, pp. 418–19, from MS Cotton Caligula C1, fol. 97.
[76] Donaldson, *First Trial*, 82.

the prosecution, spelling out the proofs of Buchanan's forensic *Narratio*.[77] Distributed in Scots, French and Latin versions, Buchanan's narrative of Mary's guilt was of inestimable value to Cecil and the English government in the years to come, deterring the French from ever coming to the aid of the queen's party in Scotland. In a memo of July 1571 considering the arguments for and against the likelihood of the king of France offering support for Mary, Cecil observes that while princes are bound to aid other princes 'as long as their lawful government continues', they are not bound to help those found guilty of 'tyrannies'. The king's party in Scotland could 'perchance' reveal matter against Mary for similar offences to those for which Brunhilde the Frankish queen (c.543–613) was torn apart by horses. 'And here it were not amiss,' Cecil notes, 'to have divers of Buchanan's little Latin books to present, if need were, to the King of France, and likewise to some noblemen of his Council. That it may be well said there is no great injury done to the Queen of Scotland, as is presupposed, in that the succession is given to her son.'[78]

The murder of Lord Darnley at Kirk o'Field on 9 February 1567 naturally caused international shock and scandal, but the queen was not immediately implicated. On the contrary, it was assumed that most of the Scottish nobility, who were known to hate Darnley, were involved. In March, the Venetian ambassador to France wrote that it was widely suspected that the principal persons of the kingdom were implicated in the murder, foremost among them the earl of Moray.[79] 'It was said that mony greit men wes consentaris to this tressounable deid', commented likewise the *Diurnall of Occurents*.[80] William Drury, governor of Berwick, reported to William Cecil in June, that there were, according to Bothwell, 'earls, barons, bishops, gentlemen, and burgesses acquainted with the death of the King'.[81] In October, Drury informed Cecil that bonds testifying to widespread involvement in the murder had been strategically destroyed, while evidence of the queen's knowledge had been preserved for accusation: '[t]he writings which comprehended the names and consents of the chief for the murdering of the King is turned into ashes … and the same which concerns her part kept to be shown'.[82] The earls of Argyll and Huntly later testified to discussions with Mary involving Moray, William

---

[77] Phillips, *Images*, 62.
[78] *CSP Scot*, IV, item 405, p. 367: 'Reasons to move the King of France to aide the cause of the Quene of Scotland, and with the answeres to the same'. Cotton Caligula C. III., fol. 412.
[79] *CSP Venice*, item 384, p. 389. [80] *Diurnall*, 106.
[81] Drury to Cecil, 27 June 1567, SP 59/13, fol. 190.
[82] Drury to Cecil, 28 Oct 1567, SP 59/14, fol. 169.

Maitland, Morton and Bothwell, as well as themselves about how she might divorce or otherwise be quit of Darnley.[83] In a detailed survey of the evidence, Gordon Donaldson concluded that 'It is beyond doubt that there was a conspiracy against Darnley to which Earls of Moray, Argyll, Huntly, Bothwell, Secretary Lethington, Sir James Balfour of Pittendreich were parties.'[84]

At issue here is not the question of Mary's complicity in the murder of her husband, but the convergence of political interests that made it essential that the queen be isolated among many assumed to be complicit. This convergence of interests – the interests of the English Crown and of the king's party, led by Moray – required not only that Mary be proven the sole agent of this political murder, but that her motives not be construed as policy or governance. She must be shown to have been motivated solely by irrational lust. Stephen Alford does not mean to be funny when he reveals why the question of the queen of Scotland's guilt merits the attention of serious English historians such as himself. 'Mary's part in the murder of Darnley has traditionally been the territory of antiquarians, amateur historians, and romantic biographers,' he says,

> but it is actually a good deal more important than it seems. England wanted a settlement based on a Moray regency, strict conciliar and parliamentary supervision and imperial control. But the regime needed solid evidence.[85]

In other words, Mary's putative part in the murder of Darnley was important because proof of it would justify settling Scotland under a Moray regency subject to English imperial control.

In the months that followed Darnley's murder there had already begun a concerted and well-orchestrated propaganda campaign, in which Buchanan's resistance theory plays a part, to establish the story of Mary as a lustful adulteress who, with her paramour Bothwell, conspired to bring about the young king's death. Tricia McElroy's remarkable and ground-breaking work on this campaign reveals the sensational success with which it exploited the literary and material potential of the broadside ballad. McElroy describes how the Confederate Lords, reliant on the English government as a covert ally,

> intuited that while Elizabeth might be interested to learn of Mary's declin-
> ing relationship with her subjects, she would not tolerate political

---

[83] Robert Keith, *History of the Affairs of Church and State in Scotland* 3 vols. (Edinburgh: Spottiswood, 1845), III.290–4; CSP Scot, II, 947.
[84] Donaldson, *First Trial*, 33.   [85] Alford, *Elizabethan Polity*, 173.

destabilization based purely on theories of resistance. Rather than support resistance to instituted authority ... the Scottish Lords fabricated the semblance of popular discontent with Mary's regime.[86]

Consequently, all through the spring and summer of 1567, broadside poems, handbills and proclamations began to appear on the market crosses and kirk doors of Scottish burghs denouncing Mary as 'an adulterous, murderous Jezebel who deserves to lose her crown'.[87] Part of the brilliance of the strategy was its ventriloquising effect: as people read the ballads, they seemed to be hearing the voices of the 'rude pepill' themselves. In these ballads, genres and motifs from fifteenth-century Scottish poetry – *chanson d'aventure*, allegory, last will and testament – shape political commentary on contemporary events in ways familiar to those versed in Scottish vernacular culture. Poetic personae seem to come alive as the voices of those wronged. A poet hears 'ane bony boy' singing 'oche and wallaway' at the death of a king, as if speaking the plight of the fatherless James. Or the ballads speak with the voices of ordinary folk, such as the Edinburgh kale market wife, Maddie. The figure of Maddie, a recurrent persona, derives from a populist medieval tradition of social protest, transforming it into a vivid reality-effect – the illusion of ordinary women speaking their minds about the queen in the Edinburgh of 1567.[88] Nor were the ballads at odds with the kind of resistance theory Buchanan was articulating in *De iure*. On the contrary, the ballad 'ane Declaratioun of the Lordis iust quarrell' sets out just such a theory, in the form of a dialogue between 'Philandrius' and 'Erideilus', setting it in the highly coloured and emotive context of the 'huire' (whore) 'Quene', whose 'awin wryting' shamefully testifies how she consented to be ravished by Bothwell, and plotted against her husband.[89] By popularising Buchanan's arguments and examples, and couching them in the 'bruit abhominable' of Mary's adultery and husband-murder, this broadside fluttering from the market crosses and tollbooths of Scottish burghs becomes, as McElroy writes, 'a material manifestation' of popular resistance theory in action.[90] Replicating the poet, who tells how he overhears '[t]wa learnit men in priuie' talking of the Queen, these burgh folk encountering the ballads were also overhearing, discussing and judging the question of tyranny and the tyrant's fate.[91]

[86] McElroy, *Executing Mary*, 19.   [87] McElroy, 'Scottis Natioun', 319.
[88] McElroy, 'Scottis Natioun', 332.
[89] *Satirical Poems of the Time of the Reformation*, ed. James Cranstoun, 2 vols. (Edinburgh, Blackwood, 1891–3), I.59, lines 51-5.
[90] McElroy, 'Scottis Natioun', 322.   [91] *Satirical Poems*, I.57, line 3.

The earl of Moray, having strategically absented himself from Edinburgh the night before the murder and then left, the following day, to 'partis beyond sea', was clearly involved, *in absentia*, in this defamation campaign.[92] Robert Sempill, author of most of the ballads that survive, was in Moray's pay. In January 1568, a Treasury payment is recorded for 'a play made by Robert Semple, and played before the Lord Regent and divers uthers of the nobilitie' in January 1568. The printer, Robert Lekpreuik, rewarded by Moray with the position of King's Printer, supported the cause until the end of the war in 1573.[93] Nor were Sempill's and Lekpreuik's ballads meant for Scottish consumption alone. Indeed, they survive uniquely in English archives. Thanks to the diligence of Sir William Drury in Berwick, they made their way swiftly and regularly to Cecil's desk in London for endorsement and filing. And Drury did more than send ballads and scurrilous pictures; he relayed gossip and ghoulish tales of Mary's poisoning her infant son, or mysterious Edinburgh nightwalkers crying for vengeance.[94] In May 1567, Drury describes 'an interlude of boys at Stirling' enacting 'the manner of the King's death and the arraignment of the Earl [Bothwell]'. Such was the intensity of feeling, Drury reports, that the consequences were nearly fatal: the boy playing Bothwell 'was in sport so long hanged that hardly in a long time could life be recovered'.[95]

Mary's imprudent conduct after her husband's murder – hastily marrying the Earl of Bothwell, failing to pursue her husband's murderers – unsurprisingly persuaded many of the Scottish lords to act against her in the spring of 1567. Their initial stated objective was to punish the murderers of Darnley, protect the infant prince and liberate the queen from Bothwell so that she could rule by the advice of her nobles, as before.[96] This rhetoric of deliverance, however, was belied by Mary's immediate imprisonment, after Carberry, on the island of Lochleven, the laird of which was Moray's half-brother.[97] Thereafter, the forcible obtaining of the queen's signature on instruments of deposition followed by the infant James's coronation seems to have taken some of her opponents by surprise. 'Within a week the confederacy began to crumble.'[98] For the powerful earl

[92] *Diurnall*, 107; CSP *Scot*, II, item 484, p. 318.
[93] McElroy, 'Scottis Natioun', 324–5; Anna Jean Mill, *Medieval Plays in Scotland* (Edinburgh, Blackwood, 1927), 191 n.3.
[94] Drury to Cecil, 15 April 1567, SP 59/13, fol. 13.
[95] Drury to Cecil, 14 May 1567, SP 59/13, fol. 88
[96] Loughlin, 'Career', 256; Webb, '"Gude Regent"?', 18–20.   [97] Webb, '"Gude Regent"?', 21.
[98] Loughlin, 'Career', 256.

of Argyll, deposition was a step too far; he defected from the Confederate Lords to support the queen. By the time of James's coronation, only about half the original Confederate Lords were present.[99]

The deposition of a queen and the crowning of her son was a very drastic step. Recanting his part in it, William Maitland likened decisions made after Carberry to being in a boat crossing the Firth of Forth which caught fire: 'ye would loupe in the sea, to flie the fyre; and finding your selfe able to drowne, ye wald preis againe to the boit'.[100] These were, in other words, desperate, unprecedented improvisations of legitimacy in a revolutionary situation. But when Mary crossed into England and appealed to Elizabeth, further legitimising strategies were required. The fiction of Mary's voluntary abdication did not persuade the English queen or the English commissioners. Their scepticism, however, forced the king's party to be complicit in the serious humiliation of their nation by acknowledging the sovereignty of English jurisdiction. Nothing else, however, could guarantee Moray's safety. Mary's commissioners at York insisted that 'they could not acknowledge Queen Elizabeth a judge over them nor the actions of Scotland'.[101] But Moray and the king's party knew that Cecil's interests and their own would converge if Mary could be proved guilty of tyrannical murder and their deposition of her legitimate.

Buchanan's *Detectioun* meets this question of dishonour to the Scottish nation – the shame of a sovereign nation's voluntarily subjecting itself to the jurisdiction of another – head on. He begins his text with a subordinate clause which disarms the reader immediately by acknowledging that it is novel, contrary to custom and, indeed, an act of insolence, for a foreign jurisdiction to require accountability from a people who are sovereign, free and *sui juris*.[102] In its Latin form, Buchanan's text is particularly pointed, for his expression, '*sui … iuris*' refers to the Roman law of persons, as expressed in Justinian's *Digest*, 1.6, attributed to Gaius's *Institutes*, which separates people into 'those who are *sui iuris*' or who exercise jurisdiction over themselves and 'those who are *alieni iuris*', 'within the jurisdiction of others [*aliens*]'. This division maps on to Gaius's primary division of persons into free and unfree, for the '*alieni iuris*' include slaves and children, who are under the *potestas* of the master or father.[103] Buchanan's opening acknowledgement of the

---

[99] Webb, '"Gude Regent"?', 27.   [100] Bannatyne, *Memorials*, 127.
[101] Herries, *Historical Memoirs*, 109–10.
[102] Buchanan, *Detectio*, sig. Aijr.
[103] *The Digest of Justinian*, trans. Alan Watson, eds. Theodor Mommsen and Paul Krueger, 4 vols. (Philadelphia, PA: University of Pennsylvania Press, 1985), I.17–18. See also Keechang Kim, *Aliens in*

present situation's irksomeness (*molestia*) in placing a people who are *sui iuris* under a foreign jurisdiction is tantamount to defining the Scottish people as an unfree people. The resonances, for Scottish readers, of Edward I's claim to have jurisdiction over the Scottish succession by virtue of overlordship must have been unmistakeable. But the sentence goes on, using the figure of *incrementum*, to diminish the shame of being subject to foreign jurisdiction by comparing it with a worse shame of being 'accompted the most wicked persons (*sceleratissimi*) that lyue'.[104] Within this move, Buchanan's argument performs a twist whereby the very worst shame of all, the necessity of disclosing faults which common decency would have kept hidden, becomes the only means by which the supposedly greater stigma of being accounted *sceleratissimi* can be overcome. In the process of this twist, the shame of disclosing faults so as not to seem *sceleratissimi* simultaneously overcomes what would otherwise seem the greatest national shame possible, that of being counted an unfree nation. By this astonishing means, Buchanan manages to dismiss as a mere bagatelle the vital constitutional and nation-defining principle at stake in yielding to a foreign monarch's jurisdiction over one's own sovereign in view of the more pressing need to adjudge one's own sovereign guilty and so cleanse the whole nation of her crime. The whole sentence in Thomas Wilson's translation reads:

> Whairas of thynges iudicially determinit within any dominioun, to haif accompte demandit by strangeris, is to sic as be not subiect to forane iurisdictionn [*sui ... iuris*], baith strange, and also for the strangenesse displeasant, to vs aboue all other it ought to be most greuous, qhua are driuen to this streight of necessitie, that quhase fautes we desire to couer, thair liues we are enforced to accuse, unlesse we will our selues be accompted the most wicked persons that lyue.[105]

Whether or not anyone was fooled by this deft sophistry, its strategy was more successful than could have been anticipated. Elizabeth, despite her frequent audiences with the earl of Moray, refused ever to give Mary a personal audience, saying that she was 'a shamed of her'.[106] In January 1572,

Medieval Law: The Origins of Modern Citizenship (Cambridge: Cambridge University Press, 2000), 2–9.

[104] Buchanan, *Detectioun*, sig. A2r. For *incrementum*, see Quintilian, *Inst.*, 8.4.

[105] Buchanan, *Detectioun*, sig. A2r.

[106] Alford, *Elizabethan Polity*, 120. Donaldson, *First Trial*, discusses at length the damage done by Elizabeth's refusal to give audience to Mary.

Sir Thomas Smith, in France negotiating Queen Elizabeth's proposed marriage with the duke of Anjou, wrote to Cecil that with respect to Scottish matters, he had 'distributed certain books of Buchanan in Latin which have done no hurt, but made the matter so plain that they be ashamed to defend her that fain would'.[107] Buchanan had successfully displaced his nation's fear of accruing shame for deposing their monarch and for submitting to a foreign jurisdiction, on to the figure of a fiend-like queen of whom it was hard not to feel ashamed. The precision of the displacement is caught by the repetition of the word '*molestia*' (irksomeness, chagrin) which, like a catchword, links the end of *De iure* to the beginning of the *Detectio*. At the very end of *De iure*, Buchanan asks if Thomas Maitland is satisfied by these arguments justifying the right of the Scottish people to overthrow tyrants. He is fully satisfied, Maitland replies, and if he can satisfy others, he will be relieved of *molestia maxima*, extremely troubled feelings (*De iure*, 162–3). At the outset of the *Detectio*, the speaker acknowledges that it is irksome (*molestum est*) for a free people to submit themselves to the jurisdiction of another. One kind of *molestia* drives out another: proving that the right Scots have to rid themselves of tyrants depends on proving the monarch's tyranny, which means (in this case) proving the nation to be unfree.

IV. Jurisdiction and the Scottish People

Part of my objective in juxtaposing these very different Scottish literary responses to the Marian crisis – Buchanan's *De iure* and *Dectio* and occasional poems in the Maitlands' MF and MQ – has been to draw attention to the former's conscious rhetorical deflections of national dishonour while foregrounding the latter's precise political and national engagements, which have been often occluded by literary criticism. It might be argued that the Maitlands' manuscript books offer a patrician view of Scotland in crisis. The MQ is, after all, readable as a laird's family's celebration of its own political survival through the years of Marian crisis. Marie Maitland married Sir Alexander Lauder of Hatton in 1586 and her son, George Lauder (1622–77) was a royalist soldier and poet. John Maitland became lord chancellor of Scotland. The family would prosper. Yet, as we will see, it might also be said that Buchanan's determination to make the *vulgus* or common people of Scotland play their assigned role as detectors and witnesses of tyranny produces a vision of Scotland less

---

[107] *CSP Foreign*, X, item 23, p.13.

attuned to the material realities of what constitutes the 'common weal' or *res publica* than that produced by the laird of Lethington.

Joanna Martin's excellent new edition of the MQ makes it easy for readers to reconstruct the political and military contexts which occasioned certain poems. Martin acknowledges a debt, shared by many scholars of Scottish literature, to the foundational scholarship of A. A. MacDonald. She diverges, however, from MacDonald's view of the MQ as nostalgic and commemorative. She proposes it might be read as a *speculum principis* for the young James VI and his counsellors: political advice for a new monarchy. The MQ was written at the beginning of James's personal reign, 'the dawn of a new period in Scottish cultural and political life', and several later poems address the young monarch and new regime. Martin's protestation that the book is therefore 'not *just* a nostalgic anthology' oddly eclipses the record of familial and national devastation that her own excellent commentary makes amply legible.[108] Not a *nostalgic* anthology, certainly. Rather, a harrowing account of the family's and nation's precarity during the wars of 1567–73. Just as William Maitland warned the English in 1570 that continued war would leave James 'no kingdom at all apt for rewll bot in place thereof a confused chaos and contrey devyded in two or three hundred kyngdoms', so his father in poem after poem of the MQ, fears that '[t]his haill land will destroyit be' if the wars continue (MQ 19).[109] The currency of a critical reading of the MQ as 'nostalgic' is a symptom of the distorting effect that neglect of England's part in the Scottish wars of 1567–73 has on Scottish literary criticism.

A. A. MacDonald has done much to encourage appreciation of Sir Richard Maitland's poetry, but he seems unaware of England's role in sixteenth-century Scottish affairs, ascribing Sir Richard's lamentation for Scotland's misery to the problems caused by the Protestant Reformation. MacDonald hence feels the need to denounce Sir Richard's 'ugly national prejudice' against the English. 'Maitland,' he writes, 'conjures up a sense of atavistic anti-English nationalism.' His evidence for this is MQ 19: 'England is glaid quhen it is tauld / Of Scottis the diuisioun'. Perhaps, hazards MacDonald, 'Maitland believed that an appeal to this rather ugly national prejudice would mitigate the acerbity of the contemporary religious factionalism, which he probably saw as by far the greater evil.'[110] But if Richard Maitland here exhibits 'ugly national prejudice' then Scottish national imagining simply becomes impossible. In fact, in this poem (MQ 19), it is not 'religious factionalism' but the Marian civil

[108] Martin, 'Maitland Quarto and Literary Culture', 67.   [109] Loughlin, 'Career', 329.
[110] MacDonald, 'Maitland and Dunbar', 147.

wars which are at issue, and the poet is equally unsparing of the reliance of the queen's party 'on France for their supplie'. He wishes the impossible, that 'all this hail countrie / Of France and England bayth wer frie' (MQ 19, ll.79–80). The poet's ironic even-handedness is also evident in MQ 25, where he mocks both parties, king's and queen's, for their dependence on England and France respectively. 'For gif that ye dependis on the King', he writes,

> For your support the Englismen inbring,
> At lenth thairof ye sall mak littill ruse.
> Think on the wordis King Edward spak to Bruse,
> 'Haue we not ellis to doe,
> But win ane rowme yow to?'   (MQ 25, ll.42–6)

Here he recalls Hector Boece's report of the naïve rebuke of Robert Bruce, grandfather of Scotland's famous king of that name, to Edward I for breaking a promise to make him king of Scotland in return for his support. As if England, with its own geopolitical interests, had nothing else to do but help the obtuse, ambitious members of the Scottish nobility in their rivalries.[111] As for the French, he warns the queen's party, 'Remember how thay pleit yow befoir. / Ye war richt red [rightly advised] thay sould yow not restoir / To your auld libertie' (MQ 25, ll.63–4).

Sir Richard's lightness of tone here, his mockery of both sides' vulnerability to being 'pleit' or played by the stronger nations with more politic governments, is one way of lyricising the sufferings inflicted on all Scots as a result of wars. After Moray's assassination, Elizabeth took the decision to launch an invasion of Scotland under the command of the earl of Sussex and Lord Hunsdon. Justified as the seeking out and prosecuting of Her Majesty's English rebels – refugees in Scotland from the failed Northern Rising – the campaign's scarcely hidden real purpose was to destroy Marian resistance and establish the earl of Lennox as Moray's successor in the regency. 'Any talk about arresting fugitive rebels was merely a guise to cloak the English design to maintain their dominance in Scotland,' wrote Pollit.[112] Ninety castles, towers and dwelling houses and three hundred towns and villages were destroyed in this brutal campaign.[113] William Maitland, Sir Richard's son, wrote scathingly to Sussex to congratulate the English on having 'reasonably well acquitted themselves of the duty of old enemies' having 'burnt and spoiled as much ground in Scotland as any army of England did

---

[111] Bellenden, *Chronicles*, II.365–7.   [112] Pollitt, 'Northern Rebellion', 10.
[113] Loughlin, 'Career', 293.

in one year these hundred years'. But rather than speaking thus about *enemies* after 'the rude fashion of Scottish people', William continued facetiously, he was content to speak English officialese and praise Sussex for not having '"been idle for two months in the pursuit of Her Majesty's rebels"'.[114] The Maitlands were just one family that suffered severe losses during Sussex's campaign. Sir Richard Maitland's poem, 'Blind man, be blythe' (MQ14), responds to the harrying and despoiling of Blyth, in Lauderdale, by English forces. Sir Richard, blind since 1561, was by this time seventy-four years old. He urges himself punningly to be blithe in the loss of Blyth, first because the land, which enemies couldn't take, may replenish itself:

> Thocht thay haue spuilyit Blyith of gude and geir,
> Yit haue they left lyand still the land …
> Therfoir, be blyith! The tyme may be at hand
> Quhen Blyith salbe yit, with Goddis grace
> Als weill pleneist ('replenished') as euer thay it fand
>
> (MQ 14, ll.9–15)

He then tries out blitheness as political prudence: don't let other perceive your 'sussie' (*souci* – concern) for your losses. Finally, blitheness is God's wisdom: 'Be thou not blyithe, quhat vaillit land or rent?' (l.27). The poem wittily ends by looking beyond all endings, substituting for the lost Blyth God's 'blyithness and ioy that is endless' (l.32). In the MF, however, the conclusion 'ffinis' after 'endless' is followed by a note, copied in the same hand as the poem, which turns the ascription of authorship 'Quod Sir Richard Maitland' into an inventory of all the material blitheness that ended:

> Quod Sir Richard Maitland of Lethington knycht, quhane his landis of the baronrie of Blyth in Lawderdaill was heriet [ravaged] be Rollent Foster, Inglisman, kapitane of Wark, with his cumpanye to the number of thre hunder men; quha spulyeit [despoiled] fra the said Richard, and fra his eldest sone, their serwandis, and tennentis furthe of the said baronie, fowr thowsand scheip, younger and elder, twa hundrithe nowlt [neat or cattle], threttie horsis and meiris, and insycht [furnishings] furthe of his howsis of Blythe, wourthe ane hundrithe pund, and the hail tennentis insycht of the haill baronrie that was tursabill [moveable]. This spulye [spoil] was committit the Xvj day of Maij, the yeir of M D.L XX yeiris. And the said Sir Richart was thre scoir and xiij yeiris of age, and growin blind in tyme of piece, quhane nane of that cuntra lippint for [expected, looked for] sic thing.[115]

Blyth was not the only casualty of the English and king's party vengeance against the Marian Maitlands. In 1571, a parliament of the king's party

---

[114] *CSP Foreign*, item 1016, p. 272.   [115] *Maitland Quarto*, ed. Martin, 315.

confiscated Lethington House. MQ 20 takes a similarly stoic and even humorous approach to the disaster. The poem's refrain, 'Thocht I be auld' carries its own pathos while shifting into ironic and playful reflections on age and youth, setting the real pain of loss (which Sir Richard expressed in a bitter but futile complaint to Queen Elizabeth in 1574) on one side.[116] Sebastiaan Verweij rightly queries the scholarly categorisation of the Maitland manuscripts as 'household books' in this context. 'Exactly what household means is insufficiently explored' he writes, when the house itself has been confiscated and the family relentlessly persecuted.[117]

In the poems of the MQ, it is the household itself, the domestic space, its inhabitants and its 'tursabill' (moveable) furnishings that are marked by political violence. As a former commissioner for the borders under Mary of Guise and a jurist and author of a book of *Practiques* or reports on legal cases, Sir Richard Maitland had spent much of his life immersed in arguing and adjudicating legal disputes involving lands, rents and goods.[118] His understanding of jurisdiction was thus administrative and practical, a poetics of the everyday, humdrum next to Buchanan's brilliant rhetorical manoeuvres. In MQ 33, a poem on the English invasion and spoiling of Edinburgh, there is, for all the unsparing attention to atrocity, a characteristic emphasis on jurisdiction and proper procedure. The victims would have 'obeyit the auctoritie' of the regent, Sir Richard quietly notes, had this man entrusted with authority (the earl of Lennox) simply sent for them by 'ane missive bill':

> I trowe wes neuer harde nor sein
> In Scotland greater miserie ...
> Craftismen and commounis ar put doun
> Be thift, reif and continuall weir [war]
> Neir herreit [ravaged] is our principall toun [Edinburgh] ...
> Sum hes thair place brint [burnt] to ane gleid [ember],
> Thair guddis spuilyit [plundered] halallie;
> Thair servands slaine, sum brint to deid,
> Thair selfis taine vncourteouslie,
> And hauldin in captiuitie,
> Quha wald haue, for ane missiue bill,
> Obeyit the auctoritie,
> And cummit at my lord Regentis will   (MQ 30, lines 4–48)

[116] *CSP Scot*, V, item 45, 'Sir Richard Maitland to Elizabeth', 24 Aug 1574, pp. 46–7.
[117] Verweij, *Literary Culture*, 196.
[118] See Verweij, *Literary Culture*, 196–7; *The Practiques of Sir Richard Maitland of Lethington, 1550-1577*, ed. Robert Sutherland (Edinburgh: Scottish Record Society, 2007).

Throughout Sir Richard's poems in the MQ we find an imaginative preoccupation with these everyday jurisdictional imaginings – a sense of the ease with which ordinary people's lands and goods are subject to 'wrang intromissioun' (illegal occupation) and violent theft. But the poet also takes pleasure in the propriety and use of ordinary possessions. The word for 'furniture' in Scots can be 'insycht' (apparently from 'insight', meaning furnishings of all kinds) or 'geir' or 'plenishing'.[119] So, in the note on Blyth the 'hail tennentis insycht … that was tursabill' (all the tenants' moveable furnishings) were taken from the baronry as well as from the house, while the poem expressed hopes that it would one day be '[a]ls weill pleneist as euer'. In 'Virgil his village Mantua', a poem on Lethington, the poet considers the work to 'plenische and fulfill' the house with 'beddis soft and tapeis fair' to be of as great 'spreit' as that of building it (MQ 68 231–2). In a poem rejoicing in the marriage of Mary Queen of Scots to the dauphin of France, Sir Richard exhorts the burgh towns to celebrate with bonfires, farces and plays, to let the market cross run wine and hang out tapestries 'as wes the custome in our elderis dayis'. 'And euerilk man', he continues, 'put on his nutptiall goun',

> Let it be sene into this borrowstoun
> That in your cofferis hes lyne this mony yeir   (MQ 6, ll.40–2)

Each man's nuptial gown, long lying in its coffer, emerges into the streets triumphantly acknowledging the Queen's wedding feast. But at the same time, in other poems, these coffers and 'kists' or chests, 'usually carved, with ornamental locks and bands' are not able to keep goods safe.[120] Border raiders are countenanced by the nobility. Civil wars enable them to 'fill thair handis / With other mennis landis / Geir, vittall and stoir' (MQ 25, ll.98–100). In an early poem on the border thieves of Liddesdale, we learn that '[t]hay leif not spindill, spone nor speit, / Bed, bolster, blanket, sark nor sheit' (MQ 3, ll.49–50). The complex internal rhymes of MQ 18 render the effects of 'this cruel ciuill weir', border thieves emboldened to ride from Liddesdale through Lothian all the way to Fife:

> Alace, this is ane miserable life
> Of sturt and stryfe, that na man can wit how
> Keep ox or kow, the theiffis ar so ryfe,
> Yea, evin to Fyfe, they ryid the countrie throw   (MQ, ll.6–9)

[119] DOST: https://dsl.ac.uk/entry/dost/insicht_n_1 .
[120] Margaret Sanderson, A Kindly Place? Living in Sixteenth-Century Scotland (East Linton: Tuckwell, 2002), 93.

Fig. 1.1 Queen Elizabeth I ('The Ditchley portrait') by Marcus Gheeraerts the
Younger. © National Portrait Gallery, London.

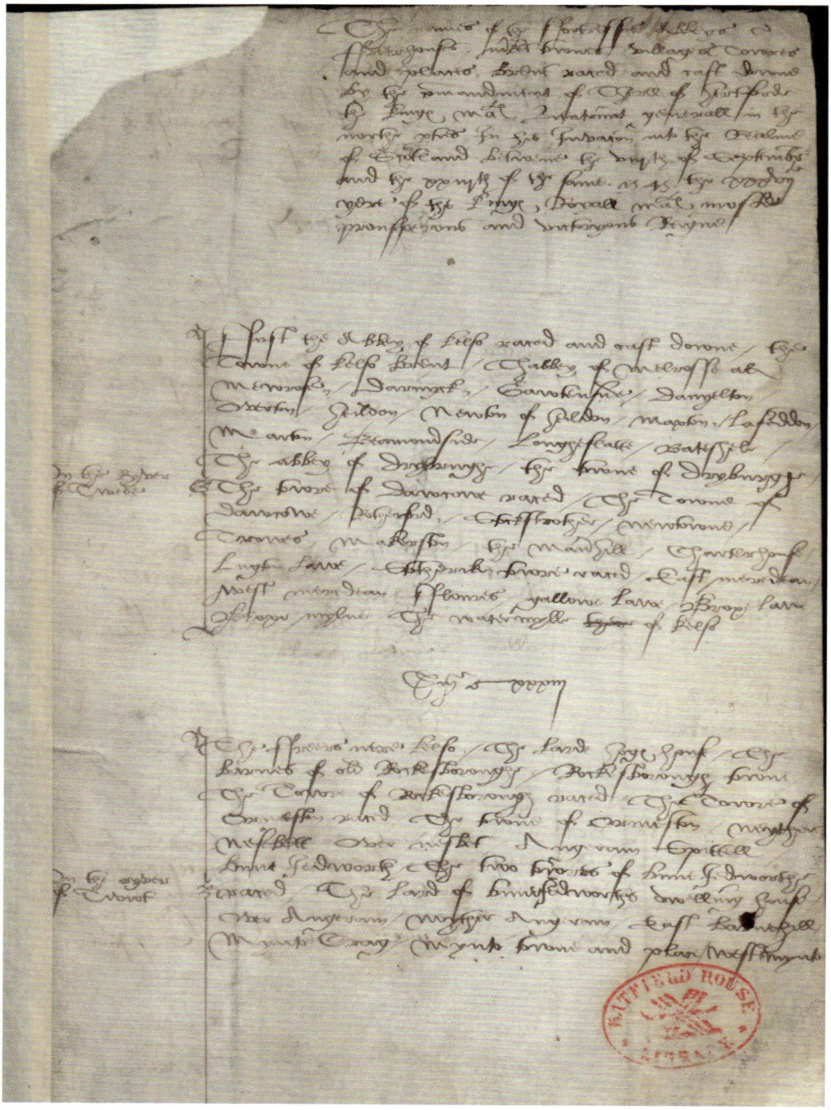

Fig. 1.2 'The Invasion of Scotland, September 23, 1545', The Cecil Papers, vol.137. fol. 116. Reproduced with permission of the Marquess of Salisbury, Hatfield House.

Fig. 2.1 Allegorical Portrait of Sir John Luttrell, Eworth, Hans, c.1520–after 1578. Reproduced with permission of the Courtauld Institute.

Fig. 3.1 Michael Drayton, *Poly-Olbion* (1613). The Bodleian Libraries, University of
Oxford, J-J Drayton d.35, frontispiece.

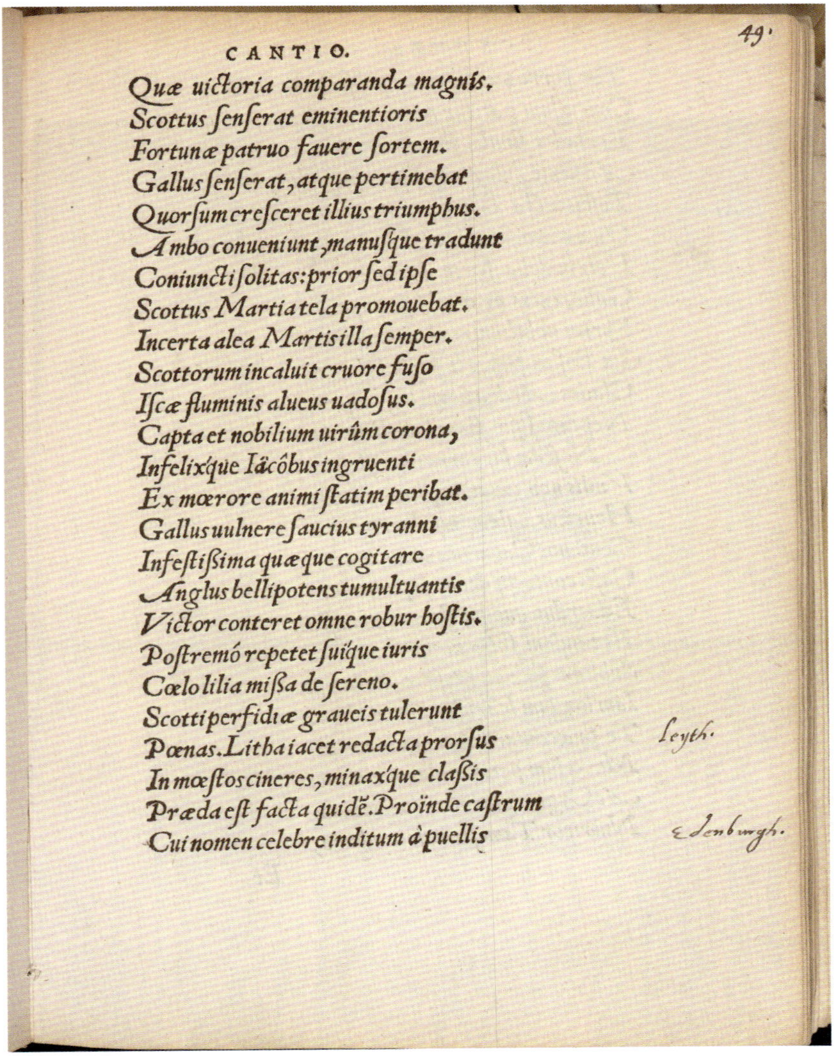

Quæ uictoria comparanda magnis,
Scottus senserat eminentioris
Fortunæ patruo fauere sortem.
Gallus senserat, atque pertimebat
Quorsum cresceret illius triumphus.
Ambo conueniunt, manusque tradunt
Coniuncti solitas: prior sed ipse
Scottus Martia tela promouebat.
Incerta alea Martis illa semper.
Scottorum incaluit cruore fuso
Iscæ fluminis alueus uadosus.
Capta et nobilium uirûm corona,
Infelixque Iácôbus ingruenti
Ex mœrore animi statim peribat.
Gallus uulnere saucius tyranni
Infestißima quæque cogitare
Anglus bellipotens tumultuantis
Victor conteret omne robur hostis.
Postremó repetet suíque iuris
Cœlo lilia mißa de sereno.
Scotti perfidiæ graueis tulerunt
Pœnas. Litha iacet redacta prorsus
In mœstos cineres, minaxque claßis
Præda est facta quidë. Proinde castrum
Cui nomen celebre inditum à puellis

Leyth.

Edenburgh.

Fig. 3.2 William Lambarde's annotations to John Leland, *Cygnea Cantio*, 1545. British Library, C.95.c.15, sig. E2 r. Reproduced with permission of the British Library.

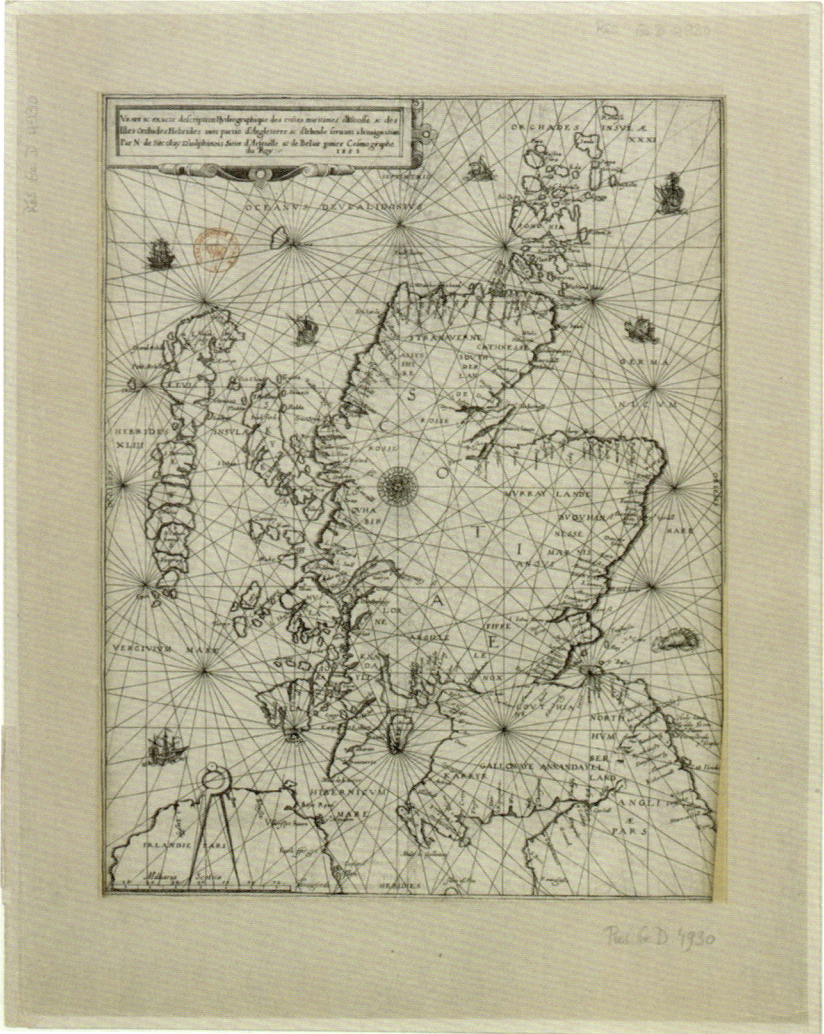

Fig. 3.5 Nicolas de Nicolay, *Vray et exacte description hydrographique des costes maritimes d'Escosse et des Iles Orchades, Hébrides, avec partie d'Angleterre.* Paris, G. Beys, 1583. Bibliotheque Nationale Français, ark:/12148/cb31016282 w.

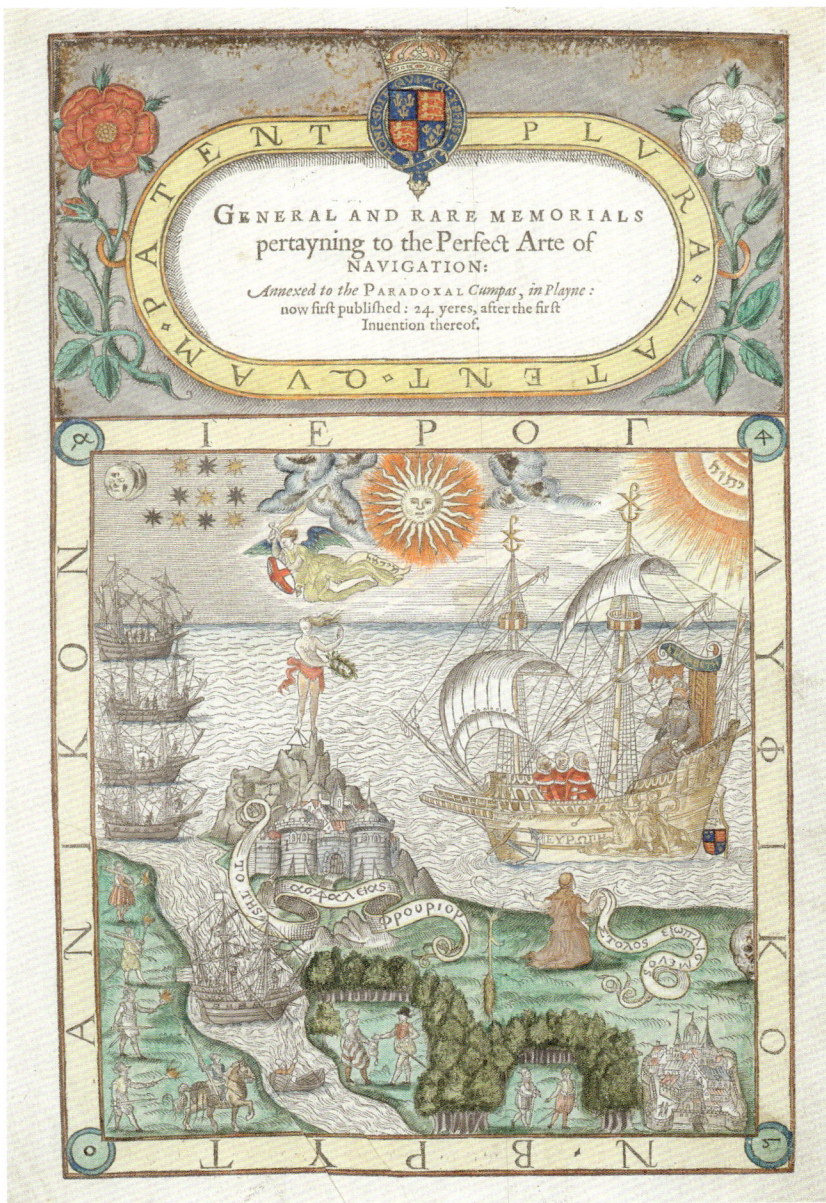

Fig. 3.6 John Dee, *General and Rare Memorials pertayning to the Perfecte Arte of NAVIGATION* (1577). The Bodleian Libraries, University of Oxford, Douce D subt. 30, titlepage.

Fig. 3.7 Mercator map of Arctic region, showing northern tip of Scotland, 1595.
Collection/Bridgeman Images Chapter 3, p. 32.

Fig. 3.8 The Drowning of Britomartis (1547–9), probably by Jean Cousin the Elder
(c.1490–1560). © The Metropolitan Museum of Art/Art Resource Scala, Florence.

Fig. 3.9 'Britomartis Se Jetant à la Mer pour Echapper à Minos' (1547–8) engraving by Etienne Delaune, France. National Gallery of Art, Washington, DC, Rosenwald Collection, 1964.8.609.

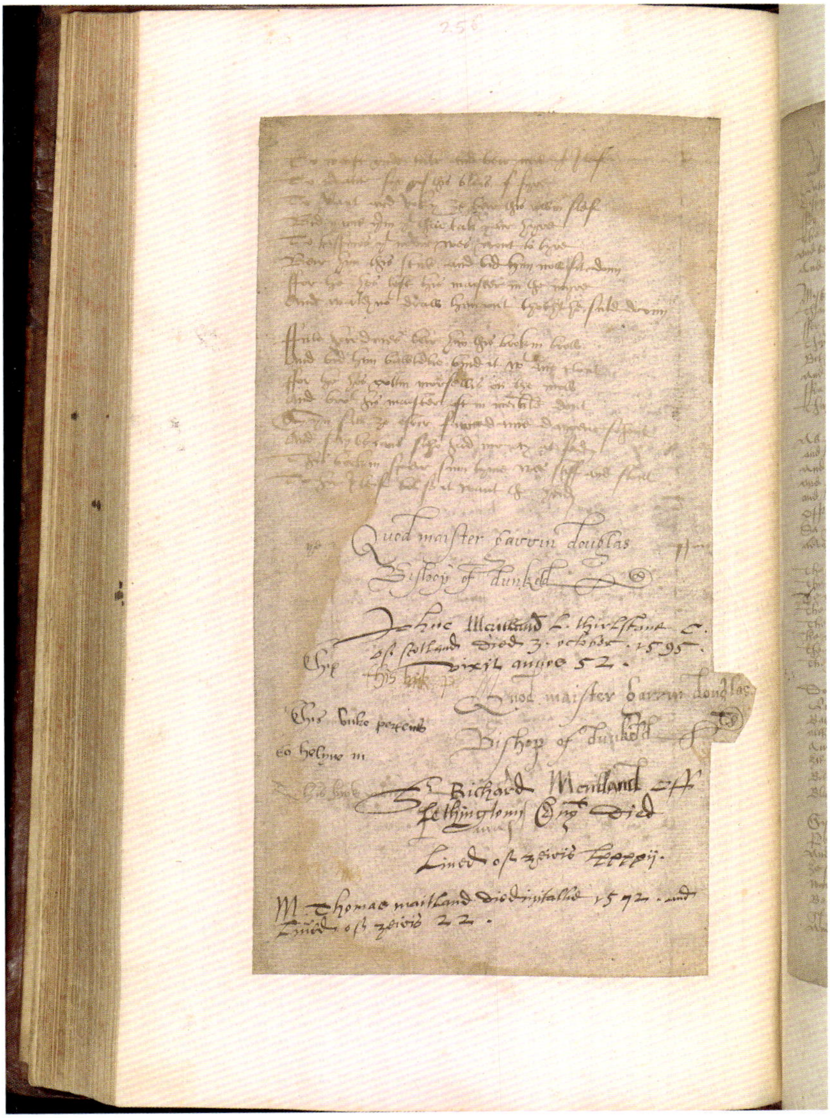

Fig. 4.1 'M. Thomas Maitland died in italie 1572. And lived of yeiris 22', Maitland Folio, Pepys Library, Magdalen College, Cambridge, MS 2553, fol. 256. By permission of the Pepys Library, Magdalene College, Cambridge.

Fig. 4.2 Lethington House, East Lothian (now known as 'Lennoxlove'), celebrated in Thomas Maitland's poem. Author's photograph.

Fig. 4.3 Sir James Wilford (1515–50), siege of Haddington, 1547 after Hans Eworth. National Trust 135561, Coughton Court, Warwickshire. © National Trust Images.

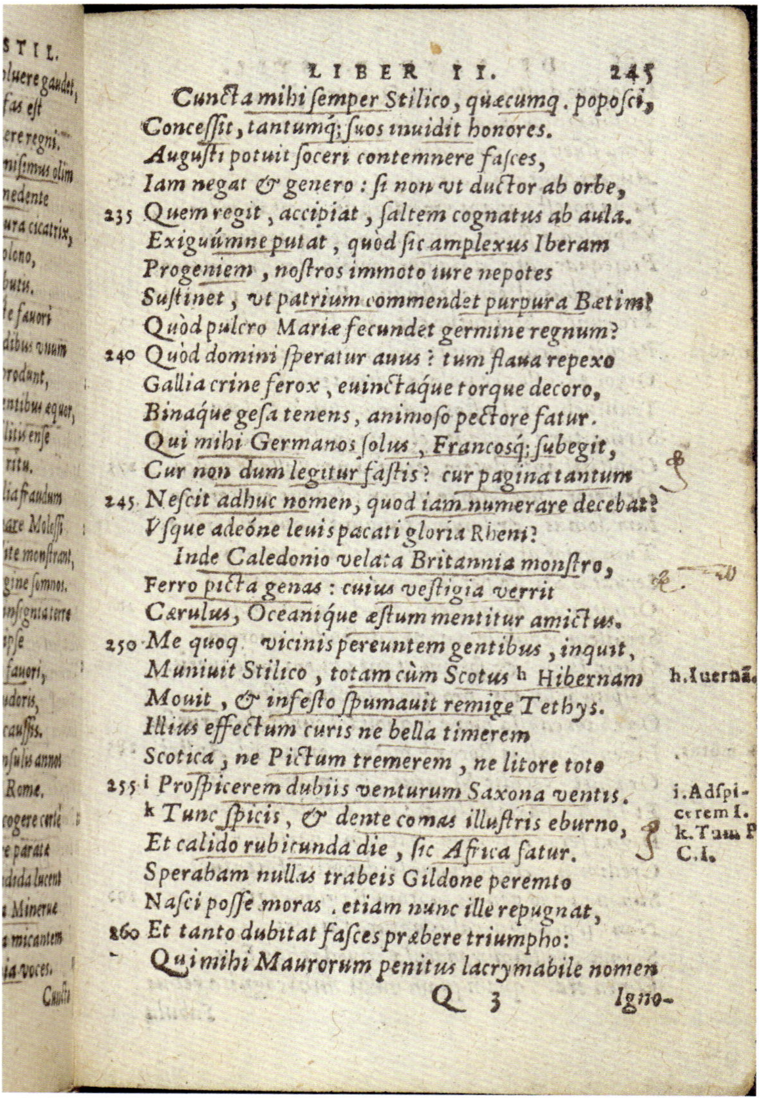

Cuncta mihi semper Stilico, quæcumq; poposci,
Concessit, tantumq; suos inuidit honores.
Augusti potuit soceri contemnere fasces,
Iam negat & genero : si non vt ductor ab orbe,
235 *Quem regit, accipiat, saltem cognatus ab aula.*
Exiguúmne putat, quòd sic amplexus Iberam
Progeniem, nostros immoto iure nepotes
Sustinet, vt patrium commendet purpura Bætim?
Quòd pulcro Mariæ fecundet germine regnum?
240 *Quòd domini speratur auus : tum flaua repexo*
Gallia crine ferox, euinctáque torque decoro,
Bináque gesa tenens, animoso pectore fatur.
Qui mihi Germanos solus, Francósq; subegit,
Cur non dum legitur fastis? cur pagina tantum
245 *Nescit adhuc nomen, quod iam numerare decebat?*
Vsque adeóne leuis pacati gloria Rheni?
  Inde Caledonio velata Britannia monstro,
Ferro picta genas : cuius vestigia verrit
Cærulus, Oceaníque æstum mentitur amictus.
250 *Me quoq vicinis pereuntem gentibus, inquit,*
Muniuit Stilico, totam cùm Scotus ʰ Hibernam
Mouit, & infesto spumauit remige Tethys.
Illius effectum curis ne bella timerem
Scotica, ne Pictum tremerem, ne litore toto
255 ⁱ *Prospicerem dubiis venturum Saxona ventis.*
  ᵏ *Tunc spicis, & dente comas illustris eburno,*
Et calido rubicunda die, sic Afrıca satur.
Sperabam nullas trabeis Gildone peremto
Nasci posse moras, etiam nunc ille repugnat,
260 *Et tanto dubitat fasces præbere triumpho:*
  Qui mihi Maurorum penitus lacrymabile nomen
             Q 3   *Igno-*

h.Iuernā.

i.Adspi-
cerem s.
k.Tum P
C.I.

Fig. 7.1 Ben Jonson underlining and noting the figures of 'Britannia' and 'Africa' with flowers and a manicule on his copy of Claudius Claudianus ed. T. Pulmann (Antwerp, 1585). The Bodleian Libraries, University of Oxford, 8° C 90 Art. Seld., p. 245.

A very minor detail in Buchanan's *Detectioun* shows how little this material and jurisdictional aspect of Scotland's commonweal matters to him. His task of incriminating Mary, undertaken according to Roman teaching on forensic narrative, is to relate events in their natural sequence, but to 'give a taste in the Narrative of everything we shall be treating in the Proof: person, motive, place, time, means opportunity'.[121] The known circumstances of events in the months before Darnley's murder are thus inflected, through lexical choices, omissions, hints and suggestions, in the direction of proving Mary's and Bothwell's neglect of Scotland's honour and welfare in the intemperance of their mutual infatuation. Mary, in McElroy's drily funny summary, consorts flagrantly with Bothwell, while Darnley wanders disconsolately around the Scottish countryside.[122] '[T]he king', Buchanan reports quite falsely, opening one such episode, 'determined to go to Jedworth to the assizes to be there holden' (*Detectioun*, sig. B3v). Bothwell at the same time 'maketh his iorney into Liddesdale' as if, Buchanan implies, playing gooseberry to the king and queen. There in Liddesdale, Buchanan goes on,

> behauing himself nouther according to the place quhairto he was called, nor according to his nobility of race and estimation, he was waunded [wounded] by a pore theefe that was him self ready to dye and carried into the castell called Hermitage. (sig. B3v)

The Queen then

> flingeth away in haste like a mad woman, by great iourneys in poste, in the sharpe time of winter, first to Melrose and then to Jedworth. Thare though she heard sure news of his life, yet hir affectioun impatient of delay cauld not temper it self, but nedis she must bewray hir outragious lust. (sig. B3v)

Scholars have long ago pointed out that October is not 'the sharpe time of winter' in Scotland and that Mary, far from hastening to see Bothwell (who had been appointed Lieutenant Warden of the Borders and Keeper of Hermitage Castle by her mother, Mary of Guise) opened the circuit court in Jedburgh on 9 October 1566 and presided over its hearings for six days, as well as holding two privy council meetings, before making the journey to Hermitage Castle on 16 October 1566. She was accompanied by several members of her privy council, including the earls of Moray, Argyll and Huntly and William Maitland, her secretary, and, after transacting some

---

[121] Quintilian, *Inst.* 4.2.55.   [122] McElroy, *Executing Mary*, 121.

business, she returned to Jedburgh the same day (about sixty miles altogether).[123] There was probably not much leisure or privacy for outrageous lust. Furthermore, the king had decidedly not 'determined to go to Jedworth'. Darnley was nowhere to be seen at assizes, having refused to go, despite Mary's entreaties. Darnley's strange, irresponsible behaviour was causing the government some embarrassment. A letter dated 8 October had been sent by Mary's privy council (among the signatories were Moray, Huntly, Argyll and William Maitland) to the queen mother of France describing the awkward difficulties of this and other quirks of Darnley who, from his father's house in Glasgow, had announced he was leaving the country to live overseas and had a ship ready in the dock. Mary, the letter explicitly stated, had requested Darnley's presence at the assizes as a matter of state, but he had refused to come.[124] Mary herself then fell dangerously ill in Jedburgh for several days. There were fears for her life and she made a will and testament, begging Moray to 'trouble nane' for practising the religion of their conscience. Still Darnley refused to journey from Glasgow to Jedburgh, 'a fault I cannot excuse', wrote Monsieur du Croc, the French ambassador.[125]

It was easy enough for Buchanan to omit these details and portray a Darnley hastening to the queen's beside only to be cast aside for Bothwell (*Detectioun*, sig. C1 r). A little trickier was the suggestion that there was something off-colour or sordid about Bothwell's being wounded while serving as warden of the borders. Buchanan argues that the earl behaved neither according to his place nor his noble race (*necque pro loco quem obtinebat, necque pro familia et expectatione*) because he was wounded 'by a pore theefe that was him self ready to dye' (*a latrone moribundo vulneratus*) (*Detectio*, 8; *Detectioun*, sig. B3v). It is as if there was something bungling and incompetent about an earl being laid low by a half-dead vagrant, or else that there was something opportune in the vulnerability of this paramour of the queen's, contriving to move himself thus into her luxury accommodation while Jedburgh shut its doors against the king. Buchanan's adjective *moribundo*, in other words, is busy stimulating dubious inferences, while another underspecification – the thief's anonymity – is itself loaded. For the man who managed to wound Bothwell after being shot by him was, as the *Diurnall* reports, none other than 'Johne Eluat [Elliot] of the Park'.[126] Far from an obscure vagrant, this man was a kind of gangster chief: the

[123] John Small, 'Queen Mary at Jedburgh in 1566', *Proceedings of the Society of Antiquaries of Scotland* 3 (1881), 210–39.
[124] Keith, *History*, II.455–9.   [125] Small, 'Mary at Jedburgh', 228, 222.   [126] *Diurnall*, 100.

leader of a border family responsible for widespread blackmail, intimidation and oppression. Each one of these great thieves, Sir Richard Maitland says in his poem on the Liddesdale raiders, is known by a 'to-name' or nickname: so is 'John of the Park'. It is he who takes not only the goods but the kists and arks (large grain chests) in which they are carefully stored:

> Thay leif not spindle, spone nor speit,
> Bed, bolster, blanket, sark [shirt] nor scheit,
> Ihone of the Park
> Rypis [robs] kist and ark,
> For all sic wark
> He is richt meit   (MQ 2, ll.49–54)

Buchanan's omission of the name of a criminal notorious all over Scotland combines with his transformation of an episode of attempted judicial arrest into the spectacle of Bothwell's effeminised and somehow squalid vulnerability to occlude the royal good governance instanced by the whole episode. For Mary was, like her mother, Mary of Guise, administering justice in the borders. Indeed, the *Diurnall* laments that with the nobles' imprisonment of the queen, the Liddesdale gangs simply took over the country:

> fra the quenis grace putting into captivitie vnto this time, the thevis of Liddisdail made greit hirschip [armed incursion] on the puir labouraris of the ground, and that throw wanting of justice, for the realme was so dewydit in syndrie factiounis and conspiratiounis that their was na auctoritie obeyit, nor justice execute.[127]

Buchanan's treatment of Mary's presiding over the assizes substitutes the adulterous streetscapes, doorways and back bedrooms of Roman elegy and comedy (the imaginative scenes of his 'hardcore humanism') for the lexicon and public spaces of judicial administration. Back in Jedburgh, Darnley belatedly turns up from Glasgow, but 'forsaken of all friendes' he 'scant with begging findeth rowme in a cottage', while

> Bothwell out of the house quhaire he was lodged befoir, as it were in triumph ouer the king (*velut de Rege triumphans*), was gloriously remoued *in sight of the pepill* into the Quenis awin lodging, and thare layed in a lower parler directly under the chamber quhaire the Queene hir self lay sick.
>   (*Detectioun*, sig. B4v, my italics)

Essentially, as McElroy has written, the people of Scotland play an indispensable role in the *Detectio*'s presentation of the proof Mary's 'tyranny',

---

[127] *Diurnall*, 125.

for it is they who are recruited to ensure that every stage of the narrative is a further proof that the murder of Darnley *could only have been motivated by the queen's personal erotic feelings*, and not by a much wider political consensus of the ruling nobles. This in turn clarifies the predication of *De iure* on the *Detectio*, for although historians of political thought debate the question of how, in practice, Buchanan imagined the electoral freedom of the Scottish people, it is clear that in this instance incontrovertible proof that Mary 'entendyt to set vp a tyrannicall regiment' has to be established by a narrative demonstrating the *popular knowledge* of the queen's alleged adulterous liaison prior to Darnley's murder.[128] Buchanan's apparent concern for the political power of *vulgus*, the common people, then, is predicated on their performing this evidentiary role in the detection of tyranny.

Sir Richard Maitland's account, as justice clerk for the borders under Mary of Guise, has more in common with the *Diurnall*'s view of what happened to the common people after Mary's deposition than with Buchanan's view of their ancient freedom. Poem after poem in the MQ ascribes the difficulty of 'Craftismen and commounis' in keeping their goods and gear safe from raids and burning to 'this greit stryif' '[a]mang the lordis', which brings 'thift, reif, and continuall weir' (MQ 30). 'Sen ye are of ane natioun all', he apostrophises the nobles of both parties, cease to strive '[T]o haue the reull of Queen or King' (MQ 30, ll.73, 84). Sir Richard's poetry of the Marian civil wars could be called a poetry lamenting the lack of state-formation at the level of judicial administration. As the magnates fight, what is lacking is a magistracy able to redress the wrongs of theft, fraud and intimidation that follow from their neglect of governance and ordinary justice. Indeed, Sir Richard's halcyon vision for peace after the victory of the king's party at the Pacification of Perth (1573) is that 'iustice be done this kinrik throw / The quhilk may gar the rasche-bus keip the cow' (MQ 58, ll.46–7). A 'rasche-bus' is a clump of rushes: Sir Richard is imagining the kingdom as a space so well governed as to have the pliant reeds and rushes of the lochs take the place of fences and coffers. But his poem also takes an easy way out, implicitly ceding the loss of sovereignty acknowledged in Buchanan's *Detectio* and in the victory of the king's party. Accepting the guilt of Scotland's queen, and the justice of her indefinite foreign imprisonment, Buchanan's *Detectio* and the Pacification of Perth establish England's jurisdiction over Scotland's succession. Sir Richard's son, John Maitland, voiced the traditional view of Scottish freedom when

---

[128] Mason surveys this debate, 'Introduction', *De iure*, lvii–lxiii.

he advised the earl of Mar (who became regent in 1571) that 'Scotland come neuer yit in servitude / sen Fergus first, bot euir hes bene frie' (MQ 44). After 1573, however, he himself knew that this was no longer true: Buchanan's writings and the victory of the king's party produced an ideology of Scottish freedom as a right of tyrannicide, but at the expense of ceding to the de facto sovereignty of English jurisdiction over its constitution.

CHAPTER 5

On the Knees of the Body Politic: Scottish Succession and English Liberties, 1567–1608

I. 'The King's Two Bodies' and the 'Disability of Foreign Birth'

'There were very great and serious advantages in the English doctrine of the King's Two Bodies', wrote Ernst Kantorowicz in his foundational study.[1] The advantages he had in mind were constitutional and revolutionary. The English revolution, unlike the French, was able to make use of the legal fiction of protecting the king's body politic (the state) while destroying the king's natural body in the person of Charles I. An essentially poetic conception – constitutional restraints on the person of the king imagined as an immortal body – thus shaped English revolutionary politics. Nor was the execution of Charles the only instance in which the doctrine exhibited its creative versatility. It was also employed in complex ways through different stages of England's adjustment to a Scottish royal succession and through subsequent debates in Parliament and the law courts over the two nations' future association under a single king. We saw in the last chapter how William Cecil justified England's prevention of Mary Stewart's restoration by appealing to a neo-Galfridian history of overlord-ship of Scotland, going back to Edward I and to the myth of Brutus. This chapter will show how the lawyer Edmund Plowden translated the same Galfridian history into the constitutionalist terms of 'the King's Two Bodies' to justify a Scottish succession controlled by the English common law. On the actual accession of the Scottish king, however, new questions arose about the legal freedoms of the new king's English and Scottish subjects. If the English common law or 'body politic' had, in a sense, emerged from Plowden's justifying arguments as the real sovereign, could the English and Scots be argued to be subjects of distinct bodies politic with discrete laws and liberties, or could they all be beneficiaries of English common law? One problem with the Galfridian residue of Plowden's

---

[1] Ernst H. Kantorowicz, *The King's Two Bodies: A Study in Medieval Political Theology* (Princeton, NJ: Princeton University Press, 1957), 23.

ingenious constitutionalising of the discourse of English overlordship was that it left the door open for the argument that the Scots were, as homagers, not aliens to the English state and might therefore enjoy English legal freedoms. This chapter will trace the course of these arguments, looking first at Plowden's deployment of 'the King's Two Bodies' in his *Treatise on the Succession* of 1567 and then going on to examine the very different framing of questions of nationhood and naturalisation after James VI and I's English accession in the Union debate of 1603–9. It will look at the subtle ways in which commitment to a history of English overlordship of Scotland (once anchored in a Galfridian story of Britain and British kings) would be reconciled with maintaining the notion of Scots as aliens, incapable of English legal freedoms and privileges.

Part of the purpose of this chapter is to unsettle the rather fixed role that the Union debate has come to play in English literary criticism. English literary critics tend to interpret the Union debate in terms of English local and constitutional resistance to King James VI and I's attempt to impose a uniform geographical identity ('Great Britain') on the whole island, an attempt seen as absolutist both in itself and in its implications for English nationhood. Thus, for example, Claire McEachern reads into the Commons' opposition to James in 1606 the same feeling of commitment to local diversity and a resistance to hegemonic 'British' identity that she finds expressed in Michael Drayton's *Poly-Olbion*. She notes that in the House of Commons in February 1607 Nicholas Fuller objected to the mutual naturalisation of English and Scots by observing that cattle will move from a lean to a fat pasture if the hedge should be torn down. This she reads as evidence of English national feeling about the effect of James's 'Great Britain'. 'Where James sought to overwhelm cultural and economic differences with the comprehensive unity of a single island geography,' she writes, 'the English cited the local texture of indigenous boundaries to property.'[2] McEachern thus translates English fears of Scottish predation into the affective resistance of an indigenous population to a foreign despot redrawing boundaries. Martin Butler similarly assumes an inherent ignorance of English law-bound monarchy in James's proposed style of 'King of Great Britain', commenting that James was a monarch 'whose Britishness seemed to put him outside inherited constitutional languages'.[3] The previous chapters in this book have shown that the idea of sovereignty over the whole island in the name of neo-Galfridian 'British' empire was very far

---

[2] McEachern, *Poetics of English Nationhood*, 144. [3] Butler, *Stuart Court Masque*, 97.

from being James's innovation. It was, on the contrary, made throughout the sixteenth century by English policy-makers and poets. Within the Tudor articulations of 'British' empire, through Cecil's memoranda on England's ancient right to decide the Scottish succession, Harrison's description prefacing Holinshed's *Chronicles*, Spenser's *The Faerie Queene*, Arthurian materials in Hakluyt's *Navigations* and John Dee's maps and plats, the key elements of this 'British' ideology were the ideas of Anglo-British indigeneity (that is, the idea that English kings had inherited indigenous British sovereignty over the whole island) and the idea of constitutionalism, the idea that 'sovereignty in the godly empire of Great Britain would ultimately rest in the king's parliament of England'.[4] To say that James's 'Britishness' put him 'outside inherited constitutional languages' is anachronistically to use 'British' in the eighteenth-century sense of an inclusive identity which the English could afford to ignore, but Scots felt obliged to cultivate.[5] In the period leading up to James's accession, however, Anglo-British ideology was decidedly *English* and exclusive. It was chorographic, antiquarian, and legal-constitutional. It asserted the antiquity and continuity of Anglo-British institutions and legal arrangements and denied Scottish nationhood by upholding the tradition of Scotland as feudally held of England since the time of Locrine and Albanact. So the question that literary critics ask of the Union debate needs to be changed. Rather than asking how English literary texts of 1604–8 register a local and constitutional English resistance to the foreign and absolutist innovation of 'Great Britain', we should be asking how 'Great Britain' came to look like the innovation of a foreign absolutist. How did it come about that a Scottish succession made the ideas of 'Great Britain' and 'British empire' (ideas advocated by English texts and policies from the 1540s to the 1590s) seem a threat to English constitutional liberties and English national identity? By what argumentative strategies did the English opponents of mutual naturalisation and freedom of trade endorse James's accession as an enhancement of English island nationhood, while maintaining that the Scots were aliens? And how might those strategies play out in literary texts?

It became commonplace in 1980s New Historicist and Cultural Materialist accounts of James's accession to stress his appropriation of the Galfridian Brutus myth and of a Roman imperial style, as well as to

---

[4] Hoak, 'Cecil and Smith', 52.
[5] Robert Crawford, 'England's Scotland', in *Literature and Union*, eds. Gerrard Caruthers and Colin Kidd (Oxford: Oxford University Press, 2018), 331–48, 333.

cite his marital metaphors for the union of himself and the island, or of England and Scotland.[6] More recent studies such as Martin Butler's magisterial account of the Stuart masque see courtly art not as a projection of James's policy, but as multivocal and critically engaged. Nevertheless, the central political *agon* still tends to be one of English constitutional caution restraining Scoto-British monarchical absolutism. Yet, as Bruce Galloway long ago showed, James did not, in 1603–9, proceed in an absolutist fashion. He accepted the Commons' arguments that a change in style might lead to confusion in the laws (though Sir Henry Savile himself thought these arguments merely 'trickes and sharpness of wit' rather than substantial objections) and as early as 1604 James forewent the change.[7] He abandoned his grand schemes for the harmonisation of laws or a new name for the kingdoms. The action he took was concrete, practical and thoroughly constitutional: he initiated the statutory establishment of a preparatory Commission, with legal, governmental and mercantile representation from England and Scotland, to sit between parliamentary sessions, empowered only to prepare proposals for both parliaments. The Commission assembled in October 1604 consisted of forty-eight Englishmen and thirty-three Scots, 'a representation in miniature of all the groups that would normally be found in an English or Scots Parliament'.[8] Sir Thomas Craig recalled the cooperative atmosphere of the Commission. It 'contributed a good deal', he wrote,

> towards forming ties of good-will and affection between the two peoples. For whereas we Scotsmen unreasonably had expected to meet with arrogance and contempt of our nation at the hands of the English, while the latter expected a fiery display of Scottish *prefervidum ingenium* (burning hot temper) . . . both proved wrong in their expectations. Each side exhibited a spirit of accommodation, a modest and conciliatory demeanour, cool and unflurried minds.[9]

The Commission debated four proposals and the results of their discussion were signed and sealed in a document called the 'Instrument' which went before both national parliaments for discussion and endorsement. The proposals were specific, practical and limited. The first two, for the abrogation of hostile laws and the administration of justice in the borders, were

---

[6] Jonathan Goldberg, *James I and the Politics of Literature* (Stanford, CA: Stanford University Press, 1989), 43–7; Terence Hawkes, *Meaning by Shakespeare* (London: Routledge, 1992), 123–4.

[7] Henry Savile, *Historical Collections*, in *The Jacobean Union: Six Tracts of 1604*, eds. Bruce R. Galloway and Brian P. Levack (Edinburgh: Scottish Historical Society, 1985), 185, 239, 208; Galloway, *Union 1603–1608*, 21.

[8] Galloway, *Union 1603–1608*, 62.   [9] Craig, *De Unione*, 277.

uncontentious. The second two, for the lifting of trade restrictions and customs duties, and for the mutual naturalisation of both nations, occasioned much controversy and were ultimately rejected by the English House of Commons. The controversies provoked by the issues of trade privileges and of mutual naturalisation were closely related, as we shall see. First, however, it is important to register a fact about the progress of the Union debate. The fact is that it went backwards rather than forwards. Issues that were already legally settled became unsettled as talks went on.

The naturalisation question embraced two groups of people, those born before James's accession on 24 March 1603 and those born after. These were known as the 'ante-nati' and the 'post-nati' (the 'born before' and 'born after'). In 1604 it was *universally accepted by all sides* – even by those writers of anti-Union treatises – that the post-nati 'were by law the natural subjects of either kingdom. This was confirmed in November 1604 by an opinion of the Crown Law Officers.'[10] That is to say that the naturalised legal status of the post-nati was already a fait accompli in 1604. The Commission's task was merely to acknowledge this and to discuss legislation to enable the naturalisation of the ante-nati. The Commission did indeed declare the post-nati *de jure* naturalised, but, as Sir Henry Neville records, this question '*begat more Debate and Contestation than all the rest*', with one side (the Scots) keen to obtain and the other (the English) seeking to exclude.[11] The Commission finally proposed

> *That it be declared by Parliament, that the Law already is, (for so the Judges have declared it) that all the Subjects of either Kingdom, born since Queen* Elizabeth's *Death, are naturallized in the other to all Intents and Purposes*; and for those born before, it is agreed that they shall be naturallized to all Purposes, and enabled to all Capacities, each in the other, *except to have Voice and Seance in Parliament, and to bear any office of the Crown, or Judicature.*[12]

So the naturalised ante-nati were to be prohibited from holding public office. But even this was too much for the House of Commons. Far from considering further legislation for this modified naturalisation of the ante-nati, the Commons rowed back the naturalisation of the post-nati, despite its being already law. Why and how did this happen? In seeking to answer that question, this chapter will in its third section examine the argumentative strategies of some especially influential treatises by Sir Henry Spelman,

---

[10] Galloway, *Union 1603–1608*, 71.
[11] Sir Ralph Winwood, *Memorials of Affairs of State*, 3 vols. (London: 1725), II.37.
[12] Winwood, *Memorials*, II.37.

Sir Henry Savile and an anonymous tract drawing on both, entitled *A Discourse of Naturalisation*. Prior to that, the second section will establish a context by showing how Edmund Plowden transformed the neo-Galfridian British history of English overlordship of Scotland into the constitutionalist doctrine of 'the King's Two Bodies' in his *Treatise on the Succession* of 1567. Another related and pertinent aspect of the developing constitutionalism of English common-law needs, however, introducing first. This aspect has to do with the emergence of the distinction between alien and natural subject as legally fundamental. The sixteenth century saw the last stage of a transformation of the law of personal status from one in which liberties and franchises were understood as specific, fungible markers of a person's status, irrespective of place of birth, to one in which 'liberty' in the abstract was held to be the common-law birthright of the *Englishman*, the thing that distinguished an 'Englishman born' from a foreigner, regardless of status.

In the Roman law of persons, the most basic distinction was, as we saw in the last chapter, that between *sui juris* and *alieni juris*, free and unfree. Keechang Kim has argued that over the course of sixteenth century, however, this division was conceptually reorganised in English common law into the modern division of nationality; that is, the distinction between '*alienigena*, an alien born, or *subditus*, a subject born'.[13] While we nowadays think of discrimination on the basis of nationality as legally fundamental, medieval Christendom had no concept of an abstract set of freedoms attaching to a particular nationality, just as there was no catch-all legal disadvantage attaching to foreign birth. Medieval legal freedoms (*libertates, privilegia*) were concrete, itemised and marketable: a merchant or appointee to a religious or administrative position might seek or be awarded liberties and privileges appertaining to specific cities and local jurisdictions, or exemptions from the imposition of local taxes and customs.[14] As Sir John Baker puts it, '[l]iberty and freedom will not be found as titles in books of common law before 1600. "Liberties" and "franchises" ... are specific privileges or exemptions, treated in effect as a form of property.'[15] No homogenous legal 'disability' or disadvantage, therefore, attached to being foreign- as opposed to English-born. In a society in which villeinage still existed (it finally disappeared in the 1570s) the question was not, 'of what nationality are you?' but 'how free are you?'[16]

---

[13] Kim, *Aliens*, 1–5.   [14] Kim, *Aliens*, 23–102.

[15] John H. Baker, 'Personal Liberty under the Common Law of England', *The Origins of Modern Freedom in the West*, ed. R. W. Davis (Stanford, CA: Stanford University Press, 1995), 178–202, 178.

[16] Kim, *Aliens*, 7; on the demise of villeinage in the 1570s, see Baker, 'Personal Liberty', 189.

Legal historians have recently traced aspects of a process whereby the various 'freedoms' afforded to subjects under the jurisdiction of English common law came to be abstracted and associated with national identity rather than social status. The obscure language of Magna Carta cap. 29 was, as Baker has shown, reinvented in the late sixteenth century as a guarantee that no Englishman should be deprived of his right to jury trial by the law of the land (*lex terrae*).[17] Paul Halliday has further demonstrated how the paradox of divine election expressed in the Old Testament story of Esau yielding his birthright to Jacob came to be applied to the idea of common law 'due process' as a sign of English elect nationhood or an English birthright.[18] Keechang Kim makes a complementary argument about the gradual shift whereby positive legal privileges of commerce and inheritance came to define the distinction between an alien and an English-born subject. Though traditional histories have located a turning point in a statute of Edward III's reign, the 1351 *De natis ultra mare* ('Of those that are born beyond the sea') as inaugurating a blanket 'disability' of foreign birth, Kim argues that this is to take at face value an ideologically loaded sixteenth-century misinterpretation of the statute, which occurred in the context of fears about Scottish succession.

The 1351 statute was designed to address specific problems of proof of inheritance experienced by the heirs of Edward III's subjects fighting for him in France. In doing so, it introduced a language which conflated faithful allegiance to the king with the reach of the common law, providing that heirs 'born out of the ligeance of the king' to parents who were of the king's faith and ligeance should enjoy inheritance rights. The bond of faith between king and subject was thus equated with English jurisdiction: 'the territorial extent of the king's legal power [was] also called *ligeance*'.[19] In the second half of the sixteenth century an influential tract of 1563 by John Hales sought to bar the accession of Mary Queen of Scots by interpreting the 1351 *De natis ultra mare* as evidence for the existence of an anterior, blanket 'disability of foreign birth' that would exclude a claimant born, as Mary was, in Scotland. The concept of an abstract 'disability' attaching to foreign birth thus, according to Kim, emerged as a back-formation. 'The moment the statute *De natis ultra mare* was presented as removing the "disabilitie of foreyne birthe",' Kim writes,

[17] John H. Baker, *The Reinvention of Magna Carta* (Cambridge: Cambridge University Press, 2017), 249–75.
[18] Paul D. Halliday, 'Birthrights and Due Course of Law', *Oxford Handbook of English Law and Literature*, 587–603.
[19] Kim, *Aliens*, 121; 138.

none of the sixteenth-century lawyers could escape from the potent grip of their own assumptions, that is: (1) foreign birth meant alien status; (2) alien status meant legal disability; and (3) no such disability should affect the king's subjects because they were guaranteed equal liberty through 'obeisaunce'.[20]

The stage was thus set for a defence of the right of a Scottish monarch to succeed to the English throne that would overcome this putative 'disabilitie of foreyne birth' by means of the doctrine of 'the King's Two Bodies'. But the emergent concept of a general disability of foreign birth, coupled as this was with the reinvention of Magna Carta as conferring a liberty that was the birthright of all 'Englishmen born', set the stage for a different drama of nationhood. In the Union debates the issue at stake was whether Scots born after James's accession to the English throne might enjoy the liberties of Englishmen. The neo-Galfridian tradition of arguing that Scotland was anciently held of England was, in this context, double-edged: might that argument have the potential to justify Scottish naturalisation? Before exploring that question, we need to understand how Edmund Plowden translated the neo-Galfridian myth of English overlordship of Scotland into a new constitutionalist political theology by the doctrine of 'the King's Two Bodies'.

II. Plowden and the Knees of the Body Politic[21]

Edmund Plowden's 1567 *Treatise on the Succession* is nothing if not indebted to Galfridian British history, though this aspect of its legacy has, like the rest of it, been largely ignored. Marie Axton, its discoverer, characterised it as 'a fresh document by Plowden, which Kantorowicz did not use, expounding the concept of "the King's Two Bodies"' to prove Mary Stewart's claim to the English throne.[22] Plowden's *Treatise* does not, however, merely appeal to the doctrine of the body politic to argue for a Scottish succession. It relies just as heavily on what in Chapter 1 I referred to as the 'feudalisation of Geoffrey' – that is, the use of Geoffrey of Monmouth's history to uphold the claim that Scotland had, since Brutus's division of Britain, been feudally held as a fief of the king of England.

---

[20] Kim, *Aliens*, 162–3.
[21] This chapter section is an abbreviated version of Lorna Hutson, 'On the Knees of the Body Politic', *Representations*, vol. 152, no. 1 (2020), 25–54, which offers a fuller reading of the *Treatise*.
[22] Marie Axton, *The Queen's Two Bodies: Drama and the English Succession* (London: Royal Historical Society, 1977), 19.

In spite of the enormous influence of Kantorowicz and the support which the *Treatise* lends to his brilliant analysis of the incarnational language of the mystical body politic, the *Treatise* itself has not attracted much attention, though this might change now that a modern edition is in preparation by Daniel Haywood.[23] Among the few studies that have attended to the *Treatise*, Alan Cromartie's *Constitutionalist Revolution* credited it, along with Plowden's *Reports*, with contributing to the constitutionalist view that 'the political powers enjoyed by English monarchs were properly rights granted by the English common law'.[24] Nevertheless, Cromartie found the doctrine's exposition in the *Treatise* more revealing about the author's convictions than necessary to the argument in hand. In the *Treatise* Plowden, as Cromartie wrote,

> argued that deficiencies in the body natural, such as infancy, or illness or (in the case of Mary) alien status could not affect the body politic; Henry VII's much more serious defect of having been attainted as a traitor proved not to be a bar to his accession.[25]

Given the relatively straightforward nature of the theoretical problem it was not clear why Plowden needed to spend five chapters setting out the 'Two Bodies' doctrine with such mystical fullness. To Cromartie 'the unnecessary elaboration with which he discussed the whole notion of a body politic' was precisely '[w]hat was revealing about Plowden's treatise'.[26] In other words, Plowden's incarnational language revealed his convictions as a Catholic constitutionalist thinker more than it served his immediate purpose.

The first five chapters of the *Treatise* do indeed lay out in surprisingly rich and emotive language a theory of the monarch's 'bodie pollitike' as a both a human legal artifice, 'constituted & devised by reason & pollicie, and of mere necessitie for preservacion of the people' and as a spiritual,

---

[23] Daniel Haywood is currently engaged in preparing a scholarly edition of Edmund Plowden's *Treatise on the Succession* (1567). For Plowden's manuscripts, see Marie Axton, 'The Influence of Plowden's Succession Treatise', *HLQ*, 37.3 (1974): 209–26 and Geoffrey de C. Parminter, 'Edmund Plowden as Advocate for Mary Queen of Scots', *Innes Review*, vol. 30 (1979), 35–53; J. H. Baker, *English Legal Manuscripts in the United States of America: A Descriptive List*, 2 vols. (London: Selden Society, 1985–1990), II. 327, 368. I will cite Bodleian Don.c.43 by page number in the text. I would like to thank Dr Anna Reynolds for her assistance in comparing the manuscripts and transcribing variants in Harley and Cotton Caligula.

[24] Alan Cromartie, *The Constitutionalist Revolution* (Cambridge: Cambridge University Press, 2006), 109. See also Christopher W. Brooks, *Law, Politics and Society in Early Modern England* (Cambridge: Cambridge University Press, 2008), 73–4; Mortimer Levine, *The Early Elizabethan Succession Question, 1558–1568* (Stanford, CA: Stanford University Press, 1966), 93–4.

[25] Cromartie, *Constitutionalist Revolution*, 95.   [26] Cromartie, *Constitutionalist Revolution*, 95.

supernatural body, 'not visible, nor tangible, a bodie impassible, not subiecte to force or violence, and is voyde of infancy and of age, and of all imbecilities and defectes that the bodie naturall sustaineth' (1). It is impossible not to feel that the insistent negation of the fleshly body's qualities and vulnerabilities – sight, touch, suffering ('passibility'), vulnerability, infancy age and imbecility – makes the political body take imaginative shape not as abstract policy and government but as divine spirituality itself. Moreover, the relationship between the two bodies is incarnational or eucharistic: the body natural is said to 'receave' the body politic (2), so that both bodies become one, each being only enhanced by the capacities of the other. The puzzle, then, is not simply the fullness of the doctrine's elaboration, but the intended role of proprioceptive emotion, the aura of sacredness, in its constitutional implications. But there is a more immediate puzzle. For this setting out of the theory of a royal Christology seems altogether surplus to Plowden's final legal argument. If the first part of Plowden's *Treatise* details the 'Two Bodies' theory to argue that 'foreigne birthe is no disabilitie to receaue the Crowne' (30), the second half seems to render that argument quite redundant. It undertakes to prove '[t]hat neither Scottland, neither the Scottes be out of the ligeance of England, nor disabled by theire byrthe to receaue inheritaunce in Englande' (78).

Why would Plowden develop a complex political-theological language to refute a legal objection of foreign Scottish birth if he then intended to argue that Scots were not foreign? From Chapter 7 to Chapter 11 of the treatise's first part Plowden argues that the law which disables persons born out of the ligeance of the king of England to inherit in England does not apply to the Crown because the Crown contains a body politic. In the second part, however, he goes on to argue that Scotland is not, in any case, out of the obedience of England: 'for yt is written and beleeued certainly', Plowden declares,

> that Scottland is holden of the kinge of England. And yt is taken that yt was first yeuen to Albanacte second son of Brute the first kinge that possessed this realme to holde of Locrine his oldest brother kinge of Englande. And ever sithens yt hath bene holden of England, as by the Cronicles and recordes & other testimonies yt maye appeare (78–9).

In this section Plowden rehearses the whole pseudo-history of overlordship, naming the usual famous English overlord kings – William the Conqueror, William Rufus, Henry I, Henry III, Edward I, Edward III and Henry V – as well as a range of chroniclers, including Polydore Virgil, William of Newbury, Matthew Paris and Thomas Walsingham. He relies fairly heavily on Henry VIII's *Declaration* which, as we saw in Chapter 1, gave Anglo-Scots history as a legal record of tenure *ab initio*. He also cites wholesale the chroniclers on whom Edward I drew for his claims of overlordship. He urges his readers to turn to Edward I's own letter to Pope Boniface for the eloquence with which it proves that England has held overlordship of Scotland since the time of Locrine and Albanact and of King Arthur.

These historical records of ceremonies of homage cited by Plowden were, as we have already seen, deceptive. At one extreme, there was John Hardyng's blatant forgery of documents of Scottish homage, not detected until 1837.[27] Alfred Hiatt's excellent scholarly detective work has detailed how, between 1422 and 1463, John Hardyng presented to successive English governments at least fourteen forged documents purporting to prove that Scottish kings acknowledged English kings as their liege-lords, the overlords of Scotland. 'As well as straightforward statements of homage,' Hiatt writes, 'the forgeries are an attempt to establish a chain of renewed submission over the reigns of a number of different Scottish kings, and to write away any evidence that the Scots could produce to assert their independence.'[28] Yet the process of manipulating the meanings of specific acts of homage had begun much earlier. For example, in 1200, the Scottish king William the Lion came to Lincoln to do homage to King John of England for lands in Northumbria, Cumberland and Westmoreland. The chronicler Roger Hoveden records the ceremony thus

> and there in the sight of all the people William king of Scots became the vassal of John, king of England, for his right and swore to him over the cross of Hubert, archbishop of Canterbury, fealty in life and limbs and his earthly honour against all men, and in the preservation of peace with him and his kingdom, saving his own right [*salve juro suo*]; with these witnesses [there follows a long list of noble and ecclesiastical witnesses].[29]

The phrase '*salve juro suo*' indicates William's rights as king of Scotland. However, as Rees Davies comments, King John clearly appreciated how, on this occasion, 'his power within the British Isles could be theatrically stage-managed for the benefit of a hand-picked audience'. 'On a great hill' outside Lincoln on 21 November 1200, as Davies reads in the chronicle,

> "in the sight of all the people, William, king of Scots became the man of John king of England for his right." The limited nature of the homage (in respect of

[27] Hiatt, *Medieval Forgeries*, 105.   [28] Hiatt, *Medieval Forgeries*, 103.
[29] Alan O. Anderson, *Scottish Annals from the English Chroniclers, A. D. 500 to 1286* (London: David Nutt, 1908), 324.

the king of Scots' lands in England) was well recognized by those in the know; but it was the physical act of homage and the resplendent assembly which remained – and was meant to remain – in the memories of those present.[30]

So already in 1200, John was carefully managing the public relations side of things so as to give the impression that the homage he received was for the kingdom of Scotland, when it was actually for northern English lands. About a century later, after the death without heirs of Alexander III of Scotland, Edward I sent to English monasteries, asking the monks to search their chronicles for evidence of English overlordship. The monks often doctored their evidence. For example, 'in the account of the homage of William the Lion to John, the words "salvo jure suo" (i.e. saving William's rights), which are included in the text of Howden [Roger Hoveden] at this point, are omitted'.[31] Such distortions were endlessly repeated. Henry VIII's *Declaration* recalls William the Lion paying homage to King John, with all the details of the hill, the sacred cross of Hubert and the multitude of witnesses.[32] The 1548 *Epitome* even inserts the mendacious clause 'for the kyngdom of Scotland':

> John the brother of this Richard was next king of England, to whom the same Willyam kyng of Scottes did the like homage *for the kyngdome of Scotland* [my italics] vpon a hill beside Lyncolne, taking his faith therefore vpon the crosse of Hubert then Archebishoppe of Cantorburye, a great nomber of people beyng there assembled for yᵉ purpose.[33]

This repetition of skewed and partial accounts naturally had a cumulative effect, as is conveyed by a rapid glance at the printed marginal notes to Grafton's 1543 edition of Hardyng. Figures 5.1, 5.2 and 5.3 show printed marginal annotations from the reigns of Edward the Confessor, William Rufus and King John which repeat the work's theme, 'homage of yᵉ Scottes', with all the subtlety of repeated hammer blows. One receptive reader has copiously underlined Grafton's dedicatory denunciation of the 'rebellious' Scots with the words, 'The proper nature of yᵉ Scottishe' (see Figure 5.4). Thomas Craig complained that Holinshed's repetition of the old lie 'that the King of *Scots* owes Homage to the King of *England* as his Liege-Lord', though unimportant, was causing European historians, such as Jean Bodin – 'very Learned Men, though unacquainted with our Affairs' to repeat this lie for historical truth.[34]

---

[30] Davies, *First English Empire*, 16.   [31] Stones and Simpson, *Edward I*, I.151.
[32] Henry VIII, *Declaration*, sig. C3r.   [33] *An Epitome*, sig. f3v.
[34] Thomas Craig, *Scotland's Sovereignty Asserted*, trans. and ed. George Ridpath (London, 1695), 3–4.

Edward.   fol C.rrb.

Homage of the Scottes.

And toke homage of him, vpon the ground
In Edwardes name, as he of right was bounde
For that ylke realme, and as his elders dyd
Suche fortune then to England was betid.

¶ The kyng Gryffyn of Wales, then was slaine
That Herefordshyre spoyled had and brent
His head set vp, at Gloucester ful plaine.
For his vntrueth, and falshed that he ment
And sone therafter, his brothers head was sent
Unto the kyng for his rebellion
So were they bothe forjuged for treason.

¶ And as kyng Edward, in his palayce of pryde
Duke Goodwyne, then sittyng at his table
Sawe the butler on his one fote slyde
And like to fal, that other fote ful stable
As he was scrupyng the kyng at his table
Then held him vp, that he fel not to ground
Kyng Edward sayd, to Goodwyn in that stound.

¶ As his one fote, ye see helpe that other
Ful wel and true, I fynde it dayly nowe
Had ye ne bene, thus had helpe me my brother
Therle then to the kyng on syde gan bowe
And sayd, yf I were cause, I pray God nowe
This bread passe not my throte, but dead I bee
And straungled here anone, that ye may see.

¶ At his prayer anone with that he dyed
For with that bread, straugled was he that stound
It might not passe his throte, as men espied
Wherfore the kyng then, bad draw out the hound
Under

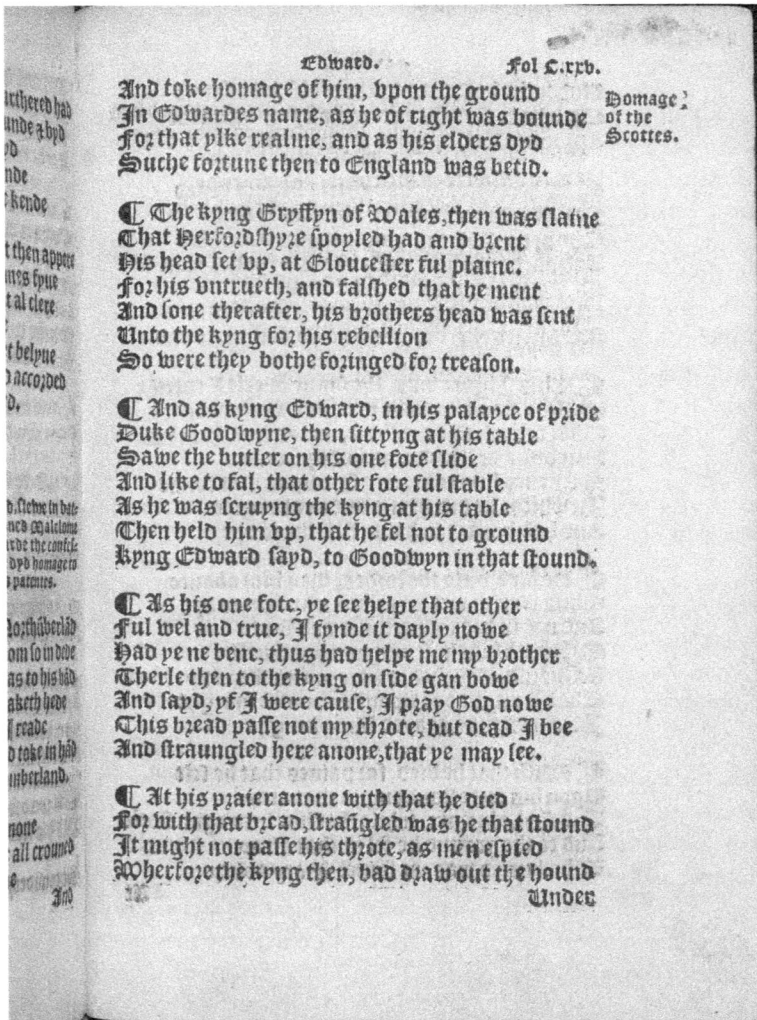

Fig. 5.1 Hardyng notes Edward the Confessor's homage from Malcolm III. *The Chronicle of John Hardyng* (London: Richard Grafton, 1543). The Bodleian Libraries, University of Oxford, 4° H 17 Art Seld, fol. 125 r.

Plowden was not unusual in believing the English exchequer was full of authentic records to prove that Scotland had been feudally held of England for centuries; William Cecil's memoranda show he held the same view. Why not rely on such arguments, then, to clinch the case for the Scottish

Rufus.   Fol.C.rrrij.

Malcolpnes brother,that to it had no right
But Dunkan, sone of Malcolpne that knowyng
With helpe of kyng Willipam, and royal might
Of Scotland, so droaue him away to flight
And crouned was, as chronicles vnderstand
And homage made to Willipam for his land

Homage
of the
Scottes.

₰Sone after,kyng Dunkan of Scotland slain
By treason was, and Dunwal restitute
Unto the croune of Scotland then againe
Whom Edgare then by succour and refute
Of kyng Willipam droue out al destitute
Of any helpe, and crouned was in Scotland
To kyng William did homage for his land

Homage
of the
Scottes.

₰Of whose homage, John Hardyng gaue the
ful clerely made, written wel and sealed   (letter
The whiche also, with other letters better
That by reason may not be reueled
The whiche,yf he would haue enbeseled
The kyng James vnto his warison
I M. marke, him hight of his discrecion

¶And in his tyme, Roes that Richard hight
The kyng of Wales, in battaile strong was slain
Besyde the castel of Brekenham, then ful right
Fro whiche tyme forthe, theyr kynges seazed ful
And princes called they were,soth to sayn   (plain
The kyng with host, on Robert Monbray rode
Who with the kyng faught, for his traytourhod.

₰And discomfite, helde Bamburgh castel then
And the kyng enduryng, ful.vij.yere
                    r.iiij.   Consen₌

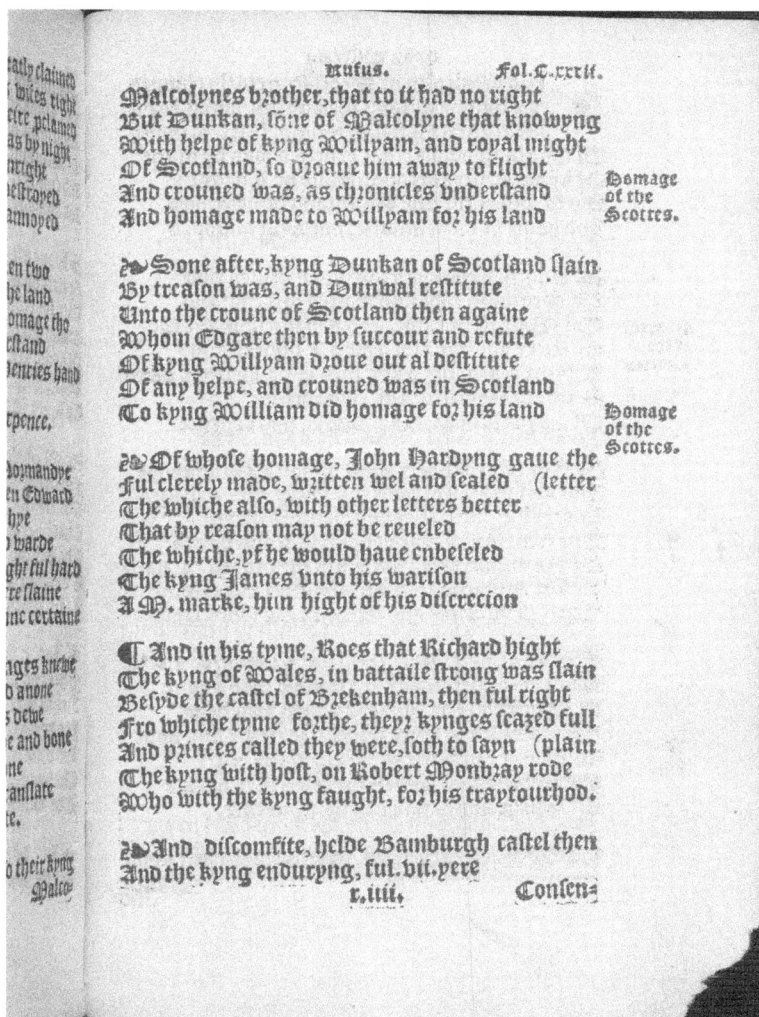

Fig. 5.2 Hardyng accuses James I of Scotland of wanting to 'embesele' (steal) his evidences of homage. *The Chronicle of John Hardyng* (London: Richard Grafton, 1543). The Bodleian Libraries, University of Oxford, 4° H 17 Art Seld, fol. 132 r.

succession? Why add the doctrine of 'the King's Two Bodies'? The answer lies in the evident constitutionalism of Plowden's thought. Plowden was chiefly concerned to refute John Hales, who, in citing *De natis ultra mare* to argue that both Mary and her father were born 'out of the ligeance' of the kyng John.   Fol.C.xlix.

In his fyrst yere, a tate he toke ful out
Of eche plough land thre shillynges full payed
For whiche the people bitterly for him prayed.

The.C.xlii.chapiter.

¶ Howe kyng Wyllyam of Scotland dyd homage liege to
kyng John at Lyncolne, the duke Arthure of Brytayne and
all the lordes of Irelande dyd the same.

IN his fyrst yere, kyng Wyllyā of Scotlād
 Made his homage, in Lyncolne his citee
 And Arthure duke of Brytayne, I under‑
Sone after, made his homage and feautee (stand
At London then, with great humilitee
The prince of Wales, there made his homage
For Wales then, that was his heritage

Homage of the Scottes.

The great Onele, and Makmurre also
And al the lordes, and kynges of Ireland
Therles also of Ulster, dyd right so
Of Ormond and Desmond, for their lande
And all estates there, as I understande
Were sworne to him, and to him did homage
For their lyuelodes, and their heritage

Homage of the Irishemen.

The kyng Philip confedered with Arthure
To rebel sore, againe his eme kyng John
And graunt him men, and power strong and sure
To get Guyon Poytou and Angeou anone
Wherfore kyng John to Normandy gan gone
And there he toke Arthure duke of Brytayn
In castle Mirable dyed, in mykel payne.

Dame Isabel the syster also of Arthure

        In

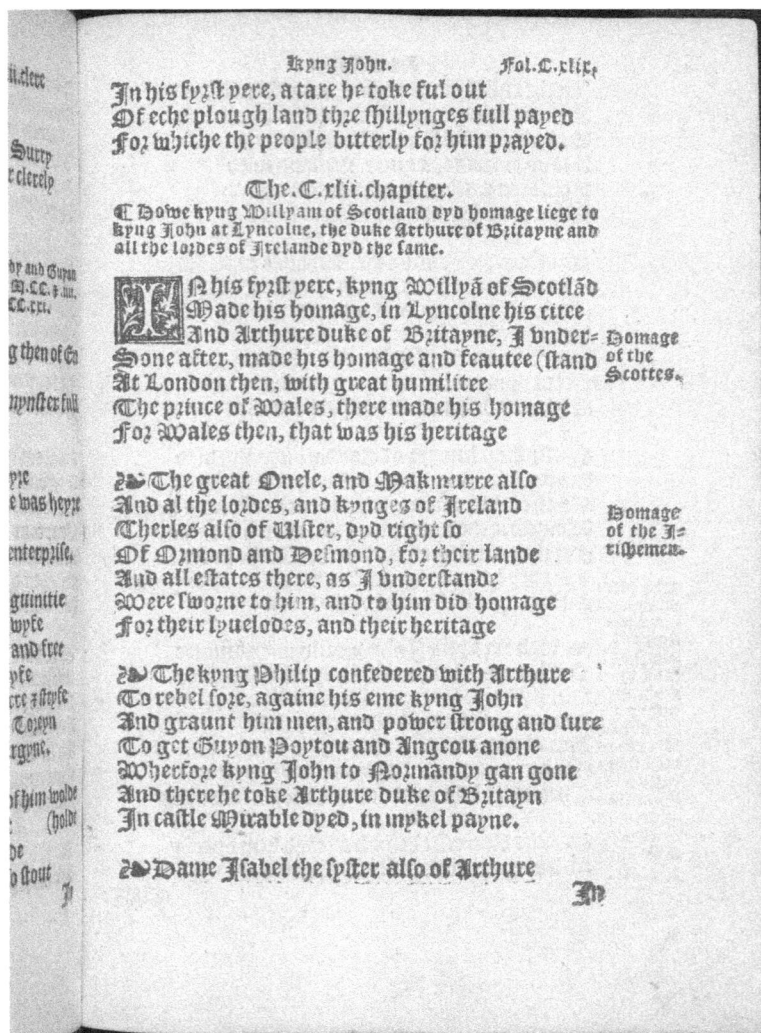

Fig. 5.3 Hardyng notes John's homage from William at Lincoln. *The Chronicle of John Hardyng* (London: Richard Grafton, 1543). The Bodleian Libraries, University of Oxford, 4º H 17 Art Seld, fol. 149 r.

English king, made an early emotional appeal to the emergent idea of the 'liberty of England': '[i]f yow will put Strangers and right *Englishe* Men in one Case', he exclaimed, 'What avayleth the Liberty of *Ingland*? What

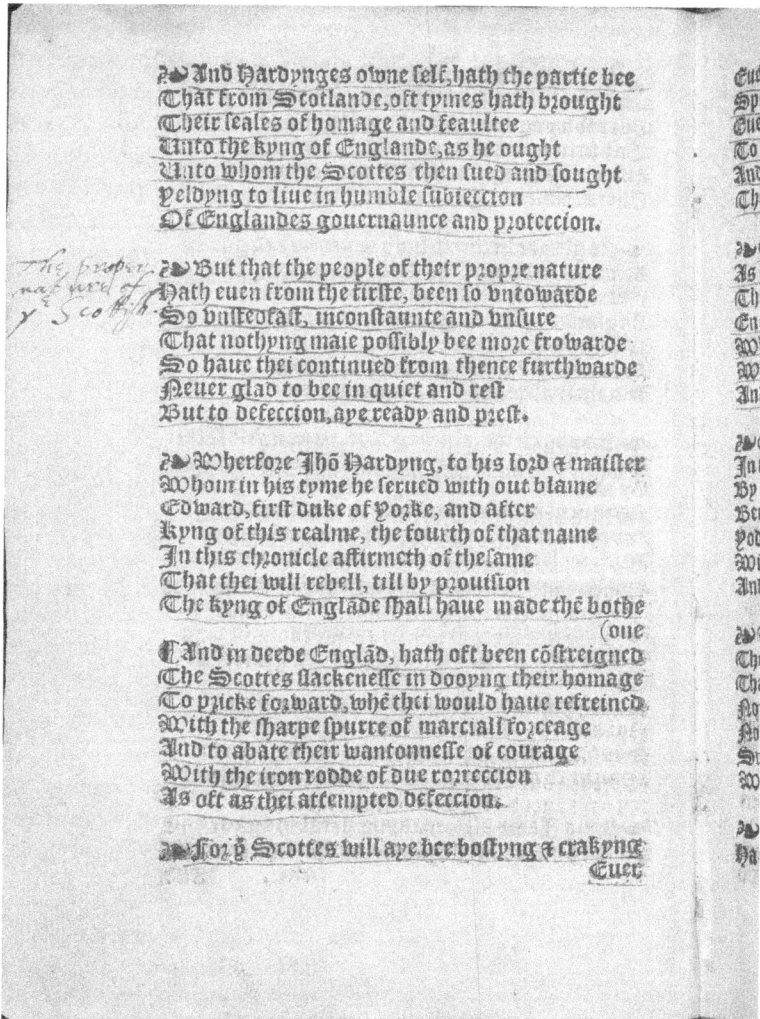

Fig. 5.4 'The proper nature of ye Scottishe', reader's annotation. *The Chronicle of John Hardyng* (London: Richard Grafton, 1543). The Bodleian Libraries, University of Oxford, 4° H 17 Art Seld, sig.§§2v.

profiteth it to be an *Englishe* Man borne?'[35] Plowden, who was collecting cases for the *Reports* he would publish in 1571, was already contributing to the 'liberty of England' by amassing the learning on equitable statute

[35] John Hales, *A Declaration of the Succession of the Crowne Imperiall of Ingland* [1563] in G. Harbin ed., *The Hereditary Right of the Crown of England Asserted* (London: 1713), xxx.

interpretation and on 'the King's Two Bodies' that would define common-law restraints on the monarch's personal power. In his *Treatise*, the exposition of that mystical doctrine becomes an ingenious way of exalting the very common-law 'liberty of England' invoked by Hales by showing that it is not threatened by a Scottish succession. Through the 'Two Bodies' theory, he shows how the common law both governs succession and grants the Scottish queen legitimacy while exercising jurisdiction over Scotland itself. An appeal to proprioception – the inner sense by which the body is aware of itself – underlies the somatic animation of Plowden's legal language in this respect. In his text, the English common law – 'a bodie constituted & devised by reason & pollicie, and of mere necessitie for preservacion of the people' – comes to occupy the ambivalent, charismatic position of the soul in medieval Catholic Christianity. In medieval Catholicism, as Guillemett Bolens explains, the body-soul opposition exists in a tension with the body-as-metaphor for the inexpressible soul:

> The idea that the body is the prison of the soul motivates practices designed to fight and overcome the flesh ... At the same time ... the central opposition between the concepts of body and soul gives rise to a series of issues bearing on the literal and figural. The body in its literality becomes the main expressive means of the soul.[36]

The same can be said for Plowden's bodies natural and politic: the natural body becomes the main expressive means of the polity in ways which not only exalt the English constitution, but grant its marvellous powers and their limits an affective force. When Plowden argues that the common law denies kings the power to determine succession by will and testament, he deprives the king's politic body of *hands*:

> And so the denyall of the lawe to the kinge to make a Testament, argueth his naturall body is not adjudged in lawe as others be. For althoughe his natural body hath handes, yet he can geve or delyver with them by the ordour of the commen lawe ... nothinge at all (21).

Conversely, the common law's capacity to lift an attainder from an heir to the throne renders the politic body a provident and cleanly housekeeper: 'Surely this body polliticke doth sweepe the house cleane wheresoever he cometh, and graunteth pardon to the naturall body by operacion in lawe as fully as he could to an other body by Charter' (28).

---

[36] Guillemette Bolens, *The Style of Gestures: Embodiment and Cognition in Literary Narrative* (Baltimore, MD: Johns Hopkins University Press, 2012), 69.

Bolens's work on the role played by kinesic intelligence and proprioception in cognition generally brings to the surface an unnoticed aspect of all literary language. Applied to a text like Plowden's, which disavows the extent of its literariness, Bolens's insistence on the importance of kinaesthetic empathy – the stimulation through language of bodily memories of movement and sensation – illuminates the source of the pervasive, if low-lying, sense of the sacred in Plowden's constitutionalist arguments. By anticipating his history of Scottish vassalage with an account of English law as an immortal politic body, Plowden can turn the historical scene of homage itself into a proprioceptively emotive allegory of Scotland's jurisdictional subordination to England. The rarity of symbolic explanations of the rites of homage in medieval documents makes Plowden's elaborate interpretation of a by then obsolete legal ritual all the more striking.[37] His final chapter brings both the *Treatise*'s strategies of proof – theological metaphor and histories of homage – together in a strange allegorical tableau in which bodies politic acquire knees, hands and mouths in order to stage a ritual of undressing, kneeling, placing hands between thighs and joining mouths in a kiss to ensure the right of the natural body of a Scottish monarch to receive the immortal body politic of England.

Historians of English law stress the legal importance of the ceremony of homage from Norman times to the fifteenth century. According to Littleton, the tenant making homage 'shal desend and hys head uncovered, & his Lorde shal sit. and the tenaunt shal kneele before him on both his knees, and holde his hands jointly together betweene the hands of his Lorde', swearing fidelity and receiving the lord's kiss.[38] By the time Plowden was writing, however, nobody was doing any kneeling or kissing for their ordinary tenancy of English lands. Land held in fee was, as J. G. A. Pocock wrote, simply 'held in a tenure which the courts recognized as heritable according to certain fixed rules', the performance of homage having ceased at some point between the time of Littleton and that of Coke.[39] John Russell Major has shown how sixteenth-century redactions and reformations of the customs of France systematically abrogate

---

[37] See Jacques Le Goff, *Time, Work and Culture in the Middle Ages*, trans. A. Goldhammer (Chicago, IL: University of Chicago Press, 1980), 239.

[38] 'Homage', *Littleton tenures in Englishe* (London, 1576), sigs. C2v-r (misfoliated); see further 'Homage and Fealty', in F. Pollock and F. W. Maitland, *The History of English Law before the Time of Edward I* (Indianapolis, IN: Liberty Fund, 2010, first published 1898), 314–24.

[39] J. G. A. Pocock, *The Ancient Constitution and the Feudal Law* (Cambridge: Cambridge University Press, 1987), 65; John Russell Major, 'Bastard Feudalism and the Kiss: Changing Social Mores in Late Medieval and Early Modern France', *The Journal of Interdisciplinary History*, vol. 17, no. 3 (1987): 509–35.

elements of intimate physical contact and bodily subjection from the requirements of homage.[40]

It is the more remarkable, then, that Plowden's concluding allegory of Scottish homage should exaggerate all these bodily gestures of physical submission and voluntarily assumed weakness and abjection. The first and most obvious of these is kneeling itself. Leah Whittington has recently reminded us in a different context that the knees were anciently associated with generativity, with the transmission of life-spirit. She cites R. B. Onians's demonstration that 'across Indo-European languages, the words for "knees" are cognate with "generation", bearing witness that "the knee was thought in some way to be the seat of paternity, of life, of generative power".'[41] Plowden glosses the meaning of kneeling to pay homage in precisely these terms. 'The kneelinge', he writes,

> sygnifieth that he enfeebleth himselfe before his Lorde, abasinge his power, and disableth himself of all strengthe, and standeth at his Lordes choice to be overthrowne yf he Lust. for when the knees be stretched out, then man hath his full strength, and in bowing them the strengthe is diminished and humilitie shewed (114).

Plowden's gloss on kneeling as a giving up of the body to be 'overthrown' in battle surely draws on the Homeric periphrasis for slaughter as a loosening of the knees of victim.[42] He then moves from a political to theological register, citing St Paul, '*In nomine Jesu omne genu flectatur, coelestium, terrestrium, et infernorum*' ('At the name of Jesus, every knee shall bow in heaven, on earth and in hell'). He comments that since neither angels nor devils have knees, the knee here signifies power *tout court*, and on a cosmic scale. The aura of theological power thus transfers itself to political allegory, as Scotland metaphorically loosens its knees before the power of England. The homager's requirement to disarm and disrobe is then described as an obligation for his loins to be 'ungyrded'. Plowden explains that men have bones or joints in their loins which, when tightly bound, make their backs strong, but which are loose and dissipated once ungirded (114–15). The spiritual association is with the sermon on the mount, from Luke 12:35, 'Let your loins be girded about', said Christ (115). The homager's slack loins thus negate the concepts of foresight and

[40] Major, 'Bastard Feudalism', 518–25.
[41] Leah Whittington, *Renaissance Suppliants: Poetry, Antiquity, Reconciliation* (Oxford: Oxford University Press, 2016), 20; R. B. Onians, *The Origins of European Thought* (Cambridge: Cambridge University Press, 1951), 174–99, 175.
[42] Onians, *Origins of European Thought*, 175, citing Homer, *Iliad*, 5.175–6; 15.291; 19.354.

providence: divine attributes, in Plowden's thinking, of the legal body politic. But the oddest aspect of Plowden's allegory of homage is his insistence that the homager place his hands between his lord's knees. The key legal gesture of homage is the handclasp, said by legal historians to be 'the very essence of the transaction'.[43] Hands between knees lays more emphasis on subordination; if hands are 'by a similitude ... taken for power' then, as Plowden explicitly says, 'the restrainte of them, purposethe imbecilitie and lacke of power' (116). If the loosening of the homager's knees recalls the possibility of being overthrown on the battlefield, his touching of the lord's knees here seems, conversely, to conjure up the secret life hidden in thighs and genitals. R. B. Onians cites Pliny the Elder on the sanctity of the knees in the usage of nations, before which, like altars, suppliants kneel and worship.[44] Plowden's strangely intimate positioning of the homager's hands thus perhaps recalls Genesis 24.1, when Abraham asks his servant to put his hand under his thigh and swear. The homager's vow to his lord seems, in Plowden's surreal scenario, to be sacred by virtue of its contact with thighs and testicles – the regions of potency, seminal life fluid, strength.

John Hales had argued that although Scottish kings had 'oft-times done their Homage ... to the Kings of *Ingland*' yet 'they have longe time forsaken their Faithe and Allegiaunce', so that Mary Stewart was born out of the allegiance of England, because her father, James V, never performed homage.[45] Plowden's theory of 'the King's Two Bodies' here comes into its own. Mary Stewart may never have bowed down before Elizabeth to offer homage, says Plowden, yet 'albeyt she [Elizabeth] have not received homage, yet she can not disclayme in the seignorie, because she enjoyeth the seignorie of Scottlande, in the right of the Crowne of England, which she enjoyeth and hath in the capacitie of her body pollitike (121).' It is no matter, he goes on, that homage was not done by James V (Mary's father) or herself,

> For the not doyinge yt, is equivalent in this case to the doyinge yt, sythens yt ought to be done: And the doer, and he to whom yt ought to be done, *be bothe bodies polliticke* [my italics]: in whiche case the not doyinge, is but a defferringe, & not a taking aware of that done, nor the bodie polliticke can devest the right therof without the assent of the realme. And so I must conclude, that the Queene of Scottes and her father were homageors to

[43] See Pollock and Maitland, *English Law before the Time of Edward I*, 314, citing Bracton, Glanville and Littleton. Numerous twelfth- and thirteenth-century illuminations show the handclasp.
[44] Onians, *Origins*, 181, 183.   [45] Hales, *Declaration*, xx–xlii, xxxi.

England, and borne within the fee & seignorie of England. And so [tou-chinge] the lawe in this poincte of disabilitie by foreine byrthe, in anye place is not a disabilitie to receave by discent the Crowne of England, muche lesse in Scottland, and least of all in the Queene of Scottes (123).

The *Treatise*'s elaboration of the theory of 'the King's Two Bodies' was, then, far from unnecessary, for its purpose was never simply the purging of a putative 'disabilitie of foreign birth' in the Queen of Scots. The neo-Galfridian history of Scotland's being feudally held, since the time of Locrine, of England had now been transformed by the 'Two Bodies' theory into a constitutional allegory. Plowden had not only asserted the jurisdiction of the common law over the natural body of England's monarch and over the succession, but over the crown and constitution of Scotland itself. In Plowden's account it was not just the Queen of Scots but the 'body politic' of Scotland, Scotland's constitution as a kingdom, that owed perpetual homage or ligeance to the body politic of the English common law. Moreover, Plowden's final allegorical scene of homage rendered the Scottish body politic as abject as any natural body. For if the body politic was defined by a lack of the 'imbecilities' of the body natural, the display of Scotland's body politic in the posture of homage was an image of its voluntarily assumed 'imbecilitie and lacke of power' (117). Plowden's tour de force of geopolitical theology was thus clearly the legal and theoretical counterpart of Cecil's policy towards Scotland during the Marian crisis of 1567–73: for all it justified a Scottish succession, it had the concept of Scottish regality on its knees before the English common law.

III.   'But some will perhaps demande why I now tearme the Scots aliens'

Understanding Plowden's assimilation of Galfridian British history to English constitutionalism helps explain why it is misleading to assume, in 1603, that the iconology of 'Great Britain' was James's foreign innov-ation, or to talk about James's 'Britishness' putting him 'outside the inherited constitutional languages'. Clearly, English legal thought could absorb a mythic history of Scottish vassalage and translate it into a constitutional language.[46] Plowden's arguments were adapted and

---

[46] Not that Plowden's arguments convinced all the lawyers. William Fleetwood wrote a treatise objecting that his friend Plowden had confused the bond of *ligeance* between a king and his subjects with that of homage between a lord and his man. See Kim, *Aliens*, 171–2; Brooks, *Law, Politics and Society*, 74–8.

popularised and his treatise was officially recognised as having helped establish James's succession when Plowden's son, Francis, presented a copy to James.[47] After 1603, however, with a Scottish monarch on the English throne, perceptions of the usefulness of Plowden's fusion of a Galfridian British history of overlordship with the constitutionalist doctrine of the 'Two Bodies' changed rapidly. Englishmen continued to believe in Scotland's historic vassalage but were wary of permitting that argument to suggest that Scots were 'within the ligeance' of the king of England's power by the common law. In February 1607 the Commons, seeking a watertight argument to challenge the *de jure* naturalisation of the post-nati, invoked the 'Two Bodies' theory without mentioning homage, arguing that Scots and English owed separate ligeance to James's separate bodies politic. The same argument was made by lawyers for the defence in *Calvin's Case* (1608) to deny the post-natus plaintiff, the three-year-old Scot Robert Colville, the right to recover lands in England.[48] It is important to note that the 'Two Bodies' argument was defeated in *Calvin's Case* but that, by the same token, the case did not naturalise James's Scottish subjects in the sense of endowing them with all the liberties of the English common law. Rather, the case asserted that a subject of one of James's royal territories beyond the reach of the common law (such as Virginia or Scotland) could come to England and, if he bought or inherited land there, could sue in the English common-law courts to vindicate his title.[49] 'Allegeance,' as Lord Chancellor Ellesmere said, 'cannot bee framed by Policie, nor put in a politike body. An oath must be sworne by a naturall bodie.'[50] If *Calvin's Case* did not naturalise the post-nati or grant the Scots free trade, but rather extended limited common-law rights to the subjects of other royal territories, it is surely worth asking why that was, and why, indeed, the case had to be brought in the first place. What accounted for the strength of the Commons' resistance to naturalisation and freedom of trade in the 1606–7 debates?

I want to turn here to influential 1604 treatises by Sir Henry Savile and Sir Henry Spelman, both of which clearly and explicitly subscribed to English overlordship of Scotland just as Plowden did (and often citing the same authorities). What they abandoned, however, was Plowden's suggestion that the history of English overlordship might be translated into

---

[47] Axton, *Queen's Two Bodies*, 19.   [48] Galloway, *Union*, 106, 151.
[49] Daniel J. Hulsebosch, 'Ancient Constitution and Expanding Empire: Sir Edward Coke's British Jurisprudence', *Law and History Review*, vol. 21, no. 3 (2003), 439–82, 458.
[50] Louis A. Knafla, *Law and Politics in Jacobean England* (Cambridge: Cambridge University Press, 1977), 246.

a contemporary constitutional relationship of bodies politic that would qualify the Scots for English legal liberties. As historians and antiquaries, both men argued from supposedly reliable instruments and archival records that Scotland had long been held in fee of England and had never been a sovereign nation. Yet this argument was not permitted to affect their treatment of contemporary Scotland as a sovereign nation whose people were aliens. That point in its turn – that Scotland was a sovereign nation and its people foreign – might be thought to offer support for the argument that James's accession had *changed* something for England. If James's accession had brought England the de facto government of another sovereign nation which had accordingly sacrificed its own king, royal court and independent foreign policy, then it might be argued that common-law liberties could be extended to Scots in recognition of this benefit to England.

However, by a strategic and circular recourse to the historical argument – that Scotland had always been held in fee of England – the value of what Scotland brought to the union was never allowed, in either of their treatises, to weigh in the calculation of whether the Scots merited common-law liberties or access to free trade. Spelman denied that Scots had anything of value to deserve reciprocal liberties, while Savile maintained that Scots' trading privileges in France rendered them too dangerous to be trusted with freedom of trade or naturalisation. The fact that Scotland was now being ruled from London was somehow subtracted, by antiquarian sleight of hand, from the calculation of material and security benefits brought to England with James's accession.

The rhetorical success of these treatises is evident in the readiness of English constitutional historians likewise to overlook the geopolitical security brought by Scotland to England at expense of the Scots having their own king and independent foreign policy. John Kerrigan has written sensitively of how '[t]he problems of regal union galvanised socio-economic discontent in Scotland' noting the 'sense that the country was "maymed" without its monarch'.[51] James's southward move undoubtedly entailed a loss of national autonomy whose adverse economic effects were exacerbated by the English refusal to admit freedom of trade between the nations. S. G. Lythe argued that Scotland's striking failure (in contrast to England) in trade and colonisation was 'attributable mainly to the anomaly of her diplomatic status ... after 1603 Scotland no longer had an independent foreign policy, and she had not yet acquired the whole-hearted

[51] Kerrigan, *Archipelagic English*, 152.

goodwill of England'.[52] Yet English arguments against mutual naturalisation and free trade seem to have rendered invisible the problem Lythe
describes: the anomaly of Scottish post-1603 'sub-national' status. English
constitutional historians are proof of the rhetorical skill of the 1604 anti-
naturalisation arguments in that they accept that the Commons' real
concern was with the threat posed by naturalisation or free trade to the
integrity of the English common law. Thus, where Bruce Galloway notes
the expediency of the House of Commons' 1607 sequence of objections to
naturalisation (invoking the 'body politic' objection in February 1607 and
moving on to 'the perfect union' objection in March), Conrad Russell sees
these arguments as principled and perfectly understandable expressions of
the English 'identification of nationality with the law, and the unitary
character of the state'.[53] Models of composite monarchy, while apparently
viable for other European states, were impossible for England, Russell
insists, because of the highly developed nature of English constitutionalism; final authority in the state had to rest with the English common law.
This leads him to argue that things would have been different had Scotland
not been a sovereign state: '[t]he fundamental inconvenient fact of Scottish
sovereignty', he argued, meant that 'Union with Scotland presented
England with a fundamental challenge to its intellectual world'.[54]

Those whose treatises most effectively undermined the case for mutual
naturalisation did not, however, believe that Scotland was a sovereign state:
they clearly stated their belief in English overlordship and Scottish sub-
regality, and they fully understood the import of Edward VI's and
Protector Somerset's British imperial project of the 1540s. The weakness
in their belief in overlordship, however, was its suggestion that Scots might
be 'within the ligeance'; that is, not aliens. And more was at stake in that
distinction than the coherence of an intellectual world. The need to
exclude the Scots from English liberties while insisting they were not
a sovereign people could lead to some awkward transitions, as when
Spelman excused the contradiction between his insistence that Scots are
aliens and his earlier argument that they have always been under English
suzerainty: 'But some perhaps will demande why I now tearme the Scottes
aliens and str[*angers*. Marginal note: "friends" in a different hand] since
before I have shewed them to have been taken as members of England', he
wrote. And he hastened to say that the Scots themselves denied their vassal

[52] Lythe, *Economy*, 75.
[53] Galloway, *Union 1603–1608*, 106–14; Conrad Russell, *King James VI and I and His English Parliaments*, eds. Richard Cust and Andrew Thrush (Oxford: Oxford University Press, 2011), 134.
[54] Russell, *James VI and I*, 138.

status and failed in their allegiance and so were clearly aliens.[55] Sir Henry
Savile, distinguishing between types of union, was adamant in Chapter 4 of
his treatise that it was 'meerly frivolous and false' to deny that '*Scotland
hath of long time bin homager to England*' (190–1). Nevertheless, he chose to
define the union as one of 'two states absolute and soveraign' (189).
Choosing to ground objections to mutual naturalisation in forms of
argument that treat the union as one of sovereign equals enabled both
Spelman and Savile to pursue comparative arguments, Spelman of benefits
to be gained, and Savile of different constitutional arrangements between
unions of states. Needless to say, Scotland proved wanting in these comparisons, undeserving of sharing the benefit of the peace between the
nations to which it had contributed. The imagining of England as an
island was thus configured anew. This time, the seas around Albion –
which included Scotland – were defined as anciently English, while the
poverty of the Scots and their liberties in France rendered naturalisation
and free trade an intolerably dangerous prospect to England, notwithstanding their shared government from London.

Savile's comparative procedure – considering the unions in Europe: that
of France and Navarre, Lithuania and Poland, Castile and Leon and,
finally, Portugal and Castile – was something of a stalking horse. Citing
Juno's plea, in Virgil's *Aeneid*, that no change of name, language, attire or
customs be forced on the conquered Latins by Aeneas's Trojan victory
(198–9), Savile agnostically rehearsed arguments for and against a change of
name.[56] As Juno was granted her plea that the defeated nation's name
(Latium) should be taken by the conquering Trojans, Savile was willing to
consider the name of 'Britain', recalling Edward VI's proposal and delving
into the credibility of Geoffrey of Monmouth (202, 210–11). Savile, however, was sceptical about Monmouth; the first reliable record he found of
an English king claiming dominion over all Britain or all Albion was that of
the Saxon King Edgar (943–75) whose significance will become clear when
we come on to Spelman's treatise (212). Leaving the question of title, Savile
proceeded swiftly to tick off the other properties of enduring union he
derived from *Aeneid* Book XII, finding that the English and Scots enjoy the
required similarities of language, attire and religion. This left him with the
last and most significant of his Virgilian precedents, '*patrios mores*',

---

[55] Henry Spelman, 'Of the Union', in *Jacobean Union*, eds. Galloway and Levack, 161–84; 174.
    Henceforward references to page numbers of Spelman's and Savile's treatises will appear in the text.
[56] Virgil, *Aeneid, VII-XII*, 2 vols., trans. H. R. Fairclough, rev. G. P. Goold (Cambridge, MA: Harvard
    University Press, 2000), XII.823–8, 834–7.

national customs, which he took to be '*lex non scripta*', unwritten law, corresponding to English common law (199).

This last and 'most important point of our union' (217) included the enjoyment of 'the same liberties and priviledges' (217). Savile considered the liberties and privileges articled in various European unions of states, coming at last to that 'likest to ours ... the union between Portugall and Castile' (229). Here he noted among other things that King Philip II endowed the Portuguese with the liberties of the Castilians in the West Indies, while denying the Castilians (the subjects of the nation where he was born) a share in Portuguese freedoms in the East Indies (231–2). The implied application to James's conduct with respect to England and Scotland (though the parallels are not close) is clear. The example, said Savile, shows that 'not only is the prince to bear himself indifferently but must deal more respectively and more tenderly with the nation where he was not born, for they will naturally stand more jealous of all his actions then his own countrymen' (232). In other words, just as Philip took care to endow Portugal with Castilian trading liberties while denying reciprocal liberties to his birth-country subjects, so the subjects of Scotland, James's birth-country, should be denied freedom of trade with England and English naturalisation. The parallel to Castilian trade privileges in the West Indies was, Savile argued, Scotland's trading privileges in France, confirmed in 1548 and 1558 (236–7). All Savile's earlier apparent concessions to union founder at the point at which he considers the economic and political danger posed to England by Scots' freedom to live and trade in France. The French, he warned ominously, 'have free liberty of fishing upon the coast of Scotland' (236). His final '*Querie, whether in this our union the league between France and Scotland, and the liberties granted, may safelie stand and not be dangerous now or hereafter*' is unequivocally answered in the negative (239).

Savile's account of the dangers of Franco-Scots trading privileges were echoed and heightened in the anonymous *A Discourse of Naturalisation* where it was argued that the combination of advantage in France and Spelman's vivid depiction of the competitive edge of Scottish parsimony in trading methods would mean that 'in a shorte tyme, all the Trade in ffraunce ... will be in the hands of the Scotts'.[57] Scots had been exempted from customs in Normandy in 1510, and in 1548 all Scots were made

<hr>

[57] National Archives SP 14/10A, fol. 40v. Further references in text. My thanks to Daniel Haywood for his transcription of the MS. For the importance of the *Discourse* for subsequent debates, see Galloway, *Union 1603–1608*, 59, 69–70, 72, 99–102.

naturalised subjects in France and vice versa, and therefore free of impositions laid on strangers.[58] These freedoms were, understandably, the object of English hostility and anxiety. The Commission dismissed the Scottish privileges as indifferent, but the *Discourse* argued that Scots could buy direct from vineyards, whereas the English had to go through a middleman. 'No mention,' as Galloway notes, 'was made of the shorter Scots sailing season or the greater travelling distance.' He observes further that 'A memorandum comparing English and Scots privileges considered the difference minimal; since Alien's Custom did not exist in France outside Normandy, the Scots advantage in Bordeaux described by the *Discourse* was illusory, while Scots privileges in Normandy were limited to goods passing into Scotland for domestic use.'[59] The idea that Scots traders might then re-export such goods to England, undercutting English traders, was refuted by Scots merchants, who explained that the voyaging costs would exceed any savings on customs.[60] It is clear from Savile's positioning of this relatively minor objection, however, that it proved much more effective as an objection to Scottish naturalisation than any arguments based on England's historic sovereignty over Scotland might have been. 'How ... maye we saye we are securely safe', exclaimed the *Discourse*, when Scotsmen naturalised in France 'shall dwell in our bosomes, and in all respects *quo ad beneficia*, be reputed Englishemen?' (fol. 42 r).

Sir Henry Spelman's *Of the Union* proved complementary to Savile's work in furnishing *A Discourse* and the Commons' debates with 'a variety of unconvincing but much-repeated arguments to show that Scots would come in time to dominate British trade' unless they continued to be treated as aliens.[61] Though their rhetorical strategies were distinct, there were parallels. Both insisted simultaneously on ancient overlordship and Scottish alien status, both made much of the Saxon King Edgar as proof of English dominion over Scotland and both set out to arouse fears for the English economy and English security, disingenuously discounting the immense improvement in the prospects of both entailed in Scotland's being under the rule of the English king.

Spelman opened his treatise with a frankly acquisitive approach to the question of Scottish naturalisation: 'As for ritches, what have they to enritche us withal? What marchandize of worthe? What freedoms, what

[58] Theodora Keith, *Commercial Relations of England and Scotland, 1603–1707* (Cambridge: Cambridge University Press, 1910), 4–5.
[59] Galloway, *Union*, 101, 70.   [60] *CSP, Domestic, James I*, 336.
[61] Galloway, *Union 1603–1608*, 43–4.

libertyes to endow us with?' (162). As he went on to disparage Scottish merchandise – wool, corn, salt, herring – the answer was predictably negative. But then Spelman seemed to adjust his priorities and to acknowledge something far more momentous, 'the strength that the uniting of Scotland bringeth unto England' (163). Here he moved, appropriately, into the topos of inexpressibility, words being inadequate to express the value of what union with Scotland has brought to England. 'Who doth not see and confesse', he wrote,

> that we (yf any nation under the sonne) ar now invincyble, for yf England alone ... hath in tymes passed invaded the most puisant kingdoms of Europe ... how much more puisant and dreadful must it of necessity now be when the populous and mighty nation of the Scots, which hitherto impeded [crossed out – 'hindered'] our victoryes and honor, is now conjoyned and associate unto us? ... We haue now no inlande enemy, no borderer, none to make roades, incursions or sudden attemptes upon us. Our enemyes must nowe come a far off and before us, for our frends are everywhere about and behind us. The sea hath taken us into her protection and sequestered our enemies and none can assayle us but with duble preparation and manifould danger. O (said Pericles) if we were an isle, we were invincible ... Therefore to conclude this pointe, the strengthe and felicity th[at] this union bringeth to England cannot be expressed (163–4).

One might assume, then, that Spelman would conclude that the strength brought by association with Scotland more than makes up for any failure of Scottish merchandise and legal liberties to be of value to English subjects. On the contrary. Separating the question of title from those of laws and privileges (164), he was quick to retract his admission of the 'strengthe and felicity' newly acquired by union. Spelman recalled that 'the comon name of Albion or Brytane' was proposed by Protector Somerset in the 1540s, but 'Britain' has, he continued, become uncertain in its reference, partly thanks to Buchanan who, in his history, argued that it sometimes refers only to England (168). Yet uncertainty about the historicity of 'Britain' – which Savile shared – is immaterial, since Spelman knew that authentic records exist to prove that the style 'King of England' was always understood to include sovereignty over Scotland. Here, like Savile, he turned to 'the stile of one of the most potent kings that ever reigned in the isle of Britain' (168), that is the Saxon King Edgar. Edgar proves an enormously significant choice for the imagining of England's imperial and commercial maritime future. The laws of Edward the Confessor, key to the myth of the ancient constitution, were ascribed to him. But most important was the defining role of the sea in the imagining of his title to Scotland. John Dee had enthusiastically set out Edgar's royal title in a cartouche in his text advocating a royal navy, *General and Rare Memorials pertayning to the Perfect Arte of NAVIGATION* (1577):

> *EGO ÆDGARUS, ANGLORUM*
> *BASILEUS, omniumque Regum Insularum,*
> *OCEANIQUE BRITANNIAM*
> *CIRCUMIACENTIS, Cunctarumque*
> *Nationum quae infra eum includuntur,*
> *IMPERATOR ET DOMINUS.*[62]

(I, Edgar ruler of the English, and emperor and lord of all the kings of the islands of the ocean surrounding Britain, and of all the peoples included within it.)

This formula, which Dee expands on for many pages, and which Spelman also sets out in full (171), was taken, as Spelman said, 'out of the foundation of the cathedral church of Worcester' (168). This was in fact a forgery, a charter known from its first word as '*Altitonantis*' ('thundering from on high').[63] It had acquired currency and fame in discourses like Dee's *Memorials* and Hakluyt's *Principal Navigations* as an authentication of England's former maritime dominion, promising a future of overseas exploration and trade. John Dee praised Edgar as the 'Saxonicall Alexander', the ideal English thalassocrat and world-conqueror, reporting that he circumnavigated all his British island dominions yearly, in a navy of '4000 Sayle at the least' so that 'he wisely knew the Ancient Bownds, and Limits, of this British Impire'.[64] Another forged charter from Ely Cathedral, also set out by Spelman, celebrates Edgar's coronation at Bath in 973, at which eight 'underkings' of Scotland, Cumbria and of the islands of the British archipelago were said to have performed their homage by physically rowing his ship up the River Dee.

Sebastian Sobecki's brilliant analysis of the topos of Edgar's navigational Anglo-British empire has traced its origins in the forgeries of the monks at Worcester Cathedral priory in the early twelfth century, when their foundation was threatened by King Stephen's creation of a new earldom of Worcester as part of his campaign against the Empress Mathilda.[65] The story of British under-kings subserviently providing the oar-power for the great English *gubernator* was probably fashioned by the Ely clerics from a literalisation of the nautical metaphors of government in Aelfric's *Life of*

---

[62] Dee, *Memorials*, 60.
[63] Sebastian I. Sobecki, 'Introduction: Edgar's Archipelago', *The Sea and Englishness in the Middle Ages: Maritime Narratives, Identity and Culture*, ed. S. I. Sobecki (Cambridge: D. S. Brewer, 2011), 1–30, 9.
[64] Dee, *Memorials*, 57.   [65] Sobecki, 'Edgar's Archipelago'.

St Swithun.[66] What Sobecki's account makes abundantly clear, however, is the centrality of Edgar's afterlife to the emergence of a mid-seventeenth century discourse of English legal liberties with respect to commerce and sea-empire. The frontispiece to Marchamont Nedham's 1652 translation of Selden's *Mare Clausum* shows Britannia seated on a rock inscribed 'Angliae respub.' with the arms of Scotland, Wales and Ireland at her feet and a charioted Neptune, heralded by Tritons, saluting her. Nedham's accompanying poem encourages England 'to adopt an imperialist policy, grounded in its naval strength', to make new discoveries and add new seas to those British seas over which Edgar ruled.[67] Sobecki gives us some sense of the afterlife of 'Altitonantis':

> In the second edition of his *Principal Navigations* (1598), Richard Hakluyt printed most of *Altitonantis* and included the entire *Libelle* [*The Libelle of Englyshe Polycy*, c.1430] besides commenting on the various sizes given for Edgar's fleet. He may have come across the latter in John Dee's *General and Rare Memorials pertayning to the Perfect Arte of NAVIGATION* (1577) . . . Next, Edward Coke printed *Altitonantis* in 1604 . . . But it is only in Selden's *Mare clausum* – printed in 1635, though written before 1618 – that the various strands of Edgar's archipelagic ambitions are brought together for the first time.

We see, then, how the antiquarian citation of the forged Worcester and Ely charters documenting Edgar's sea-empire and sovereignty over Scotland works in Spelman's *Of the Union*. Spelman had opened by weighing the value of Scottish merchandise and liberties, then he acknowledged the inexpressible strength and felicity the union brought to England in terms of maritime strength. The charters proclaiming Edgar's imperial style, however, prove that England *always had this maritime strength* and that it included dominion over Scotland. The double imperative of securing the English coastline by having no land border with a foreign country, while maintaining the integrity of 'England' in royal style and the liberty of English law is thus imaginatively achieved in the precedent of Edgar sailing round Scottish seas as part of his British empire. Spelman commented that Edgar's title of king of Albion, uses a name 'that without controversie was ever understood to comprehend all Scotland as well as England' (169). Immediately after citing Edgar's style, Spelman was then able to repeat his

---

[66] David E. Thornton, 'Edgar and the Eight Kings, AD 973: *textus et dramatis personae*', *Early Medieval Europe* vol. 10, no. 1 (2001), 49–79.

[67] Sobecki, 'Edgar's Archipelago', 4; John Selden, *Of the Dominion, or Ownership of the Sea. Two Books*, trans. Marchamont Nedham (London: 1652), frontispiece.

first questions ('What welthe the Scottes have to enriche us with? What marchandize of worth? What freedomes? What libertyes to endow us with?' 170) as if James's accession had brought no change at all to England's geopolitical security and maritime strength. Edgar models the overlordship as an English claim to the jurisdiction of the seas around Britain to which the Scots, as people, are entirely superfluous.

Spelman was then free to paint a slightly crazed picture of a Scottish nation whose risible poverty and inadequacy somehow qualified it as a serious threat to all English overseas trade, manufacturing and professions. Before James's accession, Scottish traders paid, as well as ordinary customs, a hefty alien's custom when bringing goods into England for sale. On Christmas Day 1604 this was lifted, saving considerable sums to the captains of Scottish vessels arriving in Boston, Hull or Newcastle with salt, fish, linen or *charbon d'ecosse* (Scottish charcoal) for glass-making. Spelman's objections, reiterated in the anonymous *A Discourse of Naturalisation* and dominating the Commons' debates in 1606–7, ensured that the saving was short-lived: the pre-1603 duties were soon revived.[68] Spelman warned against opening 'passage to Colchis for the goulden fleece' by lifting prohibitions against using foreign ships, '[f]or the Scottes ... being traned upp with harder lyfe and diett will performe a viage a 3d parte cheaper then the England' (177). In a lather of xenophobic indignation, the *Discourse* took up these accusations of spartan habits of mercantile voyaging (smaller ships, frugally victualled) and blended them with outrage at the tax-free Bordeaux wines Scots were rumoured to be able to have in exchange for fish and hides, to produce a horrifying scenario of naturalised Scots rapidly devouring their English counterparts. 'By ther Naturalization, the Scotts in ffraunce do trade as freely there with the same Immunyties, as the Naturall French', the *Discourse* declared and went on to complain that whereas

> The English lyue in a gentlemanlyke fashion and sett ther Shipps to the Seas in a warlyke manner, well manned, at great wadges, and plentifully vyctualled to ther great chardge: The Scotts in expences are frugall, and go meanely shipped ... yf the Scotts be naturalyzed in England ... respecting the inequallety of the expences in manner of lyveinge betwene ther marchants and ours ... yt is apparant that the Scottishe marchantes will eate out ours in a small tyme (fols. 40v-41 r).

Scots artificers and tradesmen who will 'flocke hither in such multitudes' will each of them

---

[68] Lythe, *Economy*, 202, 217; Keith, *Commercial*, 15–17.

gather vnto himselff the wealthe of his neighbours and vndermyne them in proffyte ... such is there parsimonious lyff in respect of ours, and there povertie wilbe evermore a spurr vnto them to make them industryous to thryve (fol. 41v).

Even were the parsimony and greed of Scots artificers less monstrous, England has no room for them: 'we that fynde already our countarie to narrowe for our selffs must make roome for others, and learne to lodge 7 ffryers in 6 bedds' (fol. 41v). Savile's and Spelman's arguments, redacted and circulated in the *Discourse* and repeated many times in the Commons debates of 1606–7, ensured that the *de jure* naturalisation of the post-nati was reversed and that Scots remained aliens for purposes of trade.

English literary accounts of reactions to the prospect of Union at James's accession have tended to align Union with James's absolutism, portraying English resistance either in terms of a commitment to local diversity of custom or to constitutionalist restraints on the monarch. Neither of these models permits the motivated incoherence of the English construction of Scottish nationhood to emerge into visibility. Nor do these models acknowledge that 'Britain' was not an innovative idea and that Galfridian British history of overlordship itself played a crucial role in the development of English arguments about the immemoriality of English common law and the fiction of 'the King's Two Bodies'.[69] The idea that James's 'British' project was imperialist towards Englishmen or threatened an 'enslavement' or 'conquest' of the English is entirely a product of arguments designed to defeat the proposals of mutual naturalisation and free trade.

In conclusion, this chapter has shown that Edmund Plowden's *Treatise on the Succession* deployed the doctrine of 'the King's Two Bodies' not to purge the defect of a Scottish monarch's 'disability of foreign birth', but rather to translate the spurious historical claim of England's overlordship of Scotland into a constitutionalist political theology, an account of how a Scottish succession would be controlled by England's body politic or common law. On James's accession, Plowden's constitutionalist version of overlordship seemed inadequate to counter the prospect of naturalisation and mutual free trade between England and Scotland. Accordingly, some writers of treatises produced shifting and incoherent accounts of Scottish nationhood, veering expediently between construing Scotland as an English fief and as a sovereign state with the effect of occluding

---

[69] George Garnett, '"the oulde fields": Law and History in the Prefaces to Sir Edward Coke's Reports', *The Journal of Legal History* (2013), vol. 34, no. 3, 245–84.

Scotland's contribution to English prosperity at James's accession so as to justify excluding the Scots from English liberties and free trade. These strategies have been taken at face value in a narrative which has presented James as passionately devoted to union as a personal vanity project. James's practical need as the king of Scots to resolve the status of his Scottish subjects' nationhood has been ignored. English opposition to it has been seen as an altruistic, constitutionalist resistance to foreign absolutism, even though setting up a committee and going through Parliament is hardly absolutist. As the naturalisation of the post-nati was rejected by the House of Commons, the problem of Scottish sub-nationhood remained unresolved until 1707, with detrimental effects on Scotland's prosperity. *Calvin's Case* did not achieve naturalisation; rather, it contributed, if indirectly, to the exportability of English liberties abroad. Daniel Hulsebosch has argued that in *Calvin's Case*, Edward Coke inadvertently sketched the beginnings of a jurisprudence for American colonies. Because the case proved that James's subjects in royal territories outside England owed allegiance to his natural not politic body, and that they could nevertheless sue in the common law for lands purchased or inherited in England, it opened the way for the common law to be perceived as an abstract jurisprudence operative in the Crown's colonial dominions.[70] Though Coke saw English liberties as confined to the jurisdiction of England, the effect of his decision was to establish that there were 'core English liberties – property rights and consent – that the king had to respect whenever Englishmen traveled to his non-English dominions'.[71] English liberties thus became exportable to colonies such as Virginia (of which one of Union's greatest opponents, Sir Edwin Sandys, was governor) without becoming the birthright of Scots.

This chapter is indebted to the work of the legal historians Baker, Halliday, Kim and Hulsebosch on the sixteenth-century elevation of English legal freedoms to an abstract national right enshrined in Magna Carta. It has argued that the denial of common-law liberties to James's Scottish subjects can be seen as part of that very process of abstraction and elevation to a national right. In *Calvin's Case*, the process expanded to the point at which English liberties, in Hulsebosch's words, 'began to escape their jurisdictional matrix ... to become a jurisprudence of British liberty'.[72] The process itself is, to a hitherto unrecognised extent, indexed by the rhetoric of Scottish exclusion. As Paul Halliday has shown, the

---

[70] Hulsebosch, 'Constitution and Empire', 481.   [71] Hulsebosch, 'Constitution and Empire', 466.
[72] Hulsebosch, 'Constitution and Empire', 469.

language of birthrights premised on their divine origins gave the levellers of the English Revolution 'a powerful rhetorical position' from which to correct judges and Parliament 'who seemed too ready to sell England's birthrights for the same "mess of pottage" that Esau had taken in payment for his own birthright'.[73] Forty years, before, however, precisely this language of the birthright was being used, by Sir Henry Spelman, as a powerful rhetorical argument to keep freedom *English*, not Scottish. 'The freedoms that God giveth to nations by their birth is no lighte thinge', he exhorted, 'Let us not then with Esau make a little accompte of so greate a blessing . . . Let us not, I say, exchange our ritch freedomes of England for those other of Scotland whereby so little commodity is likely to redound unto us' (183). Sir Edwin Sandys likewise objected in the Commons in March 1606 to the word 'naturalisation', saying 'The word is too Generall. That word maketh a man inheritable unto Magna Charta.'[74] These men both had colonial interests and well knew the commodity Scotland's conjunction had already brought to England in terms of maritime power. Their arguments should no longer simply be seen as a triumph of English constitutional resistance to the 'foreign absolutist' James VI and I.

---

[73] Halliday, 'Birthrights', 599.
[74] *The Parliamentary Diary of Robert Bowyer 1606–7* ed. David Harris Willson (New York, NY: Octagon, 1971), 219.

CHAPTER 6

Scotland Un-kingdomed: English History on Stage

I. Playbook History

When Fitzdotterel, the foolish Norfolk squire of Ben Jonson's *The Devil Is an Ass*, is complimented on his knowledge of English history, he confesses that he gets it all not from chronicles but 'from the playbooks'. This playbook history is 'more authentic', he adds.[1] Though Jonson is poking fun at his ignorance, there's also a sense in which Fitzdotterel has a point. For British people, Shakespeare's history plays have not only shaped a sense of their country's past, but its future. In 2016, the architect of Brexit, Daniel Hannan (now Lord Hannan) responded to the victory of the Leave Campaign by standing on a desk in his office to recite the St Crispin's Day speech from Shakespeare's *Henry V* – '"We few, we happy few, we band of brothers" – substituting the names of people who had worked on the campaign.'[2] Persuaded that Leave voters were motivated by concern for British sovereignty (rather than by worry about the economy or immigration), Hannan found in Shakespeare's St Crispin's Day speech a historical authentication of the idea of England/Britain as an island nation whose destiny lies outside Europe.

The Crispin Day speech is explicitly, of course, about *England* – it sketches an annual ritual of veteran reminiscence mutating into a prophecy of national remembrance 'From this day to the ending of the world' (4.3.58). Hannan's appropriation of the speech as a vindication of the Leave Campaign participates in what is a routine and generally unremarkable sense of the interchangeability of Britain and England, the stakes of which had, however, been somewhat raised in 2016 by the fact that a majority in Scotland voted to remain in the European Union. Yet Hannan's recourse to *Henry V* already belonged, as he no doubt knew, to

---

[1] Ben Jonson, *The Devil Is an Ass*, ed. Anthony Parr, in *CWBJ*, IV. 2.4.13–14.
[2] See Sam Knight, 'The Man Who Brought You Brexit', *The Guardian*, 29 September 2016: www .theguardian.com/politics/2016/sep/29/daniel-hannan-the-man-who-brought-you-brexit.

a tradition of modern British patriotic iconography, most notably in Laurence Olivier's film of 1944, but also in the speeches of Churchill and the criticism of E. M. W. Tillyard and G. Wilson Knight.[3] A historian might observe that in *Henry V*'s time the Scots, far from supporting the English invasion of France, were the backbone of French military resistance to England, contributing to England's eventual loss.[4] But for literary critics to object on those grounds to *Henry V*'s modern British afterlife would be to propose a crudely literal relation between chronicle and stage play. It would be to ignore the truth buried in Fitzdotterel's claim for the peculiar authenticity of playbook history, which points us towards acknowledging the reflexive nature of works of art, or the way plays invite and stimulate readers and audiences to imagine and critique the events they represent.

Literary critics have, in this respect, long been interested the play's enigmatic prolepsis of a post-1707 'British' identity incorporating English, Welsh, Irish and Scots in a single army fighting a Continental enemy. A single scene, part of the Harfleur siege, and occurring only the 1623 Folio text of the play, involves four army captains, two of which, the Welsh Fluellen and the English Gower, have more extensive roles in the play, while the other two, the Irish MacMorris, and the Scottish Jamy, exist only for the purpose of that scene.[5] It opens with a disagreement about the conduct of siege warfare, but debate founders on an apparent perception of insult encoded in the Welshman's unfinished observation about the Irish 'nation'. Teasingly opaque, this 'four captains' scene has become central to postcolonial and archipelagic readings of the play.[6] It has been persuasively interpreted as depicting the coloniser's fantasy of the willingly colonised subject, forming part of what has been referred to as 'the expansion of the national unit' of England in 1599: 'The four captains in *Henry V* bear

[3] Graham Holderness, 'Agincourt 1944: Readings in the Shakespeare Myth', *Literature and History*, vol. 10, no. 1 (1984), 10, 24–45.
[4] Jonathan Sumption, *Trial By Battle: The Hundred Years War*, 4 vols. (London: Faber, 1990), I.59–65.
[5] *Henry V* ed. Craik, 3.2. Further references to this edition will appear in the text.
[6] 'Archipelagic' here refers to literary-critical studies inspired by J. A. G. Pocock, 'British History: A Plea for a New Subject', *The Journal of Modern History*, vol. 47, no. 4 (1975), 601–21. See, for example, Philip Schwyzer and David Mealor, eds., *Archipelagic Identities: Literature and History in the Atlantic Archipelago* (Aldershot: Ashgate, 2004) and Kerrigan, *Archipelagic English*. For archipelagic readings of the play, see David Cairns and Shaun Richards, 'What Ish My Nation?' in *Writing Ireland: Colonialism, Nationalism and Culture* ed. Cairns and Richards (Manchester: Manchester University Press, 1988), 1–21; David J. Baker, '"Wildehirissheman": Colonialist Representation in *Henry V*, *ELR*, vol. 22, no. 1 (1992), 37–61; Andrew Murphy, '"Tish ill done": *Henry the Fift* and the Politics of Editing', in *Shakespeare and Ireland: History, Politics, Culture* ed. Mark Thornton Burnett and Ramona Wray (Basingstoke: Macmillan, 1997), 213–29; Schwyzer, *Literature, Nationalism*, 126–50.

testimony to the Elizabethans' growing conviction that the national unit
was not England but England, Wales, Scotland, and Ireland.'[7] Vagueness
of reference to 'expansion' here covers the fact that while there has been,
since the 1980s, a general critical consensus about the parallels, in *Henry V*,
between historic wars in France and the colonial violence of Elizabethan
campaigns in Ireland, uncertainty reigns about how to characterise
England's relation to Scotland.[8] The coloniser's fantasy of the willingly
colonised fits, in different ways, the portrayal of MacMorris and Fluellen,
not least in that hopes for the suppression of Irish 'rebellion' are expressed
in the final Chorus, while it is evident that the Welsh Fluellen expresses
(both ironically and sincerely) the Tudor monarchy's claims, through its
Welsh lineage, to rule over all Britain. In Fluellen, however, the emotive
power of Tudor claims to British-Welsh descent is relocated into a more
reflexive and humorous discourse of the ethics of warfare.[9]

How to read the implications of the 'four captains' scene for a sixteenth-
century English imagining of Scotland remains unclear, especially in view
of Henry's having earlier taken thought, before embarking for France,
about how to 'defend / Against the Scot' (1.2.136–7). Ignoring Anglo-Scots
history of the Hundred Years War altogether (no doubt to avoid a vulgar
historicism of the kind I have just mentioned), critics have focused on the
scene's implications for the Irish and Welsh as colonised subjects in
the sixteenth and seventeenth centuries, identifying as the coloniser the
Scottish Captain Jamy, taken as a figure for James VI and I and his
ambitions for British Union.[10] In this context critics invoke James VI
and I's well-known image of the island of Britain as his wife, ignoring
the tacitly Anglo-imperial grounds on which the English House of
Commons rejected Union and with it all such metaphors.[11] The colonisation of Ulster is of course an Anglo-Scots phenomenon. David Armitage
writes that 'after 1608, the Stuart composite monarchy created in 1603 ...
became, for the first time, the agent of collectively British (that is, Anglo-
Scottish) colonisation in the escheated lands of Ulster'.[12] Though this is
undeniable, Armitage does not consider the radical asymmetry of the
power distribution in the 'composite monarchy' for English and Scottish

---

[7] Jonathan Baldo, 'Wars of Memory in *Henry V*', *SQ*, vol. 47, no. 2 (1996), 132–59.
[8] Jonathan Dollimore and Alan Sinfield, 'History and Ideology: The Instance of *Henry V*', in
    Alternative Shakespeares, ed. John Drakakis (London: Methuen, 1985), 206–27.
[9] Schwyzer, *Literature, Nationalism*, 126–150; David Quint, '"Alexander the Pig": Shakespeare on
    History and Poetry', *Boundary 2*, vol. 10, no. 3 (1982), 49–67.
[10] For example, Cairns and Richards, 'What Ish my Nation?', 11.   [11] See Chapter 5.
[12] Armitage, *Ideological Origins*, 26.

nations. The year 1608, as we saw in Chapter 5, also marked the end of Scottish subjects' hopes for access to freedom of trade and legal liberties on a par with English subjects, while still being tied to English foreign policy. We saw how the English refusal of Union in 1608 left the Scots not in a colonised, but in a *sub-national state*, 'a state wherein we are not considered as subjects nor allies, nor friends, nor enemies, but all of them, only when, where, and how long our task masters please'.[13]

The identification of the bit-part of 'Captain Jamy' in *Henry V* with James VI and I (thus identifying the play's Anglo-imperialism with the Scottish Stuart dynasty) seems an unsatisfactory reading on many counts. First, it substitutes for Scotland as kingdom the privileged and exceptional figure of a Scottish *king of England* (James I, 1603–1625). Second, while it recognises that Scotland, unlike Ireland, was not subject to English colonial violence, it fails to recognise that Scotland *was* subject to the equally brutal and destabilising violence of England's military pursuit of its claims to overlordship first in the attempted conquest of the 1542–50 and then again in the Marian crisis of 1567–73. Third, it omits to note that, for Shakespeare's contemporaries, Henry V's assertion of his overlordship of Scotland in the theatre of war itself was a celebrated dimension of the success of his French campaign. Henry, as English chronicles and 1540s war propaganda reiterated, had responded to the Franco-Scots alliance by forcing Scotland's uncrowned king, James I (1406–37) to fight in the English army against his own people at the siege of Melun in 1420. This aspect of Henry's French campaign was famous. Henry VIII's *Declaration* (1542) reported that while the unruliness arising from Henry IV's deposition of Richard II allowed the Scots licence to 'play', 'Henry the v, for recovery of his right in France, commaunded the kyng of Scottis to attende vppon hym in that iourney'.[14] The *Epitome* of 1548 likewise claimed that Henry V 'had warres against the French kyng, in all whiche, this James then kyng of Scottes, attended vpon him as vpon his superior lorde, with a conuenient number of Scottes, *nothwithstanding their league with France*' [my italics].[15] Given the sixteenth-century currency of the knowledge – now thoroughly forgotten – that Henry V countered the Franco-Scots alliance by obliging the king of Scotland to fight his own nation, one question we should be asking about Shakespeare's *1 & 2 Henry IV* and

[13] William Paterson, *Proposals & Reasons for Constituting a Council of Trade* (Edinburgh, 1701), vi–v.
[14] Henry VIII, *Declaration*, sig. C4r (punctuation modernised for legibility).
[15] *Epitome*, sig. g3r.

Henry V is why these plays preclude the possibility of imagining Scotland as the ally of France or Scotland as a kingdom at all.

Before we go any further with the question of how Scotland might or might not be represented in Shakespeare's *Henry V*, however, we need to stick a bit longer with Fitzdotterel's intuition about the authenticity of playbook history. How do plays elicit and authenticate national feeling? In this context, Peter Womack's astute comments on the imagining of the nation as community in *Henry V* are worth quoting at length. Pondering the oddity of the Chorus's embarrassment at the inadequacy of 'this unworthy scaffold' to present the glories of Agincourt, Womack proposes that rather than the audience's imagination being 'enlisted in order to repair the deficiencies of the theatre', the aim here is rather 'that the deficiencies of theatre are being advanced in order to motivate the enlisting of the audience's imagination'.[16] The reason for this, he proposes, is that the audience is being asked to body forth, in imagination, an entity that is only ever purely imaginary. That entity is the *nation*: in this case, England. The nation is imaginary, he says, precisely because it is 'not a thing but a mode of connectedness'.[17] Here, of course, Womack is drawing on Benedict Anderson's celebrated theory of the rise of nationalism, *Imagined Communities*. Having shown that national belonging cannot be experienced directly, only imagined, Anderson goes on to explain how it nevertheless feels like '*community* because, regardless of the actual inequality and exploitation that may prevail in each, the nation is always conceived as a deep, horizontal comradeship'.[18] Thus, in Womack's analysis, the very inadequacies of the stage laid bare by the Chorus constitute an imaginative opportunity for the audience to experience themselves as part of a *national community*, and it is this collective freedom to imagine that constitutes the 'inward greatness' of England:

> This inward England which is greater than its outward appearance is graspable not in spite of the disjunctions between stage and kingdom, beleaguered army and nation, but through them. In piecing out the imperfections of performance with their thoughts, the spectators are at the same time piecing out the imperfections of the historical events.[19]

Womack's recognition that it is the audience's imaginative capacity which critically constitutes the nation by interpreting the modes of connectedness

[16] Peter Womack, 'Imagining Communities: Theatres and the English Nation in the Sixteenth Century', in David Aers ed. *Culture and History, 1350–1600: Essays on English Communities, Identities and Writing* (London: Harvester, 1992), 91–145, 92.
[17] Womack, 'Imagining Communities', 94.
[18] Anderson, *Imagined Communities*, 16 (italics in original).
[19] Womack, 'Imagining Communities', 95.

on offer in *Henry V* makes any challenge to its fudging of the Britain/ England distinction seem petty. For the play, as critics continually observe, offers plenty of scope for audience scepticism about the cross-class national brotherhood invoked by Henry, as well as scepticism about Henry's motives for engaging in an invasive war and for committing acts that might be defined as war crimes. To this extent, the 'inward England' of *Henry V* seems to anticipate all the critiques one might level at patriotic applications like Hannon's. The play presents Henry's charisma as a military leader in a knowing, deeply sceptical and ambivalent way, as Norman Rabkin famously argued when he likened Henry to the gestaltist's drawing that in one way looks like a rabbit and in another like a duck. Just so, Henry can look like a moral hero or a cynical manipulator, his conduct of war in France ethically principled, or barbaric and unjust.[20] The play's self-reflexive and engaging ambivalence about the justice of invasive war, about Henry's motives, about a patriotic cross-class solidarity, all seem to render pedantic any critical objection to the incoherence that has Henry prepare to defend England 'against the Scot' while having a Scot serve as captain of his troops (1.2.138; 3.2.75–6). It is like objecting that Hal and Hotspur couldn't have been young rivals in *1 Henry IV*, because Hotspur was twenty-one years older.[21] Such incoherences or inaccuracies seem not to matter in a play that so brilliantly enables critical reflection on *the meaning of nationhood* through its complex portrayal of a nation at war.

Nevertheless, it should give us pause to realise that the sixteenth-century resonances of Agincourt for the English and the Scots were diametrically opposed to the extent that Scots identified profoundly with defeated France, not victorious England. So, for example, Robert Wedderburn's extraordinary *Complaynt of Scotland* (1550), following Alain Chartier's rallying of the French in the *Quadrilogue Invectif* (1422), substitutes for Chartier's description of post-Agincourt desolation the plight of Scotland after the English victory at Pinkie in 1547. Wedderburn, whose own house was destroyed by English forces, recalls the 'cruel ande onmercyful slauthyr' of 'oure nobil barrons, & of mony vthirs of the thre estaitis' in 'the grite affliction quhilk occurrit on oure realme in september.m. v.xlvii yeris on the feildis besyde mussilburgh'.[22] Pinkie was, for sixteenth-century Scots, Scotland's Agincourt. This chapter will argue that the polarisation of

---

[20] Norman Rabkin, 'Rabbits, Ducks and Henry V', *SQ*, vol. 28, no. 3 (1977), 279–96.

[21] *King Henry IV Part 1*, ed. David Scott Kastan (London: Arden, 2002), 1.1.86-8n. Further references to this edition will appear in the text.

[22] Robert Wedderburn, *The Complaynt of Scotland*, ed. A. M. Stewart (Edinburgh: W. Blackwood and sons for the Scottish Scottish Text Society, 1979), 17–18. I am indebted to Roger Mason for this

sixteenth-century English and Scots attitudes to Agincourt matters, not because knowing that fact renders Shakespeare's *Henry V inaccurate*, but because knowing it helps us understand what was at stake in some of Shakespeare's most fundamental choices in the plotting of *1 & 2 Henry IV* and *Henry V* from his major sources, including the chronicles of Hall and Holinshed and from earlier history plays. It helps us understand how Shakespeare's history plays have themselves contributed to the illusion that Scotland's existence as a sovereign nation was a matter of no concern to sixteenth-century Englishmen.

As well as exaggerating the deficiencies of theatre so as to foreground the play's dependence on the audience's imagination, *Henry V* makes unusual demands on the audience's ethical judgement. Attending to the shared ethical transhistoricism of literary criticism and international law, Christopher Warren, indeed, characterises *Henry V* as 'an artefact prompting judgement'.[23] A growing body of critical work on *Henry V* has developed Rabkin's 'rabbit/duck' view of *Henry V* less in a characterological direction than in the context of the play's apparently deliberate troubling of ethical perspective afforded on such questions as whether Henry's cause is just; whether he was right to give the order to kill French prisoners of war; whether he gave the order in retaliation for the killing of the camp followers; whether his argument for soldiers' individual responsibility for their actions squares with his commands that they rape and kill. In *Henry V*, as Camille Slights puts it, the Reformation 'internalisation of conscience is expressed in a developing sense of nationhood'.[24] This activation of ethical judgement throughout the play signals Shakespeare's indebtedness to and knowledge of the antecedents of modern international law in the rules of medieval and early modern *jus gentium* (the law of nations) concerning the conduct of war.[25] *Henry V* has become a focus of interest for historians of international law and experts in American military defence as well as literary critics interested in related topics because of the 'point by point' exactitude with which Shakespeare's play engages the central ethical questions of the just war tradition.[26]

point. See Roger A. Mason, 'Dame Scotia and the Commonweal: Vernacular Humanism in *The Complaynt of Scotland* (1550)', *The Mediaeval Journal*, vol. 10, no. 1 (2020), 129–50.

[23] Christopher Warren, 'Henry V, Anachronism and the History of International War', *Oxford Handbook of English Law and Literature*, 710–32.

[24] Camille Wells Slights, 'The Conscience of the King: *Henry V* and the Reformed Conscience', *Philological Quarterly*, vol. 80, no. 1 (2001), 37–55, 45, 49.

[25] Janet M. Spencer, 'Princes, Pirates and Pigs: Criminalizing Wars of Conquest in Henry V', *SQ*, vol. 47, vol. 2 (1996), 160–77, 161; Meron, *Henry's Wars*, 41.

[26] John Mark Mattox, '*Henry V*: Shakespeare's Just Warrior', *War, Literature and the Arts*, vol. 12, no. 1 (2000), 30–53, 31; see also Meron, *Henry's Wars*.

If the nation is not a thing but a mode of connectedness, then the way we are asked to imagine ourselves as part of a nation in *Henry V* is crucially inflected by being engaged in the kinds of ethical discriminations that arise as a part of just war discourse, which are themselves nation-defining, being founded on discriminations between internal and international strife, between enemy aliens and rebel subjects. As we saw in Chapter 1, William Lamb's challenge to Henry VIII's right to invade Scotland in 1542, entitled *Ane Resonyng* (1548), opened with a Scot resisting an Englishman's taunt that he should be 'eschamit' of his 'natioun', and went on to invoke the law of nations in claiming that Henry VIII's invasion of Scotland was clearly unjust because his *Declaration* used 'domistical pruife' (English law) to justify his cause, without inviting proofs from the other nation.[27] The justice of invasive war and of the invading prince's right to determine it was, as Theodore Meron shows, a hotly disputed issue in the writings on the law of nations in Shakespeare's time.[28] What happens to Scotland in *Henry V*, however, is not a defeat or a national shaming in view of alliance with France, but a dispersal, fragmentation, and disintegration – a vanishing of the nation altogether from historical consciousness. William Lamb characterised the dispute over England's title to Scotland in 1548 as 'ane grit, wechtie, doubtabill questioun of weir [war] fyftene hundreth yeiris betuix two potent realmes'.[29] In Shakespeare's play, a similar doubtable question over England's title to France takes imaginary form as the geography of England's overseas expansion itself. The audience's imaginary forces are asked to call into being an England whose cliffs are drawn up for battle against those of a defiant mainland across the sea:

> Suppose with the girdle of these walls
> Are now confined two mighty monarchies,
> Whose high upreared and abutting fronts
> The perilous narrow ocean parts asunder.   (Prologue, 19–22)

The anomaly of Scotland, politically allied to France but territorially adjacent to England, would destroy the internal logic of the Chorus's brilliantly vivid image. What the audience is being asked to suppose within the walls of the theatre is not something that even the mind's eye could 'see', since what is conjured is metaphor, the evanescent sense of likeness between the facing of cliffs across the seas and the uprearing of horses in the imminence of the battle charge. No longer imaginable as a realm, let alone a potent one, Scotland in Shakespeare's play dwindles into 'the Scot',

---

[27] Lamb, *Resonyng*, 3, 19.   [28] Meron, *Henry's Wars*, 17–46.   [29] Lamb, *Resonyng*, 19.

a flickeringly intermittent ethnic identity, while England takes shape as a thalassocracy, an island poised for maritime expansion, fortified by fleets like cities 'on th'inconstant billows dancing' (3.0.15). Thus it appears that one radically innovative achievement of the *Henry IV* plays and *Henry V* is their careful precluding of any possibility of imagining Scotland as an enemy nation and significant military ally of France. This is achieved, I will argue, by ensuring that 'the Scot' exists as a supplementary figure in a drama mapping English domestic strife and disorder on to the moral reformation of England's monarch.

In the rest of this chapter, I will show how the nation imagined as a mode of connectedness in *Henry V* is indebted to what I will call the 'metaphorical plot' of a group of earlier history plays. These history plays contain what Irving Ribner labelled 'romance situations' – that is, evidently fictional scenes of a monarch's amorous or otherwise transgressive immersion in his subjects' lives and culture.[30] In evoking the concept of the 'metaphorical plot', I am drawing on Patricia Parker's discussion of the different ways in which metaphor – a figure of thought itself identified with changing place – can also be thought of as creating a plot in the sense of an expansive conceptual space which opens from within the workings of metaphor itself.[31] The Chorus's strange metaphor, in which sea-parted cliffs of two land masses resemble the charging armies of two great kingdoms, creates just such a conceptual space. A small group of English history plays about the youthful escapades of monarchs who would become great military leaders – the group includes Robert Greene's *Friar Bacon and Friar Bungay* (c.1589) the anonymous *Famous Victories of Henry the Fifth* (c.1594?) and the anonymous *Edward III* (1592/3) as well as Shakespeare's *1 & 2 Henry IV* and *Henry V* – involve narratives which seem to instantiate such a metaphor or expand within in it. For these plays invite us to align a young prince or king's inward/inland reformation with a sense of England's readiness, as an island nation, to do battle. They suggest that the monarch's reformation establishes in England a security from invasion, a way of being chaste and contained that defines England as *island-like*, defended by the sea, while the same self-government, imagined as the monarch's inward, deliberative power or military prudence, is the predicate on which England justly enters the sphere of relations between nations, since crossing the sea seems to mark international war. Within this

---

[30] Irving Ribner, *The English History Play in the Age of Shakespeare* (London: Routledge, 2005), 8.
[31] Patricia Parker, 'The Metaphorical Plot', in *Literary Fat Ladies: Rhetoric, Gender, Property* (London: Methuen, 1987), 36–53.

metaphorical plot, the 'Scot' may function within the first movement of reformation in domestic government, but 'Scotland' seems therefore by definition unable to be translated to the second, the space between the nations that raised armies, fought each other, and ransomed each other's prisoners during the Hundred Years War. In *Henry V*, Shakespeare finally achieves an identification of English national imagining with a highly critical and reflexive perspective on the laws of international war in which the possibility of thinking of Scotland as a nation has disappeared, subsumed into the analogy between the prince's moral reformation and domestic government. The artistic precision with which this effect is achieved will come into focus with an examination of the significant ways in which Shakespeare calls to mind, in *Henry V*, the rhetoric and staging of the earlier play (in which he is thought to have had a hand) of *Edward III*. Before I come on to that discussion, however, I want briefly to show the work involved in Shakespeare's extraction of Scotland and Scotland's French alliance from the materials he selected when reading the histories of Henry IV and Henry V in the chronicles of Edward Hall and Raphael Holinshed.

II. Scotland in Hall and Holinshed

Shakespeare enlists his audience's imaginary forces to suppose two monarchies as the animated confrontation of two coastlines, banishing from their minds the thought that England might have a land border with another nation. Yet danger to England from the land border with Scotland was the preoccupation of Shakespeare's company's patron, Henry, Lord Hunsdon, who was governor of Berwick in 1568–77. It was Hunsdon who, with the earl of Sussex, led the subjugation of the supporters of the queen's party in 1570 (discussed in Chapter 4) in 'a series of devastating raids on the Scottish borderlands between April and June 1570, laying waste to the country and seizing the principal castles'.[32] When Shakespeare was beginning to write plays, Hunsdon was acting as the privy council's principal advisor on Scottish affairs, remaining cautious in the extreme through the Armada years with respect to James VI's potential enmity to England.[33] One of the critics who think that that Shakespeare wrote all or part of the *The Raigne of King Edward the Third* proposes that it was written for Hunsdon, using his copy of Froissart (now

[32] Wallace T. MacCaffrey, 'Carey, Henry, first Baron Hunsdon, 1526-96', *ODNB*.
[33] MacCaffrey, 'Hunsdon', *ODNB*.

in the British Library), where Hunsdon's own marginal annotations show he took 'an especial interest in the Scottish siege of Salisbury's castle' on the borders.[34]

Moreover, for Shakespeare to choose Henry V as a subject for a play was to choose one of three monarchs – Edward I, Edward III and Henry V – who were English favourites precisely because they combined reputations as conquerors overseas with signs of their successful overlordship of Scotland and, therefore, dominion over Britain. Henry VIII's *Declaration* described how John Balliol had performed homage to Edward I before Robert Bruce began to 'usurp' Scotland's throne and then related how Edward III defeated and imprisoned King Robert's son, David II, before describing Henry V's leading James I (of Scots) into war in France.[35] The *Declaration*'s omission altogether of Edward II's humiliation at Bannockburn is an index, if one were needed, of Christopher Marlowe's audacity not only in choosing to commemorate Edward II on the English stage, but in linking the unspeakably humiliating English defeat at Bannockburn in 1314 to Edward's infatuation with Piers Gaveston.[36] The *Epitome* likewise celebrates Edward I, Edward III and Henry V in sequence, passing over Edward II and Bannockburn in silence.[37] Popular war manuals, such as Robert Barret's *The Theorike and Practike of Moderne Warres* (1598) coupled English victories in France and Scotland, celebrating 'our braue English Kings in *France, Scotland* and other places, namely at the battell of *Poytiers, Agincourt* fielde, and else where'.[38]

How did Scotland figure in the histories of Henry IV and Henry V as Shakespeare would have encountered them in Holinshed? Edward Hall's *Chronicle*, published by Richard Grafton in 1548 as part of Protector Somerset's anticipated conquest of Scotland, was closely followed and paraphrased by Holinshed. From the outset, both Hall and Holinshed keep in view a sense of the importance and desirability of conquering Scotland and uniting Britain. In the very first year of Henry's reign, it was not enough, Hall writes, for fortune to encourage his own subjects, along with the French and Welsh, to rise against him, but she 'muste in his saied firste yere also, arme the Scottes with spere and shelde against him and his

---

[34] Roger Prior, 'Was *The Raigne of King Edward III* a Compliment to Lord Hunsdon?', *Connotations*, 3.3 (1993–4), 243–64, 245–6.

[35] Henry VIII, *Declaration*, sig. C4r.

[36] See Charles R. Forker, 'Introduction', Christopher Marlowe, *Edward the Second* ed. Charles R. Forker (Manchester: Manchester University Press, 1988), 46–7.

[37] *Epitome*, sig. f6r-g3r.

[38] Robert Barret, *The Theorike and Practike of Moderne Warres* (London: 1598), sig.Q1r.

realme'.[39] Holinshed follows Hall's wording here 'It was not inough that K. Henrie was troubled now in the first yere of his reigne, with ciuill sedition, and the couert practices of Frenchmen; but that the Scots also tooke vpon them to make open warre against him.'[40] Both narrate in some detail Henry's quarrel with Robert III of Scotland. Henry, supporting George Dunbar, earl of March, against Robert III, 'gathered a great armie, and entred into Scotland, burning townes, villages and castels' including Edinburgh and Leith.[41] It was while Henry was 'foorth of the realme in Scotland' that Owen Glendower took the opportunity to cause trouble in the Welsh Marches, taking prisoner Edward Mortimer, earl of March. The Scots under Archibald, earl of Douglas, invaded Northumberland and were soundly defeated by Henry Percy, whom the Scots nicknamed Hotspur. Among Hotspur's prisoners was 'Mordacke earl of Fife', son to 'the gouernour', Robert, duke of Albany, who had taken over the government of Scotland from his brother, Robert III.[42]

Shakespeareans will recognise, at the mention of Hotspur, Holmedon and Hotspur's taking of Scottish prisoners, including 'Murdoch, Earl of Fife' (*1 Henry IV* 1.1.71), that the foregoing narrative from Holinshed leads to the place where *1 Henry IV* begins: with the Welsh capture of the earl of Mortimer, and Hotspur's defeat of the Scots at 'Holmedon' or 'Humbleton'. It should be clear, however, that what Shakespeare has done with the narrative that Hall and Holinshed give cannot simply be explained as brilliant dramatic condensation. Shakespeare shapes the material through language which occupies the metaphorical plot I described above, activating a contrast between foreign wars and internal disorder, between the 'new broils . . . in stronds afar remote' (1.1.3–4) of Henry's desired crusade, and the horrors of civil wars in the realm itself, which the king figures as a mother devouring her offspring: 'No more the thirsty entrance of this soil / Shall daub her lips with her own children's blood' (1.1.5–6). Hall's and Holinshed's narratives of foreign and domestic troubles besieging Henry – from France, Wales, Scotland and Northumberland – have been spatially reduced by Shakespeare and reorganised as the posts of messengers conveying a sense of the geographical reach of Henry's realm. News from Wales in the west and Northumberland in the north are relayed first by Westmoreland, warden of the Marches, and then confirmed by Westmoreland's invocation of the arrival from the north of Walter Blunt, whose body '[s]tained with the

[39] *Hall's Chronicle*, 23.   [40] *Holinshed*, III.16.   [41] *Holinshed*, III.16–17.
[42] *Holinshed*, III.17–21, 21.

variation of each soil / Betwixt that Humbleton and this seat of ours'
testifies to his personal witnessing of Hotspur's defeat of '[t]en thousand
bold Scots' (1.1.64–70). Figuratively and spatially, then, the kingdoms of
the French and Scots have been delicately extracted from this plot of
Henry's troubles, which we are asked to imagine as unfolding across all
the soils over which England has jurisdiction, the defiant Hotspur with his
war booty of prisoners finally galling the king with remembrance of the
closest and most intimate dimension of England's domestic disorder: the
behaviour of his unruly son and heir, Prince Hal.

   In the theatre, then, the troubles of Henry IV's early reign become
intelligible as those of a realm whose exuberant misgovernment extends
from the Welsh Marches and Northumbrian-Scottish borders to the roads
that take pilgrims and merchants from Canterbury to London via Gad's
Hill. Scots are indeed in evidence – ten thousand of them – but only as
corpses and as war prisoners, the currency or war booty by which Hotspur
measures his rivalry with the king. There is no sense of a Scottish kingdom,
or Scottish royal policy. This might be thought to represent the power
struggles within Scotland in those years: the ambitious Robert III, suffering
from ill health, had ceded government to his ambitious brother, Robert,
duke of Albany. Yet if this were Shakespeare's aim, he deliberately omits
a crucial additional fact. For it was Henry IV himself who illegally *held the
king of Scots* – Robert III's son, James I – in custody.

   Holinshed opens his account of Henry V's reign by stating this fact. He
explains that after Robert III's heir, David, was murdered by the duke of
Albany, the king then made the ill-fated decision to protect his remaining son,
James, by sending him to France, only to have him captured and 'reteined' (as
Holinshed euphemistically puts it) by King Henry IV of England.[43] While
Holinshed's euphemism thinly veils the illegal aggression of Henry's act
(imprisoning a foreign monarch in time of peace), he admits its devastating
consequences for the Scottish kingdom. The news killed Robert III, leaving the
child James at once the king of Scotland and a prisoner in a hostile realm. (The
author of the 1548 *Epitome*, less scrupulous than Holinshed, was happy to
promulgate the outright falsehood that Robert III had resigned and delivered
his son into Henry's custody 'as of his superior lord'. Far from recognising
Henry as his superior lord, Robert did not even recognise him as king of
England, addressing him in letters as 'Duke of Lancaster'.)[44]

---

[43] *Holinshed*, III.61
[44] *Epitome*, sig. g2v; Chris Given-Wilson, *Henry IV* (New Haven, CT: Yale University Press, 2016),
   167. See also Chapter 4, 134.

Both Hall and Holinshed characterise James I's eighteen years of imprisonment in England as an educational privilege, but they also acknowledge the opportunity it represented for Henry when, after Agincourt, a Scottish military alliance helped France back on her feet. Henry realised he could make use of his custody of their king to demoralise France's allies.[45] At the siege of Melun, where the town held out valiantly, thanks to the strengthening of French resistance by 'manie Scots', Holinshed writes that

> the king kept with him young James of Scotland, who sent to those Scots, that they should come out and yeeld them vnto him, and not to stand in armes against their liege lord and king; but they gaue word backe againe, they could not take him for a king, that was in the power of another, and so kept them in hold and armour still.[46]

Once secure of his victory, Henry 'caused twentie of the proudest' Scots to be hanged as rebels to their king, James.[47] Through this piece of international legal theatre, Henry forcibly asserted the overlordship his father had failed to exercise over Robert III. By executing Scots war prisoners as criminals, Henry was depriving them of foreign enemy status, denying their nationhood. Scottish historians variously registered this injustice. Walter Bower says Henry hanged 'the bravest' (*fortissimi*) Scots for not obeying a king who was 'perforce' in thrall to the English king.[48] John Mair condemned Henry for setting the captive King James against his own people, but approved of the Scots who refused to play along,

> for they knew that the stability and permanence of the Scottish kingdom did not depend upon their king, and that though the English king might make a prisoner of their king, he could not for all that make a prisoner of the kingdom of Scotland.[49]

Hector Boece invented a wonderful anecdote in which Henry, planning to take young James to France with him to fight his compatriots aiding the dauphin, found him playing in the tennis court (*'in spharisterio . . . ludebat'*) and summoned him to the council meeting, where he asked him to accompany him to France and to halt Scotland's support for France. The bare-headed James, fresh from the tennis court, replied that he'd like to

---

[45] Michael Brown, *James I* (Edinburgh: Canongate, 1994), 20–6; Christopher Allmand, *Henry V* (Berkeley, CA: University of California Press, 1992), 152–3.

[46] *Holinshed*, III.123.   [47] *Holinshed*, III.123.   [48] Bower, *Scotichronicon*, VIII.123.

[49] John Mair, *A History of Greater Britain as well England as Scotland*, trans. Archibald Constable (Edinburgh: Published at the University Press by T. and A. Constable for the Scottish History Society, 1892), 343–4.

help Henry, but that he had no authority or discretion over the Scots as subjects, as he had not been crowned and sworn a coronation oath.[50] By this anecdote, Boece enacted the historical refusal of the Scots in France to recognise James as their king as James's own prescient recognition of the contractual nature of sovereignty. Hall, interestingly, does not suppress Boece's story, but doubts its credibility, reserving his greatest indignation for the ingratitude shown by James when, once back in Scotland, he forgets all the 'kyndnesses' of his English captivity and reverts to making political common cause with France. Neither good literature, education nor a distinguished marriage could suffice to 'make this kyng Iames frendly to the realme of Englande', marvels Hall, 'After he had once taken the ayre and smelled the sent [sic] of the Scottish soyle' he 'newly alied hymself with the Frenche nacion'.[51]

There is, however, one further, crucial episode in Hall's history of Henry V's reign in which James and Scotland figure as key. This occurs in the great set-piece debate following the archbishop of Canterbury's self-interested exposure of the fraudulence of Salic law and vindication of Henry V's title to the Crown of France. At the archbishop's conclusion, Ralph Neville, earl of Westmoreland, counters his urging of French invasion with a highly wrought argument, starting from Geoffrey of Monmouth when 'the hole Isle of Britain was one entier Monarchi', working through to Robert the Bruce's league of perpetual amity with France, to argue that Henry should invade Scotland first, and conquer France by recovering his old British empire.[52] 'See what an occasion fortune hath offered vnto you' he asks, at the climax of his argument, 'is not their kyng your captiue and prisoner?' He strongly concludes that it would make strategic sense first to invade Scotland and 'conquere and ioyne that to youre Empire ... restore the renoumed Monarchy of Britayne'. With the Scots subjugated and the whole island of Britain under your dominion, he argues to Henry, conquest of France will easily follow.[53] Westmoreland's impassioned arguments are qualified, in turn, by the Duke of Exeter, who likewise trawls through the post-Galfridian arguments of Scottish homage to argue that the Scots accomplish little without French alliance and that if France were conquered, Scottish subjugation would follow, and England would hold empire over both the isle of Britain and France, just as the Romans were persuaded to look

[50] Hector Boece, *Scotorum Historia* [1575] ed. and trans. Dana F. Sutton (2010), Liber XVI.59: https://philological.cal.bham.ac.uk/boece/16lat.html.
[51] *Hall's Chronicle*, 119–20.   [52] *Hall's Chronicle*, 52.   [53] *Hall's Chronicle*, 54.

beyond their ambition in Sicily to conquer Carthage. Exeter's proposal that Henry prepare an army for France and leave Westmoreland to guard the northern Marches is, as Shakespeareans know, the winning argument in Shakespeare's *Henry V*, as it was in Hall and Holinshed.

When Hall composed the carefully worked speeches of this debate in the 1540s, hopes of conquering Scotland as a prelude to the conquest of France were at their highest. The issue debated was politically live. As the 'crux and fulcrum on which events turn' in the reign of Henry V, and through the French-backed regimes of Mary of Guise and Mary Queen of Scots in Scotland, it continued to be of vital interest for Hall's early Elizabethan readers.[54] One such reader was Christopher Watson, who in 1568 prefaced the debate to his own translation of Polybius, describing how, when his copy of Hall's *Chronicle* 'lay open . . . in the life of king Henry the fift' and he read Westmoreland's speech, he was 'rapte in minde more profoundly to digest his stately stile' and 'indissoluble' arguments.[55] Watson applied to Westmoreland's speech his own translation of Polybius, producing, in Warren Boutcher's words, 'a clear blueprint for an aggressive British policy of the kind mooted and supported by Cecil in the early years of Elizabeth's reign'.[56] Watson, in other words, reads the questions facing Henry V over Scotland and France in relation to English government policies opposing the restoration of the French-backed Mary Queen of Scots and supporting an English-backed regency in Scotland. These – the policies described in Chapter 4 – were also being actively furthered by the man who would become the patron of Shakespeare's company, Henry Carey, Lord Hunsdon, later Lord Chamberlain, who was at that time governor of Berwick and leading invasions into Scotland to subjugate the queen's party.

The debate whose eloquence and urgency dazzled Christopher Watson, prompting him to translate Polybius as a contribution to Anglo-British policy in Scotland, was not completely ignored by William Shakespeare when composing *Henry V*. But in Shakespeare's version, the debate seems to have lost its central issue and its dynamic political vitality. There is an exchange between Westmoreland and Exeter, but it takes place in an oddly truncated, banal and even redundant form, its substance already having

---

[54] Warren Boutcher, 'Polybius Speaks British: A Case-Study in Mid-Tudor British Humanism and Historiography', in *Tudor Translation*, ed. Fred Schurink (Basingstoke: Palgrave Macmillan, 2011), 101–20, 105.

[55] Polybius, *The Hystories of the Most Famous and Worthy Cronographer Polybius*, trans. Christopher Watson (London: 1568), sig. M5v.

[56] Boutcher, 'Polybius', 112.

been rehearsed in more rousing and exciting terms between Henry himself and the archbishop of Canterbury. If we look more closely, however, we can see that the entire premise of the debate has changed: it is doing something completely different. As it appears in Hall and Holinshed, the question of whether to conquer France by invading Scotland or vice versa recognises that Scotland is a player in the international theatre of war. In Hall and Holinshed, Scotland is, like France, *a kingdom to invade* and England must embrace the claims of British history and attempt to conquer Scotland in order, at length, to deprive France of the advantages of strategic power to damage England via Scotland. In Shakespeare, by contrast, Henry speaks not of an alliance between the kingdoms of France and Scotland, nor of the possibility of invading and conquering a place called Scotland, but of the need for domestic defence against an expedient and every-hungry predator called 'the Scot': 'We must not only arm t'invade the French', he cautions, 'But lay down our proportions to defend / Against the Scot, who will make road upon us, / With all advantages' (1.2.136–9). Canterbury, understandably, thinks the king must be referring to border reivers, but Henry's awkward and evasive periphrasis 'We do not mean the coursing snatchers only / But fear the *main intendment* of the Scot' (1.2.143–5, my italics) attempts a distinction which takes care to withhold any recognition of territorial sovereignty. Immediately after Canterbury's reassuring recollections of Edward III, Westmoreland offers the adage of winning France by way of Scotland, glossing it thus:

> For once the eagle England being in prey,
> To her unguarded nest the weasel Scot
> Comes sneaking in and sucks her princely eggs.   (1.2.169–71)

Long ago, William Hazlitt noted the disparity here: Shakespeare's conferring of a right on the eagle England to 'be in prey' in France, while the weasel Scot had no such right in England. Hazlitt attributed the disparity to class distinction, to the way in which, in these old times, moral rights depend on the dignity or meanness of the persons involved. And he went on to admire 'the effects of subordination in a commonwealth' in the concluding speech of the debate, the archbishop of Canterbury's praise of order and degree in the offices of the realm.[57] Though more is involved here than a simple chivalric pervasiveness of hierarchical thinking (for, as

---

[57] William Hazlitt, *Characters of Shakespeare's Plays*, ed. J. H. Lobban (Cambridge: Cambridge University Press, 1908, reprinted 2009), 158–9.

many critics have pointed out, the 'common people' play a fundamental role in the imagining of English history plays) Hazlitt was surely right to link the two speeches.[58] The archbishop's Tillyardian paeon to the cosmic and natural order figured in the well-governed state in which king, officers, magistrate, merchants and soldiers all fulfil their diverse functions concludes a debate which has, in effect, relegated what should have been a concern with Franco-Scots alliance to a concern with due subordination of roles within *English domestic government*. As Exeter says, 'we have locks to safeguard necessaries'

> And pretty traps to catch the petty thieves
> While that the armed hand doth fight abroad
> Th'advised head defends itself at home.
>
> For government, though high and low and lower
> Put into parts, doth keep in one concent,
> Congreeing in a full and natural close
> Like music   (1.2.176–83)

Thus what was, in Hall, Holinshed and Watson, a geopolitical debate on how best to break up the Franco-Scots alliance has become, in Shakespeare, part of a debate on how to order *domestic government* while pursuing wars in other realms *overseas*. In other words, the debate itself has achieved the effect of de-territorialising Scotland in the English imagination, subsuming its ordering within the agreeing parts of the music of the English commonwealth. More striking, in this respect, than analogical hierarchy in Westmoreland's opposition between the vehicles of eagle and weasel is the asymmetry of the tenors they metaphorise. For the eagle names a kingdom, 'the eagle Eng*land*', whereas the weasel is not a place, not a realm, but an apparently homeless or placeless ethnic identity. 'The weasel *Scot*' conjures a tiny predator of legendarily rapid metabolism with nowhere but its stomach to stash its winnings – with no nest like the eagle's, no suffix of 'land', as in Eng*land,* to suggest the stability of a nation. This ravenous 'Scot' has become a figure of perennial disturbance to the English commonwealth, while the kingdom that would confer the dignity of history and nationhood has disappeared. To understand this fully we must turn now to a play which, whether he had a hand in writing it or not, Shakespeare clearly knew intimately. That play is *The Raigne of King Edward the third*.

---

[58] On the importance of 'the people' to the English history play, see Helgerson, *Forms of Nationhood,* 195–245; Annabel Patterson, *Shakespeare and the Popular Voice* (Oxford: Blackwell, 1989).

III. Impounding the King of Scots

I earlier mentioned Shakespeare's indebtedness, in *1 & 2 Henry IV* and *Henry V*, to the metaphorical plot of a group of history plays which align the idea of England's geopolitical security with a story of the young monarch's moral reformation, seen as preparative to performance on the international stage of war. One such play is the anonymous *Edward III*, which some scholars argue was part-authored by Shakespeare, largely on the grounds that lines and phrases from Shakespeare's *Sonnets* (1610) appear in its scenes of amorous courtship.[59] Shakespeare's numerous recollections of *Edward III* in *Henry V* certainly show, as one critic has put it, that he knew the play 'as well as he knew Holinshed's *Chronicle* or North's *Plutarch* or Ovid's *Metamorphoses*'.[60] A particularly salient moment of recollection in *Henry V* occurs when the archbishop of Canterbury reassures Henry that he may make war in France without fearing Scotland. Henry says that histories of his great-grandfather's expeditions into France prove that he could never cross the Channel without the Scot 'pouring like a tide into the breach' and besieging castles and towns,

> That England, being empty of defence
> Hath shook and trembled at th'ill neighbourhood. (1.2.153–4)

Canterbury replies, taking up Henry's personification of England,

> She hath been then more feared than harmed, my liege.
> For hear her but exampled by herself:
> When all her chivalry hath been in France
> And she a mourning widow of her nobles,
> She hath herself not only well defended,
> But taken and impounded as a stray
> The King of Scots, whom she did send to France
> To fill King Edward's fame with prisoner kings
> And make her chronicle as rich with praise
> As is the ooze and bottom of the sea
> With sunken wrack and sunless treasuries. (1.2.155–65)

This resoundingly triumphant refutation of Henry's fears refers to the period of Edward III's long siege of Calais in 1346 when Philip VI of

[59] See Giorgio Melchiori, 'Authorship', in *King Edward III*, ed. Giorgio Melchiori (Cambridge: Cambridge University Press, 1998), 9–17. Further references to the play in this edition will appear by act, line and scene in the text.

[60] E. Pearlman, '*Edward III* in *Henry V*', *Criticism*, vol. 37, no. 4 (1995), 519–36, 519.

France, having already suffered defeat at Crécy, asked David II of Scotland to help him by invading England 'in the hopes', as John Mair put it, 'that Edward would then desist from siege'.[61] The Scots themselves, after the death of their King Robert the Bruce and during the minority of his son, the boy-king David II, had long suffered invasions by Edward III and his puppet king Edward Balliol. As England and Scotland were already at war, the Scots were ready to help their French allies. In 1346, David II led an army to Newcastle but found it well defended, before, at the Battle of Neville's Cross, he was wounded by an arrow in the face, but refused to surrender and was taken prisoner in hand-to-hand combat by John Coupland.[62]

Canterbury's thrillingly hyperbolic account of David's being sent to France to 'To fill King Edward's fame with prisoner kings' alludes, however, to not to any source in Froissart or Holinshed, but to the climactic final scene of the play *Edward III* which forms a tableau of the English royal family at Calais with their prisoner kings, as Edward's son, the Black Prince, brings on the French king as his captive, while Philippa, Edward's queen, disputes with John Coupland or Copland for the right to present Edward with the captured King David of Scotland (5.1). Critics have noted the significance of Shakespeare's reproduction of a stage-memory as if it were history, but the implications of Canterbury's example go much further. For while Henry's words animate an England shaking and trembling at Scottish incursions, it is Canterbury who feminises England as a 'mourning widow', bereaved of her noble aristocracy, a widow who doesn't only imprison but *impounds* the intruder, claiming him as domestic property. This is not, in other words, just a stage memory, but a recollection of *Edward III*'s entire metaphorical plot.

Canterbury's feminisation of England first identifies England with a memory of the role played, in *Edward III*, by Edward's queen, Philippa. Froissart tells how the pregnant Queen Philippa fell on her knees and pleaded with her husband, King Edward, to spare the six burghers of Calais who surrendered the keys on behalf of the city.[63] *Edward III* translates this feminine labour of intercession into England's domestic defence of herself. At the siege of Calais, Edward receives the news from Northumberland: the 'painful travail' of his pregnant queen has

[61] Mair, *History*, 292.
[62] Ranald Nicholson, *Scotland: The Later Middle Ages* (Edinburgh: Mercat Press, 1974), 145–7.
[63] John Froissart, *Chronicles of England, France, Spain and adjoining countries*, trans. Thomas Jones, 2 vols. (London: Routledge and sons., 1868), II.188.

been a labour not of childbirth, but of fending off an intruder, her husband 'being absent from the realm':

> David of Scotland, lately up in arms
> Thinking belike he soonest should prevail,
> Your highness being absent from the realm,
> Is, by the fruitful service of your peers
> And painful travail of the queen herself,
> That, big with child, was every day in arms,
> Vanquished, subdued and taken prisoner.   (4.2.39–46)[64]

While Canterbury's figure of England as a doughty widow seems clearly taken from the hyperbolic effect of this apposition of a king 'taken prisoner' as if by a queen 'big with child and every day in arms', it also recalls the earlier movement of the play's plot, which has Edward embark for France only after his attempted seduction of the countess of Salisbury, lately besieged by Scots in her border castle, is resisted by her arguments of matrimonial fidelity. This plot, which takes up the whole of the second movement of *Edward III* (after Edward's declaration of war against France, but before his embarkation), aligns the reformation of Edward's moral judgement with the geographical movement of the dramatic action to the scene of war between nations, vividly indicated by a sea-battle witnessed from the northern French coast. The romantic and casuistical subplot of the king's love for a countess in a castle on the Scottish borders makes possible a governing imaginative distinction between the bounded integrity of the chaste 'island' of England ('hear her but exampled by herself') and the 'overseas' sphere of international war. This is the metaphorical plot that the archbishop of Canterbury animates by invoking a feminine England impounding a Scottish king like a stray animal.

Edward III is not the only English history play to align the idea of England as a securely defended island with the moral education of a conquering monarch. Other plays that do so are the Queen's Men's *Famous Victories of Henry the Fifth* (c.1588) – from which, Giorgio Melchiori argues, *Edward III* borrows its plotting, and Robert Greene's *Friar Bacon and Friar Bungay* (c.1589), also played by the Queen's and the Admiral's Men.[65] *Bacon and*

---

[64] Neither Edward III nor Edward Balliol were able to turn victory at Neville's Cross into the reconquest of Scotland, though they took back much of what David had recently regained (Nicholson, *Scotland: Later Middle Ages*, 147–8). Describing 'the burnt Candlemas' – Edward III's later wasting of Lothian with fire (1356) – John Mair wrote that although Edward III 'held the king of Scotland a prisoner in England, yet he did not make his way into Scotland more than twenty leagues' (Mair, *History*, 297).

[65] See Melchiori, 'Appendix: The Use of Sources', *Edward III*, 178–9.

Bungay is an instructive example for the way it achieves an imaginative equivalence between the reformation of the young monarch's transgressive amours and the sense that England has integrity as a whole island and can therefore defend itself from invasion. Greene's play weaves together two loosely related plots. In one, Henry III's son, Prince Edward (later Edward Longshanks, the great conqueror of Scotland and Wales), spends his time chasing a beautiful innkeeper's daughter from Suffolk, Margaret of Fressingfield, thereby evading the diplomatic and dynastic imperative that he wed the daughter of the prince of Castile. As Margaret will entertain no suit but marriage, Edward is persuaded by his licentious fool, Rafe, that the only 'perfect plot' of her amorous debauchery must be by recourse to Friar Bacon's magic arts.[66] Meanwhile, in Oxford, Friar Bacon declares his ambition to use his necromantic arts patriotically, in aid of King Henry III. His plan is to ensure England's geopolitical containment and security by 'compass[ing] England with a wall of brass' (ii.30). Henry III's own address to monarchs visiting from western Europe, the emperor of Germany, and king of Castile, emphasises the natural defences of navigable seas. He welcomes his guests, the 'Great men of Europe, monarchs of the west, / Ringed with the walls of old Oceanus / Whose lofty surge is like the battlements / That compassed high-built Bable in with towers' to 'England's shore, whose promontory cleeves [cliffs] / Shows Albion is another little world' (iv.1–7). Bacon's ambition to render England impregnable harkens back to the days of the Roman conquest of Britannia, promising such days will never return. 'I will', he declares, 'strengthen England by my skill',

> That if ten Caesars lived and reigned in Rome,
> With all the Legions Europe doth contain,
> They should not touch a grass of English ground   (ii.58–61)

Todd Borlik has persuasively linked Greene's play to an upsurge in interest in English coastal fortification around the time of the Spanish Armada. Sir Francis Walsingham, patron of writers on fortification, 'helped establish the Queen's Men, the very playing company that first performed *Friar Bacon and Friar Bungay* sometime around 1589'.[67] Though Borlik argues that Bacon's failure to realise the magic wall 'does not diminish the ideological

[66] Robert Greene, *Friar Bacon and Friar Bungay* in *Drama of the English Renaissance: I The Tudor Period*, eds. Russell A. Fraser and Norman Rabkin (New York, NY: Macmillan, 1976), i.120. Further references to this edition by scene and line number will appear in the text.
[67] Todd Andrew Borlik, 'Building a Wall Around Tudor England: Coastal Forts and Fantasies of Border Control in *Friar Bacon and Friar* Bungay', *Early Theatre*, vol. 22, no. 2 (2019), 67–88, 77.

potency of what it represents', he seems not to consider that the wall might nevertheless be realised metaphorically in a no less ideologically potent form in Prince Edward's moral awakening to embrace the Britomart-like chastity of dynastic and diplomatic marriage. 'Just as Bacon abandons his dream of the wall, Prince Edward must relinquish Margaret, the "fair maid of Fressingfield", to his friend Lacy and instead marry Eleanor of Castile to promote peace with this Spanish kingdom,' writes Borlik.[68] Indeed, but Edward's marriage thereby walls England round with the inviolability of Chastity's good faith and good international diplomacy as a bedrock of strong government, and it is this that renders Bacon's magic wall as unnecessary as it seemed hubristic. Witnessing the tragic consequences to which his prospective glass can lead, Bacon renounces necromancy altogether in a recognition which corresponds precisely with the moral awakening of Prince Edward, who, having used Bacon's 'prospective glass' (magic looking glass) to spy on his friend Lacy's matrimonial courtship of Margaret of Fressingfield, eventually repents of his lust and murderous jealousy. Confronting the lovers, Edward is ready to kill his friend until their fidelity to one another moves him to reflect on and feel ashamed of his own licentious passions. As he renounces Margaret and blesses her union with Lacy, she thanks and praises him for a 'conquest ... as great / In conquering love, as Caesar's victories' (viii.138–9). Clearly, as will be the case in *Edward III*, the moment of Chastity's victory activates the metaphorical plot with which we are becoming familiar: the plot in which the imagining of England as a continent, well-governed island becomes equivalent to imagining England as ready to perform justly and victoriously on the international stage, an equivalence expressed in the imaginative act of *crossing the seas*.

   Just so, in the later play of *Edward III*, the king awakens, morally, to the Countess's preference for death over his proposed violation of their marriage bonds by elevating this chaste heroine over the Roman Lucrece:

> Even by that power I swear, that gives me now
> The power to be ashamed of myself,
> I never mean to part these lips again
> In any words that tend to such a suit.
> Arise, true English lady, whom *our isle*
> May better boast of than ever Roman might
> Of her, whose ransacked treasury hath tasked
> The vain endeavour of so many pens.
>
>   (2.2.188–195, my italics)

---

[68] Borlik, 'Builing a Wall', 73.

The violated Lucrece's 'ransacked treasury' deserves little praise compared with the continent and chaste integrity of 'our isle', as guaranteed by the 'true English lady's' power to make Edward ashamed of himself and thereby able to take ship from 'our isle' across the sea into the ethical space of *jus in bello*, the space in which the just conduct of war and peace between the nations is debated and enacted. 'I am awakened from this idle dream', he announces, commanding his followers, 'straight to sea' (2.2.198, 202). In *Friar Bacon and Friar Bungay* there is no corresponding embarkation, but Prince Edward's readiness, the instant he has renounced his pursuit of Margaret, to marry Eleanor of Castile, clearly promotes, as Borlik says, 'England's participation in pan-European, even global commerce' that is celebrated in the exotic feast prepared by Bacon to celebrate the diplomatic marriage.[69] Although *Bacon and Bungay* makes no explicit reference to Edward I's later conquests of Wales and Scotland, the play's final speech makes explicit the Anglo-imperial idea of 'Britain' that underwrites the play's celebration of England's chaste insularity. Asked by Henry III what will come of Edward's and Elinor's marriage, Bacon prophesies the advent of Elizabeth Tudor, a bud which will grow from Edward and his queen 'here where Brute did build his Troynovant' (xvi.44) – in other words, in the garden of an English island of Britain. Edward's moral awakening, his recognition of the worth of Margaret's chastity and the importance of marriage to government, renders the necromantic brazen wall as redundant as it would have been self-defeating: England becomes, in the imaginative vision of the play, a British island fortified by the chastity and integrity of its monarch's government, on which, in turn, may be predicated the island's future of expansive trade and heroic conquest.

In *Bacon and Bungay* we see emerge the conceptual equivalence between the young monarch's inward reformation and the image of England as an island nation entering on to the world stage. Christopher Marlowe's *Edward II* (c.1592) deserves more space than I can give it here for the way its utter subversion of this conceptual equivalence testifies to its emergent power. With a thrillingly hyperbolic insouciance *Edward II* turns the mighty island kingdom of England to flotsam. Before he will part with his 'sweet Gaveston', he declares, '[t]his isle shall fleet upon the ocean / And wander to the unfrequented Inde' (1.4.48–50). The historical Edward II was most despised for the loss, at Bannockburn, of all that his father had won in Scotland, though his poor generalship, 'unwisely order[ing]' his

[69] Borlik, 'Building a Wall', 73.

men and 'confound[ing] their ranks' was nothing to do with Gaveston, who had already been put to death.[70] Yet Marlowe fuses Edward's erotic misgovernment and military mismanagement in Mortimer and Lancaster's blaming of Bannockburn on Edward's love for Gaveston, vividly recollecting a king whose soldiers marched into Scotland 'like players', earning the mockery of the Scots scorning the loss of English manhood (2.2.181–94). But Marlowe's play bears witness, by subversion, to this metaphorical association of the monarch's chaste reformation with the achievement of an English island.

Recent readings of *Edward III* and *Henry V* have been rather quick to move from noting the plays' exposure of 'the personal shortcomings of Edward and Henry' to seeing in them equivalent critiques of monarchy and the justice of invasive war.[71] As I have tried to suggest, however, the space of unresolved doubts about the conduct of international war is precisely where these plays develop their discourse and feeling of nationhood. This space of conscience and doubt enhances rather than critiques the English monarchy and its French invasions. This can be seen in the way the 'four captains' scene in *Henry V* thematises as part of a discourse on the disciplines of the wars the difficulty of the question of what a nation actually is and who may speak of it. And the fact that, in *Henry V*, the archbishop of Canterbury can reassure Henry V about the Scottish threat with a figure which condenses the story of Edward III's reformed adulterous love into the domestic autonomy of the widow impounding the Scottish intruder is itself a tribute to the ease with which the model of monarchical reformation can turn a monarch's 'personal shortcomings' into an image of English domestic good government.

It is undoubtedly the case, however, that despite generations of readers' unease about the rejection of Falstaff (and, more recently, unease at the bullying of the drawer, Frances) the story of Henry V's reformation through *1 & 2 Henry IV* has produced, in *Henry V*, a more successful blend of sceptical patriotism, a more successful 'imagined community' of England at war than has *Edward III*. One obvious distinction between the plays involves the uses of laughter. While both plots of moral and governmental reformation link the prince's transgressions to the licence and pleasures of wit (in the Elizabethan 'prodigal son' mode) laughter in the mainly humourless *Edward III* is exclusively directed against 'the Scot',

[70] *Holinshed*, II.553; Forker, 'Introduction', 46–7.
[71] Amy Lidster, 'Challenging Monarchical Legacies in *Edward III* and *Henry V*, *English*, vol. 68, no. 2 (2019), 126–42, 132, 142; Huw Griffiths, 'Passports and the Locations of Sovereignty in *The Reign of Edward III*', *English Studies*, vol. 96, no. 7 (2015), 747–71.

whereas in Shakespeare's *1 & 2 Henry IV* and in *Henry V* the irresistible banter and conviviality of Hal's licentious English life translates, on the battlefields of France, into a range of demotic, ethnically accented and critical perspectives on war discipline (including the disciplining of the Eastcheap soldiers) and on the king himself. While Captain Jamy's Scots accent confers no privileged position of criticism – unlike Fluellen's Welsh accent, which enables him to liken Henry to 'Alexander the Pig' – neither does it make him a target of mockery.[72] This may be, as Giorgio Melchiori has argued, because *Edward III* was the object of a complaint from Scotland. If Shakespeare's *Henry V* thus learns from *Edward III* not to engage in the overt mockery of Scottish kings, his achievement nevertheless renders the kingdom of Scotland more invisible than ever.

As critics have noticed, the opening action of *Henry V* follows that of *Edward III* quite closely in broad outline: the king learns of his dynastic claim to the French crown, defies humiliation by a French embassy and pauses over the question of a threat of Scottish invasion. In *Henry V*, this last question is partly dealt with by an allusion to Edward III whereas in the play *Edward III* we have the unfolding of that plot and its implications in the French war. Derived from Froissart, the story of Edward's love for the countess of Salisbury was made into a novella by Bandello and translated by Pierre Boiastuau as the opening novel in *Histoires Tragiques* (1559) and by William Painter in *The Palace of Pleasure* (1566).[73] For Boiastuau, the story shows how English kings have been not only prodigal of human blood, but that 'la lasciueté a esté le sceptre de leurs royaumes' ('that sensuality has been the sceptre of their kingdoms').[74] In a manner typical of the Elizabethan prodigal narrative, however, the English story uses Edward's youthful lasciviousness to stage a moment of introspection ad awakening conscience, a recognition of his love's sinful violation of the bonds of fidelity sacred in matrimony and in the just conduct of war. As usual, love and beauty act as stimulants of princely wit. The Scots having already departed from their siege of the castle, Edward, who should be mustering soldiers for France, sits around mustering arguments of love. For a fortnight he hides in the castle's summer arbour or 'council house' with

---

[72] See Quint, 'Alexander the Pig'. For the 'prodigal son mode', see Richard Helgerson, *The Elizabethan Prodigals* (Berkeley: University of California Press, 1976).

[73] Melchiori, 'Introduction', *Edward III*, 36–9. Melchiori omits Boiaistuau, whose story of 'Edouard, Roy d'Angleterre' opens the very first volume of his *Histoires Tragiques* (1558). See *XVIII Histoires Tragiques . . . par Pierre Boisteau . . . par Franc. de BelleForest* (Paris, 1570), fols. 6r-19v. I am not persuaded by Melchiori that the Countess of Salisbury scenes are a late addition to the play.

[74] Boaistuau, *Histoires*, fol. 6r.

Lodowick, his secretary, writing sonnets. These scenes of poetry-making foreground not only the licentious casuistry of Edward's witty invention, but the sense in which wit can, conversely, be a medium in which the conscience becomes active in making ethical discriminations and refining self-knowledge in relation to ethical principles. When the countess's father, Warwick, finds himself trapped into swearing an incautious oath of utmost service to his king, he does indeed fulfil his oath by offering *sententiae* to persuade his daughter that adultery with a king is forgivable, but then wittily deploys opposing sentences to 'unsay again' all that he has said. Among Warwick's 'unsaying' sentences is the famous line from Shakespeare's ninety-fourth sonnet, 'Lilies that fester smell far worse than weeds' (2.1.452). And it is through the countess's wit that Edward comes to recognise the evil implications of his desire. She proposes (after offering many other protesting arguments) that in order to enjoy her love, Edward must remove two lives that stand in the way: those of his wife, Queen Philippa, and of her husband, the count of Salisbury. After some opportunistic and hyperbolic allusions to himself as a Leander ready to swim 'though a Hellespont of blood' (2.2.154) and to her beauty as 'guilty of their death', Edward comes to his senses as the sight of the two knives with which the double murder must be performed (2.2.171). Ashamed and conscientious at last, within a few lines he has assigned the countess's father, Warwick, the wardenship of the North, and commanded the Prince of Wales to sea for France.

By educating Edward in the honouring of those on whom his command in war depends – his wife, his son and such captains as the earl of Salisbury serving in Brittany – the countess herself turns wit into something like military prudence. The play's final two acts involve the intricate interweaving of scenes of good faith and trust upheld between English captains and prisoners of war with contrary French failings of the same, all vividly imagined as part of the earl of Salisbury's journey from Brittany to Calais via Poitiers, where Edward's son, the Black Prince, faces overwhelming odds in the form of 'multitudes of millions' of massed French soldiers (4.4.6). The effect of this unhistoric juxtaposition is to heighten emotion and suspense about the Black Prince's fate. Salisbury, arriving in Calais, offers a tour de force description of how 'like a bear fast chained unto a stake' Edward's son fought, 'still expecting when the dogs of France would fasten on his flesh' (5.1.143–5). This dreadful news elicits maternal tears from Queen Philippa, who has already arrived in Calais with the imprisoned king of Scots. Her weeping turns to joy as the Black Prince enters, contrary to all expectation, with the king of France as his prisoner.

The final scene of national victory thus has an oddly domestic flavour as Edward, his queen and son are sentimentally and triumphantly reunited, accompanied by the captive kings of France and Scotland. They all apparently anticipating a happy sea-voyage back to England, that 'little isle' in which 'many princes more' will be '[b]red and brought up' (5.1.241, 220–1).

I began this chapter with Peter Womack's account of how Henry V invites the audience to imagine themselves as part of a nation through the disjunctions of history and its theatrical performance. I linked Womack's analysis to those of critics who have seen, in the unresolved doubts the play raises about Henry's actions on the battlefield, the audience's conscientious engagement in questions of justice in war. I have tried to show that the space of *jus gentium* or of the ethical decision-making that defines nations at war is predicated on a prior imaginative movement from a private or 'domestic' reformation of conscience involving the prince's transgressive behaviour which, in turn, helps define England as a securely governed island home, precluding the entry of Scotland on to the stage of the Hundred Years War. In chronicles Henry V was, of course, no less famous than Edward III for youthful licence and subsequent reformation. And though, in *1 & 2 Henry IV*, Prince Hal's transgressions are dramatised in relation to a different set of fantasies – the playfulness, excess and convivial banter of the tavern, as well as theatricality itself – they are nevertheless, as Stephen Greenblatt and Steven Mullaney have shown, figured as exercises in humanist wit, or, to put it in our own terms, exercises in cultural mastery through the learning of languages and customs. Greenblatt brilliantly likens Hal's ruthless game with the monotonous replies of the apprentice tavern-drawer, Francis, to the glossary of the Carolina Algonquian language compiled by English astronomer-ethnographer Thomas Harriot during his 1585 voyage to Roanoke Island, while Mullaney read Hal's 'time in the taverns of Eastcheap' as 'a literal as well as figurative language lesson', 'a prodigality of a different order – the sign not of errant youth but of power, making a far from traditional passage through the margins and subcultures of its domain'.[75]

One lesson Shakespeare seems to have learned from *Edward III*, however, was where to direct the mocking games of such language-learning with impunity. Prince Hal may be ruthless with the tavern apprentice,

---

[75] Stephen Greenblatt, *Shakespearean Negotiations* (Berkeley, CA: University of California Press, 1988), 45. Steven Mullaney, *The Place of the Stage* (Chicago, IL: University of Chicago Press, 1988), 79, 81–2. For Harriot, see Thomas Harriot, *A briefe and true report of the new found land of Virginia* (London: 1590).

Francis, but the love of Edward III for the countess of Salisbury turns on a shared pleasure in mocking the incivility of the Scottish ruling classes. More than her beauty, it is the countess's mimicry of the 'broad' unsubtle language of her Scottish besiegers that moves Edward's love for her. 'She is grown', he muses,

> more fairer far since I came hither,
> Her voice more silver every word than other,
> Her wit more fluent – what a strange discourse
> Unfolded she, of David and his Scots?
> 'Even thus', quoth she, 'he spake' – and then spoke broad
> With epithets and accents of the Scot
> But somewhat better than the Scot could speak.
> 'And thus quoth she' – and answered then herself –
> For who could speak like her?   (2.1.25–33)

Indeed, the countess's own grief before the king's arrival is expressed not as fear of physical harm or sexual shame at the hands of the Scots, but as a horror of their gross inarticulacy. Rather than distinguishing courteous wooing from brutal rape, her words link courtship and sexual violence as alike grievous to the 'scornful captive to a Scot' who must submit '[e]ither to be wooed by broad, untuned oaths / Or forced by rude, insulting barbarism' (1.2.7–8). The verbal inanity of which the countess complains is all too evident in the only scene in which King David II and Douglas appear, a scene which just gives them time to boast vainly, repeat the word 'bonny', squabble greedily and flee with cowardly haste before the arrival of the English (1.218–66). A letter sent in 1598 by Queen Elizabeth's agent in Edinburgh, George Nicolson, to Lord Burghley, reported that it had been regretted to him 'in quiet sort that the comedians of London should in their play scorn the King and people of this land and wished that it might be speedily amended . . . lest the worst sort getting understanding thereof should stir the King and country to anger thereat'.[76] If Melchiori is correct in identifying *Edward III* as the offending play, then we can perhaps see, in Shakespeare's adaptation of the metaphorical plot I have identified – in which a prodigal prince's inward reformation prepares an island nation for international war – a domestication of the figure of 'the Scot' which deliberately avoids overt linguistic mockery.

In Westmoreland's contrast, in *Henry V*, between 'the eagle England' and 'the weasel Scot', I noted the asymmetry of the metaphorical tenors of

---

[76] George Nicolson to Lord Burghley, 15 April 1598, SP 52/62 f.19; see Melchiori, 'Introduction', *Edward III*, 12.

'England' and 'Scot'. The word 'Scotland' occurs nine times across *1 & 2 Henry IV* and once in *Henry V*. Three of those times it specifies a place of refuge for the earl of Northumberland. The word 'Scot' occurs sixteen times – almost twice as many – across *1 & 2 Henry IV* and *Henry V*. This is significant because 'Scot' does work indifferently as a collective or singular noun across the class registers for which there is no English equivalent. As 'English' is an adjective, it is impossible to use it refer to 'the English people' or 'the English king' in the way that 'the Scot' might stand indifferently for the king or the people or even the kingdom. One effect of the frequency of the term 'Scot' in *1 & 2 Henry IV* is to suggest fungibility or exchange-value. By no means all the epithets applied to 'the Scot' in *1 Henry IV* are mocking or disparaging; on the contrary, as critics have noticed, Archibald Douglas is praised as 'the ever-valiant and approved Scot' (1.1.54). Nevertheless, there is a prevailing sense in which, as figures in a dispute over the king's sovereign right to prisoners of war, the 'Scot' is associated with the currency of honour, power and even sovereignty. The repeated play on 'scot' as a small sum of money – which, in a circular fashion, mid-twentieth century editorial notes ascribe to the disparagement of the Scots as a people – strengthens this impression.[77] Thus Hotspur rages 'By God, he [Henry IV] shall not have a scot of them; / Not if a scot would save his soul he shall not' (1.3.212–3) while Falstaff can't resist joking that he was forced to pretend to be dead at the Battle of Shrewsbury or 'that hot termagant Scot had paid me, scot and lot, too' (5.4.112–3). The *Henry IV* plays and *Henry V* are thus not innocent of the depiction of an English lesson in the witty mastery of languages that by definition will come to exclude Scotland as 'the Scot' from the scene of international war. In *1 Henry IV* the noble Hotspur fails strategically because his wit, though apprehensively extravagant, is not sufficiently judicious or calculating. As Worcester says, 'He apprehends a world of figures here / But not the form of what he should attend' (1.3.208–9). It is, accordingly, to Hotspur that Hal's mind turns after he has played his ruthless game of forcing Francis the drawer to the desperate, barren repetition of 'Anon, anon, sir' (2.4.95). 'That ever this fellow should have fewer words than a parrot,' muses Hal, 'and yet the son of a woman!'

> His industry is upstairs and downstairs, his eloquence a parcel of reckoning. I am not yet of Percy's mind, the Hotspur of the North, that kills me some

---

[77] *King Henry IV Part 1*, ed. A. R. Humphreys (London: Methuen, 1960), 1.3.212, glossing Hotspur's 'By God he shall not have a Scot of them', by citing Fuller, '"That is, *we will lose nothing, how inconsiderable soever* . . . This *Proverb* began in the *English borders*, when . . . they had little *esteem* of, and less *affection* for, a *Scotch-man*" (*Worthies*, 1662, ii.303)'.

six or seven dozen of Scots at a breakfast, washes his hands, and says to his
wife, 'Fie upon this quiet life! I want work.' 'O my sweet Harry,' says she,
'how many hast thou killed today?' 'Give my roan horse a drench,' says he,
and, answers, 'Some fourteen,' an hour after, 'a trifle, a trifle.' (2.4.96–106)

Where Francis's eloquence is nothing but a 'parcel of reckoning', Hotspur
reckons his deeds too sparely. The mismatch between the parsimony of his
words and extravagance of his prowess in killing is expressed in the small
change of Scots – 'some six or seven dozen . . . at a breakfast'. In this casual,
though not overtly offensive, reduction of 'the Scot' to the measure of
Hotspur's value to the English Crown – and thus, by definition, Hal's own
(since, as he promises his father, 'Percy is but my factor, good my lord, / To
engross up glorious deeds on my behalf' 3.2.147–8) – we can see how it is
that the lesson of the fatally humourless play, *Edward III*, was absorbed by
Shakespeare with respect to the problem of domesticating Scotland, so as
to prevent it from appearing as France's ally, and as one of the fighting
nations in the Hundred Years War.

Where the secure English isle identified by the monarch's reformation in
Greene's *Bacon and Bungay* and *Edward III* is linked with chastity, Hal's
reformation, as many critics have pointed out, rather polarises a fraternity of
idleness and theft against one of dignified work. In the famous 'I know you
all' speech of *1 Henry IV*, he punctures the Eastcheap fantasy of endless play
by telling us that 'To sport would be as tedious as to work' if all days were
holidays (1.2.194–5). When, in *Henry V*, the archbishop of Canterbury
concludes the Westmoreland-Exeter debate on Scotland by likening the
kingdom of England to a beehive, he sings a hymn of praise to order and
industry which ends in the execution of the 'lazy yawning drone' (1.2.204).
And in the St Crispin's Day speech it is a brotherhood of work that binds
together those who stand at Agincourt against the 'gentlemen in England
now abed' (4.3.64) or against those who, like Pistol, 'to England steal' to live
by cutting purses, counterfeiting wounds and by theft (5.1.88). In this version
of the metaphorical plot of monarchical reformation, the characterising of the
kingdom of Scotland as pure predation, pure theft, as in 'the weasel Scot', has
a disproportionate ideological force. From being the currency of Hotspur's
squandered powers of rebellion, 'the Scot' has become, in *Henry V*, all that
must be excluded by the mode of connectedness that is the working brotherhood of Agincourt. And yet, by the nature of its engagement of the audience's
imagination and judgement, the play's evocation of 'Englishness' feels reflex-
ively sceptical and inclusive. It is notable, in conclusion, that the words 'king
of Scotland' occur not at all in *1 & 2 Henry IV* and *Henry V*, and 'king of

Scots' only once – and in that once it refers to David II 'impounded as a stray' (1.2.160). The refusal of Shakespeare's *1 & 2 Henry IV* and *Henry V* even once to name the king of Scotland, James I (1406–1437), who was himself a poet, and who played an enforced role leading Henry's forces in France (inherently dramatic as a potential war crime), has made the kingdom itself seem to disappear from this period of English history.[78] And if the bland and entirely dispensable part of 'Captain Jamy' was intended as an allusion to the real King James I, it has successfully compounded that effect.

---

[78] Rona Munro cleverly opens her dramatisation of the reign of James I with the confrontation of Henry V and the Scottish prisoners of war at the siege of Melun. See *The James Plays* (London: Nick Helm Books, 2014), 3–17.

CHAPTER 7

Race-Making in the Invention of Britain: The Masque of Blackness

I. Jonson's Masque

Critical discussion of Ben Jonson's *Masque of Blackness* (1605) has emerged out of two distinct subfields. One of these derives from debates about the relation of art to royal power, and the extent to which the masque was a spectacle of power, the servant of absolutism. In this context, Martin Butler has countered New Historicist readings with a stress on political dialogue, pointing to negotiations over the question of British Union as 'the ideological crucible out of which the masques were made'. Butler thus reads *Blackness*, with its discovery of the island name 'Britannia' as endorsing James I's project of 'Great Britain' in such a way as left 'less space for negotiation' for English constitutional objections to Union.[1] Critical work on premodern race, however, has been differently preoccupied with questions how and where modern categories of racialised thinking emerge.[2] This work sets *Blackness* within a long (and exploitative) tradition of Moorish masquerade at European courts, while acknowledging its newly imperial message of Britannia's power to manage and dispose racial difference, embodied in the queen and her ladies as 'daughters of Niger'.[3] Discussions in both contexts acknowledge each other, but in general the meaning of the intimate relation between the two remains elusive.[4] Yet

---

[1] Butler, *Stuart Court Masque*, 95. Butler's study revises such accounts as Stephen Orgel's *The Illusion of Power* (Berkeley, CA: University of California Press, 1975).

[2] For example, Ania Loomba and Jonathan Burton, 'Introduction', *Race in Early Modern England: A Documentary Companion* (Basingstoke: Palgrave, 2007), 1–36; Geraldine Heng, *The Invention of Race in the European Middle Ages* (Cambridge: Cambridge University Press, 2018), 1–54; Sujata Iyengar, *Shades of Difference: Mythologies of Skin Color in Early Modern England* (Philadelphia, PA: University of Pennsylvania Press, 2005).

[3] See Anthony G. Barthelemy, *Black Face, Maligned Race* (Baton Rouge, LA: Lousiana State University Press, 1987), 18–41; Kim F. Hall, *Things of Darkness* (Ithaca, NY: Cornell University Press, 1995), 128–141; Bernadette Andrea, 'Black Skin, the Queen's Masques: Africanist Ambivalence and Feminine Author(ity) in the Masques of *Blackness* and Beauty', *ELR*, vol. 29, no. 2 (1999), 246–81.

[4] An exception is Mary Floyd-Wilson, *English Ethnicity and Race in Early Modern Drama* (Cambridge: Cambridge University Press, 2003), 111–31.

there is no doubt that the masque makes the questions of Britain and black masquerade mutually dependent. The masque's riddling invention of the name 'Britannia', figured as an oceanic voyage discovering Britannia's hidden, gem-like insularity, is predicated on a devastating trivialisation and negation of African racial difference. Its opening arguments for the intrinsic beauty of Ethiopian nobility dwindle into a tired old figure for overcoming impossibility: washing the Ethiop white. The surrounding seas that define Britannia's claims to insular unity morph into a skin-cleansing advertisement: that 'wholesome dew, called rosmarine' which 'with . . . soft and gentler foam' will wash Niger's daughters.[5] By time we get to these lines, blackness has lost its initial poetic engagement with the idea of Africa and has become wittily and deprecatingly conflated with its own theatrical device. No longer signifying racial difference, blackness, by the end of the masque, is reduced to artificial pigment, the matter of soluble black paint on white skin.[6]

In this book I seem constantly to be encountering trivialisation strategies of one kind and another, so I once again recall Joe Moshenska's helpful observation that trivialisation strategies are not in themselves trivial, that their complexity is buried in the very means by which they achieve their aim of being overlooked.[7] In this chapter, I want to take seriously Jonson's trivialising reduction of racial difference to the artifice of theatrical greasepaint by looking at a race-making innovation in the discourse of British Anglo-imperialism which occurs in Jonson's chief source, Camden's *Britannia* (1586). This chapter brings together the two contexts that have hitherto been somewhat distinct in determining critical readings: debates over the *nationes* or peoples in the British Isles and the 'cultural, historical and material basis of the Africanist trope that became current in the court (and public) theater of seventeenth-century England'.[8] Both English and Scottish courts through the sixteenth century had shown a penchant for entertainments that made a spectacle of black skin, sometimes involving black people, such as Elen, 'the Quenis blak maiden', at the court of James IV and Margaret Tudor in 1512, and sometimes involving black masquerade, as when Mary Queen of Scots was met by fifty young men in yellow taffeta, their faces black 'in the maner of

---

[5] *The Masque of Blackness* ed. David Lindley in *CWBJ* II. 505–28; 525, 297–8. Further references to this edition will be given by line number in the text.
[6] See Andrea Stevens, *Inventions of the Skin: The Painted Body in Early English Drama, 1400–1642* (Edinburgh: Edinburgh University Press, 2013), 87–100 and below, 000.
[7] Moshenska, *Iconoclasm*, 20.   [8] Andrea, 'Black Skin', 248.

Moris' at her royal entry into Edinburgh in 1561.[9] With respect to the latter tradition, the material difference – and the scandal – of Jonson's masque, commanded by Anne of Denmark, was that the royal and noble women playing in it were not dressed in seemly black velvet, but had their skin, draped in diaphanously revealing costumes, painted with black pigment.[10] The *Masque of Blackeness* was, then, to borrow Andrea Stevens' phrase, 'an invention of the skin'. Rhetorically speaking, it was also an invention of *the invention* – in the Renaissance sense of 'discovery' (from Latin, *invenio*, 'I find, I discover') – of an island called *Britannia*. But even in this rhetorical and chorographical way, *Britannia* was simultaneously 'an invention of the skin'. For Camden – who was Jonson's reverend teacher – produced in his *Britannia* a new account of the racial origins of the inhabitants of Britain that distinguished them not by their heroic narratives of Brutus and Gathelus, but by linguistic evidence for skin-painting. Although turning from the skins of Niger's daughters to those of ancient Britons, Scots and Picts might seem like leaving behind the history of the African presence in early modern Britain, this chapter is concerned to analyse what Toni Morrison called the 'theatrical presence of black surrogacy' as a crucial element in the construction of the literature of British and American whiteness.[11] It will try to offer an explanation for why the imagining of painted skin and then the projecting of that paint's removal to define Britain's inhabitants as all alike *unpainted* might have been understood as a unifying strategy in 1605. And it will consider the disturbing implications thereby entailed, including the production of unpaintedness as whiteness and the positioning of residual blackness – the blackness that is *not paint* – as beyond the waves and the shore that admit entrance to Britain.

The very passage of Camden's *Britannia* which supplies Jonson's conceit of the masque's riddling 'discovery' of a united Britain was itself a new departure from the Galfridian derivation of Britain from the Trojan Brutus. As F. J. Levy was the first to acknowledge, Camden's two great historiographical innovations in *Britannia* were to replace Geoffrey of Monmouth's myth of Trojan-British origin with an ethnographic account of British racial origins and to interpret the past chorographically, moving through space, not through narrative time.[12] Not (as we have seen) that chorography itself

---

[9] Imitaz Habib, *Black Lives in the English Archives 1500–1677* (Aldershot: Ashgate, 2008), 31, 293; Stevens, *Skin*, 91; *Diurnall*, 67.
[10] Stevens, *Skin*, 91–94.
[11] Toni Morrison, *Playing in the Dark* (New York, NY: Random House, Vintage Books, 1992), 13.
[12] F. R. Levy, 'The Making of Camden's Britannia', *Bibliothèque d'Humanisme et Renaissance*, vol. 26, no. 1 (1964), 70–97.

was new, but that Camden's antiquarian perambulations, unlike those of previous chorographers, were structurally unified by a prefatory linguistic ethnography of the island's earliest *nationes* or races.[13] *Britannia* moves from a linguistic-ethnographic identification of the most ancient inhabitants of Britain towards topographically organised perambulations through the island which territorialise the past in relation to the book's introductory ethnography.[14] Where earlier chorographers had tied their antiquarian investigations to the Galfridian tradition of Trojan-British origins, Camden rendered this origin story obsolete, substituting for it a new ethnography of a pre-Roman race of Gallic Britons and a new antiquarian interest in the material remains of Roman Britain.

Camden's linguistic ethnography thus departed sharply from such antecedent chorographers as John Leland (1540s), Humphrey Llwyd (1572) and William Harrison (1577), all of whom combined antiquarian topographical description with an endorsement of the Galfridian tradition which underwrote England's suzerainty over Britain as the consequence of Brutus's division of the kingdoms.[15] The predecessor whose methods most closely anticipate Camden's was George Buchanan in his *Rerum Scoticarum Historia* (1582).[16] Buchanan was the first to propose with any evidential precision that the ancient inhabitants of Britain spoke related dialects, suggesting a common origin in Gaul.[17] But where Buchanan used linguistic ethnography to identify *three* Gaulish-derived British nations – the Britons, the Scots-Irish and the Picts – Camden chose, in a radical departure from all previous historians to argue for an ethnic identification of the Britons and the Picts as *a single racial group*, the original inhabitants of the island, on the evidence that they *painted their skins*. I propose that by identifying the painted Picts as painted ancient Britons, Camden was able to extend the habitation of the Britons to the very northernmost parts of the island. The consequence was an imaginative de-territorialising of Scottish antiquity. Scots no longer figured as an ancient British nation on a par with Britons/Picts in spite of the fact that Scots and Picts both

---

[13] William Rockett, 'The Structural Plan of Camden's *Britannia*', *Sixteenth Century Journal*, vol. 26, no. 4 (1995), 829–41.

[14] Rockett, 'Structural', 831–2.

[15] Leland, *Arthure*; Leland, *Cygnea Cantio*; Humphrey Llwyd, *Commentaroli Britannicae Descriptionis Fragmentum* (London, 1572), trans. Thomas Twyne as *The Breviary of Britain*, ed. Philip Schwyzer (London: Modern Humanities Research Association, 2011); Harrison, 'Description', *Holinshed*, I.1–220. Further references to these texts will appear in the text by page or folio.

[16] Buchanan, *Rerum Scoticarum Historia* (Edinburgh: 1582); Buchanan, *The History of Scotland Translated from the Latin of George Buchanan*, trans. James Aikman (Glasgow, 1827), 4 vols.

[17] Buchanan, *History*, I.1–148.

begin to be mentioned in Latin sources at about the same time (c.350–400 AD). Camden denied Scots ethnic parity with Picts as *primi incolae* on the grounds that he could find nothing to prove beyond doubt whether they came from Ireland, Scythia or elsewhere. He translated his uncertainty ('I have affirmed nothing') into a figure for ethnic miscellaneity, proposing Scots to be 'a mishmash of sundry nations which conflowed into Ireland, and thereupon gat that name … For that is called a Scot, which from sundrie thinges groweth into one heape.'[18] Uncertainty with respect to 'Pict', on the other hand, turned into a positive, if conditional, conjecture: but for the contrary arguments of Bede, he wrote, 'I would think that the Picts … were verie natuall Britons themselves' (1610:115; 1587: 40). As these Picts were thought to have been completely wiped out by Kenneth McAlpin (Cinaed mac Alpín) in the ninth century, Camden's new ethnography effectively sets an indigenous ancient British claim to the whole island which tacitly but very effectively denies ethnic legitimacy to the present inhabitants of the northern kingdom.[19] Far from gesturing, in the twenty years before James's accession, towards a tactful 'inclusivity' of the Scots as ancient British *natio* or nation, I propose that Camden's *Britannia* cleverly reasserts, at the implicit, conjectural level of racial imagining, the English claim over the whole island of Britain that had once been made through stories of Brutus and Arthur.[20]

In this chapter, I will first indicate the nature of Jonson's debt to Camden in associating the name of Britain with a race of people who painted their skin. I will then show how radically Camden's argument for the ethnic unity of Britons and Picts as painted peoples transformed the Galfridian model of earlier Anglo-Welsh chorographies. By way of recent work which recognises George Buchanan as the first humanist scholar to consider the relations of Gaelic, Brittonic and Pictish languages in the British Isles, I will argue that Camden was aware of Buchanan's ethnolinguistic methods, and that he transformed their conclusions in order to assert the dominance, in ancient times, of a single 'British' race in place of

[18] Camden, *Britain*, 124; Camden, *Britannia*, 51. Further references to these two editions will appear in the text, by date and page number.

[19] On the probable peaceful transition of cultural power from Pictish to Alban kings around the time of Cinaed, see Woolf, *Pictland*, 87–121.

[20] The pervasive assumption is that Camden aimed to be racially inclusive, but was impeded by the 'facts'. Juliet Fleming's comment is revealing: 'In discussing the history of the Scots, Camden underlines his purpose in arguing for the racial unity of the peoples of Britain, and incidentally demonstrates the difficulty of producing a tactful account of Britain's past', Fleming, *Graffiti and the Writing Arts in Early Modern England* (London: Reaktion, 2001), 119. Here Camden's abjection of the Scots is rewritten as the tact of the disinterested scholar.

Buchanan's three distinct races. Finally, I will turn back to the questions of representing peoples with painted and tattooed skin in the context of debates over 'Great Britain' at the time of the accession of a Scottish king to the English throne, asking how we should read Jonson's sceptical trivialisation of origin myths and racial difference in *Blackness*.

II. The Painted (*Picti*) Britons: Camden's Great Innovation

At its opening, Jonson's *Blackness* expresses a surprising scepticism about the Europeans' tendency to indulge in discourses of the 'origins' of back skin. When asked by Oceanus why he has travelled so far from Ethiopia to 'these . . . shores' (94), the River Niger gives an account of the loveliness of his daughters, 'the first-formed dames of earth' (98), whose beauty inheres 'in their black' (104) precisely because of its aboriginal, inalterable nature: it does not change with age or death. Belief in these 'arguments' (111) however, has been shaken by European poets, who 'infect all climates' with 'wingèd fictions' (119–20) of Ethiopian blackness having a contingent, historical origin in the moment when Phaëton lost control of the sun's chariot and, in Ovid's words, '*Sanguine tum credunt in corpora summa vocato / Aethiopum populus nigrum traxisse colorem*' ('It was then, as men think, that the peoples of Aethiopia became black-skinned, since the blood was drawn to the surface of their bodies by the heat').[21] Niger's analysis is brilliantly inflected to suggest how, within European Petrarchan poetry, the competitive figures of antithesis and similitude ('eyes like stars', etc.) relegate this newly contingent 'blackness' to the status of flexible, evaluative foil.[22] The fiction of Phaëton implies that

> Before his heedless flames were hurled
> About the globe the Ethiops were *as fair*
> *As other dames*, now black with black despair;   (122–4)

Hovering between sensory colour perception ('light coloured') and comparative measure of beauty ('as fair / As other dames'), the word 'fair' here exemplifies the formal, race-making power of poetry as it both defines beauty *against* blackness and makes blackness beauty's essential definitional resource. As the sun, in Niger's account, was both formal cause and 'best judge' of Ethiopian beauty (101), restoration of faith in the judgement of

---

[21] Ovid. *Metamorphoses, Volume I: Books 1–8*. Translated by Frank Justus Miller. Revised by G. P. Goold (Cambridge, MA: Harvard University Press, 1916), 76–77, lines 235–6, translation adjusted.

[22] See Hall, *Things of Darkness*, 62–122.

beauty needs to be restored by the riddling discovery of a sunless land, a land whose

> ... termination (of the Greek)
> Sounds –*tania*   (150)

In this mysterious place 'bright Sol, that heat / Their bloods, doth never rise or set' but 'leaves that climate of the sky / To comfort of a greater light, / Who forms all beauty with his sight' (148–55). This 'greater light' is, of course, James; in this new place, beauty will be formed by shared political allegiance to James, not by climate. Following the 'tania' clue, Niger and his daughters have, as they explain to Oceanus, wandered through lands whose names connect descriptions of peoples with the word '-*tania*':

> In search of this have we three princedoms passed,
> That speak out –*tania* in their accents last;
> Black Mauritania first, and secondly,
> Swart Lusitania; next we did descry
> Rich Acquitania; and, yet, cannot find
> The place unto these longing nymphs designed.   (156–61)

The riddle is solved as the goddess Ethiopia appears and reveals to Niger's daughters that they have arrived in a land which has recently recovered its ancient name, 'Britannia'. Ethiopia's rhymes emphasise that the recovery of this 'ancient dignity and *style*' produces the insular rarity and wonder of 'this bless'd *isle*' which is, in Virgil's words, '*A world divided from the world* ...' (192–202).

Jonson's source for his riddling voyage of discovery comes from the passage in which, in the first and subsequent editions of *Britannia*, Camden revealed his etymology of the name 'Britain'. The passage concludes a wide-ranging discussion of the possible derivations of the name 'Britain' (including Geoffrey of Monmouth's story of Brutus and Humphrey Llwyd's '*Pryd Cain*') by pulling, as if out of a hat, a startling new proposition. 'What if I should conjecture,' he asks, 'that they were called Britans of their depainted bodies?' ('*quid si à depictis corporibus Britones dictos fuisse coniecturam?* 1610; 26; 1587: 24). And he continues: 'For, whatever is thus painted and coloured, in their ancient countrey speech, they call *Brith*' ('*Quidquid enim depictum & coloratum*, Brith *patria & antiqua lingua appellant*'; 1610: 26; 1587: 24). Arguing by analogy with the western kingdoms of Mauritania, Lusitania and Aquitania, Camden then proposes that Greek merchants, learning the name

'Brith' from the Gauls (who spoke the same language as the Britons: '*vel à Gallis quibus una eadem lingua*') then coined the name *Brith-tania*, which was taken over by the Romans. This section on 'Britanniae Nomen' (1587: 21–27) is followed by several pages with the running head 'Romani in Britannia' (1587: 28–39), which are followed in turn by the running heads '*Picti*' (43–46) and then a new heading, '*Scoti*' (46). Camden introduces the Picts as '*primas in antiquitate . . . post Britannos*' (1587:40; 1610:114) and then announces that he is able to prove 'that the Picts were the very British indeed' (*quod Picti ipsi Britanni fuerint*) on the basis of their customs, name and language (*more, nomine, & sermone*), especially the custom of 'painting and staining themselves with colours' (*ritus ille pingendi, & coloribus se oblinendi*, 1587:41; 1610: 114–15). Camden's ethnic identification of Picts with Britons lies at the heart of his etymology of Britain as '*Brith-tania*', land of the painted or coloured people.

The radical novelty of Camden's identification of the Picts as the same race as the ancient Britons seems to have escaped modern critical attention. Yet no medieval or early modern historian before Camden asserts the kinship of Britons and Picts. Up until the late sixteenth century, as we have seen from previous chapters, British histories, chronicles and romances make the Picts kin not to the Britons but to the Scots.[23] Indeed, the sharpest possible racial distinction between Britons and Picts is essential to the discourse of Scoto-Pictish abjection that energises British history's important prophetic strain (the promised return of Arthur and recovery of British empire). Scots and Picts, according to this tradition of British history, are paired as liminal, extremely savage foreign peoples who repeatedly threaten Britain's northernmost regions, preventing, by their incursions, the true *Briton* heirs to the island from properly occupying their *British* island homeland. Thus, Geoffrey of Monmouth repeatedly describes 'Scotia' and 'Albania' as uncivilised regions, hospitable only to Saxon and Norwegian invaders, who, aided by these savage Scots and Picts, make the northern regions uninhabitable for the Britons.[24] Indeed, Geoffrey prefaces his history with a '*descriptio insulae*' that makes this

---

[23] See also Andrew Hadfield, 'Bruited Abroad: John White and Thomas Harriot's Colonial Representations of Ancient Britain', in *British Identities*, ed. Baker and Maley, 159–77.

[24] Geoffrey of Monmouth, *The History of the Kings of Britain*, trans. Neil Wright, ed. Michael D. Reeve (Suffolk: Boydell Press, 2009), VI.91–92; VIII.120. This edition divides Geoffrey's work into books and chapters, which I follow in citation. These are not page numbers. See the editor's 'Introduction', lx.

topographical-historical plot explicit. *'Britannia, insularum optima'*, it begins, 'Britain, best of islands', and concludes:

> It is, finally, inhabited by five peoples, the Normans, the Britons, the Saxons, Picts and Scots: of these Britons once occupied it from shore to shore (*a mari usque ad mare*) before the others, until their pride brought divine retribution down upon and them and they gave way to the Picts and the Saxons.[25]

Geoffrey's was a history originally directed at an Anglo-Norman audience with prophetic hopes of Welsh resurgence, but it was soon repackaged, along with its claims of prior occupation 'from shore to shore', as an Anglo-imperial history, justifying successive English attempts to conquer Scotland on the grounds of ancient title to sovereignty.[26] In the Arthurian romances that spread over Europe in the wake of Geoffrey's history, Picts and Scots went on being associated with liminality and danger to Arthur's Britain – in Marie de France's *Lanval*, King Arthur returns from fighting 'les Escoz e pur les Pis / ki destrueient le païs' (the Scots and the Picts, who were destroying the land).[27] Scottish histories, on the other hand, offered positive if complex and semi-mythic narratives of a sovereign and autonomous Scottish kingdom emerging from intermarriages, alliances and mutual expulsions of Scots and Picts.[28] In no account until Camden's, as far as I know, is there ever any suggestion of an ethnic identification between the Britons and the Picts.

It needs emphasising that not only medieval chroniclers but also modern English chorographers before Camden all founded their topographical descriptions of Britain on a sharp racial distinction between 'homeling' Britons and marauding foreign Picts/Scots. Camden's immediate predecessors, Humphrey Llwyd's *Commentarioli Britannicae Descrptionis fragmentum* ('Fragment of a little commentary of the description of Britain', 1572) and William Harrison's 'An Historical Description of the Iland of Britaine' (1577 and 1587) both emphatically distinguish Britons from Picts,

---

[25] Geoffrey, *History*, 'Description of the Island', 5.
[26] Gillingham, 'Context', 99–118; Mason, 'Scotching the Brut'; Goldstein, *Matter of Scotland*; Stones and Simpson, *Edward I*; Merriman, *Rough Wooings*, 265–89.
[27] *Lais de Marie de France* trans. and ed. Alexandre Micha (Paris: Flammarion, 1994), 142.
[28] See Dauvit Broun, 'The Picts' Place in Kingship's Past before John of Fordun', in Edward J. Cowan and Richard J. Finlay, *Scottish History: The Power of the Past* (Edinburgh: Edinburgh University Press, 2002), 12–28; also Roger A. Mason, 'Civil Society and the Celts: Hector Boece, George Buchanan and the Ancient Scottish Past', in *Scottish History*, 95–120; Ulrike Hogg and Martin MacGregor, 'Historiography in the Highlands and Lowlands', in Nicola Royan ed., *The International Companion to Scottish Literature, 1400–1650* (Glasgow: Scottish Literature International, 2018), 100–23; Mason, 'Scotching the Brut'.

associating the latter with the Scots as predators from northern seas. As the topographical description providing a structural 'British' coherence to Holinshed's *Chronicles* of England, Scotland and Ireland, Harrison's *Description of Britaine* performed the usual English claim to Britain not only by endorsing Brutus's mythic division of the kingdoms, but by arguments of Scoto-Pictish foreignness, belatedness and savagery. Here Harrison drew on the 'SCOTIA' section of Llwyd's *Commentariolum*. Llwyd had earlier endorsed the myth of Brutus's threefold division of Britain into Lhoegria, Albania and Cambria (fol. 8v), offering topographical descriptions of Lhoegria (fols. 12 r-29v) and Cambria (fols. 41 r-77 r). His section marked 'SCOTIA' (fols. 29v-39 r), however, is not a comparable topography, but a refutation of claims for the antiquity of Picts and Scots within Britain. Principally concerned to refute Boece's narratives of Scottish and Pictish kingdoms stretching back to 330 BC, Llwyd draws two sharp lines of distinction between the ancient Britons and the Picts. First, he refutes the Latin etymology of 'Pict' and second, he creates an inland cultivator/coastal predator distinction between south and north. The term 'Pict', he insists, has nothing to do with Latin, '*pictum*', 'painted'. Rather, it comes from Gaelic 'Phichtaid'. His Picts are not, then, *painted people*. They are most emphatically not 'the Britons, of whom Caesar and others do report, that they were wont to paint their bodies with woad, that they might appear more terrible to their enemies' (*Breviary*, 85; *Commentariolum*, fol. 30v). Llwyd cites Gildas reporting nations which lived by piracy (*pyraticam quandam gentem*, fol. 30v) which came out of Norway or Sweden into Albania/Scotland and, thereafter, 'in their little leathern boats ("*suis coreaceis*") . . . along Scotland were wont to rob and spoil shepherds and fishermen' (though Lwyd's Latin gives '*pastoribus & agricolis*', shepherds and farmers; fol. 31 r; *Breviary*, 85).

As we saw in Chapter 3, Harrison's *Description of Britain* first tells a story of metamorphic British indigeneity, of the British race surviving successive invasions by the Romans, the English, the Normans and the Danes. Britain's 'natural homelings', the British, joined 'in mariage with the Englishmen' so that 'their whole race' did not perish, but survived subsequent conquests, he writes (13–14). He goes on to refute the claims of Scots and Picts to have been comparably ancient nations in the island: 'How and when the Scots and Picts, a people mixed of the Scithian and Spanish blood, should arriue here out of Ireland, and when the Picts should come vnto vs out of Samaria, or from further north & the Scithian Hyperboreans, as yet it is vncerteine,' he writes (10). Scottish histories boast their antiquity, but Harrison judges them to have recently 'stolne in hither'. 'The Scots did often aduenture hither to rob and steale out of Ireland' until, helping the Picts (whom he does define as 'painted') these Scots 'so planted themselves in these parts, that vnto our time that portion of the land cannot be cleansed of them' (10). In both accounts, the island's topography remains essentially Galfridian: a civilised core anciently inhabited by Britons, threatened from late classical times by influxes of thieving Scots and Picts. Harrison's language of ethnic cleansing of 'the land' testifies to the strength of feeling behind the refutation of Scottish claims to historic nationhood within the island.

III. How Camden Read His Buchanan

Camden respectfully departed from the chorographies of Llwyd and Harrison and the antiquarian work of Leland, rejecting the myth of Britain's having been discovered by Brutus the Trojan, just as, he said, 'the wiser sort' of Scots have rejected their stories of Gathelus and Scota (1610: 8–9). He adopted a new linguistically based ethnography, arguing for the identification of the Picts as ancient Britons on the strength, as we saw, of three kinds of evidence – their customs, name and language (*more, nomine, & sermone.* 1587: 41; 1610: 114–15). In this he concurred with the methodological innovations of George Buchanan, whose *Rerum Scoticarum Historia* (1582) he seems to have read with close attention. John Collis, William Ferguson and Guto Rhys have shown how Buchanan based his radically new style of inquiry into the origins of British peoples on very principles that Camden later adopted, examining 1) the languages of the people being investigated (*sermones*); 2) their customs and religious practices (*mores*); and 3) the names of places, especially enduring ones, such as those of towns and rivers (*nomina*).[29]

Buchanan's aim, in the first three books of his *Rerum Scoticarum Historia*, was to discredit the dismissal of Scottish antiquity evident in the 'SCOTIA' section of Llwyd's *Commentariolum*, and to redirect serious linguistic-ethnographic attention to the north, as well as the south and west, of the British Isles. He observed the way in which English and Welsh

---

[29] See John Collis, 'George Buchanan and the Celts in Britain', in *Celtic Connections: Proceedings of the Tenth International Congress of Celtic Studies, Volume I: Language, Literature, History, Culture*, volume 1, ed. William Gillies, Ronald Black and Roibeard Ó Maolalaigh (Edinburgh, 1999), 91–107; William Ferguson, *The Identity of the Scottish Nation: An Historic Quest* (Edinburgh: Edinburgh University Press, 1998), 79–97; Guto Rhys, 'Approaching the Pictish Language: Historiography, Early Evidence and the Question of Pritenic', Unpublished PhD thesis, University of Glasgow (2015), 64–8.

chorographers, following Caesar, Pomponius Mela, Livy and others, rendered the north insubstantial by describing Britain's shape as triangular. The Roman conception of Britain's triangularity, he observed, had been disproved by Tacitus's recording of Agricola's exploits in the region north of the Forth-Clyde isthmus.[30] Insisting on the extent and breadth of northern Britain, and disambiguating the shape of the whole island from the designation of 'that part of the island which was a Roman province' (I.12; 1582, fol. 3v), Buchanan made imaginative space for the habitation of the island of Britain by other races (*nationes*), exposing the *trompe l'oeil* by which descriptive geography, effacing the topography of Britain's north, helped make it seem insubstantial and unimaginable, an amorphous, sea-encroached region of landless marauders. Buchanan made good on this demystification with a substantial, detailed and original topographical description of Scotland, whose influence and importance within Scotland Roger Mason has demonstrated.[31]

Then Buchanan moved on to language. He performed humanistic demolitions of both the British-Trojan and the Scottish-Graeco-Egyptian tales of origin. Of the former, he observed that Geoffrey of Monmouth's oracle of Diana spoke in Brutus's very own idiom and style, exposing the wish-fulfilment of its promise of British empire. Of the latter, he expressed surprise that the Scottish inventors of the Greek prince Gathelus had not even taken care, in the interests of plausibility, to give him a Greek name. But though he mocked Llwyd for simultaneously espousing the Brutus legend and deriving the name 'Britain' from the Welsh words '*Pryd*' and '*Cain*' ('beauty' and 'white'), Buchanan was far from being uninterested in the languages of the island. Rather, he insisted on the credibility of Latin (rather than Brittonic or Gaelic) sources and on the importance, when reconstructing linguistic affinities through place names, of discriminating, limiting deduction to 'name-elements whose meaning could be plausibly deduced and whose occurrence was not confined to one or two cases'.[32] Here Buchanan made, according to Ferguson, Collis and Rhys, his most important discoveries. 'His great innovation,' writes Rhys, 'was to investigate both ancient and contemporary place names and compare them with Gaelic and

---

[30] See, for example, Harrison, 'Description', 5; Tacitus, *Agricola, Germania, Dialogus*, trans. M. Hutton and W. Peterson, revised R. M. Ogilvie, E. H. Warmington, Michael Winterbottom (Cambridge, MA: Harvard University Press, 1970), Introduction, 17; *Agricola*, 3–5.

[31] Roger A. Mason, 'From Buchanan to Blaeu: The Politics of Scottish Chorography, 1582–1654', in *George Buchanan: Political Thought in Early Modern Britain and Europe*, ed. Caroline Erskine and Roger A. Mason (Farnham: Ashgate, 2012), 13–47.

[32] Collis, 'Buchanan and Celts', 101.

Welsh words ... He considered areas south of the Forth-Clyde estuary to
have been Pictish ... and noted that rivers named *Avon* corresponded to
Welsh, *afon*, "river", Aberbrothock ..., Aberdone, Aberdene ... were correctly equated with Brythonic *aber*, "estuary" and Ptolemy's "Scottish"
Cornavii with Cornwall.' This, Rhys concludes, 'marked the beginning of
an objective and informed approach to Celtic linguistics and the language of
the Picts'.[33]

From these elements and from the observations of Caesar and Tacitus,
Buchanan argued that all the nations who anciently settled in Britain came
from either Gaul, Spain or Germany, and that Spain and Germany were
themselves populated by colonies of Gaulish speakers (Celtiberi, Gothuni
and Cimbri). These Gaulish colonies, he wrote, had acquired literacy from
the Greeks of Marseilles, but used writing not to record history, but only
for mercantile reckonings and transactions. '*Graecis quidem figuris elemen-
torum, sed sermone Gallico*', he wrote, 'the letters were Greek, but the
language was Gaulish' (I.64; 1582, fol. 14 r).[34] Against Llwyd, Buchanan
maintained that the bards of these Gaulish nations were not true historians
and that the only reliable witnesses were therefore the Romans who
recorded observations about their customs and languages.

As Caesar and Tacitus bore witness to the spread of Gaulish-speaking
peoples across Europe, Buchanan proposed that the whole of Britain's
ancient inhabitants spoke various Gaulish dialects and he named *three*
ancient nations: Britons, Picts and Scots (I.82; 1582, fol. 18 r). From Caesar
and Tacitus, Buchanan laid out his evidence for thinking that Britons, Scots
and Picts all derived from Gaulish colonies. He explained Caesar's mistaken
belief that the British are indigenous as Caesar's inference from the fact that
the Britons had no written memorial. Noting that both Caesar and Tacitus
remark on the similarities between British and Gaulish customs and languages, he hypothesised that the Britons came from the *Belgiae*, who were
Gaulish speakers around the sea-coasts. The *Scoti* in the west of course, are
one with the Irish; these Tacitus said had come from Spain, which, as
Buchanan reminds us, was full of Gaulish colonies (I.83–5; 1582, fol. 18 r–v).
In sum, then: Buchanan argued that the three ancient peoples of Britain all
came from Gaulish colonies and spoke different Gaulish dialects; this he

---

[33] Rhys, 'Pictish Language', 66.
[34] For the consequences of James Aikman's misleading translation of '*sermone Gallico*' as 'Gothic', see
William Ferguson, 'George Buchanan and the Picts', *Scottish Tradition*, vol. 16 (1991), 18–32, 26–29.
This and other passages from Buchanan appear without specific acknowledgement and in a severely
distorting fashion to produce a Scythian origin for the Scots in Spenser's *View of the Present State of
Ireland*.

supported by citing Caesar and Tacitus on the similarities of custom between the Britons and the Gauls; and finally, as Collis demonstrates, he offered a wealth of discriminating evidence from place names for his contention that there was 'in the pre-Roman period a common Gallic language spoken across Western Europe, which was also spoken by the earliest inhabitants of Britain, who must therefore have originated in Gaul'.[35]

No one who reads both Camden and Buchanan can fail to be struck by the very strong similarity between Camden's methodology and Buchanan's. Camden conjectures that Greek merchants learned the name 'Brith' from the Gauls who spoke the same language as the Britons (1587: 25) from which the Greek merchants coined the name 'Brith-tania'. This chimes with Buchanan's argument that the Gauls learned letters from the Greeks, with whom they traded. On the resemblance between British peoples and Gauls, based on language and customs, Camden cites exactly the same evidence from Caesar and Tacitus as Buchanan does. Noting these similarities, however, Guto Rhys thinks that Camden came to his conclusions independently of Buchanan, because he mentions Buchanan only his *Scoti* chapter, not in his chapter on *Picti*.[36] This may well be true, but the evidence might equally bear the opposite construction. In the *Scoti* chapter, it is in Camden's interests to draw attention to Buchanan's misreading of '*scuta*' (shield) as '*Scota*', '*Scot*', in a passage from Seneca's *Apocolocyntosis*. This upholds Llwyd's contention that Scots are unknown in ancient sources before Vespasian's time and gently suggests that Buchanan should stick to writing poetry (1587: 51–2; 1610:124–5). Naming Buchanan here makes sense, since the whole chapter sets out to refute Buchanan's claim that the Scots are an ancient British nation (1610: 124). In the chapter on *Picti*, however, where Camden wishes to prove Britons and Picts to be the sole ancient nation of Britain, mention of Buchanan, far from serving Camden's purpose, might have exposed some problems with his presentation of the evidence. There are reasons for thinking that Camden might have been deliberately setting out to refute Buchanan. A letter from Thomas Savile to Camden rejoices that the latter has been able to 'disarm the aging rhetorician', Buchanan, (*senescentem Rhetorem exarmare*) without too much work, while a draft letter of Camden's to Savile, mocks Buchanan's *fabulae refellendae* (refutable fables) and describes him as a poet lacking sobriety and strength.[37]

---

[35] Collis, 'Buchanan and Celts', 101.   [36] Rhys, 'Pictish language', 67.
[37] *Gulielmi Camdeni . . . Epistolae* (London: 1691), 11; BL Add MSS 36294, fol. 6v. These comments are noted and translated in Stephanus Parmenius, *The New Found Land of Stephen Parmenius* trans. David B. Quinn and Neil M. Cheshire (Toronto: University of Toronto Press, 1972), 113.

Camden's argument in his *Picti* chapter registers consciousness of
Buchanan's arguments both by what it includes and what it takes care to
omit. Both Buchanan and Camden had to contend with Bede's famous
identification of five different languages spoken in Britain in his own day:
English, British, Scots, Pictish and Latin.[38] Having argued that three
ancient British languages – British, Scots and Pictish – were all derived
from Gaul, Buchanan suggested that Bede might here be referring to
different dialects rather than absolutely distinct languages. He then traced
many affinities between place-name elements in different parts of Britain
and across the Gaulish colonies of Europe. As we have seen, he noted that
'Avon' signified a river in both Scots and Welsh; that 'Dun' was a frequent
element in the names of towns among the Gauls, in ancient Britain, and
among modern Welsh, Cornish and Scots and that the 'Aber' in
'Aberdene' meant 'a bay or road for a ship' while 'Strath' in the ancient
Scottish language meant the vale through which a river takes its course
(I:29, 32, 37, 109; 1582: fols. 6v,7v, 8 r, 23–4).

Bede's account of the Scythian origins of the Picts posed a problem for
Camden, but in working out how to overcome it, he must have found
Buchanan's linguistic arguments for the affinities between all the ancient
languages of Britain extremely helpful. Buchanan had, effectively, set the
stage for arguing 'that the Picts were perhaps not so distinct linguistically
from Britons'.[39] When Buchanan explains the place-name element 'Strath'
as anciently signifying a river valley ('*Strat enim regionem ad fluminum
decursum iacentem appellare solent*', 1582: fol. 6v), Camden translates this
linguistic insight to his *Picti* chapter: '*The Vale of* . . . comming of *Strath*,
which in the British tongue betokeneth a Valley' ('*à* Straith, *quod
Britannicè vallis est*', 1587: 43). 'Aber' likewise is said by Camden to be
'the British word, Aber, which signifieth a mouth' (1610: 117). Buchanan's
'*vetere Scotorum lingua*' becomes, Camden, '*Britannicè*', British.

A similar consciousness of Buchanan's work, evinced through omission,
may be read into Camden's use of Latin sources for identifying Picts and
Britons as 'painted people'. The repertoire of ancient sources alluding to
a British or Pictish customs of dyeing the skin blue, or sporting tattoo-like
designs, was not enormous; the same texts were repeatedly cited. The earliest
references, in the historical and geographical writings of Caesar, Pomponius
Mela, Tacitus and Pliny, are to a blue dye, possibly for purposes of inspiring

---

[38] Bede, *Ecclesiastical History, Volume I: Books 1–3*, translated by J. E. King (Cambridge, MA: Harvard
      University Press, 1930), 16–17.
[39] Rhys, 'Pictish language', 66.

fear in battle; Propertius, Ovid and Martial make playful allusions to this British custom. Later writers, such as Solinus, Herodian and Claudian, however, refer to a practice of using iron to ornament the body with animal designs. Claudian, in particular, refers to people so marked as 'Picts'.[40]

How did early modern scholars perceive the differences between dyeing the skin a single colour and tattooing lifelike forms on it? One property of the tattoo, as we perceive it now, is its permanence. Juliet Fleming ventriloquises the sense of affront to modern liberal sensibilities: 'The "problem" with tattoos, we say (as if we were all being forced to get one, this minute) is that they are indelible – "You can never get a tattoo off".'[41] But, as she shows, it is unclear whether early moderns had the same strong sense of the tattoo's indelibility. Thomas Harriot's chapters accompanying De Bry's engravings of Picts, reproduced in the *Briefe and True Report of the New Found Lande of Virginia* (1590) describe Pictish women as having their shoulders 'painted with griffon heades', while their daughters 'did paint themselues of sondrye kinds of flours', implying either ignorance of a tattoo's permanence or, perhaps, teasing his readers. ('A tattoo is forever, a virgin is not', Fleming comments.)[42] Buchanan, however, did not share this indifference: for him, the distinction had high racial stakes. The Britons, he said, painted (*pingebant*) and stained themselves (*se inficiebant*) with paint from herbs to seem terrible in battle, but the Picts variagated their skin using iron (*ferro cutem variarent*) and inscribed it with diverse figures of animals (*ac diuersorum animalium figuris inscriberent*) for the purpose of ornament (I:88; 1582: fol. 19 r). It is this key difference that prompts Buchanan to seek the for evidence of such practices among the Gaulish *Gothuni* or *Cotini* on the Danube whom Tacitus says were not Germans, for they spoke the Gallic tongue and who were thought to have marked themselves with iron. William Ferguson explains how Buchanan was long misconstrued as having therefore said that the Picts were German Goths.[43]

As the derivation of the word 'tattoo' from Polynesian languages would suggest, European consciousness of tattooing is generally dated with some precision to James Cook's voyages of 1769, an 'encounter phenomenon', as Fleming puts it (though she herself seeks its alternative, indigenous history in

---

[40] Gillian Carr, 'Woad, Tattooing and Identity in Later Iron Age and Early Roman Britain', *Oxford Journal of Archaeology* vol. 24, no. 3 (2005), 273–92, Appendix 288–9.

[41] Fleming, *Graffiti*, 81.

[42] Fleming, *Graffiti*, 105; Thomas Harriot, *A briefe and true report of the new found land of Virginia* (London: 1590), 'Some Picture of the Pictes', sigs. E2v, E3v.

[43] Tacitus, *Germania* in *Agricola, Germania, Dialogus*, ch.43, 200–1: 'As for the Cotini and the Osi, the Gallic tongue of the first and the Pannonian of the second prove them not to be Germans'. See, on the importance of this, Ferguson, *Identity*, 90–1.

Camden's *Britannia*).[44] What this implies is that sixteenth- and seventeenth-century historians reading classical authors on ancient Britain would not readily have distinguished the practice of painting from that of pricking the skin with a sharp iron or bronze implement and imparting pigment, not least because Latin *pingere* can range in meaning from colour to figurative adorn-ment and needlework (embroidery). Thus, Buchanan's distinction between ephemeral British war-paint and indelible Pictish symbolic ornament was not easy to convey either in Latin or English. Camden, for example, cites Isidore on needle-pricking and glosses it as 'painting' (*pigendi*; 1587: 42; 1610: 115). There are, however, other ways in which Camden frames the evidence as if con-sciously resisting Buchanan's distinction. For example, one of the most striking of Claudian's references to the Picts in *De bello Getico*, is recited after the Battle of Pollentia (402 AD) at which Stilicho held back the advance of Alaric and the Goths.[45] Claudian describes the Roman Legion left in Britain who

> kept the fierce Scots in check, and gazed upon the
> lifeless forms marked by iron upon the dying Pict.
> *quae Scotto dat frena truci ferroque notates*
> *perlegit examines Picto morientes figuras.*[46]

Here, Claudian's language beautifully specifies as Pictish the use of iron to mark the body with living forms which seem, pathetically, to die along with their host. The poet also, here as in almost all of his references to the Picts, juxtaposes them with the Scots. In his panegyric of Honorius, Book III, Claudian refers to Stilicho subduing 'the painted Pict, not falsely named' (*nec falso nomine Pictos*) and pursuing 'the Scot'.[47] When Camden cites Claudian in his *Picti* chapter, however, he omits any men-tion of Scots, thus: '*Nec falso nomine Pictos / Edomuit. Et alibi Perlegit examines Picto moriente figuras*' (1587: 41–42; 1610: 115). After omitting Claudian's Scots, Camden proves his identification of Picts as Britons by quoting Isadore of Seville's *Etymology*:

> *The Nation of the Picts* (saith he) *have a name drawne even from their bodies, for that by the artificiall pricking therein of small holes with a needle, the workman wringing out a juice of greene grasse, encloseth the same within, that their Nobilitie and Gentrie thus spotted, may carrie these starres about them, in their painted pounced limmes, as badges to be knowen by.* (1610:115; 1587:42)

---

[44] Fleming, *Graffiti*, 88–9.
[45] Alan Cameron, *Claudian: Poetry and Propaganda at the Court of Honorius* (Oxford: Clarendon Press, 1970), 180.
[46] Claudian, tr. Maurice Platnauer (Cambridge, MA: Harvard, 1922) 2 vols., II.156–7, lines 417–8. I am following Cameron in referring to the poem as *De bello Getico*.
[47] Claudian, I.274–5, lines 54–5.

'Shall wee thinke now', concludes Camden (explicitly *contra* Boece, but surely thinking of Buchanan's *Gothuni*) 'that these Picts were Germans . . . or rather the very Britons themselves?' (1610:115). What he doesn't tell us is that Isadore's *Etymology* actually names not the Picts but the Scots, and that the colour they mark themselves is not blue-green, but black: 'The Scotti . . . in their own language receive their name from their painted (*picta*) . . . bodies, because they are marked by tattoos of various figures made with iron pricks and black pigment (*atramentum*)' (*Scotti propria lingua nomen habent a picto corpore, eo quod aculeis ferreis cum atramento variorum figurarum stigmate adnotentur*).[48]

IV. Back to Blackness

Recent archaeological analyses of pendant bronze cosmetic grinders found in Britain and dating back to the Iron Age conclude, *contra* Buchanan, that no sharp division between painting and tattooing need exist: 'It is entirely possible that many methods of body painting and tattooing were used at the same time.'[49] My aim, however, has not been to argue for the accuracy of either Buchanan's or Camden's linguistic ethnographies, but to draw attention to the poetic, imaginative work involved in Camden's redefining of the racial make-up of ancient Britain as the early moderns understood it. Many of the consequences of Camden's redefinition are familiar. Artists and engravers associated with New World discovery – John White, Jacques Le Moyne, Theodore de Bry – paint and engrave, post-Camden, figures of Britons and Picts alongside those of Algonquian and Timuca Indians.[50] The appendix on 'Som Picture of the Pictes' which concludes Harriot's *Briefe and True Report*, begins 'In tymes past the Pictes, habitans of one part of great Bretainne, which is now nammed England'.[51] Thus Picts, long associated with North-East Scotland are now specifically said to come from *England*. The frontispiece of John Speed's *Theatre of the Empire of Great Britaine*

---

[48] *The Etymologies of Isidore of Seville*, trans. Stephen A. Barney, W. J. Lewis, J. A. Beach and Oliver Berghof, ed. Muriel Hall (Cambridge: Cambridge University Press, 2006), 198. IX.ii.103.

[49] Carr, 'Woad', 282.

[50] Paul Hulton explores the complex relation between John White's 1585 watercolours labelled 'Picts' and their publication as part of De Bry's *America*, see Hulton, *America 1585: The Complete Drawings of John White* (University of North Carolina and British Museum Publications, 1984), 17–18. The caption, 'Pict', was added to the engraving of White's original 1585 watercolours by Harriot or De Bry for the 1590 publication. See K. Sloan, *A New World: England's First View of America* (London: British Museum, 2007), 153–5.

[51] Harriot, *briefe . . . report*, sig. E1v.

sports, just above a cartouche inscribed 'Britannia', the figure of an ancient Briton, whose shoulder sports an animal face tattoo.[52]

The consequences of Camden's work – which traded the aggrandising myth of Trojan Brutan origin for the new vision of ancient British tattooed nakedness – have tended to be discussed in terms of the English having to coming to terms with their own barbarism vis-à-vis the Romans. Yet Camden's redefinition might also be read as having taken advantage of Pictish ethno-nemesis in order to produce a monoracial account of ancient Britain, translating older Galfridian myths of English sovereignty into the register of race and ethnicity. In the years before 1586, when Camden was working on *Britannia*, the succession was far from certain and hostility to the idea of a Scottish succession had been mitigated by Edmund Plowden's revival of the Galfridian argument that, Scotland being a vassal state, any such eventuality would not imply equality, but would continue the status quo of English suzerainty. Doing away with the Galfridian argument was, in this respect, somewhat risky, but Camden mitigates the risk by establishing a way of imagining the British past as one in which painted Britons, also called Picts, anciently inhabited the entire length of the island, from Cornwall to Caithness, only to have been replaced in the north by a more recent, heterogeneous set of immigrants, the 'mishmash' Scots. This newly racialised topographical history of Britain compensates imaginatively for the loss, in discarding the Brutus myth, of England's argument of ancient sovereignty over Scotland.

This proposition may seem more probable in the light of Chapter 3, which demonstrated the extent to which the emergence of English anti-quarianism and chorography was tied up with the pursuit, by way of Galfridian British history, of English claims to sovereignty over Scotland. We have seen how the 1540s war to conquer Scotland generated a much reprinted and cited propaganda literature which pressed the Galfridian myths of Trojan origin (Brutus's division of 'the' kingdom) into service both as support for arguments of Scotland's vassal status and for God's purpose for a united Great Britain. We saw in Chapter 1, too, from Edward VI's negotiations with Scottish prisoners, that an Anglo-imperial 'Great Britain' was proposed, in which the two realms would be

> united and reduced into one empire which shall be forever called and named the empire of Great Britain and the prince and master of it the Emperor of Great Britain.[53]

[52] John Speed, *The Theatre of the Empire of Great Britaine* (London: 1627).
[53] de Selve, *Correspondence*, 268–70, my translation.

The emergence of English antiquarian history and chorography, as was shown in Chapter 3, was intimately bound up with these Anglo-imperial ambitions, a fact rarely if ever registered by its historians. The influence of Richard Helgerson's interpretation of chorography as motivated by a devotion to the local, a resistance to sovereignty and empire is seen, for example, in the way in which Lesley Cormack's *Charting an Empire* exempts chorography from the imperialism which she sees as otherwise driving new developments in English geography in the sixteenth century.[54] But it is clear that English antiquarianism and chorography actively pursued the Anglo-imperial project of recovering British empire from the start, as we saw from Leland's inauguration of antiquarianism in his defence of Arthur and his inception of English chorography with *Cygnea Cantio*, both texts insistent on British Trojan origins and English sovereignty over Scotland. We saw that Cecil's 'British policy' of securing England's control of the coastlines of Britain was furthered by Laurence Nowell, the Anglo-Saxonist and cartographer whose map of Scotland marks it as conquered territory. John Dee's advocacy of cartographic and navigational improvement went hand in hand with his researches in Galfridian British history to assert English jurisdiction over the Scottish coastline. Humphrey Llwyd denied the antiquity claimed for the Scots by Hector Boece, while himself championing the equally unhistorical story of Brutus's division of the island, while Harrison's description of Britain, prefacing and framing Holinshed's *Chronicles*, concludes its extensive chorography with a chapter tracing England's sovereignty within the island back to Brutus.[55] Camden himself, in his own river poem, adorns the marriage chamber of Tame and Isis with imperial spoils of British and English kings, including 'What mighty Arthur from the Saxons won / What Edward from the Scots'.[56] Thus, though Camden keeps the Galfridian British history and its underwriting of English sovereignty over Scotland out of his prose, he acknowledges it in the vatic strain of his poetry.

To dispense, definitively, with Brutus, Locrine and Arthur, then, required that the long and widely held assumptions of England's ancient sovereignty over the Scots be rewritten more subliminally, in racial terms. The redefinition of the Picts as Britons in Camden's history ensured this, while disavowing any imperial intent. Imperial intent, indeed, was

<hr />

[54] See above, Chapter 3, 71–77, 83–89.   [55] Harrison, *Description*, 196–214.
[56] These lines first appeared in Latin in the 1607 edition of *Britannia*, 272–3, sigs. Cc2v-Dd1r. I think Dr Emily Mayne for researching its first published appearance.

promptly transferred to James VI and I, whose understandable concern to sort out the mutual legal standing of his two peoples is consistently read as a tone-deaf insistence on fulfilling a personal wish to be king of Great Britain. Martin Butler's welcome emphasis on the masque as an art of dialogue with the monarch, the key to which was 'to find formulae ... defining areas of agreement and accepting mutual constraints' finds most interest in masques which urge the king to be cautious. 'In contrast to these cautious masques,' he writes, alluding to Samuel Daniel and Thomas Campion, 'Ben Jonson's entertainments for 1605 and 1606, *The Masque of Blackness* and *Hymenai*, developed a radical perspective that left less space for negotiation.'[57]

What, then, of Jonson's decision, in *The Masque of Blackness*, to have the recovery of Britannia's 'ancient style' take the form of a voyage of discovery through countries connoting colour as substance ('black', 'swart', 'rich') to find an island anciently named for its 'depainted bodies'? What did it mean to move from an encomium of black as the very definition of intrinsic, permanent beauty ('fixed colour', a 'hue' that '[c]an never alter', 105, 110) to the discovery, on reaching Britannia, that black is merely a superficial 'veil' on the skin, a surface that dissolves in water (288)? Does this unfixing of the fixed colour, this altering of the unalterable hue, offer an ironic comment on Camden's own proposition that to be British is to be painted? Or does the figuring of political integration as the island's dissolving of the substance of blackness rather transform the masque into a proposition about the necessary place of blackness in the resourcing of a future British empire?

Could Jonson have known of Buchanan's attempt to distinguish between Pictish scarification and British war-paint? Perhaps not: his own copy of Buchanan's *Rerum Scoticarum Historia* probably post-dates *Blackness*, as it was a gift from William Drummond.[58] He also, however, owned and heavily annotated a copy of the poems of Claudian, whose panegyrics on Stilicho's governorship of the Roman empire he was imitating, as Victoria Moul notes, in works around 1603–4.[59] Jonson's extensive annotations – underlinings, but also marginal drawings of flowers and pointing hands – show how carefully he attended to Claudian's poetry of

---

[57] Butler, *Stuart Masque*, 29, 109.
[58] David McPherson, 'Ben Jonson's Library and Marginalia', *SP*, vol. 71, no. 5 (1974), 1–106, item 30, 32–3.
[59] Victoria Moul, 'England's Stilicho: Claudian's Political Poetry in Early Modern England', *International Journal of the Classical Tradition* (2019), n.p., note 10: https://doi.org/10.1007/s12138-019-00529-z

multiracial global empire, including the very sources interpreted by Buchanan and Camden as indicators of race. The lines cited by Camden in his *Picti* chapter which omit mention of the Scots are, indeed, underlined by Jonson in such a way as to recognise the importance of the Scoto-Pictish pairing:

> *Ille leues Mauros, <u>nec falso nomine Pictos</u>*
> *Edomuit. <u>Scotumque</u> vago mucrone secutus*[60]

> (He conquered the fleet Moors and <u>Picts not falsely named</u>; <u>the Scots, too</u>, his roaming sword pursued)

Jonson clearly noticed that Claudian routinely associates Picts and Scots. He also noticed Claudian's rhetorical contrasts of Picts, Scots and Britons on the one hand, and African or Libyan Moors on the other, indicating the climactic and geographic extremities of the empire over which Stilicho extended his reach.[61] In the following poem, Theodosius is said to have weathered Caledonian snows and Libyan summers, to have 'struck terror to the Moors, <u>subjected the coasts of Britain</u>' ('*Terribilis Mauro, <u>debellatorque Britanni</u> /litoris*') another phrase underlined by Jonson, who, a couple of lines later, underlined a further reference the warming of these cold northern regions with the blood of slaughtered Picts and Scots.[62] An exceptional passage, where Britannia, clad in an ocean-rivalling blue, her cheeks marked with iron (*ferro picta genas*), is joined by the figure of a sunburnt Africa (*calido rubicunda*), each to beg Stilicho to be their consul, is not only underlined by Jonson, but marked with several marginal flowers and a manicule (see Figure 7.1 in plate section).[63] Such an empire-evoking pageant might just have inspired Jonson to turn Queen Anne's request to dance as a blackamoor into his vision of an entertainment in which '*Niger, in form and colour of an Ethiop*' could appear with '*Oceanus ... the colour of his flesh blue*' to usher in the rediscovery of Britannia-as-island and the transformation of Ethiopian dames into Britons (28, 31).

Jonson's extraordinary conception of an African river's westward voyage, ending not in the discovery of a new world, but the recovery of Britannia's ancient Roman nomination or 'style', may owe something to

---

[60] *Claudius Claudianus, T. Pulmanni diligentia & fide summa, è vetustis codicibus restitutus* (Antwerp, Plantini, 1585). Bodleian Seld 8° C 90, 166.
[61] See Jessie Martiz and J. A. Maritz, 'The Classical Image of Africa: Evidence from Claudian', *Acta Classica*, vol. 43 (2000), 81–99.
[62] *Claudianus*, 172.   [63] *Claudianus*, 245.

Claudian. If it does we must, I think, see it as an extraordinarily confident reversal. Where Claudian's Roman empire is a centre whose periphery extends from people with painted skins in a frozen north (the Picts and Scots in Britannia) to an Africa whose skin is 'rubicund' with the heat, and who carries wheat in her hair, and an ivory tusk, Jonson's 'Britannia' has now been invented or discovered as a future imperial centre, set amid the world's oceans, like a diamond set in a ring.[64] Jonson implies Britons will no longer be *picti,* painted, and that *imperium* will radiate from their unpainted skin. It is the isle's discovery and naming by Africa – Niger's daughters and the goddess Aethiopia – and the retention of the daughters on the isle that supposedly instantiates its new identity.

At the same time, Jonson's poetry sceptically foregrounds the quality of *poiesis* that renders his master Camden's race-making conjectures plausible. When Niger complains of the sorrow his daughters feel, being deprived of their beauty by a new myth of racial origin, he says that poets let their 'wingèd fictions fly / To infect all climates' (119–20). In the seventeenth century, 'infect' carried the primary sense of 'to instil an opinion or belief', especially a pernicious one, but it was also used to mean 'to dye, to colour, to stain or steep in', a participle from the Latin *inficere*. Buchanan contrasted the Britons who stained themselves blue (*se inficiebant*) with the Picts who inscribed figures on their skin with iron (I.88; 1582, fol. 19 r) and Camden, whom Jonson followed closely, defined the Britons, from '*Brith*' as '*infecti*' and '*colorati*', 'dyed' and 'coloured' (1587:24). In Niger's complaint that poetry 'infects' all climates, a sense of resistance to the masque's central conceit of blackness as paint or dye irrupts with momentary if somewhat incoherent reflexive force. To build arguments of racial origin on stories of how skin came to be *infecti* or *colorati* is, Jonson seems to quip, globally *infectious*.

For all that Jonson revered Camden, his former master's Elizabethan concern with demarcating Britain's races or managing Anglo-Scots relations was not, in 1605, part of his poetic vision. The widespread belief that concern with 'Britain' was *not political* until 1603 and that Camden's *Britannia* was therefore undertaken in 1586 in a spirit of 'disinterested antiquarian enquiry' which only acquired a 'political charge' after 1603, naturally leads to readings of Jonson's masque as being concerned, in the way Martin Butler describes, with the alarming consequences of Anglo-Scots miscegenation and racial mixing as the result of a too-hasty British

---

[64] Martiz and Martiz, 'Classical Image of Africa', think Claudian imagined Africa as Phoenician white, her face burnt red by the sun, 93–4.

'union'.[65] But Anglo-Scots relations were not Jonson's concern. He under-stood perfectly well the race-making effects of Camden's arguments about the colourful skins of Picts and Britons. However sceptically, he takes Camden's work as read, playfully inflecting its conceit of Britannia as the land of painted people through an appropriation of the poet Claudian's vision of a multiracial Roman empire, stretching from Moors to Picts, Libya to Thule, Africa to Britain. But because, in Jonson's vision, this empire-to-be centres on the shared *political* allegiance of all James's sub-jects to the monarch's sun-like personal sovereignty (separate nations within the island notwithstanding) the rites of integration that give admis-sion to its administrative centre take place at the British island's ocean boundary. Here is where we see the importance, for the study of early modern racial thinking, of Jonson's apparently trivialising reduction of racial difference to the material substance of *paint*. Jonson's *Blackness*, as Andrea Stevens has argued, innovates scandalously in its material methods: Queen Anne and her ladies were *painted black* like professional actors, rather than, as would be usual for courtiers, wearing black fabric.[66] Such an innovation, for all its flaws (the paint seems to have proved difficult to remove, so the masque lacks a revelation of the women's underlying whiteness) permits the process of political integration to be figured as the washing-off of painted dyes and infectious fictions, while becoming subject to the sun-like monarch's discriminating gaze. What this figuration, in turn, produces is an unassimilable residue: racial 'blackness' acquires a defining substantiality insofar as it can be removed, *washed off*.

Thus, Britain-as-future-empire emerges, in Jonson's vision, as defined by its global reach over territories and peoples who *may not be assimilated*. Their unassimilable quality is abstracted as *blackness itself*. Indeed, Jonson's use of the unusual abstract noun, 'blackness', is itself telling in this respect, for 'blackness' as a substantive describing 'the state of being black' in material ingredients (for example, in alchemical contexts) appears with greater frequency between 1350 and 1650 than 'blackness' meaning 'dark skin colour'.[67] In Jonson's masque, the fiction of the whitening of Niger's daughters at the island's bounds, while Niger himself returns, unchanged, to Africa, conjures the vision of a multiracial empire radiating out from a future Britain as it once radiated from Rome. But beyond the centre, the putative empire is pre-emptively marked out and identified by the unalterable hue of all those who remain

[65] Angus Vine, 'Copiousness', 228; Butler, *Stuart Masque*, 111–15. [66] Stevens, *Skin*, 91–3.
[67] 'Blackness' as a substantive describing 'the state of being black' in material things (for example, in alchemical contexts) appears with greater frequency between 1350 and 1650 than 'blackness' meaning 'dark skin colour', according to the *OED*. See *OED*, 'Blackness', n1 and n2.

beyond the island's circumference. The concluding invitation to fulfil the rites of passage that will admit them to Britannia – these rites consist of steeping their bodies in the seas about the island, 'the wholesome dew called rosemarine' – works its unifying magic by undoing the divisiveness of histories of painted peoples in Britain, but in its place seems to constitute the removal of pigment as the price of admission to Britain. The echoes and reverberations of this implication down the centuries to the present day seem to haunt the masque, as if it were presciently defining generations who would, from beyond Britannia, produce and sustain the greatness and wealth of the unpainted Britons of the future. What we can be certain of, however, is that tracing the masque's play with rites of exclusion and inclusion that constitute the skin's pigment as a *removable material ornament* becomes a way of understanding, in Toni Morrison's words, 'the nature – even the cause – of literary "whiteness"'.[68] *The Masque of Blackness* helps us see how high are the stakes and how rich and complex the layers of artifice in the rhetorical and performative 'discovery' or 'invention' of *whiteness* as the underlying 'cause' of Britain's unity as an island nation.

---

[68] Morrison, *Playing*, 9.

CHAPTER 8

Divisions and Kingdoms: Oedipal Britain from Gorboduc *to* King Lear

I. Britain Between King Lear and King James

We seem to be at Gloucester's house, in Act 2 of *King Lear*. We have only just heard Lear ask if the horses are ready for his sudden departure from the house of his daughter, now duchess of Albany (Scotland) to take up residence with his other daughter, now duchess of Cornwall. Yet now we seem to be somewhere in between Albany and Cornwall, at the residence of the duke of Gloucester. The duke's son Edmund, hearing rumours of 'likely wars' between Albany and Cornwall, makes immediate use of this news. 'Have you,' he asks his brother Edgar ominously, 'not spoken 'gainst the Duke of Cornwall aught? – He's coming hither now, i'the night, i'the haste ... Have you nothing said / Upon his party 'gainst the Duke of Albany? / Advise yourself.'[1] But as Edmund persuades Edgar to flee, this fear of having even inadvertently offended one or other side in this sticky web of whispering malice pales before the reprisals threatened by Edgar's own father. 'All ports I'll bar,' exclaims Gloucester,

> the villain shall not scape;
> The Duke must grant me that. Besides, his picture,
> I will send far and near, that all the kingdom
> May have due note of him; and of my land,
> Loyal and natural boy, I'll work the means
> To make thee capable   (2.1.80–3)

A slight ambiguity stirs in the idea of Gloucester 'barring all ports'. The word means both 'doors' or 'gates' and 'harbours', conjuring both domestic and insular points of entry, the integrity of both home and island. In this play in which closest kin are thrust out of doors 'barring all ports' might suggest Gloucester's expelling Edgar from his home or preventing his leaving the

---

[1] *King Lear*, ed. R. A. Foakes (London: Arden, 1997), 2.1.24–8. Further references to this edition will appear in the text.

estate. But Gloucester's plan to broadcast Edgar's picture pulls the word 'port' in a kingdom-wide direction. So we might instead imagine him trapping Edgar in the island, blocking all seaports, forcing his son to improvise house-like hideouts in the wilderness ('the happy hollow of a tree', 2.2.173) and transforming his own casing – skin, hair, speech – to survive. Either way, this vision of a landscape without refuge becomes most claustrophobic and chilling as we register Gloucester's anxiously assuring himself of his permission for this vigilantism: 'The Duke must grant me that.' This moment of self-assurance is horrible not just in its intimation of the appetite he has for violence against his own son, but in his precipitate acceptance of Cornwall's absolute rule. As soon as Cornwall arrives, he confirms Gloucester's confidence in the punitive cruelty at his disposal: 'If he be taken, he shall never more / Be feared of doing harm, make your own purpose / How in my strength you please' (2.1.111–13). We know how gruesomely this will end. The terrible eye-gouging scene likewise compounds the thought of escape routes (ports) from homes and islands when Cornwall, fearing that Gloucester is headed for Dover, permits his own absolute power to overlook the forms of justice and to 'do a courtesy' to his wrath against the father himself, *in his own home* (3.7.26). What crazy dystopia is this? What kind of Britain, ancient or otherwise, is being imagined here and performed before the king at Whitehall at Christmas, 1606?

For some time now, the scholarly consensus has been that James in some sense *is Lear*: that in precipitating a grotesque crescendo of internecine hostilities by dividing the kingdom, Lear mirrors James's high-handed absolutist hubris – with who knows what consequences – overriding national sensibilities and bizarrely insisting on welding together England and Scotland as 'Great Britain'. More recently, this general argument has been given a further impetus by work on the contribution of cartography to the cultural production of space. In general, this has meant that the Folio text's command, 'Give me the map there' (1.1.36) has been taken to signify the identification of Lear's/James's absolutism with the new spatial imperialism of cartography: 'a whole nonliterate, incorporeally conceived culture shockingly reduced to and treated as a visual diagram', as Terence Hawkes wrote in 1989.[2] The objection to a critical identification of Lear's division of his one kingdom with James's attempt to unify his two kingdoms is no less longstanding, however. Dividing and uniting are not just different but opposite kinds of action. As R. A. Foakes pointed out, James himself drew on the

Galfridian British history from which the Lear story came to warn his son against 'the seed of division and discord' sown by Brutus's division of the kingdom.[3] Yet some sort of identification between Lear and James remains a tantalising critical possibility. In an ingenious reading from which I will diverge in some important respects, Philip Schwyzer discerns a covert critique of James's 'Great Britain' in *Lear*, a project which he sees as both 'hopelessly premature' and at the same time, old-fashioned, 'reliant on a nostalgic spirit of [British] nationalism'. There is, as he astutely observes, something ominous and strange about staging a tragedy of the division of Britain in which name 'Britain' never occurs at all (in striking contrast with *Cymbeline*).[4] John Kerrigan's magisterial study registers the scholarly consensus that the play somehow 'engages ... with the debate about Anglo-Scottish union that raged between 1603 and 1607' though he cautions that '[i]t would be fatuous to claim that the irregular, overloaded, speculative world of this tragedy can be reduced to topicality'.[5]

That the intensity of the experience *King Lear* offers cannot be reduced to a commentary on the acrimonious Union debates of 1605–6 is undeniable. Yet, as Kerrigan suggests, it is hard to resist the feeling that Shakespeare was somehow responding, with this tragedy, to the fraught question of relationship between two kingdoms now united in loyalty to the person of one king, though divided politically about what that should mean. After all, Shakespeare and his fellow-actors were members of the royal household, they were 'the King's Men'. They could hardly not have been cognisant of the vertiginous turns of political feeling at the centre of power. And there is the obvious point that although Shakespeare, after the death of Elizabeth, went on drawing on material from Holinshed's *Chronicles*, his shaping of this historical material changed radically in both a generic and affective sense. After James's accession, Shakespeare's reading in Holinshed and other histories furnished him not with the material for history plays, but with material he shaped into *tragedies*, drawing on Greek and Latin models, especially Seneca. Colin Burrow makes an explicit link between James's accession and Shakespeare's experimentation in Senecan tragedy:

> The accession of King James in 1603, and the subsequent transformation of the Lord Chamberlain's Men into the King's Men did, however, put an instant pressure on Shakespeare to rethink how he wrote in general and how

---

[3] Lear, ed. Foakes, 'Introduction', 15, 91.
[4] Philip Schwyzer, 'The Jacobean Union Controversy and *King Lear*', *The Accession of James I: Historical and Cultural Consequences* ed. Glenn Burgess, Roland Wymer and Jason Lawrence (New York, NY: Palgrave, 2006), 34–44, 34, 45, 39–40.
[5] Kerrigan, *Archipelagic English*, 17.

he registered the presence of Seneca in particular . . . The result of all this, briefly put, was a phase in Shakespeare's career in which he experimented in what might be called British Senecanism. The tragedies of *Macbeth* . . . and *King Lear* were the main results.[6]

Burrow's sense that Senecan thought pervades Shakespeare's dramatic writing more thoroughly after 1603 is borne out by innumerable studies of *Hamlet*, *Othello*, *Macbeth* and *Lear* as well as by Burrow's own compelling readings. His further intuition, however, that there might be a specific affinity between Senecan tragedy and the topic of ancient Britain is extremely suggestive. It helps break the impasse Kerrigan identifies in recognising that *Lear* responds to contemporary debates about Britain and union but transcends mere topicality.

For in fact, as this book has throughout been trying to show, there was nothing merely topical about an interest in Galfridian history's plotting of ancient Britain's successive divisions and reunifications. Brutus's legendary division of the island between Locrine, Albanact and Camber was, as we saw in chapters 1, 2 and 4, regularly cited as the origin of England's title to Scotland. In 1540s war propaganda it was urged as the reason why Scots should yield to Edward VI and Protector Somerset, who proposed a united 'Great Britain', a fact often recalled by both sides in the Union debate.[7] Not that Geoffrey's stories were always accurately or fully conveyed. Henry VIII's *Declaration* (1542) went straight from Brutus's division and Locrine's overlordship to William the Conqueror, skipping Leir and the rest. The *Epitome* (1548) was more comprehensive, but the author muddled Geoffrey's history of King Leir's reign, making Goneril's and Regan's sons, Marganus and Cunedagius, into brothers rather than cousins, who once again divided the realm. He related how they 'brotherly' divided the realm, so that Cunedagius had 'Logres' (England) and Marganus had 'Albania' (Scotland). Inevitably, war broke out and Cunedagius killed Marganus. The kingdom was thus united once more under Cunedagius and his son, Rivallo, 'untill after the reigne of Gorbodian, who had issue two sonnes, Ferres and Porres', and there was, yet again, division and violence.[8] A reader of the British Library copy STC 31962612 has corrected 'brother' to 'cosyn' three times in the margin. Some contemporary knew Geoffrey's King Leir a little better than the author. But the very mistakes

[6] Colin Burrow, *Shakespeare and Classical Antiquity* (Oxford: Oxford University Press, 2013), 187.
[7] See Craig, *De Unione*, 256–7; Spelman, *Of the Union*, in *Jacobean Union*, eds. Galloway and Levack, 168, 173; Savile, *Historical Collections*, in *Jacobean Union*, 207–8.
[8] *Epitome*, sig. A8r-v.

and corrections here point us towards the recognition that Shakespeare is not just being *topical* in shaping one of the many episodes of ancient Britain's division to the question of England's relation to Scotland. People had been writing and reading and correcting one another about this history through the sixteenth century because *they felt it mattered*. Just as the geopolitical problem of Scottish nationhood did not suddenly erupt onto English consciousness in 1603, neither did adaptations nor reworkings of Geoffrey of Monmouth's stories of the division of 'the' unitary kingdom called Britain.

There is a further point. What Burrow calls 'British Senecanism' was not a new development with the accession of James and the problem of Union, either. The *Epitome*'s swift move from Leir's murderous grandsons to the fratricidal sons of 'Gobordian' or Gorboduc should remind us that the very first classical tragedy in English was nothing other than a Senecanised episode of Galfridian British history – an example of 'British Senecanism'. This was Thomas Norton's and Thomas Sackville's *Gorboduc*, performed in 1561.[9] Not only, then, had Geoffrey's Britain long been held to be an exemplary source of stories of division which implied England's right to the whole island, including Scotland, but these narratives had also long been felt to have some affinity with Senecan tragedy – particularly with Seneca's treatment of the Sophoclean or Euripidean 'matter of Thebes': the stories of Oedipus' murder of his father, Laius, and marriage with his mother, Jocasta, of his subsequent self-blinding and exile with Antigone, and of the curse of their warring sons, Eteocles and Polynices.

Reading *Lear* as a response to the Union crisis has seemed reductive because it seemed merely topical. Assuming James's proposal to unite the two kingdoms as 'Great Britain' was an unheard-of political innovation rather than a long-cherished Anglo-imperial ambition and policy, critics have not much considered the place of Galfridian stories of the division of Britain in the emergence of Elizabethan genres of insular imagining. Literary scholars encounter earlier Galfridian British stories as pick-and-mix extracts in Geoffrey Bullough's *Narrative and Dramatic Sources of Shakespeare*. They accordingly underestimate the emotional and symbolic centrality of such stories to Elizabethan national self-definition, especially in relation to the abjection of Scotland. The incoherence of

---

[9] Thomas Norton and Thomas Sackville, *Gorboduc* in *Early English Classical Tragedies* ed. John W. Cunliffe (Oxford: Clarendon Press, 1912), lxxxi. Further references to act, scene and line in this edition will appear in the text.

proceeding from the assumption that James's project of 'Great Britain' was novel and tyrannous – and therefore like Lear's division – is clear from the prominence of Britain, Troynovaunt, Brute, Arthur and the rest within Elizabethan epic poems, chorographies, historical narratives, masques, plays and other cultural forms. Readers before 1603 could have enjoyed literary reworkings of Geoffrey's 'division of Britain' narratives, including the Leir story, in the *Chronicle* of John Hardyng (1543); in the *Briton moniments* in Book II, Canto x of Spenser's *The Faerie Queene* (1590); in John Higgins's additions to *The Mirror for Magistrates* (1574, 1578); in Holinshed's *Chronicles* (1577, 1587) or in William Warner's *Albion's England* (1589) among others. In all these reworkings the atrocities precipitated by Britain's division are moving and meaningful as part of the prophetic purpose of Geoffrey's history, which predicts the return of the whole island to a single *natio* (the native British) who once occupied it '*a mari usque ad mare*', from shore to shore.[10] In Spenser's *The Faerie Queene*, as we saw in Chapter 2, a troubled history of succession divisions of the kingdom by Brutus, Leyr, Gorbogud and the rest is key to the promise-filled 'Arthurian moment' of the poem's action, as Prince Arthur, in Book II, reads the *Briton moniments* until the text breaks off at the accession of his father, Uther Pendragon, whose last battle against the Saxons marks the beginning of Britomart's adventures in Book III.

There were also the already-mentioned handful of attempts to handle the Galfridian division of Britain as Senecan Oedipal tragedy. As well as *Gorboduc* in 1561, Shakespeare would have known of George Gascoigne and Francis Kinwelmarsh's Euripidean *Jocasta* (1566) which, though not British in theme, clothed the Oedipus story in an English idiom which recalled Galfridian Britain.[11] And in 1587, a Galfridian story of Britain's division was once more cast as Senecan tragedy in *The Misfortunes of Arthur*, composed by the lawyers of Gray's Inn.[12] In these plays the Galfridian topos of 'division' is Oedipalised; the rupture in the native land (whether Thebes or Britain) is figured as the curse of fraternal enmity or incest. But in them also the unity of 'Thebes' or 'Britain' is assumed – it is only on that basis that division between brothers (Ferrex and Porrex, Eteocles

[10] Geoffrey, *History*, ed. Reeve, tr. Wright, 'Description of the Island', 5. Further references to Geoffrey's *History* in this translation will appear by book and chapter in the text.
[11] George Gascoigne, *Jocasta* in *A Hundreth Sundrie Flowres*, ed. G. W. Pigman (Oxford: Clarendon Press, 2000), 59–140, 509–48. Further references to act, scene and line will appear in the text.
[12] Thomas Hughes, *The Misfortunes of Arthur* in *Early English Classical Tragedies*, ed. Cunliffe, 217–96. Further references to act, scene and line will appear in the text.

and Polynices) or between father and son (Arthur and Mordred) becomes tragic. The kingdom is mono-national, of one nativity. Division is the catalyst of tragedy, as royal siblings, parents and children destroy one another. In *Jocasta*, Thebes is saved from the Argives as Creon rules, but in *Gorboduc* and *Misfortunes*, Britain becomes prey to the Scots, who are imagined (as they are in Geoffrey) as a hostile foreign power. In *Gorboduc*, the king's failure to have secured the succession through parliament to one born within the 'natiue land' leads to fraternal division, war and the destruction of the royal line, so that 'Brittaine realme is left an open pray' (5.2.191) to the 'heauie yoke of forreine gouernance' of Fergus, duke of Albany, or Scotland (5.2.172). Similarly, after the great King Arthur and his son have slaughtered one another in *Misfortunes*, the 'medowes, fieldes, and pleasant plaines' of Britain will be enjoyed by foreigners: Saxons, Normans, Danes 'and *Scottes*' (4.4.46–7). These tragedies' indebtedness to Senecan reworkings of the Oedipus plays of Sophocles and Euripides reveals itself in language that throughout plays on the etymology of 'nation' (*natio*), returning it to 'nativity' (also *natio*), meaning birth, the emergence from the womb.

Thinking, as one of the King's Men, about the debates raging through 1605–6 on the question of those born before and born after, those nati, ante- and post-, Shakespeare could not but have been aware of how deeply problematic Galfridian stories of the 'division of Britain' would be for a new piece of theatre that year. The question of most serious dispute between king and Commons in 1605–6, as we saw in Chapter 4, was not one of name, or map-related boundary change but of national freedoms and birth rights. Should Scots and English be mutually naturalised and enjoy freedom of trade, or should they continue to live under a single king on a single island as alien nations? Critics tend to talk of James's 'Great Britain' project as one to which both English and Scots were implacably opposed. If one sees the dispute the way contemporaries did, however – turning on the question of mutual naturalisation – there was absolutely no opposition in Scotland.[13] The Scots had lost their sovereignty, control over foreign policy and the presence of their king; they hoped, as a compensating benefit, not to remain without freedoms in the nation to which they were now tied. Equally, although pro-Union propaganda might celebrate King James as tracing his genealogy back to Brutus, there was no possibility of making Galfridian British history inclusive of the whole Scots nation. Nor, indeed, was there a desire among the English, in this political moment, to speak of the Scots as other than aliens, even if this meant sacrificing cherished

[13] Galloway, *Union 1603–1608*, 129.

Galfridian arguments of vassalage to England. Witness Sir Henry Spelman's volte-face in his treatise of 1604: 'But some perhaps will demaunde why I now tearme the Scottes aliens and str[angers]* since before I have shewed them to have been taken as members of England' (174). 'Division of Britain' stories deriving from Geoffrey of Monmouth would thus seem, in 1606, inherently problematic as material for contemporary tragedy not, *pace* Schwyzer, because the 'British' propaganda around James was peddling a nostalgic nationalism, but because Galfridian British history was structurally antagonistic to the Scots as a nation, and a similar antagonism was at that very moment fuelling the conflict between the king and the House of Commons.

Whether or not it is reductive to analyse *Lear* in the context to the 1605–6 disputes over naturalisation, then, my tentative proposal in this chapter is that a reductive account of these disputes has made it hard to see how *Lear* – a tragedy in which unthinkable depths of cruelty lie just beneath apparently banal and reasonable calculations of self-interest and propriety – might have been conceived as a response to them. My first proposition, however, is that Galfridian British history had a powerful affective logic throughout Elizabeth's reign as an English national discourse, quite irrespective of its waning credibility as history. This affective logic was enhanced when lawyers and men close to government became poets and pioneered vernacular experiments in the genre of Senecan tragedy, adapting the Galfridian division-of-the-kingdom accordingly. Yet Shakespeare's devastating alterations to the ending of the Leir story destroy the possibility of reading the Galfridian division-of-the-kingdom narrative, even in its more recent Senecan tragic form, as an English national discourse. In the conclusion to this first section of my chapter, I will show how this is so. In the following section I will show that *Lear* was not new in recasting Galfridian British history as Senecan tragedy. I will show how Elizabethan British tragedies produce an affective identification of place and birth, of Britain as the womb and home of a single, indigenous nation which cannot include the Scots. Yet this identification is powerfully resisted in *Lear*. In the next section, I will take up recent cartographic criticism of *Lear* alongside recent discussions of Shakespeare's Senecanism. Here I will show that the uncanny and claustrophobic way in which space contracts and draws in during the action of *Lear* precludes any sense of enmity as identified with distance or foreignness: the real enemy feels intimate and close. I will then return to the question of the womb and birthplace in *Lear*, arguing that Shakespeare's doubling of the Oedipus story is a move which resists the reading of its tragic consequences as national. In conclusion, I will examine Shakespeare's handling of the

French invasion and the final custodianship of the realm to Edgar and Albany, an ending which, I propose, makes its own comment on the high stakes being attached to the importance of England and Scotland remaining two separate nations within an island kingdom in 1605–6.

II.   The Deaths of Goneril and Regan

'Division' is the tragic engine of narrative in Geoffrey's *History of the Kings of Britain* because the drive of the whole history is prophetic, pointing to the promised reunification of Britain at the return of Arthur, once and future king. So if the hero of Geoffrey's narrative is the integrity of the island as anciently possessed by the British people, it is hardly surprising that, in reign after reign, the story of the island kingdom's vulnerability repeatedly takes the form of an ill-advised division, leading either to invasion or internecine war. In Geoffrey himself, the logic is clear: first we have Brutus and his sons, the invasion of Humber and killing of Albanact (II.23); then Leir, who, rejecting Cordeilla, divides Britain between Maglaunus, duke of Albany and Henuinus, duke of Cornwall, married to his daughters, Gonorilla and Regau, who subsequently dispossess him. Cordeilla and her husband, King Aganippus of France, manage to win back the British kingdom for Leir. Cordelia rules Britain after her father's and Aganippus's death (II.31). But then Gonorilla's and Regau's sons, Marganus and Cunedagius, defeat her and, and divide the kingdom again, with Marganus taking the north '*trans Humbrum . . . uersus Katanesiam*' ('from the Humber to Caithness') and Cunedagius taking the south (II.32). Believing he should rule the whole island, Marganus attacks Cunedagius, but the latter defeats and kills him, so the island kingdom remains unified under his rule for three generations until the old age of King Gorbodugo, whose sons, Ferreux and Porrex, quarrel over which of them should succeed him. When Porrex kills Ferreux in battle their distraught mother compounds the horror by killing her fratricidal son, ensuring division and civil strife for generations (II.33). After several more divisions of the kingdom, the arrival of the Saxons in the south brings a corresponding change to the area to the north of Humber. From this point on, the area from Humber to Caithness is repeatedly described as inhospitable and uncivilised, a 'receptacle' (*receptaculum*) for foreign (*alienegena*) peoples, mainly Picts and Scots, aided by Saxons (VIII.120). These unruly peoples are confronted first by Uther Pendragon, and then by his son Arthur. On Uther's death, Arthur is hastily crowned so that he can destroy these peoples, which he does, ruthlessly, but he himself is then destroyed by his Pictish nephew, Modred, son of Loth of Lothian, who, while Arthur is away defeating Romans, lays claim both to his queen, Guenevere, and to the throne of Britain (IX.149; X.164). The end of Arthur's Britain is shot through with prophecies of a greater British empire, as Cadualdrus hears an angel foretell that Arthur will one day return to recover the island for the British people (XI.205). The summaries I have given here come from Geoffrey's own text but, as I have indicated, these stories were accessible to Elizabethan readers and audiences in many forms and genres. The point I want to stress is that whenever and however these stories of Britain's division are adapted in Elizabeth's reign – whether as heroic history, proof of vassalage or Senecan tragedy – some trace of Geoffrey's prophetic design is present, in however etiolated or shattered a form, to make sense of the conception of 'Britain' as the island kingdom of the British-English, imagined as the readers and audiences of these texts.

For *King Lear* to be a national tragedy in the Galfridian British tradition, then, one would expect atrocities: violence between siblings, parents and children and defeat in war, with moralising against the evils of division and the realm's vulnerability to invasion by foreigners. But the alterations Shakespeare makes to the ending – taking more liberties with the chronicle material than he does in any other play – takes his tragedy of Britain in a completely different direction. To have all three daughters die before their father, and to have Goneril and Regan die *without giving birth* is to strip away the Galfridian historical future. Margreta de Grazia has proposed that the play's BC setting enables Shakespeare to produce an exceptionally bleak ending, negating all Christian promise of redemption.[14] I suggest it also negates the nationally redemptive promise central to the affective structure of Galfridian British history, even in that history's admonitory form as Elizabethan Senecan tragedy. The deaths of Goneril and Regan without offspring (Regan's son was the great-grandfather of 'Gorbodugo' or Gorboduc) are a fulfilment of their father's Senecan curses, an ostentatious evacuation of *natio* in the senses both of nation and nativity. While Goneril's sororicide and self-slaughter take place offstage, stage directions in both the Quarto and the Folio insist that her's and Regan's dead bodies be brought onstage to flank the entry of Lear with the dead Cordelia in his arms. In Act 3 in the Folio, the fool offered a parody of social satire as popular Galfridian prophecy – a 'prophecy Merlin shall make', he teases (3.3.1) – but even the

---

[14] Margreta de Grazia, 'King Lear in BC Albion', in *Medieval Shakespeare: Pasts and Presents*, ed. Ruth Morse, Helen Cooper and Peter Holland (Cambridge: Cambridge University Press, 2013), 138–56.

wit and irony of this has been aborted by the tragedy's close, in which the future line of British kings stretching to Merlin has been wiped out.[15] Indeed, if one of the ways in which *Lear* feels uncompromisingly true, emotionally speaking, is its sense of drawing out an exhausted spatio-temporality, a blank, futureless end-time ('the oldest hath borne most; we that are young / Shall never see so much, nor live so long' 5.3.324–5) then this, I suggest, may itself be Shakespeare's comment not on James's Union project, but on the obsolescence of these Galfridian materials in this affective form. 'This is a play without memories and without children', Philip Schwyzer has commented, seeing it as refusing 'to be borne along on the tide of British nationalist propaganda'.[16] I rather see it as a response to the extremity of divisions over questions over the meaning of *natio* – nation or birth – on the island of Britain. The end of *Lear* is a negation, a turning to bleak absurdity, of an implicit, underlying identification of Britain as maternal place of origin. Such a homology had shaped nationalist emotion in Elizabethan Senecan tragedies of the division of Britain, but this Elizabethan 'British nationalism', unlike the tide of Union propaganda to which Schwyzer is referring, had long defined itself against the Scots as foreign enemies.

III.   Oedipal Britain on Stage 1561–1588

In its insistence on denying the maternal futures of Lear's daughters and in figuring Britain as what Janet Adelman described as a 'landscape of maternal deprivation', Shakespeare's *King Lear* eschews the most prom-inent and powerfully nationalist emotional effect of earlier Senecan tragedies on the division of the kingdom.[17] For the identification of the divided kingdom – Britain or Thebes – with a birthplace or 'native soil' was a principal feature of the Elizabethan Senecan tragedies with which Shakespeare would have been familiar. These earlier experiments in Senecan tragedy performed at the Inns of Court through Elizabeth's reign – *Gorboduc, Jocasta* and *The Misfortunes of Arthur* – all arrange their Galfridian or Oedipal materials to produce an overwhelmingly affecting identification of the land as a lost mother. In them an English community of feeling is produced as the imagining of the mourning of

[15] On the fool's prophecy, see Terence Hawkes, 'The Fool's "Prophecy" in *King Lear*', *Notes and Queries*, vol. 7, no. 9 (1960), 331–2.
[16] Schwyzer, 'Union Controversy', 45.
[17] Janet Adelman, *Suffocating Mothers: Fantasies of Maternal Origin in Shakespeare's Plays, Hamlet to the Tempest* (London: Routledge, 1992), 104.

a maternal land, a birthplace, a home and native soil, destroyed by her children and laid open to foreign invasion and occupation. In the British tragedies, the island of Britain is identified as native, as a mother and birthplace for the English, while the Scots, with some geographical haziness, are represented as threatening foreign invaders.

Gorboduc, performed at the Inner Temple and at Whitehall at Christmas 1561/2, is well known both as the first English Senecan tragedy and as a warning of the dangers of Scottish succession. Its plot rounds out Geoffrey's brief sentence on hostilities between King Gorboduc's sons, Ferrex and Porrex, with motivation drawn from Geoffrey's account of Gonorilla's and Regau's sons, Marganus and Cunedagio, who fell out when mischief-makers incited the elder to feel he should have the whole kingdom (1.2.161–4; 1.2.275–81). In *Gorboduc*, it is the queen, Videna, who incites her elder son thus; she has rightly been read as a Clytemnestra or Medea figure. However, by the fourth act, after Porrex has invaded Ferrex's realm and killed his brother, Videna makes an extraordinary speech which links her with the Jocasta as depicted in a tragedy by Seneca on the story of Oedipus which is called, variously, *Thebais* or *Phoenissae*. 'If after bloud, so eigre were thy thirst,' she begins, addressing, in imagination, her fratricidal son

> And murderous minde had so possessed thee,
> If such hard hart of rocke and stonie flint
> Liued in thy brest, that nothing els could like
> Thy cruell tyrants thought but death and bloud:
> Wilde sauage beasts, mought not their slaughter serue
> To fede thy gredie will, and in the middest
> Of their entrailes to staine thy deadly handes
> With bloud deserued, and drinke thereof thy fill?
> Or if nought els but death and bloud of man
> Mought please thy lust, *could none in Brittaine land* (my italics)
> Whose hart betorne out of his panting brest . . .
> Suffice to make a sacrifice to peaze
> The deadly minde and murderous thought in thee?
> But he who in the selfe same womb was wrapped,
> Where thou in dismall hower receiuedst life?
> Or if nedes, nedes, thy hand must slaughter make,
> Moughtest thou not haue reached a mortal wound,
> And with thy sword have pierced this cursed wombe,
> That the accursed *Porrex* brought to light,
> And geuen me a iust reward therefore?   (4.1.36-57)

Sackville (who wrote this speech) here uses a trope known as *incrementum*, a figure of scalar ascent or descent, evaluating degrees of wrongdoing.[18] The ascent of the scale of guilt traces, however, a counter movement into intimacy and pathos. We travel from distance to proximity through imagined victims of Porrex's bloodlust, from hunting to homicide. It is an easy turn from a Briton to a brother and thence to the mother herself, who 'wrapped' both boys 'in the selfe same womb'. Videna's final hopeless wish that Porrex's sword had been directed at her uterus remembers Jocasta in Seneca's *Phoenissae. Phoenissae* exists in fragmentary form, but what we have articulates a contrast between Oedipus, who will not dissuade his sons from the destruction of Thebes because he wants them to fulfil the curse of his guilt, and Jocasta, who interposes her own body to prevent her sons' mutual destruction. Oedipus uses *incrementum* to prove that his sons are destined to immolate the kingdom. Going over his own guilt, he climbs the scale of horror from parricide (murder of his father Laius) to incest, making the former '*leve*' or trivial, by comparison with the latter, and then, in a ghastly climax, locating the worst crime in his mother/wife's fertility: 'My deed against my father is trivial; into my bedroom was led my mother; lest that be not criminal enough, a *fecund* mother. Nature can bear no greater crime than this.'[19] But having asserted this as the greatest crime, he triumphantly conceives an even greater one: he has produced the sons who will destroy the kingdom. By contrast Jocasta, as she tries to prevent her sons killing each other, repeats the figure as self-sacrifice to prevent Thebes's destruction. 'That I am guilty is a trivial (*leve*) thing', she says 'I have made others guilty. / This, too, is trivial: I have borne sons who are guilty' (367–8). Though Jocasta's womb thus becomes the locus of Oedipus' guilt as well as her own, she realises her guilt as expiation, asking her sons not to kill each other but to 'aim at this belly that produced brothers for my husband' (447).[20]

Sackville adapts the hint of pathos in Jocasta's use of the figure to produce a more substantial imagining of inhabited land as maternal space or birthplace. Videna's belated wish that her womb had taken Porrex's sword, coupled with the movement of her speech through the

[18] See Jeanne Fahnestock, *Rhetorical Figures in Science* (Oxford: Oxford University Press, 1999), 91–2; Alex Davis, 'Revolution by Degrees: Philip Sidney and *Gradatio*', *Modern Philology*, vol. 108, no. 4 (2011), 488–506; Quintilian, *Inst.*, 8.4.

[19] Seneca, *Phoenissae*, in *Tragedies*, vol. VIII, trans. John G. Fitch (Cambridge, MA: Harvard University Press, 2002), lines 270–3, pp. 300–1. Further references will appear by line number in the text. See Elaine Fantham's excellent, 'Nihil Iam Iura Naturae Valent: Incest and Fratricide in Seneca's *Phoenissae*', *Ramus*, vol. 12, nos. 1-2 (1983), 61–76.

[20] H. A. Watts's notes in Cunliffe's edition, links Videna's speech to Seneca's *Phoenissae*, 443-7; see *Classical Tragedies*, 304.

beating hearts of animal and human bodies, has us apprehend a Britain filled with endangered yet cognate life. As tragic events pile on, Britain is increasingly imagined as the fulfilment of Videna's wish: a mother murdered by her own children. This is a figure which itself makes all Britons kin. The people who 'headlong' rebel and kill Gorboduc and his queen are said have destroyed the 'wombe' and 'natiue soile' (5.2.20-1) of Britain, 'the common mother of us all' (5.2.98). This place of nativity then lies open to an invader, '*Fergus*, the mighty duke of Albanye' (5.2.76) who threatens the 'natiue land' (5.2.99). The *Nuntius* describes Fergus lodged in a field with twenty thousand men, marching to conquer 'Brittayne land' (5.2.137) and subject it to 'forreine thraldome' (5.2.120). Yet Fergus appears, in 5.1, as one of the British nobility. So why is he not another rebellious, matricidal child of 'Brittaine land the mother of ye all' (5.2.135)? Perhaps there is a deliberate spatial ambiguity of Gorboduc's earlier command, '*Humber* shall parte the marches of theyr realmes' (1.2.345), a strategic omission of 'Caithness' from the usual Galfridian formula, making unclear the boundaries of the island.[21] Certainly, Norton and Sackville were experimenting with a way of dramatising Geoffrey's 'Britain' as an affective identification, the structuring of a feeling of belonging to the land which needed both to lay claim to the whole island and to define a part of it – Albany or Scotland – as if that part beyond the bounds of the island of Britain and so the nation's foreign and predatory foe.[22] The novelty in their way of structuring this feeling of national belonging lay in its Senecan emphasis on Britain as place of birth, a development of the notion that 'division' in the kingdom was the catalyst of violence against the mother.

Seneca's *Phoenissae* was itself a reworking of, among other things, Euripides' tragedy by the same name. Lodovico Dolce's Senecanised adaptation of Euripides' *Phoenissae* as *Giocasta* (1549) was Englished as *Jocasta* by George Gascoigne and Francis Kinwelmarsh, who in the process made its 'Senecan echoes more accurate', injecting 'an additional dose of Seneca'.[23] It was presented at the Inns of Court at Christmas 1566–7, at the

---

[21] Jaecheol Kim's 'The North-South Divide in *Gorboduc*: Fratricide Remembered and Forgotten', *SP*, vol. III, no. 4 (2014), 691–719, interprets *Gorboduc* in relation to the Northern Rebellion rather than Scotland, but, as we saw in Chapter 3, the two crises were related for the English government.

[22] On *Gorboduc* as political tragedy, see Jessica Winston, 'Expanding the Political Nation: *Gorboduc* at the Inns of Court and Succession Revisited', *Early Theatre*, vol. 8, no. 1 (2005), 11–34. Levine, *Elizabethan Succession* treats it as a succession tract, 30–43.

[23] Yves Peyré, 'Eclecticism and Syncretism in Gascoigne and Kinwelmarsh's *Jocasta*', *Translation and Literature*, vol. 29 (2020), 44–58, 49; Lodovico Dolce, *Giocasta* (Venice, 1549). See also Sarah Dewar-Watson, 'Jocasta: "A Tragedy Written in Greeke"', *International Journal of the Classical Tradition*, vol. 17, no. 1 (2010), 22–32.

height of concerns about a Scottish succession and just as Plowden was writing his treatise.[24] Judging by the attention Shakespeare devoted to Gascoigne's *Supposes* (which he rewrote as the subplot of *The Taming of the Shrew*) he is likely to have read *Jocasta*. And however cursorily he might have read it, he could not have failed to notice the centrality of the play's identification of divided kingdom and the maternal body of Jocasta, the titular heroine and *mater dolorosa*. The action opens with Jocasta grieving over the siege of Thebes by Polynices, who has led an Argive army against his home because his brother, Eteocles, has refused to grant him his turn to rule according to their agreement. From the outset Jocasta identifies the city's self-division with her flesh:

> Seying this towne, seying my fleshe and bloude,
> Against it selfe to levie threatning armes.   (1.1.8–9)

The first two acts slowly develop this identification by unfolding to us the powerful affection of Polynices, exiled and outcast, for his mother and the 'native soil' of Thebes. Jocasta alerts us to the extremity of what Eteocles has done to Polynices, not merely denying him his chance to rule, but banishing him from his home. 'Drunke with the sugred taste of kingly raigne,' Eteocles

> Not onely shut his brother from the crowne
> But also from his *native country soyle*.
>
>   (1.2.172–4, my italics)[25]

The play's second scene surveys the action around the besieged city; in Euripides, it takes the form of a 'viewing from the walls', a *teichoskopia*, in which an old family servant points out the soldiers of the Argive army to an apprehensive Antigone.[26] Gascoigne and Kinwelmarsh transform this scene into further evidence of Polynices' remembered affection for his home. Instead of pointing out the Argive soldiers, the servant narrates an emotion-filled reunion with Polynices and his mother outside the city walls. 'At sight of me,' says Bailo, 'his colour straight he changed / And like a loving childe in clasped armes / He caught me up, and frendly kist my cheke' (1.3.160–3). At the threshold of Thebes, the enemy, Polynices, is embraced as the city's and his mother's 'loving childe'.

---

[24] See Pigman's commentary, Gascoigne, *Hundreth*, 512–13.

[25] Translating Dolce's '*natio terren*', *Giocasta*, fol. 7v.

[26] See Helene P. Foley, *Ritual Irony: Poetry and Sacrifice in Euripides* (Ithaca, NY: Cornell University Press, 1985), 117–19; Euripides, *Phoenician Women*, trans. David Kovacs (Cambridge, MA: Harvard University Press, 2002), 88–201.

Act 2 stages the strangest truce and parley between the brothers within the walls of Thebes, encouraging an emotional identification between the space of the parley – Thebes itself – and the body of the mother. As he enters, now an enemy to Thebes, Polynices is overwhelmed. 'Loe here', he says on entering, 'mine own citie and native soyle. / Loe here the nest I ought to nestle in' (2.1.1–2).[27] He cannot, says, behold without grief the 'lovely lodge wherein I fostred was: / From whence driven out' (2.1.111–12). In dialogue with his mother, Polynices emphasises the poverty and abjection of his outcast state; his brother's harsh command that he return to live in the swamps or 'mustie Moores' (2.1.569, translating Dolce's 'palude') makes him anticipate the figure of Edgar in *Lear*.[28] Eteocles, meanwhile, with misogynistic obscenity, demands his mother what 'queynt commoditie' has persuaded her to 'yelde the gates wide open to my foe' (2.1.257-9) as if Polynices' arrival were a compounding of the incest which gave him birth. He denies Polynices the right to say 'mother', while commanding him out of the city's gates.

After Jocasta has committed suicide, dying in sorrow amid the sons who have killed each other, the pathetic identification of mother and 'native soil' continues as Creon commands that Polynices, whose last wish was to be buried within Thebes, be cast out unburied into the fields. The final scene of *Phoenissae* is thought by classicists not to be Euripidean, because, among other things, it incoherently presents Antigone wanting 'both to follow her father into exile and stay in Thebes to bury her brother'.[29] For Gascoigne's and Kinwelmarsh's audience, however, there would seem no incoherence in this ending. Antigone's wish to not to 'denye these guiltlesse bones / Of *Polinice*, theyr grave in countrey soyle' (5.5.84–5) and her wish to accompany her father 'Ychased from his native countrey soyle' (5.5.244) are the culmination of the tragedy of a divided kingdom named for the maternal body and place of birth with which all the passions of division were identified.

A final, spectacular example of Seneca-meets-Geoffrey-of-Monmouth before Shakespeare's own occurs with the extraordinary *Misfortunes of Arthur* performed in February 1588 before the queen at Greenwich by the gentlemen of Gray's Inn. The authors included Thomas Hughes, Francis Bacon, Christopher Yelverton (who had contributed an epilogue to *Jocasta*) and William Fulbecke. This play – also said to be 'indirectly modelled on Euripides' *Phoenissae*' – went immediately into print.[30]

[27] Translating Dolce's '*il mio diletto nido*', *Giocasta*, fol. 13r.   [28] Dolce, *Giocasta*, fol. 22r.
[29] See Kovacs, 'Introduction', Euripides, *Phoenician Women*, 208.
[30] Rebecca Bushnell, *Tragedies of Tyrants* (Ithaca, NY: Cornell, 1990), 104, though William A. Armstrong, 'Elizabethan Themes in *The Misfortunes of Arthur*', *Review of English Studies* vol. 7,

Although mocked even in its own time for being cut-and-paste Seneca and Lucan (swan's feathers stuck on a goose), *Misfortunes* does achieve some affecting and exciting moments. Occasionally, the authors hit on phrases so striking as to prompt thoughts that they influenced Shakespeare. Gueneuora's Medea-like 'Come spitefull fiends . . . my breast / Raues not inough: it likes me to be filde / With greater monsters yet' (1.2.38–40) seems to anticipate Lady Macbeth.

More intriguing, in terms of the Oedipal links of *Lear*, however, is the authors' decision to turn the most famous of all Galfridian kings of Britain – King Arthur – into the tragic, tyrannous, shame-filled figure of Oedipus. The play's story of how Arthur returned from a wildly improbable defeat of the Roman empire to find his nephew, Mordred, in possession of his queen, Ganhumara, and his kingdom of Britain comes out of books VIII–XI of Geoffrey's History. Many of the main Galfridian characters are present in forms unmediated by later Arthurian romance: Arthur's allies, Cador of Cornwall, Hoel (*Hoelus*) of Brittany, Gawain (*Gwalgainus*); his enemies, the Saxon Cheldric (*Chelricus*) and Gillamor (*Gillamurius*), king of Ireland.

But the authors of *Misfortunes* make two significant changes. The first is to Arthur's relation to Modred (whom they call Mordred). In Geoffrey, Modredus is the son, along with Gawain, of Loth of Lothian, to whom Arthur's father, Uther Pendragon, gave his daughter, Anna, in marriage; his brother is Gwalgainus or Gawain.[31] The authors of *Misfortunes*, however, follow Malory in making Mordred Arthur's *son* by incest with his sister, Anna. As Arthur himself was the illegitimate son of Uther's dalliance with Igrene, the wife of Gorlois of Cornwall, this addition to his shame cues Arthur's echo of Oedipus from *Phoenissae*. '*Leve est*', 'it is trivial', Oedipus begins, as does Arthur, 'For were it light, that eu'n by birth my selfe / Was bad, I made my sister bad: nay were /That also light, I haue begot as bad (3.4.16–22). Arthur's incestuous begetting of Mordred is fated

---

no. 27 (1956), 238–49, sees more Seneca. For a full account of the play, see *The Misfortunes of Arthur: A Critical, Old-Spelling Edition*, ed. Brian Jay Corrigan (New York, NY: Garland Publishing, 1992).

[31] There is, in Geoffrey's text, some confusion as to whether Modredus is Arthur's nephew or cousin. See Geoffrey, *History* ed. Reeve, trans. Wright, VIII. Anna is said to be Arthur's sister at VIII.138.534 and she appears to be given in marriage to Loth of Lothian (*Loth de Lodonesia*) at VIII.139.547: '*Probitate ergo ipsius acclamante, dederat ei rex Annam filiam suam regnique sui curam dum infirmitati subieceret*', 'Impressed by his talents, the king [Uther] had given him his daughter Anna's hand and stewardship of the realm when he was ill'. However, at IX.152.205-8, Loth is said to have married the king's sister in the reign of Aurelius Ambrosius – in other words, Uther's and Ambrosius's sister – and fathered Gawain and Mordred. Scottish historians noticed this discrepancy. See Fordun, *Chronicle*, I.102, 'Geoffroy, however, writes that Mordred and Galwanus were the sons of Anna, sister of Aurelius, Arthur's uncle . . . But, further on, he calls Arthur the uncle of Galwanus.'

to fulfil its curse and destroy the kingdom, just as the incestuous sons of Oedipus will destroy Thebes. His use of the figure of *incrementum*, however, expresses not a perverse triumph in the abomination, but rather the pathos of exile and loss.

The second change which the authors make concerns the chronology of Arthur's conquest of the Scots. Its importance lies in the way in which it once again facilitates an identification of Britain as the native soil and home of the English, while figuring the Scots as recent foreign invaders. Brian Jay Corrigan repeats Henry Carson Grumbine's assertion that the play could serve as an index to books VIII, IX and X of Geoffrey's *Historia Regum Britanniae*, but this is not quite true.[32] For in the *Historia*, Arthur's coronation follows fast on Uther's death – this would be just after the 'Arthurian moment' of Spenser's *The Faerie Queene* – and Arthur rushes north, with Cador, duke of Cornwall and Hoelus of Armorica to fight the Scots, Picts and the Irish. This, the major campaign of Arthur's life, culminates in a near-genocide of the Scots and Picts is what establishes him as king of Britain, celebrated in the homage paid to him at Caerleon. John Dee, in his copy of Geoffrey, underlined Arthur's campaign to 'wipe out the Scots and Picts with incomparable ruthlessness' (*delere gentem Scotorum atque Pictorum, incomparabili saeuitae indulgens*).[33] It is after this campaign that Arthur enjoys a prosperous overlordship of the Britain he has recovered, only later deciding to go abroad to defy the Roman empire. He entrusts the running of the country to his nephew, Modredus, son of Loth and brother of Gwalgainus, and to his queen, Ganhumara, (X.164) and sails off. After his defeat of the Romans in epic battles, Arthur hears of Modredus' treacherous usurpation and Ganhumara's adultery and rushes back. Modredus tries to prevent Arthur's landing at Richborough near Dover, but Arthur succeeds in pursuing him to the river Camblan in Cornwall, where, in a fearful battle with devastating casualties on either side, Modredus is slain and Arthur, mortally wounded, is transported to Avalon (XI.177).

While this chronology seems superficially to resemble that of *Misfortunes*, the key difference is the authors' conflation of the first conquest of the Scots and Picts on which Arthur's sovereignty over all Britain rests, and the second battle to defeat Modredus, whose claim to the island (as Scots historians, particularly Hector Boece, interpreted Geoffrey)

---

[32] Thomas Hughes, *The Misfortunes of Arthur*, ed. Harvey Carson Grumbine (Berlin: Verlag von Emil Felber, 1900), 32.

[33] Geoffrey of Monmouth, *Britanniem vtriusque Regum*, owned by John Dee, now in Christ Church College special collections W.b5, 12, sig. k1r. fol. XXXIIv.

comes not through being Arthur's British son, but through the greater legitimacy of his descent from Uther Pendragon. For he was the son of Loth (whom Boece makes king of the Picts) by way of Anna, Uther's daughter and Arthur's sister.[34] Mordred thus represents, for Scots historians such as Boece, a figure for Britain's historical multinationality, the challenge of a legitimate Pictish-Scottish claimant to the throne of all Britain, against the illegitimate British Arthur. Fordun had already hinted that 'Mordred had legitimate cause to take up arms against Arthur'. Boece 'removed any sense of civil war since Mordred was a king in his own right and not Arthur's vassal'. By making Loth king of the Picts and having his son Mordred's succession rights rebuffed by Britons 'as men of foreign blood', Boece epitomised in the Arthur-Mordred conflict Britain's multi-nationality, not its incestuous civil wars.[35]

In *Misfortunes*, the combined effect of making Mordred Arthur's son by incest and conflating two battles within the isle of Britain into one is chiefly rhetorical. It is imaginatively constitutive, for an English, Elizabethan audience, of a mononational British island. By substituting the first conflict for the second, the tragedy produces a perfect topographical/emotional antithesis between Arthur's heroic conquests which now all take place 'abroad' (against the Romans, beyond Britain's shores) and his Oedipal love for the flesh and blood of his island 'home' (Britain) against which, though it now wants to destroy him, he can hardly bear to take up arms. By erasing the Arthurian conquest that the Elizabethans found most significant and credible – the near-extermination of the Picts and Scots – and by turning Mordred from Arthur's nephew from Lothian into a son begotten on his own sister, the authors of *Misfortunes* produce the perfect Oedipal Britain, the perfect tragic identification of 'Britain' with a deep and tender love for the unattainable and forbidden reunion with the place of origin. At the same time, their transposition of Modred's paternity from Loth of Lothian to Arthur himself erases the multinationality of Arthur's Britain (Modred's Pictish otherness) as well as what the Scots historians had annoyingly argued was Modred's legitimate claim to the throne of Britain. In arguing thus, I want to complicate Curtis Perry's fine reading of *Misfortunes* as 'our most detailed and suggestive literary evocation of Elizabethan anti-imperial thinking'.[36] While Perry rightly sees that the play

[34] See the excellent account by Elizabeth Hanna, 'A "Scottish Monmouth"? Hector Boece's Arthurian Revisions', in *Latin Culture*, 105–26.

[35] Hanna, '"Scottish Monmouth"?', 112, 116, 111; see Fordun, *Chronicle,* I.102–3.

[36] Curtis Perry, 'British Empire on the Eve of the Armada: Revisiting *Misfortunes of Arthur*', *SP*, vol. 108, no. 4 (2011), 508–37, 519.

frames Mordred's rebellion and Britain's civil war as caused by 'Arthur's absenteeism, his failure to attend to matters at home', he does not consider that this displacement of all Arthur's imperial conquests 'abroad', produces the promised 'home' – 'Brytain land the promist seate of Brute' (2.1.2) – as purely and indigenously English-British in a manner that would be belied if Mordred were Loth's son. None of this undermines Perry's argument that the gentlemen of Gray's Inn might be making an anti-imperial argument to Elizabeth 'out of a concern with the implication of imperial ambition for the maintenance of domestic order and the preservation of liberty'.[37] What it does, however, is to expose the predication of an English domestic order and liberty on the fantasy of a pan-British 'home', a domestic empire that defines the Scots as foreigners to the island.

So in turning the story of Arthur into a Senecan tragedy which not only acknowledges Arthur's illegitimacy, but, in the speech of the ghost of Gorlois, relishes it as the 'shamefull lust' of Pendragon, prologue to the begetting of worse and worse ('Let th'ofsprings sinne exceed the former stocke', 1.1.23), the authors of *Misfortunes* have cleverly carved out a new emotional space in which the matter of Britain can become tragic and claim all Britain for England in a properly classical way. Just as, in *Jocasta*, emotion is generated through the painful antithesis of Polynices' return to destroy his longed-for home, so in *Misfortunes*, pathos emerges from Arthur's return from exploits 'abroad' to reach at last his 'natiue soyle' and home, only to find his wife estranged and son amassing troops against him (2.1.4). 'For lo,' as the Nuntius says at the opening of the second act, 'when forreine soiles and seas were past /With safe returne, and that the King should land: / Who, but his onley sonne (O outrage rare) / With hugie host withstoode him at the shoare? (2.1.55–8). Through the first act, Gueneuora's and Mordred's vacillating and impassioned arguments return again and again to the antithesis of 'home' and 'abroad'. 'Though neither seas, nor lands, nor warres *abrode* / Sufficed for foyle', the indignant Gueneuora threatens her straying husband, 'yet shall thou finde /Farre worse at *home*' (1.2.25–6, my italics). 'Since *Arthur* thus hath ransackt all abroade,' admonishes Cador, 'What meruaile ist, if *Mordred* rave at home?' (3.1.26–7, my italics). Mordred sees that his threat to Arthur is psychological, a defeat of the self by the self: 'What though he vanquisht haue the Romaine troupes? / That bootes him not: him selfe is vanquisht here' (2.3.58–9). And it is this sense of self-vanquishment, of Arthur's emotional defeat from within, that dominates the play. His commanders try to

---

[37] Perry, 'British Empire', 536.

persuade him to defy Mordred, but he expresses extreme, visceral reluctance: 'But as for warres, insooth my flesh abhorres / To bid the battle to my proper bloud', he protests (3.1.39–40); 'To spoile my sonne were to dispoile my selfe' (3.1.89). The antithesis of foreign wars and peace at home recurs frequently, structuring the sympathy with which Arthur's reluctance to fight is portrayed:

> Can *Arthur* please you no where but in warres?
> Be witnesse Heauens how farre t'is from my minde,
> Therewith to spoile or sacke my natiue soile   (3.1.230–2)

As in *Jocasta* the 'native soil' of home is the forbidden womb; there the mother of Oedipus' sons and brothers, here of Arthur's beloved nephew/son. It is a figure of yearning, a home not to be attained:

> What corner (ah) for all my warres shall shrowde
> My bloodless age: what seate for due deserts?
> What towne, or field for ancient soldiers rest?
> What house? What rooffe? What walls for wearied lims?
>
> (3.3.39–42)

In this speech we see the emotional work performed by the occlusion of Arthur's first and most famous conquest, the one that created Britain as the sheltering home, the native land. Here the contrast between 'all my warres' and the corner that might shroud him in old age is a variant on empire, which is located definitively 'abroad', and an island imagined as the most modest of demands, a familial shelter for the warrior's old age. His defeat anticipates the overrunning of this now ruined, roofless shelter called Britain by marauding Picts, Scots and Irish. These are not the settled inhabitants of a multination Britain (i.e. Mordred's subjects in Pictavia/Lothian), but foreign invaders: 'The *Scots* may now their inrodes olde renew' (4.3.14). By transforming Mordred into the most beloved child – Arthur calls him, 'My Sonne, my Nephew, yea each side my selfe' (3.4.14) *Misfortunes* produces what Arthur longs for from Mordred and Britain as something not unlike the dream of old age denied to Lear, when he furiously justifies his repudiation of Cordelia to Kent: 'I loved her most, and thought to set my rest / On her kind nursery' (1.1.123–4). Yet *Misfortunes* produces this feeling as the affective structure of English-British nationalism; that is, it forms the imagining of an exclusively English claim to Britain as birthplace. This was a structure of feeling that could make no sense when Shakespeare was thinking about *King Lear* in 1605–6.

IV.   Why Is *Lear* Not a 'national tragedy'?

When Shakespeare wrote *King Lear* in the first years of the new king's reign, he followed these earlier Elizabethan experiments insofar as he shaped the British story of the old king and his three daughters to fit the Senecan treatment of Oedipus, the tyrant king who discovers that he has sired on his mother a cursed and destructive generation. Recent re-evaluations of Shakespeare's knowledge of Greek and Latin tragedy, including Senecan tragedy, remind us how saturated the language and conceptual structure of Shakespeare's *King Lear* is in 'deep and continued thinking about Seneca'.[38] Curtis Perry, as part of an important re-evaluation of Shakespeare's Senecanism, has shown that *Lear* owes particularly close and detailed debts to Seneca's two plays about Oedipus, *Oedipus* and *Phoenissae*. *Lear*'s famous speech cursing Goneril in Act 1, scene 4, in which he threatens to pluck out his own eyes, ashamed of their weeping, derives from the messenger's report, in Seneca's *Oedipus*, of Oedipus reacting to the feeling the tears on his cheeks with the imperative that his eyes be expelled with their tears.[39] Like Perry, John Kerrigan has pointed to the similarities between the virtual landscape of death (the imagined 'Dover cliff') to which Edgar leads his blind father in 4.6 and the death-haunted ridge of mount Cithaeron where Antigone leads the eyeless Oedipus at the opening of Seneca's fragmentary *Phoenissae*.[40] Reminiscences of this interaction also, as Perry notes, inform the scene of *Lear*'s bewildered and remorseful encounter with Cordelia.[41] Both Edgar and Cordelia, like Antigone in *Phoenissae*, attempt to alleviate the self-isolating shame and despair of their fathers, one of whom strays, like Oedipus, blindly seeking a precipice of death, while the other wanders in his wits, imagining the felicity of incarceration with his daughter. Janet Adelman reads *Lear* as Oedipal in the Freudian sense, saying that Cordelia's refusal of Lear's impossible demands 'creates a rage in Lear that we might agree to call Oedipal, and to gender male, insofar as it seems to have its roots in the son's frustrated desire for the mother's exclusive sexual attention'.[42] Carol Thomas Neely surveys the last half-century's 'remediation' of *Lear* as a work primarily about familial incest, acknowledging its Senecan

---

[38] Burrow, *Classical Antiquity*, 198.
[39] Curtis Perry, *Shakespeare and Senecan Tragedy* (Cambridge: Cambridge University Press, 2021), 117; Seneca, *Oedipus*, in *Tragedies*, vol. IX, trans. John G. Fitch, (Cambridge, MA: Harvard University Press, 2004), 954–6.
[40] Kerrigan, *Shakespeare's Originality*, 63–5; Perry, *Senecan Tragedy*, 120.
[41] Perry, *Senecan Tragedy*, 112, 134–40. Perry also sees the concluding scene of Seneca's *Hercules Furens* as informing the reunions in *Lear*.
[42] Adelman, *Suffocating Mothers*, 125.

precedents.[43] And criticism interested in Shakespeare's creative response to the Queen's Men's play of the Lear story, *The True Chronicle Historie of King Leir* (which was probably composed around the same time as *Misfortunes*, in 1587–8) also stresses the 'Senecan' and Oedipal quality of Shakespeare's revision.[44] The older *Leir* play featured well-motivated intrigue and characterisation, suspense, pathos and comedy. Shakespeare stripped it of all but the most minimal motivational circumstance, doubling the plot and heightening the power of its rage and its mockery. Shakespeare's Lear, as Meredith Skura notes says, is 'less like the old Leir than like Seneca's Oedipus in power, rage and tragic stature'.[45] One of the changes Shakespeare made was to excise any reference to Lear's dead queen as a remembered character. The old *Leir* play opens with mourning for a beloved wife and mother: Leir's 'deceast and dearest Queene' (1.2). The effect of Shakespeare's excision is uncanny, pervasive and spatial: Lear's kingdom becomes, in Adelman's already-cited words, a 'landscape of maternal deprivation'.[46]

Everything, then, seems to point to what Shakespeare's *Lear* should share with earlier adaptations of Geoffrey of Monmouth's stories of the ruinous division of Britain. *Lear* should, by this account, produce an identification of Englishness with sorrow for the impossibility of being able to return to that native soil, that sheltering home, that island of Britain. Yet *Lear* does not create this feeling. In one sense it obviously can't, because the earlier tragedies created their identification of Britain as longed-for birthplace through an explicit othering of the Scot as foreign invader. This would be nonsensical in 1606 when English political objectives had shifted from wanting to claim the island of Britain as an exclusively English or Anglo-Welsh birthplace to wanting to resist a Scottish king's proposals for a united island of Great Britain. What, then, is Shakespeare up to with his Senecan Oedipalisation of the Lear story? Why does he create an Oedipus in Lear, if not to create a pathos around the idea of national belonging, the idea of the island of Britain?

[43] Carol Thomas Neely, '*King Lear* and Incest, 1969–2016: *in Medias Res*', *Borrowers and Lenders*, vol. 13, no. 1 (2020).

[44] See Grace Ioppolo, ' "A Jointure more or less": Re-measuring *The True Chronicle Historie of King Leir and His Three Daughters*', *Medieval & Renaissance Drama in England*, vol. 17 (2005), 165–79; Geoffrey Bullough, *Narrative and Dramatic Sources of Shakespeare*, vol. VII (London: Routledge and Kegan Paul, 1973), 337–402, further references in the text.

[45] Meredith Skura, 'Dragon Fathers and Unnatural Children: Warring Generations in *King Lear* and its Sources', *Comparative Drama*, 42.2 (2008), 121–48, 124.

[46] Adelman, *Suffocating Mothers*, 104.

V. Forget the Map

One problem with beginning to answer that question is that insufficient attention has been paid, in Shakespeare criticism, to the distinction between Britain and England, even in the context of historicist readings of Lear's high-handed cartographic division as being equivalent to James's high-handed unification. Most surprisingly, there has been little attempt at the disambiguation of England and Britain in the new and influential spatial turn of Lear criticism. Before I return to the question of the Oedipal in *Lear*, then, I need to consider the important body of critical work which has brought to early modern English drama a new concern with the question of what map-making does to the human perception of space.[47] This criticism reads *Lear*'s scene of kingdom-division, and the subsequent sensory disorientations and mortifications of Edgar as Poor Tom, of Lear in the storm and of blind Gloucester believing himself on Dover cliff as part of a phenomenological critique of the illusion and abuse of power inherent in the cartographic gaze.[48] It sees *Lear* as a response to the cultural impact of the imperialistic 'new geography' of the Elizabethan universities with its 'hugely influential semantic transfer of organic into functional space'.[49] The 'new geography', as Bernhard Klein has elegantly explained, separates the body from the hazards of spatial experience, linking comfort and security to the human subject's visual control of space as depicted, for example, in Vermeer's superb 1668 painting, 'The Geographer'.[50] Drawing on cognitive ecology and phenomenology, several critics have offered persuasive readings of Gloucester's and Lear's experiences of sensory disorientation as meditations on the fragility of the embodied and perceptual experience of being-in-space, being as the sensory *location* of the self. No longer able to exercise their illusory power over abstracted, cartographic or legal space (kingdom or estate) the patriarchs struggle to orient themselves as they are made wretched, deprived of their senses and of the power to interpret sensation as a coherence of subjectivity. ('Methinks the ground is

---

[47] Broadly deriving from Henri Lefebvre, *The Production of Space*, trans. Donald Nicholson-Smith (Oxford: Blackwell, 1991).

[48] See John Gillies, 'The Scene of Cartography in *King Lear*', *Literature, Mapping and the Politics of Space in Early Modern Britain*, ed. Andrew Gordon and Bernhard Klein (Cambridge: Cambridge University Press, 2001), 109–37. For other 'cartographic' readings of *Lear*, see F. T. Flahiff, 'Lear's Map' *Cahiers Elisabéthains*, vol. 30 (1986), 17–33; Hawkes, 'Lear's Maps'; Gillies, *Geography of Difference*; Sullivan, *Drama of Landscape*; Gillies and Vaughan eds., *Playing the Globe*; Peter Holland, 'Mapping Shakespeare's Britain', in *Shakespeare's Histories and Counter-Histories* ed. Dermot Cavanagh, Stuart Hampton-Reeves and Stephen Longstaffe (Manchester: Manchester University Press, 2006), 198–218.

[49] Klein, *Writing of Space*, 5.   [50] Klein, *Writing of Space*, 2.

even' 'Horrible steep' (4.6.3); 'I will not swear these are my hands: let's see – / I feel this pinprick.' (4.7.55–6).)[51]

Yet proponents of this important and illuminating new critical turn have shown surprisingly little interest in the geographical distinction between England and Britain. Nor have they, for all their interest in English cartographic imperialism, registered its provenance in the attempted conquest of Scotland in the 1540s and in John Dee's and Richard Hakluyt's Galfridian-based British claims of England's jurisdiction over Scotland's coastline.[52] As we saw in Chapter 3, plans and platts of Scottish fortifications and harbours, crucial to the English effort to conquer Scotland, led to advances in English cartography, while Dee's cartographical innovations were predicated on researching Galfridian claims to British title over Scotland as first steps to maritime global empire.[53] Cartographic criticism thus seems to perpetuate the older critical move of equating Lear's division of the kingdom with James's proposal to style himself king of Great Britain, implying that James, like an imperial cartographer, has translated organic into functional space and deprived English people of cherished local and regional differences, of their embodied experience of emplacement. John Gillies alludes to the older critical tradition that with Lear's division 'Shakespeare was making a complimentary allusion to James I's campaign', so that in elaborating what he takes to be the tragedy's moral and phenomenological critique of the map in the stripping and abjection of the body, he implies that the tragedy critiques a cruelty and inhumanity inherent in James's proposed change of name.[54] Peter Holland, who is explicit about how his thinking about *Lear* has been influenced by Gillies, clinches the identification of James as imperial cartographer when he writes that for the audience of *Lear*, 'The map had changed. The people's history had been rewritten in the new geography of the King of Great Britain.'[55] Here the pathos of cartography's cultural tragedy – the map's abstraction of the embodied experience of space – attaches to the English, referred to simply as '*the people*'. Their

---

[51] See, for example, Andrew Bozio, *Thinking Through Place on the Early Modern English Stage* (Oxford: Oxford University Press, 2020), 98–122; Steve Mentz, 'Strange Weather in *King Lear*', *Shakespeare*, vol. 6, no. 2 (2010), 139–52.

[52] See 24–5, 83–9.

[53] See Chapter 3, 83–9; Marcus Merriman, 'The Platte of Castlemilk, 1547', *Transactions of the Dumfriesshire and Galloway Natural History and Antiquarian Society*, 44 (1967), 175–81; Tyacke and Huddy, *Saxton*, 11–15; For the imperialism of the 'new geography', see Cormack, *Charting an Empire*.

[54] Gillies, 'Scene of Cartography', 115; see also Hawkes, 'Lear's Maps', 136–7; Sullivan, *Drama of Landscape*, 107.

[55] Holland, 'Mapping', 215.

authentic 'history' is threatened by a 'new geography' associated with a king whose own country, Scotland, had in fact been a classic victim of Elizabethan new geography's cartographic imperialism.

Critics link the 'cartography scene' in *Lear* to the advances in surveying techniques represented by Christopher Saxton's maps for Thomas Seckford, omitting to note that Saxton's innovative skills were applied only to maps of England and Wales. The entire point of Lear's having a kingdom to divide is that it is supposed to be the whole island, not just England and Wales.[56] Analysing the portion assigned to Goneril, with its 'shadowy forests', 'champaigns riched', 'plenteous rivers' and 'wide-skirted meads' (1.1.64–5), Gillies invokes the 'landscape effect of a Saxtontian map'. Garrett Sullivan likewise calls Saxton's atlas 'a model not only for *Lear*'s cartographic representation of his kingdom, but also for Lear's geographic descriptions of land'.[57] Yet if we understand Goneril's portion to be Albany or Scotland, that part of Britain was never rendered by Saxton as an innovative landscape effect. Saxton's Atlas, the so-called 'Burghley Atlas' in the British library (Royal MS 18 D III), consists of 119 folios filled with coloured manuscript maps of English and Welsh locations and lists of JPs, into which is pasted in a map of Scotland based on George Lily's of 1546. The map has been taken out of a printed book by John Leslie, bishop of Ross.[58] Though Scotland appears here as a foreign supplement to Elizabeth's kingdom, Burghley lays claim to it, as the atlas is prefaced by his own manuscript notes on Brutus and Galfridian history.[59]

To note that Saxton never mapped Scotland is not, of course, to invalidate cartographic criticism's direction of our attention to the moral and phenomenological critique of the map enacted in *Lear*'s scenes of bodily exposure and sensory disorientation. But if such critiques are not to reproduce older moralising tales of James's tyrannous unification of space, a more discriminating attention to English cartography's relation to Scotland and 'British history' is needed. Gillies, for example, asserts that 'the major spatial idea in *Lear* is mobilised around the bodily opposition of housedness and unhousedness', but this seems to me misleading.[60] Just as close kin are unkind in *Lear*, so the interiors of houses are hard-hearted. Gloucester's house is '[m]ore harder than the stones whereof 'tis raised' (3.2.64). The cruellest of exposures, murders and mutilations threaten, with hallucinatory suddenness, from spaces

---

[56] See Tyacke and Huddy, *Saxton*, 23–45.
[57] Gillies, 'Scene of Cartography', 117; Sullivan, *Drama of Landscape*, 107.
[58] Royal MS 18 D III, fol. 122r.
[59] Royal MS 18 D III, fol. 2v, '2390 a° [anno] Mundi Brutus venit in britanniam'.
[60] Gillies, 'Scene of Cartography', 123.

of closest familiarity and intimacy – from children, parents and guests in the home: 'Good my friends, consider, you are my guests', pleads the shocked Gloucester, hearing Cornwall's command to bind him fast; 'I am your *host*', he repeats, appalled to find himself humiliated and violated, his beard plucked (3.7.30, 39, my italics). Moreover, one of the most striking things about the play's tragic form is its *suppression* of any sense of the territorial regions of Britain and especially the suppression of any sense of a north-south divide. John Kerrigan says Shakespeare's audience was 'invited to question how wise' Lear was to split the kingdom 'into the traditional realms of the north . . . the Celtic West . . . and fertile southern England', but the audience is given no sense of such climatic, geographical, cultural or political distinctions in the play.[61] We're invited to react to people in courtly households, but clues about location are elusive and distance collapses. The play ostensibly requires us to imagine that both Oswald and Kent set out from Goneril's house in Scotland one evening and, arriving at Regan's in Cornwall the same night, change course and travel to Gloucester, where they arrive before dawn (all this is supposed to happen between Act 1, scene 5 and the beginning of Act 2). In practice, it seems pedantic to notice this, because we just don't think about it. (W. W. Greg thought, for example, that Albany might be 'living somewhere in the West like the others' to facilitate all the journeying to and fro; his assumption of Scotland's needing to be in the vicinity is telling and speaks, I think, to every reader's and audience's impression.)[62] This is a play with 'no specific geographical reference' to anywhere in Britain except Dover, a play in which, as F. T. Flahiff has written, 'we are almost always in the company of characters whose names provide at least a vicarious sense of place'. These are, moreover, characters to whom Shakespeare has given no first names: Albany, Cornwall, Gloucester and Kent.[63]

VI. Oedipus and His Double

The significance of 'a vicarious sense of place' emerging only through the proximity and presence of named characters in *Lear* brings us back to the question of intimate human relations, of parents and children, and the question of what Shakespeare is doing with Seneca's Oedipus plays. Why is Shakespeare's Senecan-Oedipal reshaping of a Galfridian story of kingdom-division not a tragedy of the nation? For geographical territorial

---

[61] Kerrigan, *Archipelagic English*, 16.
[62] W. W. Greg, 'Time, Place and Politics in *King Lear*', *The Modern Language Review*, vol. 35, no. 4 (1940), 431–46, 431.
[63] Flahiff, 'Lear's Map',19.

division is not, in *Lear*, the cause of the escalation of violence. In *Lear*, 'division' is not imagined territorially and geographically even to the extent that it is in *Gorboduc*, where the planting of the two sons, Ferrex and Porrex, in the 'furder parts' of their distant realms (1.2.313) is emphasised; this makes them set about gathering intelligence about one another's kingdoms in Act 2, precipitating an escalation of violence. In *Lear*, by contrast, such antagonism as there is between Albany and Cornwall does not feel catalysed by the cartographic event. Curran's 'likely wars toward' between the dukes (1.II–12) and Kent's words in the Folio about 'division / Although as yet the face of it is covered / With mutual cunning, 'twixt Albany and Cornwall' (3.1.19–21) may inform a sense of competitive *realpolitik*, but it does not describe the direction taken by events. Thus 'division', far from feeling like an event, let alone a cartographically inspired one, feels like a structural dynamic within human relations, a human disposition. It begins not with Lear's 'even from this line to this' (1.1.63), but with the apprehension we have, from Kent's and Gloucester's ambient gossip, that what really matters is who is currently uppermost in a king's affections and how one can introduce the children of one's more embarrassing, not to say shameful, sexual liaisons, into advantageous society without losing too much face. And here we have the key to how Shakespeare's adaptation of Seneca's Oedipus plays in *Lear* enables him to eschew the identification of tragic feeling with national feeling. For in weaving the tragedy of Gloucester and his two sons so tightly into the story of Lear and his three daughters, Shakespeare has ensured that 'division' cannot be interpreted solely as a sovereign decision, the action of an absolutist or a cartographic imperialist. It's also the mundane predicament of humdrum adultery, 'the codpiece that will house', as the fool says (3.2.26–7), the prick insouciantly procreating and disavowing, joking, blustering, feeling ashamed. Gloucester had an affair, it was good sport, 'the whoreson must be acknowledged' (1.1.22–3), it could happen to everyman. Shakespeare has, indeed, as Perry and others have shown, thought deeply about Seneca's Oedipus plays in composing *King Lear*. And as part of that thinking he has complicated the alignment of rage, grief and guilt with the tragedy of the kingdom (Thebes, Britain) as well as complicating the generic purity of tragedy itself by doubling the story of Oedipus and his children.

Lear has a child who, like Antigone in Seneca's *Phoenissae*, is kind and natural to him, despite his brutal repudiations and the overwhelming shame that prevents him from accepting her kindness. As Oedipus marvels that a child of his unspeakable (*nefanda* – abominable, monstrous) house might be kind and natural (*pius*, 80–2), so Kent marvels that 'one self mate and make' could 'beget / Such different issues' as Cordelia and her sisters (4.3.35). In the same scene, Kent explains that although Cordelia has returned from France and Lear knows this, he will not 'yield' to see her because 'a sovereign shame so elbows him. His own unkindness / That stripped her from his benediction' (4.3.43–4). Curtis Perry's fine reading of the way in which the 'powerful antisocial energies' of Senecan drama inform Lear's and Cordelia's relation endorses and illuminates both Janet Adelman's psychoanalytic reading of it as structured by Lear's repressed desire and Stanley Cavell's reading of it as structured by the avoidance of love. Glossing Oedipus in *Phoenissae*, Perry comments, 'Cavell's themes of shame and avoidance are here so central to the action as to become effectively the play's entire story.'[64]

But Lear also has, in Goneril and Regan, the Eteocles and Polynices whose cruelty will spectacularly outdo his own tyranny, destroying the kingdom and themselves. Lear's speech in 3.2 addressing the storm ('Rage, blow! / You cataracts and hurricanoes, spout / Till you have drenched our steeples, drowned the cocks! . . . Crack nature's moulds, all germans spill at once', 3.2.1–8) is quite properly read in the contexts of Senecan cosmic *sumpatheia*, Lucretian atomism or ecological disequilibrium, but it bears comparison, too, with Oedipus' response to the Nuntius who, in *Phoenissae*, begs him to dissuade his sons from fighting. Oedipus refuses and urges them to an immolation of buildings and seeds that seems the fiery equivalent of a tempest's drowning and cracking open: 'Bring weapons, attack the penates with firebrands, reap the grain of your native land with fire . . . hurl all into destruction, fling the city walls down . . . let the city be cremated – and let the fire begin first in my marriage chamber' (340–7). In a final resistance to the appeal to him to try and reconcile his sons and bring peace, Oedipus insists on staying incarcerated in the woods, listening for 'the words of straying rumours' (361) from the political world. Quoting from Thomas Newton's 1581 translation, Perry persuasively links this moment to Lear's fantasy of listening, from prison, to 'poor rogues / Talk of court news' (5.3.13–14).[65] Gloucester, of course, is likewise derived from Seneca's Oedipus, perhaps even more obviously. Both Kerrigan and Perry, as I have mentioned, persuasively argue that Shakespeare models Edgar's leading of Gloucester to 'Dover Cliff' on Antigone leading the blind Oedipus in *Phoenissae*. But Gloucester's Edgar is also the Polynices of Euripides' *Phoenissae* and Gascoigne and Kinwelmarsh's *Jocasta* – a poor

[64] Perry, *Senecan Tragedy*, 134, 121.   [65] Perry, *Senecan Tragedy*, 140.

outcast dweller in muddy swamps and pools, who, usurped by his Eteoclean brother, will return in arms to kill him.

Profound effects arise from Shakespeare's doubling of the tragedy of Oedipus in the figures of Lear and in Gloucester. One of these is registered by Stanley Cavell in his unforgettable reading of Act 4, scene 6, in which the mad Lear and blind Gloucester encounter one another and Lear, in recognising Gloucester, begins to break through his madness. Cavell asks what Lear is confronted by in acknowledging Gloucester:

> What is difficult to show is that this is not merely or vaguely symbolic, and that this is not merely an access of knowledge which Lear undergoes. Gloucester has become ... Lear's double; he does not merely represent Lear, but is psychologically identical to him ... we have the ... double or mirror image of everyman who has gone to every length to avoid himself, caught at the moment of coming upon himself face to face.[66]

Cavell introduces the idea of the double, of Lear coming face to face with *himself*, to explain the scene's 'particular terror', its 'psychotic power'.[67] But the 'double' and the 'everyman' are generically disturbing, too: they are disruptive of tragedy, of the sovereign uniqueness of the self, and the dignity of majesty, the king standing for his people, the nation. Bakhtin talks about the double – insanity, the split personality, confrontational dialogue with the self – as a characteristic carnivalesque element in the ancient genre of Menippean satire, a disruption of man's 'finalised' quality.[68] Though terrifying, grotesque and pitiable, there is also something fantastically inventive and absurd about Lear's saying to Gloucester, 'If thou wilt weep my fortunes, take my eyes. / I know thee well enough; thy name is Gloucester' (4.6.172–3). Jan Kott's reading of *Lear* in the company of Ionesco and Beckett is apposite here.[69] More importantly, Shakespeare's doubling of the tragedy of Oedipus in the figures of Lear and in Gloucester both disrupts the generic integrity of its Senecan tragic model and undermines British Senecan tragedy's potential – as it is exemplified in *Gorboduc*, *Jocasta* or *Misfortunes* – to identify the ruin of the nation and with the pathos of a lost birth-home, a lost place of national origin. The doubling of the Oedipus story is a part

---

[66] Stanley Cavell, *Disowning Knowledge in Six Plays of Shakespeare* (Cambridge: Cambridge University Press, 1987), 52.

[67] Cavell, *Disowning*, 52.

[68] Mikhail Bakhtin, *Problems of Dostoevsky's Poetics*, trans. and ed Caryl Emerson (Minneapolis, MN: University of Minnesota Press, 1984), 116–17.

[69] Jan Kott, *Shakespeare Our Contemporary*, trans. Boleslaw Taborski (New York, NY: Doubleday, 1966), 127–68.

of an irreverent and wonderful generic democratising and bringing low – down to the level of eel pies and shelled peascods, worsted stockings, erections, codpieces, tadpoles and cow-dung, rustling silk, brothels, dice and lenders' books – that infiltrates the play's tragic grandeur from many directions: from the language of the Fool, of Kent as serving man, of Edgar as that figure of theatrical generativity, the bedlam beggar, Poor Tom.[70] All this vulgarity, this 'slum naturalism' as Bakhtin might call it, is a commentary on the way that, through Gloucester's becoming Lear's double and suffering identically, Lear's plight has ceased to be intelligible as a national tragedy of kingdom-division and has become the plight of 'everyman'.[71] The effects of this may be seen in Lear's developing horror at the thought of procreation, his cursing of wombs and germination and genitals. Oedipus returns again and again to the horror of his return to his mother's womb, the crime of incest which he and Thebes condemn more than parricide. He imagines the cliffs and crags of Cithaeron, in *Phoenissae*, as filled with the memories of mothers who, in using its gloomy depths and dangerous heights to destroy their sons, seem to him better than the mother who spared him to endure the curse of returning to her womb (*Phoenissae*, 10–26). When Lear, by contrast, gets started on the horrors of the female genitals – 'there's hell, there's darkness, there is the sulphurous pit, burning, scalding, stench, consumption!' (4.6.123–5) he, like, Edgar talking of the 'dark and vicious place' of Edmund's getting (5.3.170), performs the routine misogynistic gesture of conflating sexual promiscuity and women as birth-givers. The whole trajectory of Shakespeare's tragedy is indeed birth-related: legitimate offspring are inexplicably unkind, we 'came crying hither' (4.6.174). But birth is not related to *natio* in the sense of nation. Lear's carnivalesque inversions of justice are almost wholly taken up with a gleeful cynicism in this respect ('To't, luxury, pell-mell' 4.6.115; 'Why dost thou lash that whore?' 4.6.157; 'None does offend, none', 4.6.164). Although there may be irony in Lear's urging, in Edgar's and Gloucester's hearing, that copulation should thrive because 'Gloucester's bastard son was kinder to his father / Than were my daughters got 'tween the lawful sheets' (4.6.112–14), there is, precisely because of this doubling, no moral here to be drawn that links birth to birthplace or suggests that the division of the kingdom has led to a loss of the island's British identity or made it vulnerable to foreign (Scottish) invasion and predation.

[70] Simon Palfrey, *Poor Tom: Living 'King Lear'* (Chicago, IL: University of Chicago Press, 2015).
[71] Bakhtin, *Problems*, 115.

VII. Albany and Edgar

At this stage I seem hardly to have advanced the argument about how Shakespeare's *Lear* might have been engaging with the debates going on in 1605–6 about Anglo-Scots union, except to say 1) that these debates were less about 'union' imagined territorially than about naturalisation, and so birthplace and birth rights; and 2) that by doubling the story of Oedipus in his *Lear*, Shakespeare ironised the alignment, in Galfridian British tragedies, of English national identity and the island of Britain as birthplace and home. I will try, in conclusion, to relate these arguments through a consideration of Shakespeare's characterisation of Albany, his naming of Edgar, and his handling of French invasion.

Shakespeare's dramatic treatment of the French invasion of Britain and of the battle between the British and Cordelia's and Lear's French forces in Act 5, is notoriously evasive and baffling.[72] References to the invasion and battle are much more muted than in *Leir*, where the Gallian king, Cordelia and Leir triumphantly arrive on British shores, obtain the goodwill of the watch and townsfolk, and fight, in the name of both Saint Denis and Saint George, against Gonorill and Ragan and their British (Cambrian and Cornish) dukes (2549). Because Shakespeare intends a tragedy, he muffles the battle and references to the invasion and the slow amassing of troops on either side. There are considerable variations between the explicitness of references to the landings of the French in the Quarto and the Folio. Critics argue both over why revisions might have been made and whether French or British troops are being referred to.[73] But our bafflement is not merely an effect of referential ambiguity: it is a moral/national confusion. 'Stop a minute and ask yourselves in simple-minded terms,' says Stephen Booth, 'whether the battle in Act V is won by the good or the bad side.'[74] His question speaks partly to the tortuous effects of Shakespeare's characterisation of the duke of Albany. In Geoffrey of Monmouth and in the old Leir play both dukes – both husbands of Goneril and Regan – are unequivocally 'bad guys' (usurpers) and both are defeated by Lear, Cordelia and the Gallic forces. But Shakespeare decides to endow one of these figures – the duke of Albany – with a sense of outrage at the atrocities

[72] See Richard Knowles, 'Cordelia's Return', *SQ*, vol. 50, no. 1 (1999), 33–50; Gary Taylor, 'Monopolies, Show Trials, Disaster and Invasion', in *The Division of the Kingdoms: Shakespeare's Two Versions of King Lear*, eds. Gary Taylor and Michael Warren (Oxford: Clarendon Press, 1983), 75–119.

[73] Knowles, 'Cordelia's Return', 35–7; 38 n.15.

[74] Stephen Booth, 'On the Greatness of *King Lear*', in *Twentieth-Century Interpretations of King Lear*, ed. Janet Adelman (Englewood Cliffs, NJ: Prentice-Hall, 1978), 98–111, 108.

perpetrated against the king and Gloucester. This means that Albany's position in the developing military confrontation is extremely complicated, not to say impossibly contradictory, as the contortion of his language to Edmund (revised out of the Folio text) reveals. 'For this business,' Albany says to Edmund, 'it touches us as France invades our land / Not bolds the King, with others whom I fear / Most just and heavy causes make oppose' (5.1.24–7). These clotted, inept words imply support for Lear and Gloucester, but they simultaneously contradict that support by implying a commitment to military resistance to the French, who are invading as Lear's allies. It would seem that Albany has to fight both *against* Lear and Cordelia and somehow *for* them at the same time. Goneril impugns his lack of military manhood and political acuity: 'Fools do those villains pity who are punished / Ere they have done their mischief. Where's thy drum? France spreads her banners in our noiseless land' (4.2.55–7). The audience, however, is vague about the battle and warms to Albany's appalled registering of Gloucester's tragedy, relayed to him as a mere circumstantial detail in the important political event of Cornwall's death: 'Gloucester's eyes? . . . But, O, poor Gloucester / Lost he his other eye?' (4.2.73, 81–2).

In the final scene of the play, Albany, Kent and Edgar have survived the deaths of Lear's daughters, Edmund and the king himself. Albany invites Kent and Edgar to 'Rule in this realm and the gored state sustain', but Kent is preparing for death (5.3.319). The decision to hover over these two figures – one character called 'Albany' and one called 'Edgar' – as custodians of this exhausted, devastated political aftermath is surely significant. 'Edgar', as we have seen, was the name of the Saxon king most conjured with in cartographic-imperialist discourses of English sea-empire that made claim, through Galfridian British history, to Scotland's coastline. And Edgar was becoming the darling of English anti-unionists. Treatises opposing Scottish naturalisation argued that King Edgar, with his vast navy, had circumnavigated the British isles annually and established an imperial rule over Scotland without even needing to name the country. He was '*Aedgarus, totius Albionis Basileus*', Edgar, King of all Albion, the 'Saxonicall Alexander' as John Dee called him.[75] This Edgar, as Sir Henry Spelman wrote, justified the argument that kings of England had always had title to Scotland because he 'sheweth himselfe to be supreme Lorde of Scotlande, yet he nameth not Scotland particulerly' (169). To take a name of an English king so charged with Anglo-imperial mystique as a great thalassocrat and have him impersonate a naked bedlam beggar in

---

[75] Dee, *Memorials*, 57.

the muddy heart of a dystopian Britain seems ironically inspired. But surely so, too, is the decision to leave the imagined future – evacuated of all Galfridian prophecy – in the hands of this humbled, 'nursing' Edgar (5.3.180) along with another man who 'bear[s] a cheek for blows' (4.2.52) and is named for the country – Albany – so often demonised as the foreign threat, the invader that confirms Britain's Englishness.

It is worth remembering that in the debates of 1605–6, English opponents of Scottish naturalisation simultaneously argued that the island was now a single nation in the sense that both peoples born in it must fight for it, and, at the same time, that it was two nations in the sense that rights of being born English must not be shared with Scots. Thus Spelman enthused at the increase of strength enjoyed by the two nations as one. 'The sea hath taken us into her protection and sequestered our enemies and none can assayle us but with double preparation' (164), he wrote, urging that the Scots should with the English 'joyne . . . in the straightest knottes of amity for defence of the whole ileland' (183). Yet these co-defenders should not share in English birth rights: 'The freedomes that God giveth to nations *by their birth* is no lighte thinge' (my italics) (183). Sir Thomas Craig identified the injustice of these contradictions. He argued that it was not right to expect a set of native inhabitants to fight and die to defend an island while being excluded by birth to its freedoms and modes of access to honours, promotions and livings. 'Scotsmen, who live in the same island (*qui in eadem insula vivunt*), will feel that they are despised,' he wrote, 'if for reasons of the nationality (*ratione gentis*) or locality (*soli*) of their birth, they are excluded from access to honourable modes of living, they will not see why they should defend the island in war.'[76] In resisting and ironising the alignments of emotion and nation-as-birthplace that characterise Galfridian British tragedy and precariously placing the 'gored state' between Albany and the man he calls a *friend of his soul*, Edgar, Shakespeare can certainly be seen as making a comment on this debate. And rather than seeing such a comment as reductive in its topicality, I have tried to show that the shaping of feelings of English and Scottish national belonging through British history and Latin and Greek tragedy has a long history of its own, which helped to bring about *King Lear*.

[76] Craig, *De unione*, 92–3, 330.

Coda: Macbeth. 'Alas, poor country'

This book has been about the Elizabethan erasure of the idea of Scotland as a sovereign historic kingdom. Chapter 6 showed how Scotland's agency as a kingdom, present in English chronicle narratives of the Hundred Years' War, vanished in Shakespeare's history plays. Not once do the characters in these plays refer to 'the king of Scotland' or 'the kingdom of Scotland'. The term 'Scot' stands in, indifferently and with productive ambiguity, for territory, king, rebel and currency. Yet Shakespeare did, of course, write one very famous play in James VI and I's reign, in which there can be no doubt that Scotland as a kingdom and a land has substantial imaginative presence. In it the phrase 'king of Scotland' occurs three times and the words 'Scotland' and 'country' occur in close and iterated proximity.[1] Indeed, modern theatrical superstition demands that the play be referred to by a sort of euphemism as 'the Scottish play' as if to confirm the equivalence of the play and the nationality it dramatises. Does *Macbeth*, then, disprove the argument of this book?

Macbeth is admired as a play which puts us on intimate terms with the excitement, tension and fear involved in the committing of terrible crimes. Emrys Jones described the play's mood as one of 'profound inwardness'. The action opens so abruptly and develops so swiftly, he says, that the audience or reader is 'surprised into assuming an attitude of secret, perhaps unconscious, complicity with the hero which nothing later in the action can wholly destroy, not even the murder of Lady Macduff and her children'.[2] Part of what draws us in is a certain oblique, almost aporetic working of meaning both at the level of scenic sequence and of individual speeches. The movement of scenes across time and the figurative

---

[1] *Macbeth*, eds. Sandra Clark and Pamela Mason (London: Bloomsbury Arden, 2015), 1.2.28; 5.9.25; 5.9.29; 4.3.7, 4.3.31, 4.3.46, 4.3.100, 4.3.114, 4.3.164. Further references to this edition will appear in the text.

[2] Emrys Jones, *Scenic Form in Shakespeare* (Oxford: Clarendon Press, 1971), 195.

movement of language are both very rapid, forcing us to conjecture as we can, accepting a certain level of mysteriousness and incomprehension, until, as Jones says, we feel that at the end of the play 'we have travelled a distance almost incredibly incommensurate with the brevity of the text'.[3] Individual speeches, especially Macbeth's own, are marked by a complexity of figurative sequence – one figure quickly succeeding another – that Brian Cummings has, in a brilliant essay, discussed as examples of metalepsis. Cummings interprets metalepsis as the swift transition from one figure to another, leaving out intervening stages, so that it comes to stand for the imaginative energies released across a succession of metaphors, as one gives way to another. Cummings shows how Macbeth's own speeches repeatedly enact this mysterious transitional process, taking us (in imagination) over the borderline between imagining terrible things and enacting them:

> If it were done, when 'tis done, then 'twere well
> It were done quickly. If the assassination
> Could trammel up the consequence, and catch
> With his surcease, success: that but this blow
> Might be the be-all and the end-all, here,
> But here, upon this bank and shoal of time,
> We'd jump the life to come.   (1.7.1–7)

The lines, comments Cummings, 'are like a metalepsis in explanation of metalepsis, not in some reductive self-referential aporia but in a recognition of the way that every life is lived in an interplay between language and action'.[4]

The effects Jones and Cummings describe are not only discernible in the intense double effort of self-scrutiny and evasion that characterises Macbeth's language of introspection but also in the differently puzzling and doubtful working of the language of the Scottish nobles in scenes which comment obliquely on Macbeth's actions (2.4; 3.6). William Empson has described the effects of these scenes well: 'It seems to me,' he writes, 'that all the lords are meant to be "ambiguous" in the quite flat vague sense that we feel that any one of them may be playing his own game during this period of confusion, though we never get it clear.'[5] He quotes from Ross's response to Lady Macduff's horrified realisation that her husband has left her to the mercy of Macbeth's hit-men. She accuses her husband of not loving her and their children. Ross defends Macduff and

[3] Jones, Scenic, 198.   [4] Cummings, 'Metalepsis', 233–4.
[5] William Empson, Essays on Shakespeare, ed. David M. Pirie (Cambridge: Cambridge University Press, 1986), 143.

prevaricates: 'I dare not speak much further / Cruel are the times, when we are traitors, and do not know ourselves' (4.2.17–19). Such hiding in obliquity feels desperately inadequate just as the murderers' boots are on the threshold, but this, as Empson points out, *is* how people speak under the threat of a violent regime, when no one can risk candour and openness. It still makes us uneasy: 'we feel any one of them may be playing his own game'.

I begin with these relatively formal analyses because I want to resist conflating the effects of the extraordinary Shakespearean techniques I have just indicated with an ostensible Scottish history of violence that is said to have justified English hostility to a 'Union'. According to *Macbeth*'s most recent Arden editors, Sandra Clark and Pamela Mason, Scotland is no longer 'hidden from view' in *Macbeth* criticism.[6] Much depends, however, on the kind of analytical visibility it has. As I have shown throughout this book, a myth of *English indifference to Scotland*, which can be traced even in the rhetoric of the immensely costly and effortful attempted conquest of the country from 1542 to 1550, has been so successful as to occlude from today's literary critics the fact that English government policy was, throughout Elizabeth's reign, intensely preoccupied with achieving a compliant and English-dependent regime in the country. Enormous intelligence and military efforts went into the management of Scotland's constitutional crisis in 1567–73 to ensure that the Scottish monarch was not restored and that a series of regencies under English surveillance and presumed jurisdiction (at least according to Cecil's memoranda) were instead installed. Throughout Elizabeth's reign, as this book has shown in detail, legal, geographical and literary discourses were at once continuous with and quietly transformative of the literature of overlordship. This produced the unspoken and incoherent common-sense image – still prevalent today – of an early modern island of Britain in which Scotland is always already subsumed within the *a priori* equivalence of England and Britain while intermittently forcing itself on English consciousness as a foreign supplement, an ever-erupting 'border region' threatening England's peace.

Given the history traced in this book, especially with respect to the English belief in England's historical overlordship of Scotland, it is not enough to contextualise English attitudes to Scotland in terms of the combination of a long and vague history of Anglo-Scots hostility, suddenly made urgent and real by an apparently unanticipated and unwanted

---

[6] Clark and Mason, 'Introduction', 21, citing Willy Maley and Andrew Murphy, eds., *Shakespeare and Scotland* (Manchester: Manchester University Press, 2004), 8.

prospect of Anglo-Scots union. This is, however, largely what the visibility of Scotland in *Macbeth* criticism amounts to. The Arden editors cite critics on 'popular attitudes of hostility towards Scotland'; 'intense English dislike of the Scots', all galvanised in this particular historical moment by opposition to Union ('Introduction', 25–6). This potent combination of evidence for an unhistoricised 'hostility' and 'dislike' with evidence for opposition to a coercive royal policy of 'Union' encourages a conflation of the visibility of the polity of Scotland in the moment of *Macbeth*'s production with the visibility of the Scotland dramatised in *Macbeth*.

In the dominant critical discourse that subsumes the urgent questions of Anglo-Scots constitutional relations post-1603 into a Union bee in James's bonnet, it becomes easy to adduce, from the Scottish materials on which Shakespeare drew, evidence for a sense of *Macbeth*-like barbarity and evil as pathologically present in Scottish national culture. Some of the Arden editors' locutions show signs of this. For example, the critic Jonathan Baldo credits Shakespeare with 'seeming to support James's case for union' while signalling to anti-unionists 'the hazards of joining their nation to one whose history' was, 'in the least charitable estimation' nothing but 'a monotonous tale of violence and regicide'.[7] The Arden editors misquote Baldo as saying that *Macbeth* warned English audiences of 'the hazards of joining a nation with Scotland's violent history' (34). It is a small point, but Baldo's language carefully differentiated unsympathetic English readings of Scottish history from an essential violence ascribable to the national character. In the editors' minor rearrangement of Baldo's words, however, Scotland simply has a 'violent history' to which Shakespeare refers when composing his play and against which he warns his compatriots.

In a similar almost imperceptible shift, the editors build tellingly on a phrase from Herbert Grierson's and J. C. Smith's edition of *Macbeth* in 1914, a phrase reiterated in Kenneth Muir's Arden edition of 1951. Discussing Shakespeare's reading in Scottish history, Clark and Mason quote Grierson and Smith to the effect that 'the overriding influence' of Holinshed on Shakespeare was 'the atmosphere "of violent deeds and haunting remorse" that Holinshed creates from a succession of stories "of men driven by an irresistible impulse into deeds of treachery and bloodshed but haunted when the deed was done by spectres of conscience and superstition"' (83).[8] From this Clark and Mason conclude that '[i]

---

[7] Jonathan Baldo, '"A Rooted Sorrow": Scotland's Unusable Past', *Macbeth: New Critical Essays*, ed. Nick Moschovakis (London: Routledge, 2008), 88–117, 91.

[8] H. J. C. Grierson *Macbeth* (Oxford: Clarendon Press, 1914), xviii–xix; Kenneth Muir ed., *Macbeth* (London: Methuen, 1951, repr. 1972), xl.

n Holinshed Shakespeare found a medieval Scotland which was war-torn and primitive and desperately in need of the civilizing hand of England' (83).

Whatever Shakespeare found in Holinshed it was not primitive Scotland under Macbeth desperately in need of a civilising hand from England under Edward the Confessor. That is what Shakespeare *made* of what he found. But what drew him to dramatise this conjunction of reigns in 1606? What opportunities did the connections between Edward the Confessor and Malcolm III offer to a King's Men's playwright? Like King Edgar (959–75), King Edward the Confessor (1042–66) was a name to conjure with in the early seventeenth century. The laws Edward introduced (building on Edgar's laws) were supposed to be proof of a direct continuity, unbroken by the Norman conquest, between Saxon and seventeenth-century English liberties. They were a vital link in the chain of proof of the ancient constitution, the myth that the English common law and its institutions had originated in the immemorial customs of the people. Prominent opponents of Scottish naturalisation such as Sir Henry Spelman subscribed to this view.[9] In addition, English military support for the vanquishing of Macbeth and enthroning of Malcolm made Malcolm's homage performed to Edward (for Cumberland) seem an especially good example of homage as voluntarily and gladly performed; it looked like a grateful Scottish acknowledgement of sub-regal dependency. The *Epitome* (1548) thus relates Edward's defeat of the usurper Macbeth and the coronation of Malcolm, after which Malcolm 'did homage to this king Edwarde *for the kyngdome of Scotland*' (my italics).[10] Holinshed reports that Edward sent Siward of Northumberland north where, in helping Malcolm to the throne he 'vanquished the Scots'.[11]

What Shakespeare would have found in the first instance, then, was vital proof of Scotland's admission of the overlordship of an English king whose star was just then riding as high as it could, symbolising England's ancient constitution and the English common law. But the English belief in a history of overlordship was not to be voiced in the hearing of a Scottish king. In this case, as it happened, there was scope for reconceiving the relationship as a different kind of grateful dependency: the sick patient's deliverance from suffering by the charismatic healer. For a hagiographical tradition attributed to Edward a miraculous curative touch. Stow's *Annals*

[9] Janelle Greenberg, *The Radical Face of the English Constitution: St Edward's 'Laws' in Early Modern Political Thought* (Cambridge: Cambridge University Press, 2001), 147.
[10] *Epitome*, sig. e5v–e6r.   [11] Holinshed, I.749.

(1592) include the tale of Edward's gentle and efficacious laying of hands on the face of a woman with terrible scrofula; his touch purged her skin of the corruption, curing her both of the disease and of her barrenness.[12] Holinshed reports that Edward bequeathed the power to cure this disease, called 'the King's Evil', 'as it were a portion of his inheritance unto his successors the kings of this realme'.[13] Edward's 'real' constitutionalist legacy – the introduction of laws 'afterwards called the common lawes' (747) – was thus symbolically assimilated to the idea of miraculous medical cure, so that an evidently voluntary Scottish acceptance of vassalage to England, acknowledged in homage 'for the kingdome of Scotland' could be expressed as the nation's symptoms of need for that cure, the 'perturbation in nature' (5.1.9), the ecstasy of unrest that afflicts not only the Macbeths but the whole country, so that Scotland seems 'desperately in need of the civilizing hand of England' (83).[14] This is part of the story of how we get *Macbeth*.

But it is evidently not the whole story. There is the question of what Shakespeare found in Holinshed's history of Scotland and how he dramatised those findings. Scotland in Holinshed's account of Macbeth's reign was hardly more 'war-torn and primitive' than England in Edward the Confessor's.[15] In both narratives there is war, there are Danish or Norwegian invasions, portents, indiscriminate murders, the introduction of laws (Macbeth is also a maker of good laws) and, centrally, the clandestine murder of an heir to the throne (Earl Godwin is said to have murdered Edward's elder brother, Alfred, to place Edward, 'more meeke and simple than apt for the gouernement of the realme', on the throne).[16] The most striking distinction between the narratives lies not in their degrees of primitivism and civility but in their degrees of literariness. The English narrative is shapeless and almost annalistic ('in the yeere 1047, there fell a marvellous great snow'), but the Scottish one has considerable elegance.[17] This is because Holinshed's narrative of early Scottish history derives from the brilliant *Scotorum Historia* (1527) of Hector Boece by way of a translation by the poet, John Bellenden. It is, however, precisely the greater literariness of the Scottish history that makes it susceptible to a psychological rather than political-constitutional dramatic development.

[12] Henry Summerson, 'Tudor Antiquaries and the Vita Ædwardi Regis', *Anglo-Saxon England*, vol. 38 (2009), 157–84, 176–7.
[13] Holinshed, I.754.   [14] Holinshed, I.747.
[15] See Andrew Hadfield, 'Macbeth, IV.iii.140-158, Edward the Confessor and Holinshed's *Chronicles*', *Notes and Queries* (2002), vol. 49, no. 2, 234–6.
[16] Holinshed, I.739.   [17] Holinshed, I.741.

For Hector Boece, as John-Mark Philo has shown, turned to the great Roman historian, Livy, to fill in the blanks of Scottish history, while his translator Bellenden had himself translated Livy's history of the Roman republic into Scots during the reign of James V, in 1533.[18] Boece modelled his tyrant 'Maccabeus' or Macbeth, as Philo demonstrates, on Livy's Tarquinus Superbus, Tarquin the Proud. Boece's narrative is richly analytical and causal, so portents and apparitions are adduced in explanation of the psychology of tyranny. Macbeth administers the state extremely well for ten years, but he is 'troubled by furies', as happens to tyrants and to those who have come by their 'republics' by evil means (*per scelus respublicas occupantibus*), and these agitated him 'with constant fear that what he had done would be done to him by someone else'.[19] Furthermore, as in the case of Livy's Tarquin, fear breeds hatred: 'indeed when Maccabeus understood that he was an object of fear, and that he was feared by everyone, he himself in turn started to fear everyone. From this rose an implacable hatred of everyone.'[20] Macbeth's credulity is, as Philo notes, presented sceptically in Boece's prefatory index, which refers to Maccabeus' 'stupid confidence in prophecies he did not understand' (*stultam fidutiam in fatis non intellecti*s).[21] Rather than saying that Shakespeare found in Holinshed 'a medieval Scotland which was war-torn and primitive', we might say that Shakespeare, himself a student of Livy's Tarquin, found in the Holinshed translation of Bellenden and Boece the charismatic form of a story of the psychology of tyranny, both as experienced inwardly by the tyrant and as it spreads to infect a whole regnal community.

Yet there is an even earlier layer of a classically influenced, rationalising history of Macbeth and Macduff which protrudes somewhat in Shakespeare's play as slightly anomalous, in spite of having been assimilated by Boece and translated by Bellenden and Holinshed. This is Act 4, scene 3, the only scene in the play which does not have the swift and oblique arrow-like flight of the rest of the play, the only scene which is not 'compressed to the utmost degree'.[22] It is framed by two scenes of intense emotion: one of dread and horror (the arrival of the murderers at Macduff's castle in 4.2) and the other of sorrow and pathos (the witnessing of Lady Macbeth's mental distress in 5.1). The scene is thus vital in shaping the transition between these emotional experiences, deterring us from noticing

---

[18] John-Mark Philo, *An Ocean Untouched and Untried: The Tudor Translations of Livy* (Oxford: Oxford University Press, 2020), 115–41.

[19] Philo, *Ocean*, 119; Boece, *Scotorum Historia*, Book XII.15. https://philological.cal.bham.ac.uk/boece/

[20] Philo, *Ocean*, 118.   [21] Philo, *Ocean*, 117 n.8.   [22] Jones, *Scenic*, 197.

that we have gone from mourning the victims of the Macbeths, to feeling the sorrows of their killers. The intervening scene also contains the greatest concentration of the name 'Scotland' used to refer to the land as a country, challenging my broader argument about the erasure of Scotland in Elizabethan English literature as a sovereign, historic nation. So I want to conclude with an examination of the emotional work being done by the invocation of the name of Scotland in that scene, and of how Shakespeare's invocation of the name transforms its emotional resonance in the earlier Scottish histories.

Act 4 scene 3 is set in England, presumably somewhere in the vicinity of Edward the Confessor's court. It features Macduff's attempt to persuade Malcolm to return to Scotland as rightful heir to the throne, to lead an uprising against the usurper. Malcolm, however, is extremely wary and suspicious of Macduff, who he believes may have been sent by Macbeth to entrap him. He therefore tests Maduff's commitment to Scotland's good governance by professing himself to have faults as bad as or worse that the incumbent tyrant. When Macduff finally admits disgust with the faults Malcolm claims to possess, Malcolm is persuaded of the purity of his patriotism and agrees to go north with him. A doctor then unexpectedly pops in to describe Edward's miraculous powers of healing, quickly succeeded by the ubiquitous Ross hotfoot from Scotland, who urges the propitiousness of the time for mustering resistance to Macbeth and then with, painful hesitation, reveals to Macduff the slaughter of his wife and children.

Critics and directors complain of the tedium and artifice of this scene. Jones, however, thought it necessary as 'the testing of Macduff's humanity', which, he went on,

> is always a turning-point in a performance of *Macbeth*, since it is the first time that strong tragic emotion is released in the audience ... the emotion released by Macduff and his family is then transferred, or rather extended, first to Lady Macbeth, and then to the tyrant himself.[23]

In Jones's account, the scene channels the horror we are left to imagine at the end of 4.2, as the murderers stab the child and pursue his mother, into a feeling first of sympathy for Macduff and then for Lady Macbeth, as we watch her 'slumbery agitation' and hear her woefully discharge her 'infected mind[s]' (5.1.11, 5.1.72). For this transfer of our sympathies from victim to perpetrator it is important that the language of the Macbeths has

---

[23] Jones, *Scenic*, 221.

made us feel on more intimate terms with their thoughts and affections for one another than with anyone else in the play. This is one effect of the distinction between the mysterious complexity of Macbeth's metaleptic language of introspection and the kind of 'flat' ambiguity that Empson finds in the oblique, gap-filled exchanges of the Scottish nobility. It is important, then, that while we feel sorry for Macduff, uneasy questions hover over his sudden departure from Fife. 'He loves us not', says Lady Macduff, with reason (4.2.8), and Malcolm asks, 'Why in that rawness left you wife and child . . . Without leave-taking?' (4.3.26–8). Malcolm's suspicion of Macduff's 'motives' is supposed to be political, but though the dialogue proves to his satisfaction that Macduff is not Macbeth's instrument (and Ross's account of the murder of the whole family would corroborate this) the question of why Macduff would be so unnatural as to leave his wife and children in such obvious danger has been explicitly raised never to be answered. It remains part of what Empson calls the 'fog', its resistant opacity surely contributing to the movement of audience sympathy from the Macduffs to Lady Macbeth.

The provenance of this odd scene offers yet another example of how far from primitive was the Scottish historiography of the nation during the reign of Macbeth. It derives, as Sally Mapstone has shown, from John of Fordun's *Chronicle of the Scottish Nation* (c.1363–87).[24] Fordun's rationalising account of Macbeth's tyranny does not mention slaughter but focuses with legal precision on the breach of procedure involved in Macbeth's formal proclamation of outlawry on Macduff and seizure of his lands and properties without trial or legal process.[25] This illegality outrages the nobility and causes Macduff to flee to England find Malcolm. Fordun then devotes an extraordinary six chapters to what is, in effect, a dialogue on kingly government, an exercise in political theory. The tripartite structure, though much cut, is followed precisely by Boece, Bellenden, Holinshed and – with one vital difference – Shakespeare. In Fordun's version, Malcolm and MacDuff vie with one another in adducing historic examples to prove their case. As Malcolm declares he is lecherous, he cites examples of lechery as the downfall of kings – the inevitable Tarquin and Sardanapalus, but also the Frankish king Chilperic, England's Edwy and Scotland's late king Culen. MacDuff replies with a theory of pragmatic accommodation of private sexual incontinence, exemplified (from

---

[24] Sally Mapstone, 'Shakespeare and Scottish Kingship: A Case History', *Rose and the Thistle*, ed. Mapstone and Wood, 158–93.
[25] Fordun, *Chronicle*, I.181–83.

Suetonius) by the Roman Emperor Octavian whose womanising did not eclipse his legacy as Rome's rebuilder. So might Malcolm, sexual appetite notwithstanding, restore and rebuild Scotland – and so forth.[26] What appears to have escaped the notice of Shakespeareans, however, is not that Shakespeare, following Holinshed, much abbreviated this testing dialogue with its tripartite structure of kingly vices, but that he completely evacuated its political-theoretical content.

In Fordun, as in Boece, Bellenden and Holinshed, the tripartite struc- ture of the testing dialogue proves something about government. Macduff finds ways of accommodating the personal vices incident to monarchs and emperors: lechery and (with more difficulty) avarice. But when it comes to the third vice – unfaithfulness, promise-breach, treachery – Macduff can find no pragmatic accommodation.[27] Trust, it would seem, is the *sine qua non* of monarchical government – this is, in effect, a theory of the contract between king and people. When Macduff learns that Malcolm plans to be treacherous and break his faith with his subjects, councillors and allies as a matter of policy, he is silent for a long time and breaks out in a speech of despair about the evils Scots must now incur: 'we must either lose our wives and children, and all our earthly goods, and, as wanderers, undergo perpetual banishment; or serve a tyrant king'. It is at this point that he begins to weep, 'groaning deeply' and 'looking mournfully northwards' with the words 'Scotland, farewell for ever'.[28] The contrast with Shakespeare is immediately obvious. In Shakespeare, Malcolm caps the two vices which Macduff is prepared to tolerate with the declaration that he is a compound of all vices, abounding 'in the division of each several crime / Acting it many ways' (4.3.96–7). As a climax, this is completely vacuous. It subtracts any possible political lesson from the exercise, redu- cing it to pure formality. Malcolm's testing discovers nothing about the nature of the kind of polity and government to which they are both committed, it is merely a confirmation of the atmosphere of distrust created by Macbeth's tyranny.

Shakespeare's evacuation of the scene's political content makes perfect sense for his own dramatic purposes: it ensures that the testing does little to

---

[26] Fordun, *Chronicle*, I.185–90.

[27] Fordun, *Chronicle*, I.189, 'I am false, though I hide it; ingenious in contriving cunning deceits'; Boece, *Scotorum Historia*, XII.23, trans. Sutton, 'I greatly rejoice in lying', '*mendacio in tantum gaudeo*'; Bellenden, *Chronicles*, II.272, 'I am ful of lesings and dissait, and rejosis in nathing sa mekle as to betrays all thaim that gevis me credit or traist'; Holinshed, 5275–6, 'I am furthermore inclined to dissimulation, telling of leasings . . . I naturallie reioice in nothing so much as to betraie & deceiue such as put any trust or confidence in my woords'.

[28] Fordun, *Chronicle*, 189, 190.

dispel Empson's 'fog' of distrust contaminating the relations of the Scottish ruling classes – we still don't know why Macduff left his wife and children in that terrible rawness – and this, in turn, permits the diversion of the current of tragic emotion that Jones describes. What Shakespeare has done, in effect, is to internalise the political tragedy, to locate 'the action in a region deep in our minds'.[29] The effect may be seen in the peculiar resonance of the iteration of 'Scotland' in 4.3. The scene begins with Malcolm and Macduff like choric figures in a classical tragedy lamenting the plagues of the city: 'Each new morn,' says Macduff, 'New widows howl, new orphans cry, new sorrows / Strike heaven on the face, that it resounds / As if it felt with Scotland and yelled out / Like syllable of dolour' (4.3.4–8). 'Bleed, bleed, poor country', he continues, responding to Malcolm's suspicions of him (4.3.31). Malcolm also refers to his 'poor country' (4.3.46). When Malcolm accuses himself of all vices combined Macduff exclaims 'O Scotland, Scotland' and, angrily accusing Malcolm: 'These evils thou repeat'st upon thyself / Hath banished me from Scotland' (4.3.112–13). Then Ross appears. 'Stands Scotland where it did?', asks Macduff. Ross replies:

> Alas, poor country,
> Almost afraid to know herself. It cannot
> Be called our mother, but our grave. Where nothing,
> But who knows nothing, once is seen to smile;
> Where sighs and groans, and shrieks that rend the air,
> Are made, not marked; where violent sorrow seems
> A modern ecstasy. The deadman's knell
> Is there scarce asked for who, and good men's lives
> Expire before the flowers in their caps,
> Dying or ere they sicken.   (4.3.164–173)

In this astonishingly vivid, pathos-filled *prosopopoeia* the patriotic tears and groans of the Macduff of Fordun and the Scottish historians become something quite other. How can a country, a polity, be 'almost afraid to know itself?' (Yet in this phrase we hear the echo of Ross's evasiveness over Macduff's desertion of his wife: 'Cruel are the times, when we are traitors, and do not know ourselves', (4.2.17–19)). In the figure of the mother who drains life away rather than nurturing her children we have, of course, the subliminal transition from the witches who bubble up from the Scottish earth to the Lady Macbeth who would fill her breasts with gall and do violence to her suckling infant – except that she is afraid, afraid to know

---

[29] Jones, *Scenic*, 195.

this in herself. The conceit of Heaven struck on the face, yelling out its inarticulate 'syllable of dolour' is this infant again, the victim of the mother's diseased mind, the terrible sorrow rooted in the memory. It is this speech of Ross's, not Macduff's 'O Scotland, Scotland', that defines for us the emotion we associate with the idea of this nation. And where Macduff's deep sorrow, as shaped by Fordun's history, was the sorrow of patriotism, of a love for the country, that expressed by Ross, which collects up and anticipates so many of the charged associations of Shakespeare's tragedy, is a sorrow of pathos, encouraging us to feel for Scotland as we would for the woman 'swol'n and ulcerous, pitiful to the eye' who visited King Edward and was cured of her shameful disease (4.3.151).[30]

What English constitutionalist thinkers derived, in the early seventeenth century, from Edward the Confessor's laws was a theory of the contractual relation between ruler and ruled and a right to resist (even kill) a king who broke the terms of his agreement with the people.[31] Fordun's scene of Malcolm's testing of Macduff preparative to the resistance of Macbeth composes a similar mythos reiterated in the Scottish historical tradition (and finally developed into full-blown popular resistance theory by Buchanan). When Fordun's Macduff weeps and wrings his hands, uttering 'Scotland, farewell for ever', the emotion expressed is for a nation bereaved of its chance to restore law-bound monarchical government. Shakespeare replaces this mourning for the constitution, as it were, with Ross's figure of Scotland as a mother so deeply disturbed as to be incapable of rearing her children. Shakespeare gives us a tragic topography, a people unable to sustain themselves as a nation. This was what the dramatist brilliantly made of the Scottish histories of the tyrannical reign of Macbeth and his defeat by Macduff of Fife and Malcolm Canmore. It was not the Scotland he found in those histories. We should beware of mistaking the sublimity of *Macbeth* as tragedy for the state of the nation – either in the eleventh or sixteenth and seventeenth centuries – that it purports to depict. For all that the opponents of union in the House of Commons spoke about the violence of the Scots and Scottish history, it was Scottish householders – lords, lairds and humbler folk – who had, throughout the sixteenth century, experienced violence from English military aggression. Most of the Scottish writers examined in this book had their houses burnt down or plundered by English forces (James Henrisoun, Robert Wedderburn, Sir Richard Maitland). Indeed, in conclusion, we might remind ourselves of

---

[30] Summerson, '*Vita Ædwardi* Regis', 176–7.   [31] Greenberg, *Radical Face*, 4.

this poem of Sir Richard Maitland, describing Scotland around 1570, as a contrast to Ross's 'state of Scotland' speech in *Macbeth*:

> I trowe wes neuer harde nor sein
> In Scotland greater miserie . . .
> Craftismen and commounis ar put doun
> Be thift, reif and continuall weir [war]
> Neir herreit [ravaged] is our principall toun [Edinburgh] . . .
> Sum hes thair place brint [burnt] to ane gleid [ember],
> Thair guddis spuilyit [plundered] halallie;
> Thair servands slaine, sum brint to deid [burnt to death],
> Thair selfis taine vncourteouslie,
> And hauldin in captiuitie,
>
> (MQ 30, lines 4–48)

In establishing the historical context of English hostility to Scotland and understandable reluctance to join with a nation 'with Scotland's violent history' (34), the Arden editors cite Sir Christopher Piggott's famous anti-Scottish outburst in the House of Commons on 13 February 1607:

> Many of the English saw the Scots as an inherently violent people. In 1607 Sir Christopher Piggott outraged the King in an attack on the Scots during a series of parliamentary debates on the union of the kingdoms, when he declared what was generally believed, that the Scots 'have not suffered above two kings to die in their beds, these two hundred years' (30).[32]

This account of Piggott's statement outraging the king simultaneously locates the opinion of Scottish barbarity in a lack of respect for monarchy and suggests the failure of a Scottish monarch's tolerance of the critical speech that marks the superiority of the English political law-bound constitution. Sir Thomas Craig's measured summary of Piggott's speech gives a little more context:

> [Piggott] did not scruple to declare in Parliament that Scotland is the barrenest country in the world; that Scotsmen are the most perfidious and barbarous of all nations, devoid of an altar of faith, as the saying is, not to be tolerated in the courts of kings, and of a bloodthirsty and treacherous disposition; that the only possible relation between the two countries would be that of judge and thief, the one decreeing, the other undergoing the penalty; and that in public representations of comedy a Scotsman is always treated as a fitting subject of ridicule – a statement which is false.[33]

---

[32] On Sir Christopher Piggott's speech, see Neil Cuddy, 'Anglo-Scottish Union and the Court of James I', *Transactions of the Royal Historical Society*, vol. 39 (1989), 107–24, 114–15.
[33] Craig, *De unione*, 356.

It would be very interesting to know if Craig saw *Macbeth* and, if he did, whether he thought it better or worse that it represented the Scots not as ridiculous but as tragically incapable of nationhood.

Shakespeare's *Macbeth*, in sum, does not disprove this book's argument about the erasure, in Elizabethan literary, legal and chorographical texts, of Scotland's sovereign nationhood. It is rather a striking example of how tightly and invisibly the threads of a residual medieval ideology of Scottish vassalage are woven into the richly psychological dramatic fictions and subtly moralised national spaces that are English literature's legacy to the world. Nothing so obvious as the ubiquitous ridicule of Scotsmen alleged by Piggott is required: the erasure of Scottish nationhood is both more pervasive and less detectable, inseparable from what the world most values in the English literary and legal-constitutional achievement. Richard Helgerson was characteristically astute in identifying as collective 'forms of nationhood' the disparate legal, chorographical, geographical and historical writings of sixteenth-century Englishmen. Extending his vision to include Scotland, however, and seeing these writings not as national but as covertly and subtly *imperial* (i.e. 'forms of island empire' rather than 'forms of nationhood') can only increase our appreciation of their poetic power. To that extent, this book can be seen as taking up the challenge posed by Victoria Kahn's proposal that 'the radical, constructive implications of the humanists' rhetorical conception of literature have still not been fully digested'.[34] The humanists' rhetorical conception of literature was radically constructive in that it was committed to making rhetorically probable or believable the human motives, causes and circumstances that are the materials of vivid and powerful storytelling. This could produce new ways of imagining national belonging or of configuring the island space or, as in *Macbeth*, new and vivid ways of psychologising and pathologising the sub-national status to which Scotland was to be consigned.

It is finally worth stressing, then, at this moment in the history of English Literature as a discipline, that a critical revelation of the covertly imperial dimensions of Elizabethan poetry and drama does not detract from an emotional response to that poetry and drama's aesthetic and affective richness and complexity. To say this is to qualify or even contradict Rita Felski, for whom the demystifying critical revelation of covert rhetorical effects in literary texts is incompatible with an attentive openness to the text's imaginative and affective plurality. Felski argues that sceptical critique limits imaginative response and ultimately imprisons the text in

---

[34] Victoria Kahn, *The Trouble with Literature* (Oxford: Oxford University Press, 2020), 21.

the malodorous prison of historical context (or, as she puts it, citing Bruno Latour, 'context stinks!').[35] As I have shown, however, an appreciation of the truly radical and subversive possibilities of the Elizabethan literary text can reveal the extent to which what we think of as 'context' is itself an effect of humanist poetic world-making: for example, the way in which Spenser's *The Faerie Queene* has determined the future scope of its own 'real-life' referentiality.

Recognition of the ingenious ways in which English literary, chorographic and legal texts are, in this period, making covertly imperial claims over the whole island and its surrounding seas enriches our understanding of English literature, history and law. With respect to Scottish literature, dismantling the myth of English indifference to Scotland reveals the extent of the former's military and propagandistic intervention in the latter, both in the 1540s and in the crisis of Mary Stewart's deposition. This, in turn, permits a more nuanced understanding of the scope within which we are to understand Scottish literary expressions of religious and political affiliation or national consciousness. Finally, this book emphatically refutes the claim of Hugh Trevor-Roper that 'in Scotland, myth has played a far more important part in history than it has in England'.[36] On the contrary, this book has shown that a residual myth of Anglo-British island overlordship has been so subtly woven into English literary, legal and geographic consciousness that it remains conceptually dominant and determinative within British politics, culture and the academy to this day.

[35] Rita Felski, *The Limits of Critique* (Chicago: University of Chicago Press, 2015), 151–185, 152.
[36] Hugh Trevor-Roper, *The Invention of Scotland: Myth and History* (New Haven and London: Yale University Press, 2008), xx.

Works Cited

Manuscripts

Edinburgh, Edinburgh University Library Special Collections
MS De. 4. 22.

Cambridge
Pepys Library, Magdalen College, MS 2553.

Kew, The National Archives

State Papers Domestic, James I; SP 14/ 10 (A)
State Papers Scotland: Border Papers; SP 59/ 13
State Papers Scotland: Border Papers; SP 59/ 14
State Papers, Scotland Series, Elizabeth I; SP 52/ 62

London, British Library

MS Additional 6128
MS Additional 36294xr
MS Additional 59681
MS Additional 62540
MS Cotton Caligula B IV
MS Cotton Caligula B VII
MS Cotton Caligula B X
MS Cotton Caligula C I
MS Cotton Caligula C III
MS Cotton Vespasian D XVIII
MS Harley 849
MS Royal 18 D III

Oxford

Oxford, Bodleian Library, MS Don C 43
Oxford, Christ Church, MS Wb. 5. 12

Primary Printed Sources

XVIII Histoires Tragiques... par Pierre Boisteau... par Franc. de Belle Forest. Paris, 1570.

A Collection of State Papers, ed. Samuel Haynes. London, 1740.

A Declaration, conteyning the iust causes and consyderations of this present warre with the Scottis, wherin also appereth the trewe and right title, that the kinges most royall maiesty hath to the souerayntie of Scotland. London, 1542.

A Diurnall of Remarkable Occurents, that have passed within the country of Scotland, ed. T. Thompson. Edinburgh, 1833.

A Praier for Victorie and Peace. London, 1548.

Ariosto, Ludovico. *Orlando Furioso*, trans. Barbara Reynolds. 2 volumes. Harmondsworth: Penguin, 1975.

Anderson, Alan O. *Scottish Annals from the English Chroniclers, A. D. 500 to 1286.* London: David Nutt, 1908.

Bannatyne, Richard. *Memorials of Transactions in Scotland 1569–72*, ed. R. Pitcairn. Edinburgh, 1836.

Barret, Robert. *The Theorike and Practike of Moderne Warres.* London, 1598.

Beaugué, Jean de. *L'Histoire de la Guerre D'Escosse.* Paris, 1556.

Bede. *Ecclesiastical History*, trans. J. E. King. Cambridge, MA: Harvard University Press, 1930.

Bodrugan, Nicholas (alias Adams). *An Epitome of the title that the Kynges Maiestie of Englande hath to the sovereigntie of Scotlande.* London, 1548.

Boece, Hector. *Scotorum Historia* [1575] ed. and trans. Dana F. Sutton (2010), Liber XVI.59: https://philological.cal.bham.ac.uk/boece.
    The History and Chronicles of Scotland written in Latin by Hector Boece, Canon of Aberdeen and Translated by John Bellenden, Archdean of Moray and Canon of Ross, ed. Thomas Maitland. 2 volumes. Edinburgh: W. and C. Tait, 1821.

Bowyer, Robert. *The Parliamentary Diary of Robert Bowyer, 1606–7*, ed. David Harris Willson. New York, NY: Octagon, 1971.

Bower, Walter. *Scotichronicon*, ed. D. E. R. Watt. 9 volumes. Aberdeen: Aberdeen University Press, 1987–98.

Buchanan. George. *Ane Detectioun of the duinges of Marie Quene of Scottes, touchand the murder of hir husband, and hir conspiracie, adulterie, and pretensed mariage with the Erle Bothwell. And ane defence of the trew Lordis, mainteineris of the Kingis graces actioun and authoritie.* London, 1571.
    De Maria Scotorum Regina, totaque eius contra Regem coniuratione ... tragica plane Historia. London, 1571.

Rerum Scoticarum Historia. Edinburgh, 1582.

Georgii Buchanani Scoti, poetarum sui seculi facile principis, Opera Omnia, ed. P. Burman. 2 volumes. Leiden: Langerak, 1725.

The History of Scotland Translated from the Latin of George Buchanan, trans. and ed. James Aikman. 4 volumes. Glasgow: Blackie, Fullarton & Co., 1827.

Vernacular Writings of George Buchanan, ed. Peter Hume Brown. Edinburgh: W. Blackwood and sons for the Scottish Text Society, 1892.

George Buchanan: The Political Poetry, eds. Paul J. McGinnis and Arthur H. Williamson. Edinburgh: Scottish History Society, 1995.

A Dialogue on the Law of Kingship among the Scots: A Critical Edition and Translation of George Buchanan's De Iure Regni Apud Scotos Dialogus, eds. Roger A. Mason and Martin S. Smith. Aldershot: Ashgate, 2004.

Camden, William. *Britannia*. London, 1587.

Britain: Or, a Chorographicall Description of the most flourishing Kingdomes, England, Scotland, and Ireland, trans. Philemon Holland. London, 1610.

Gulielmi Camdeni. . . Epistolae. London, 1691.

'Poems by William Camden: With Notes and Translations from the Latin', ed. George Burke Johnston, *SP*, vol. 72, no. 5 (1975), iii–143.

Claudius Claudianus, T. Pulmanni diligentia & fide summa, è vetustis codicibus restitutus. Antwerp, Plantini, 1585.

Claudian. *Claudian*, trans. Maurice Platauer. Cambridge, MA: Harvard University Press, 1922.

Coleridge, Samuel Taylor. *Coleridge's Miscellaneous Criticism*, ed. Thomas Middleton Raynor. London: Constable, 1936.

Cope, Anthony. *The Historie of Two the moste noble Capitaines of the Worlde, Anniball and Scipio*. London: Berthelet, 1544.

Corona Borealis: Scottish Neo-Latin Poets on King James VI and His Reign, 1566–1603, eds. Steven J. Reid and David McOmish. Glasgow: The Association for Scottish Literary Studies, 2020.

Craig, Thomas. *Scotland's Sovereignty Asserted*, trans. and ed. George Ridpath. London, 1695.

De Unione Regnorum Britanniae Tractatus, trans. and ed. Charles Sanford Terry. Edinburgh: Scottish History Society, 1909.

de France, Marie. *Lais de Marie de France*, trans. and ed. Alexandre Micha. Paris: Flammarion, 1994.

de Merval, Louis. *L'entrée de Henri II Roi de France a Rouen au mois d'octobre 1550*. Rouen: Henry Boissel, 1868.

de Selve, Odet. *Correspondance Politique de Odet de Selve Ambassadeur de France en Angleterre (1546–1549)*, ed. Germain Lefèvre-Pontalis. Paris: Félix Alcan, 1888.

Dee, John. *General and Rare Memorials pertayning to the Pefect Arte of NAVIGATION*. London, 1577.

The Limits of the British Empire, eds. Ken MacMillan and Jennifer Abeles. Westport, CT: Praeger, 2004.

Delitiae Poetarum Scotorum. University of Glasgow Bridging the Continental Divide, 'Neo-Latin and Its Cultural Role in Jacobean Scotland, as Seen in the Delitiae Poetarum Scotorum (1637)': www.dps.gla.ac.uk.

Dolce, Lodovico. *Giocasta*. Venice, 1549.

Drama of the English Renaissance, eds. Russell A. Fraser and Norman Rabkin. 2 volumes. New York, NY: Macmillan, 1976.

Early English Classical Tragedies, ed. John W. Cunliffe. Oxford: Oxford University Press, 1912.

Elyot, Thomas. *The dictionary of syr Thomas Eliot*. London, 1538.

Bibliotheca Eliotae. London, 1545.

Euripides, *Phoenician Women*, trans. David Kovacs. Cambridge, MA: Harvard University Press, 2002.

Fordun, John. *John of Fordun's Chronicle of the Scottish Nation*, trans. Felix Skene, ed. William F. Skene. 2 volumes. Lampeter: Llanerch Publishers, 1993.

Froissart, John. *Chronicles of England, France, Spain, and the Adjoining Countries*, trans. Thomas Johnes. 2 volumes. London: George Routledge and sons, 1868.

Fulwell, Ulpian. *The Flower of Fame*. London, 1575.

Gascoigne, George. *A Hundreth Sundrie Flowres*, ed. G. W. Pigman. Oxford: Clarendon, 2000.

Hakluyt, Richard. *The Hakluyt Handbook*, ed. D. B. Quinn. 2 volumes. London: Hakluyt Society, 1974.

Hall, Edward. *Hall's Chronicle* [*The Union of the Two Noble and Illustre Famelies of Lancaster and Yorke*, 1548]. London: 1809; New York, NY: AMS Press, 1965.

Harriot, Thomas. *A briefe and true report of the new found land of Virginia*. London, 1590.

Harryson, James. *Exhortation to the Scotts to conforme themselves to the honourable expedient and godly union betwene the two realmes of England and Scotland*. London, 1547.

Herries, John Maxwell. *Historical Memoirs of the Reign of Mary Queen of Scots and a Portion of the Reign of King James the Sixth*, ed. R. Pitcairn. Edinburgh: Abbotsford Club, 1836.

Hughes, Thomas. *The Misfortunes of Arthur*, ed. Harvey Carson Grumbine. Berlin: Verlag von Emil Felber, 1900.

The Misfortunes of Arthur: A Critical, Old-Spelling Edition, ed. Brian Jay Corrigan. New York, NY: Garland Publishing, 1992.

Innes, Thomas. *A Critical Essay on the Ancient Inhabitants of the Northern Part of Britain or Scotland* [1729]. Edinburgh: William Patterson, 1885.

Justinian. *The Digest of Justinian*, trans. Alan Watson, eds. Theodor Mommsen and Paul Krueger. 4 volumes. Philadelphia, PA: University of Pennsylvania Press, 1985.

Keith, Robert. *History of the Affairs of Church and State in Scotland*. Edinburgh: Spottiswood, 1845.

L'entrée de Henri II à Rouen 1550, ed. Margaret McGowan. Amsterdam: Theatrum Obis Terrarum, 1973.

Lamb, William. *Ane Resonyng of ane Scottish and Inglis Merchand betuix Rowand and Lionis*, ed. Roderick J. Lyall. Aberdeen: Aberdeen University Press, 1985.

Lambarde, William. *A Perambulation of Kent*. London, 1576.

Leland, John. *Assertio inclytissimi Arurij Regis Britanniae*. London, 1544.

  Cygnea Cantio. London, 1545, trans. Dana Sutton: https://philological .cal.bham.ac.uk/swansong/.

  The laboryouse Journey & Serche of Johan Lelande, for Englandes Antiquitees, geuen of hym as a newe yeares gyfte to kynge henry the viii. in the .xxxvii. yeare of his Reygne, with declaracyons enlarged: by Johan Bale. London, 1549.

  A Learned and True Assertion of the original, Life, Actes, and death of… Prince Arthure, King of great Brittaine, trans. Robert Robinson. London, 1582.

Littleton, Thomas. *Littleton tenures in Englishe*. London, 1576.

Llwyd, Humphrey. *Commentaroli Britannicae Descriptionis Fragmentum*. London, 1572.

  The Breviary of Britain, trans. Thomas Twyne, ed. Philip Schwyzer. London: Modern Humanities Research Association, 2011.

Lyndsay, David. *Sir David Lyndsay: Selected Poems*, ed. Janet Hadley Williams. Glasgow: The Association for Scottish Literary Studies, 2000.

Lynam, Edward. *The Map of the British Isles of 1546*. Jenkintown, PA: George H. Beans Library, 1934.

Mair, John. *A History of Greater Britain as well England as Scotland*, trans. Archibald Constable. Edinburgh: Published at the University Press by T. and A. Constable for the Scottish History Society, 1892.

The Maitland Folio Manuscript, ed. W.A. Craigie. 2 volumes. Edinburgh: W. Blackwood and sons for the Scottish Text Society, 1919–27.

The Maitland Quarto: A New Edition of Cambridge, Magdalene College Pepys Library MS 1408, ed. Joanna M. Martin. Woodbridge: Boydell Press for the Scottish Text Society, 2015.

Maitland, James. *Maitland's Narrative of the Principal Acts of the Regency*, ed. W. S. Fitch. Ipswich, 1842.

Maitland, Richard. *The Practiques of Sir Richard Maitland of Lethington, 1550–1577*, ed. Robert Sutherland. Edinburgh: Scottish Record Society, 2007.

Marlowe, Christopher. *Edward the Second*, ed. Charles R. Forker. Manchester: Manchester University Press, 1988.

Monmouth, Geoffrey of. *The History of the Kings of Britain*, trans. Neil Wright, ed. Michael D. Reeve. Suffolk: Boydell Press, 2009.

Moore, Stewart A. *A History of the Foreshore and the Law Relating Thereto*. London: Stephens and Haynes, 1888.

Munro, Rona. *The James Plays*. London: Nick Hern Books, 2014.

Nicolay, Nicolas de. *La Navigation dv Roy D'Escosse Iaqves Cinqviesme*. Paris, 1583.

Ovid. *Metamorphoses*, trans. Frank Justus Miller, revised by G. P. Goold. Cambridge, MA: Harvard University Press, 1916.

Paget, William. *The Letters of William Lord Paget of Beaudesert 1547–1563*, eds. Barret L. Beer and Sybil M. Jack. Camden Miscellany, vol. XXV. London: Royal Historical Society, 1974.

Parmenius, Stephanus. *The New Found Land of Stephen Parmenius*, trans. David B. Quinn and Neil M. Chesire. Toronto: University of Toronto Press, 1972.

Paterson, William. *Proposals & Reasons for Constituting a Council of Trade*. Edinburgh, 1701.

Patten, William. *The Expedicion into Scotlande*. London, 1548.

Peele, George. *The Life and Works of George Peele*, ed. Charles Tyler Prouty. 3 volumes. New Haven: Yale University Press, 1952–70.

Polybius. *The Hystories of the Most Famous and Worthy Cronographer Polybius*, trans. Christopher Watson. London, 1568.

Quintillian. *Instituto Oratoria*, trans. and ed. Donald A. Russell. Cambridge, MA: Harvard University Press, 2001.

Satirical Poems of the Time of the Reformation, ed. James Cranstoun. 2 volumes. Edinburgh: W. Blackwood for the Scottish Text Society, 1891–93.

Scott, Walter. *Tales of a Grandfather*. London: Routledge, 1828.

Selden, John. *Of the Dominion, or Ownership of the Sea. Two Books*, trans. Marchamont Nedham. London, 1652.

Seneca. *Tragedies*, trans. John G. Fitch. 2 volumes. Cambridge, MA: Harvard University Press, 2002–04.

Seville, Isidore of. *The Etymologies of Isidore of Seville*, trans. Stephen A. Barney, W. J. Lewis, J. A. Beach, Oliver Berghof, ed. Muriel Hall. Cambridge: Cambridge University Press, 2006.

Seymour, Edward. *An Epistle or exhortacion, to unitie and peace, sent from the Lorde Protector... to the Nobilitie, Gentlemen, and Commons... of the Realme of Scotlande*. London, 1548.

Epistola Exhortatoria ad Pacem. London: Reginald Wolf, 1548.

Shakespeare, William. *Select Plays of Shakespeare*, eds. H. J. C. Grierson and J. C. Smith. Oxford: Clarendon Press, 1914.

Macbeth, ed. Kenneth Muir. The Arden Shakespeare, Second Series. London: Methuen, 1951.

King Henry V, ed. T.W. Craik. The Arden Shakespeare, Third Series. London: Routledge, 1995.

King Lear, ed. R.A. Foakes. The Arden Shakespeare, Third Series. London: Arden, 1997.

King Edward III, ed. Giorgio Melchiori. Cambridge: Cambridge University Press, 1998.

King Henry IV Part 1, ed. A. R. Humphreys. The Arden Shakespeare, Second Series, London: Methuen, 1960.

King Henry IV Part 1, ed. David Scott Kastan. The Arden Shakespeare, Third Series. London: Arden Shakespeare, 2002.

King Richard II, ed. Charles R. Forker. The Arden Shakespeare, Third Series. London: Arden Shakespeare, 2002.

Macbeth, eds. Sandra Clark and Pamela Mason. The Arden Shakespeare, Third Series. London: Arden Shakespeare, 2015.

Smith, Thomas. *A Discourse of the Commonweal of This Realm of England*, ed. Mary Dewar. Charlottesville, VA: University of Virginia Press, 1969.

Speed, John. *The Theatre of the Empire of Great Britaine.* London, 1627.

Spenser, Edmund. *The Faerie Queene*, ed. A. C. Hamilton. London: Longman, 1977.

Stones, E. L. G. *Anglo-Scottish Relations, 1174–1328: Some Selected Documents.* Oxford: Oxford University Press, revised edition, 1970.

Stones, E. L. G. and Grant Simpson. *Edward I and the Throne of Scotland, 1290–1296: An Edition of the Record Sources for the Great Cause.* 2 volumes. Oxford: Published for the University of Glasgow by the Oxford University Press, 1978.

Tacitus. *Agricola, Germania, Dialogus*, trans. M. Hutton and W. Peterson, revised R. M. Ogilvie, E. H. Warmington, Michael Winterbottom. Cambridge, MA: Harvard University Press, 1970.

The Acts of the Parliaments of Scotland, 1124–1707, eds. Thomas Thomson, Cosmo Innes and Archibald Anderson. 12 volumes. Edinburgh: Great Britain Record Commission, 1814–75.

The Bannatyne Miscellany: Containing Papers and Tracts, Chiefly Relating to the History and Literature of Scotland. 3 volumes. Edinburgh: Ballantyne and co., 1827–55.

The Complaynt of Scotlande, ed. James A. H. Murray. Early English Text Society. London: Printed for the Early English Text Society, 1872.

The Hereditary Right of the Crown of England Asserted, ed. G. Harbin. London, 1713.

The Jacobean Union: Six Tracts of 1604, eds. Bruce Galloway and Brian Levack. Edinburgh: Scottish History Society, 1985.

The Zurich Letters, ed. Hastings Robinson. 2 volumes. Cambridge: Parker Society, 1845.

Thucydides. *The Peloponnesian War: The Complete Hobbes Translation*, trans. Thomas Hobbes, ed. David Grene. Chicago, IL: University of Chicago Press, 1989.

Tudor Tracts 1532–1588, ed. A. F. Pollard. London: Constable, 1903.

Virgil. 2 vols., trans. H. R. Fairclough, revised G. P. Goold. Cambridge, MA: Harvard University Press, 2000.

The Warrender Papers, ed. Annie Cameron with intro. by Robert S. Rait. 2 volumes. Edinburgh: Scottish History Society, 1931–2.

Wedderburn, Robert. *The Complaynt of Scotland*, ed. A. M. Stewart. Edinburgh: W. Blackwood and sons for the Scottish Text Society, 1979.

Winwood, Ralph. *Memorials of Affairs of State.* 3 volumes. London: T. Ward, 1725.

Secondary Sources

Adelman, Janet. *Suffocating Mothers: Fantasies of Maternal Origin in Shakespeare's Plays, Hamlet to the Tempest.* London: Routledge, 1992.

Alford, Stephen. *The Early Elizabethan Polity: William Cecil and the British Succession Crisis, 1558–1569.* Cambridge: Cambridge University Press, 1998.

Allmand, Christopher. *Henry V.* Berkeley, CA: University of California Press, 1992.

Altman, Joel. *The Tudor Play of Mind: Rhetorical Inquiry and the Development of Elizabethan Drama*. Berkeley, CA: University of California Press, 1978.

'"Preposterous Conclusions": Eros, Enargeia, and the Composition of *Othello*', *Representations*, vol. 18 (1987), 129–57.

Anderson, Benedict. *Imagined Communities*. London: Verso, 1983.

Andrea, Bernadette. 'Black Skin, the Queen's Masques: Africanist Ambivalence and Feminine Author(ity) in the Masques of *Blackness* and *Beauty*', *ELR*, vol. 29, no. 2 (1999), 246–81.

Anglo, Sydney. 'The British History in Early Tudor Propaganda', *Bulletin of the John Rylands Library*, vol. 44, no. 1 (1961), 17–48.

Armitage, David. *The Ideological Origins of the British Empire*. Cambridge: Cambridge University Press, 2000.

Armstrong, William A. 'Elizabethan Themes in *The Misfortunes of Arthur*', *The Review of English Studies*, vol. 7, no. 27 (1956), 238–49.

Axton, Marie. 'The Influence of Edmund Plowden's Succession Treatise', *HLQ*, vol. 37, no. 3 (1974), 209–26.

The Queen's Two Bodies: Drama and the Elizabethan Succession. London: Royal Historical Society, 1977.

Baker, David J. '"Wildehirissheman": Colonialist Representation in Shakespeare's *Henry V*', *ELR*, vol. 22, no. 1 (1992), 37–61.

Between Nations: Shakespeare, Spenser, Marvell, and the Question of Britain. Stanford, CA: Stanford University Press, 1997.

Baker, David J. and Willy Maley, eds. *British Identities and English Renaissance Literature*. Cambridge: Cambridge University Press, 2002.

Baker, John H. *English Legal Manuscripts in the United States of America: A Descriptive List*. 2 volumes. London: Selden Society, 1985–90.

'Personal Liberty Under the Common Law of England', in *The Origins of Modern Freedom in the West*, ed. Richard W. Davis. Stanford, CA: Stanford University Press, 1995. 178–202.

The Reinvention of Magna Carta 1216–1616. Cambridge: Cambridge University Press, 2017.

Bakhtin, Mikhail. *Problems of Dostoevsky's Poetics*, trans. and ed. Caryl Emerson. Minneapolis, MN: University of Minnesota Press, 1984.

Baldo, Jonathan. 'Wars of Memory in *Henry V*', *SQ*, vol. 47, no. 2 (1996), 132–59.

'"A Rooted Sorrow": Scotland's Unusable Past', in *Macbeth: New Critical Essays*, ed. Nick Moschovakis. London: Routledge, 2008. 88–117.

Barber, Peter. 'The Minister Puts His Mind on the Map', *British Museum Society Bulletin*, vol. 43 (1983), 18–19.

Barringer, Judith M. *Divine Escorts: Nereids in Archaic and Classical Greek Art*. Ann Arbor, MI: University of Michigan Press, 1995.

Barthelemy, Anthony G. *Black Face, Maligned Race*. Baton Rouge, LA: Louisiana State University, 1987.

Bath, Michael. *Renaissance Decorative Painting in Scotland*. Edinburgh: National Museums of Scotland Publishing, 2003.

Bennett, Josephine Waters. *The Evolution of 'The Faerie Queene'*. Chicago, IL: University of Chicago Press, 1942.

Benton, Lauren. *A Search for Sovereignty: Law and Geography in European Empires, 1400–1900*. Cambridge: Cambridge University Press, 2010.

Berger, Jr., Harry. 'Two Spenserian Retrospects: The Antique Temple of Venus and the Primitive Marriage of Rivers', *Texas Studies in Literature and Language*, vol. 10, no. 1 (1968), 5–25.

Revisionary Play: Studies in the Spenserian Dynamics. Berkeley, CA: University of California Press, 1988.

Bolens, Guillemette. *The Style of Gestures: Embodiment and Cognition in Literary Narrative*. Baltimore, MD: Johns Hopkins University Press, 2012.

Booth, Stephen. 'On the Greatness of *King Lear*', in *Twentieth Century Interpretations of King Lear*, ed. Janet Adelman. Englewood Cliffs, NJ: Prentice-Hall, 1978. 98–111.

Borlik, Todd Andrew. 'Building a Wall Around Tudor England: Coastal Forts and Fantasies of Border Control in *Friar Bacon and Friar Bungay*', *Early Theatre*, vol. 22, no. 2 (2019), 67–88.

Boutcher, Warren. 'Polybius Speaks British: A Case-Study in Mid-Tudor British Humanism and Historiography', in *Tudor Translation*, ed. Fred Schurink. Basingstoke: Palgrave Macmillan, 2011. 101–20.

Bozio, Andrew. *Thinking Through Place on the Early Modern English Stage*. Oxford: Oxford University Press, 2020.

Brackmann, Rebecca. *The Elizabethan Invention of Anglo-Saxon England: Laurence Nowell, William Lambard and the Study of Old English*. Cambridge: D. S. Brewer, 2012.

Braden, Gordon. 'riverrun: An Epic Catalogue in *The Faerie Queene*', *ELR*, vol. 5, no. 1 (1975), 25–48.

Brooks, Christopher W. *Law, Politics and Society in Early Modern England*. Cambridge: Cambridge University Press, 2008.

Broun, Dauvit. *The Irish Identity of the Kingdom of the Scots in the Twelfth and Thirteenth Centuries*. Woodbridge: Boydell, 1999.

Scottish Independence and the Idea of Britain. Edinburgh: Edinburgh University Press, 2007.

Brown, Michael. *James I*. Edinburgh: Canongate, 1994.

Buisseret, David, ed. *Monarchs, Ministers and Maps: The Emergence of Cartography as a Tool of Government in Early Modern Europe*. Chicago, IL: University of Chicago Press, 1992.

Bullough, Geoffrey. *Narrative and Dramatic Sources of Shakespeare*. 8 volumes. London: Routledge and Kegan Paul, 1957–75.

Burlinson, Christopher. *Allegory, Space and the Material World in the Writings of Edmund Spenser*. Cambridge: D. S. Brewer, 2006.

Burrow, Colin. *Epic Romance: Homer to Milton*. Oxford: Clarendon Press, 1993.

'C. S. Lewis and *Allegory of Love*', *Essays in Criticism*, vol. 53, no. 3 (2003), 284–94.

Shakespeare and Classical Antiquity. Oxford: Oxford University Press, 2013.

Bushnell, Rebecca. *Tragedies of Tyrants: Political Thought and Theatre in the English Renaissance*. Ithaca, NY: Cornell University Press, 1990.

Butler, Martin. *The Stuart Court Masque and Political Culture*. Cambridge: Cambridge University Press, 2008.

Cairns, David and Shaun Richards, eds. *Writing Ireland: Colonialism, Nationalism and Culture*. Manchester: Manchester University Press, 1988.

Cameron, Alan. *Claudian: Poetry and Propaganda at the Court of Honorius*. Oxford: Clarendon Press, 1970.

Carley, James P. 'John Leland's *Cygnea Cantio*: A Neglected Tudor River Poem', *Humanistica Lovaniensia: Journal of Neo-Latin Studies*, vol. 32 (1983), 225–41.

'John Leland in Paris: The Evidence of His Poetry', *SP*, vol. 83, no. 1 (1986), 1–50.

'Arthur and the Antiquaries', in *The Development and Dissemination of Arthur in Medieval Latin*, ed. Siân Echard. Cardiff: University of Wales Press, 2011. 150–78.

Carr, Gillian. 'Woad, Tattooing and Identity in Later Iron Age and Early Roman Britain', *Oxford Journal of Archaeology*, vol. 24, no. 3 (2005), 273–92.

Cavell, Stanley. *Disowning Knowledge in Six Plays of Shakespeare*. Cambridge: Cambridge University Press, 1987.

Clark, T. J. 'Aboutness', *London Review of Books*, vol. 43, no. 1 (2021).

Collis, John. 'George Buchanan and the Celts in Britain', in *Celtic Connections: Proceedings of the Tenth International Congress of Celtic Studies, Volume I: Language, Literature, History, Culture*, ed. William Gillies, Ronald Black and Roibeard Ó Maolalaigh. East Linton: Tuckwell Press, 1999. 91–107.

Cormack, Lesley. *Charting an Empire: Geography at the English Universities, 1580–1620*. Chicago, IL: University of Chicago Press, 1997.

Coughlan, Patricia. '"Some secret scourge which shall by her come into England": Ireland and Incivility in Spenser', in *Spenser and Ireland: An Interdisciplinary Perspective*, ed. Patricia Coughlan. Cork: Cork University Press, 1989. 46–74.

Cowan, Edward J. and Richard J. Finlay. *Scottish History: The Power of the Past*. Edinburgh: Edinburgh University Press, 2002.

Cowan, I. B. 'The Marian Civil War, 1567-1573', in *Scotland at War: AD 79–1918*, ed. Norman Macdougall. Edinburgh: John Donald, 1991. 95–113.

Crawford, Robert. 'England's Scotland', in *Literature and Union: Scottish Texts, British Contexts*, eds. Gerrard Carruthers and Colin Kidd. Oxford: Oxford University Press, 2018. 331–48.

Cromartie, Alan. *The Constitutionalist Revolution*. Cambridge: Cambridge University Press, 2006.

Cuddy, Neil. 'Anglo-Scottish Union and the Court of James I', *Transactions of the Royal Historical Society*, vol. 39 (1989), 107–24.

Cummings, Brian. 'Metalepsis: The Boundaries of Metaphor', in *Renaissance Figures of Speech*, eds. Sylvia Adamson, Gavin Alexander and Katrin Ettenhuber. Cambridge: Cambridge University Press, 2007. 217–33.

Davies, R. R. *Domination and Conquest: The Experience of Ireland, Scotland and Wales 1100–1300*. Cambridge: Cambridge University Press, 1990.

The First English Empire: Power and Identity in the British Isles, 1093–1343. Oxford: Oxford University Press, 2002.

Davis, Alex. 'Revolution by Degrees: Philip Sidney and *Gradatio*', *Modern Philology*, vol. 108, no. 4 (2011), 488–506.

Davis, Harold. 'John Brende: Soldier and Translator', *HLQ*, vol. 1, no. 4 (1938), 421–6.

Dawson, Jane E. A. 'William Cecil and the British Dimension of Early Elizabethan Foreign Policy', *History*, vol. 74 (1989), 196–216.

de Grazia, Margreta. '*King Lear* in BC Albion', in *Medieval Shakespeare: Pasts and Presents*, eds. Ruth Morse, Helen Cooper and Peter Holland. Cambridge: Cambridge University Press, 2013. 138–56.

Dempsey, Scott. 'The Evolution of Edward I's Historical Claim to Overlordship of Scotland, 1291-1301', in *Fourteenth-Century England XI*, eds. David Green and Chris Given-Wilson. Woodbridge: Boydell and Brewer, 2019, 1–30.

Dewar, Mary. 'The Authorship of the "Discourse of Commonweal"', *Economic History Review*, 19, no. 2 (1966), 388–400.

Dewar-Watson, Sarah. '*Jocasta*: "A Tragedy Written in Greeke"', *International Journal of the Classical Tradition*, vol. 17, no. 1 (2010), 22–32.

Dollimore, Jonathan and Alan Sinfield. 'History and Ideology: The Instance of *Henry V*', in *Alternative Shakespeares*, ed. John Drakakis. London: Methuen, 1985. 206–27.

Donaldson, Gordon. *The First Trial of Mary Queen of Scots*. London: Batsford, 1969.

    All the Queen's Men: Power and Politics in Mary Stuart's England. London: Batsford Academic, 1983.

Doran, Susan and Paulina Kewes, eds. *Doubtful and Dangerous: The Question of Succession in Late Elizabethan England*. Manchester: Manchester University Press, 2014.

Duffy, Eamon. *The Stripping of the Altars: Traditional Religion in England*. New Haven, CT: Yale University Press, 1992.

Eden, Kathy. *Poetic and Legal Fiction in the Aristotelian Tradition*. Princeton, NJ: Princeton University Press, 1986.

Empson, William. *Seven Types of Ambiguity*. London: Chatto and Windus, 1930.

    Essays on Shakespeare, ed. David M. Pirie. Cambridge: Cambridge University Press, 1986.

Fahnestock, Jeanne. *Rhetorical Figures in Science*. Oxford: Oxford University Press, 1999.

Fantham, Elaine. 'Nihil Iam Iura Naturae Valent: Incest and Fratricide in Seneca's *Phoenissae*', *Ramus*, vol. 12, nos. 1–2 (1983), 61–76.

Farnsworth, Jane. 'Voicing Female Desire in "Poem XLIX"', *Studies in English Literature*, vol. 36, no. 1 (1996), 57–72.

Felski, Rita. *The Limits of Critique*. Chicago: University of Chicago Press, 2015.

Ferguson, William. 'George Buchanan and the Picts', *Scottish Tradition*, vol. 16 (1990/91), 18–32.

The Identity of the Scottish Nation: An Historic Quest. Edinburgh: Edinburgh University Press, 1998.

Flahiff, F. T. 'Lear's Map', *Cahiers Elisabéthains*, vol. 30 (1986), 17–33.

Fleming, Juliet. *Graffiti and the Writing Arts in Early Modern England.* London: Reaktion, 2001.

Flower, Robin. 'Laurence Nowell and the Discovery of England in Tudor Times', *Proceedings of the British Academy*, vol. 21 (1935), 45–73.

Floyd-Wilson, Mary. *English Ethnicity and Race in Early Modern Drama.* Cambridge: Cambridge University Press, 2003.

Foley, Helene P. *Ritual Irony: Poetry and Sacrifice in Euripides.* Ithaca, NY: Cornell University Press, 1985.

Fulton, Thomas Wemyss. *The Sovereignty of the Sea: An Historical Account of the Claims of England to the Dominion of the British Seas.* Edinburgh and London: William Blackwood, 1911.

Galloway, Bruce. *The Union of England and Scotland, 1603–1608.* Edinburgh: John Donald, 1986.

Garnett, George. '"The ould fields": Law and History in the Prefaces to Sir Edward Coke's Reports', *The Journal of Legal History*, vol. 34, no. 3 (2013), 245–84.

Gillies, John. *Shakespeare and the Geography of Difference.* Cambridge: Cambridge University Press, 1994.

'The Scene of Cartography in *King Lear*', in *Literature, Mapping and the Politics of Space in Early Modern Britain*, eds. Andrew Gordon and Bernhard Klein. Cambridge: Cambridge University Press, 2001. 109–37.

Gillies, John and Virginia Mason Vaughn, eds. *Playing the Globe: Genre and Geography in English Renaissance Drama.* Madison, NJ: Farleigh Dickinson University Press, 1998.

Gillingham, John. 'The Context and Purposes of Geoffrey of Monmouth's *History of the Kings of Britain*', *Anglo-Norman Studies*, vol. 13 (1990), 99–118.

Given-Wilson, Chris. *Henry IV.* New Haven, CT: Yale University Press, 2016.

Goldberg, Jonathan. *James I and the Politics of Literature.* Stanford, CA: Stanford University Press, 1989.

Goldstein, R. James. *The Matter of Scotland: Historical Narrative in Medieval Scotland.* Lincoln, NE: University of Nebraska Press, 1993.

Greenberg, Janelle. *The Radical Face of the English Constitution: St Edward's 'Laws' in Early Modern Political Thought.* Cambridge: Cambridge University Press, 2001.

Greenblatt, Stephen. *Shakespearean Negotiations: The Circulation of Social Energy in Renaissance England.* Berkley, CA: University of California Press, 1988.

Greenlaw, Edwin. *Studies in Spenser's Historical Allegory.* Baltimore, MD: Johns Hopkins University Press, 1932.

Greg, W. W. 'Time, Place and Politics in *King Lear*', *The Modern Language Review*, vol. 35, no. 4 (1940), 431–46.

Griffiths, Huw. 'Passports and the Locations of Sovereignty in *The Reign of Edward III*', *English Studies*, vol. 96, no. 7 (2015), 747–71.

Gunn, Steven. *Charles Brandon, Duke of Suffolk, c. 1484–1545*. Oxford: Blackwell, 1988.

Habib, Imitaz. *Black Lives in the English Archives 1500–1677*. Aldershot: Ashgate, 2008.

Hackett, Helen. *Virgin Mother, Maiden Queen: Elizabeth I and the Cult of the Virgin Mary*. Basingstoke: Macmillan, 1995.

Hadfield, Andrew. 'Briton and Scythian: Tudor Representations of Irish Origins', *Irish Historical Studies*, vol. 28 (1993), 390–408.

Literature, Politics and National Identity: Reformation to Renaissance. Cambridge: Cambridge University Press, 1994.

Edmund Spenser's Irish Experience: Wilde Fruit and Salvage Soyle. Oxford: Clarendon Press, 1997.

'Bruited Abroad: John White and Thomas Harriot's Colonial Representations of Ancient Britain', in *British Identities*, ed. Baker and Maley (2002), 159–77.

'Macbeth, IV.iii.140-158, Edward the Confessor and Holinshed's *Chronicles*', *Notes and Queries* (2002) vol. 49, no. 2, 234–6.

Shakespeare, Spenser and the Matter of Britain. Basingstoke: Palgrave Macmillan, 2004.

Hadley Williams, Janet. 'The Earliest Surviving Text of Lyndsay's *Tragedie of the Cardinall*: An English Edition of a Scottish Poem', in *Literature, Letters and the Canonical in Early Modern Scotland*, eds. Theo van Heijnsbergen and Nicola Royan. East Linton: Tuckwell Press, 2002. 22–34.

Hall, Kim F. *Things of Darkness*. Ithaca, NY: Cornell University Press, 1995.

Hanna, Elizabeth. 'A "Scottish Monmouth"? Hector Boece's Arthurian Revisions', in *The Impact of Latin Culture on Medieval and Early Modern Scottish Writing*, eds. Alessandra Petrina and Ian R. Johnson. Kalamazoo, MI: Medieval Institute Publications. 105–26.

Hawkes, Terence. 'The Fool's "Prophecy" in *King Lear*', *Notes and Queries*, vol. 7, no. 9 (1960), 331–2.

'Lear's Maps: A General Survey', *Deutsche Shakespeare-Gesellschaft West Jahrbuch* (1989), 134–47.

Meaning by Shakespeare. London: Routledge, 1992.

Hazlitt, William. *Characters of Shakespeare's Plays*, ed. J. H. Lobban. Cambridge: Cambridge University Press, 2009.

Helgerson, Richard. *The Elizabethan Prodigals*. Berkeley: University of California Press, 1976.

Forms of Nationhood: The Elizabethan Writing of England. Chicago, IL: University of Chicago Press, 1992.

Heng, Geraldine. *The Invention of Race in the European Middle Ages*. Cambridge: Cambridge University Press, 2018.

Herendeen, Wyman H. *From Landscape to Literature: The River and the Myth of Geography*. Pittsburgh, PA: Dusquene University Press, 1986.

Hiatt, Alfred. *The Making of Medieval Forgeries: False Documents in Fifteenth-Century England*. London: British Library, 2004.

Hile, Rachel E. 'The Limits of Concord in the Thames–Medway Marriage Canto of *The Faerie Queene*', *SP*, vol. 108, no. 1 (2011), 70–85.

Hoak, Dale. *The King's Council in the Reign of Edward VI*. Cambridge: Cambridge University Press, 1976.

    'Sir William Cecil, Sir Thomas Smith and the Monarchical Republic of Tudor England', in *The Monarchical Republic of Tudor England*, ed. John F. McDiarmid. Aldershot: Ashgate, 2007. 37–54.

Hoekstra, Kinch. 'Thucydides and the Bellicose Beginnings of Modern Political Theory', in *Thucydides and the Modern World: Reception, Reinterpretation and Influence from the Renaissance to the Present*, eds. Katherine Harloe and Neville Morley. Cambridge: Cambridge University Press, 2012. 25–54.

Hogg, Ulrike and Martin MacGregor. 'Historiography in the Highlands and Lowlands', in *The International Companion to Scottish Literature, 1400–1650*, ed. Nicola Royan. Glasgow: Scottish Literature International, 2018. 100–23.

Holderness, Graham. 'Agincourt 1944: Readings in the Shakespeare Myth', *Literature and History*, vol. 10, no. 1 (1984), 24–45.

Holland, Peter. 'Mapping Shakespeare's Britain', in *Shakespeare's Histories and Counter-Histories*, eds. Dermot Cavanagh, Stuart Hampton-Reeves and Stephen Longstaffe. Manchester: Manchester University Press, 2006. 198–218.

Holland, Tom. 'How Alex Salmond's Alba Party Reveals England's and Scotland's Shared Ideals', *New Statesman*, 3 May 2021.

Hulsebosch, Daniel J. 'Ancient Constitution and Expanding Empire: Sir Edward Coke's British Jurisprudence', *Law and History Review*, vol. 21, no. 3 (2003), 439–82.

Hulton, Paul. *America 1585: The Complete Drawings of John White*. Chapel Hill, NC: University of North Carolina Press, 1984.

Hutson, Lorna. 'Fortunate Travelers: Reading for the Plot in Sixteenth-Century England', *Representations*, no. 41 (1993), 83–103.

    The Invention of Suspicion: Law and Mimesis in Shakespeare and Renaissance Drama. Oxford: Oxford University Press, 2007.

    Circumstantial Shakespeare. Oxford: Oxford University Press, 2015.

    ed., *The Oxford Handbook of English Law and Literature, 1500–1700*. Oxford: Oxford University Press, 2017.

    'On the Knees of the Body Politic', *Representations*, vol. 152, no. 1 (2020), 25–54.

Ioppolo, Grace. '"A Jointure More or Less": Re-Measuring *The True Chronicle Historie of King Leir and His Three Daughters*', *Medieval and Renaissance Drama in England*, vol. 17 (2005), 165–79.

Iyengar, Sujata. *Shades of Difference: Mythologies of Skin Color in Early Modern England*. Philadelphia, PA: University of Pennsylvania Press, 2005.

Jones, Emrys. *Scenic Form in Shakespeare*. Oxford: Clarendon Press, 1971.

Kahn, Victoria. *The Trouble with Literature*. Oxford: Oxford University Press, 2020.

Kantorowicz, Ernst H. *The King's Two Bodies: A Study in Medieval Political Theology*. Princeton, NJ: Princeton University Press, 1957.

Keith, Theodora. *Commercial Relations of England and Scotland, 1603–1707*. Cambridge: Cambridge University Press, 1910.

Kendrick, T. D. *British Antiquity*. London: Methuen and Co., 1950.

Kerrigan, John. *Archipelagic English: Literature, History and Politics, 1603–1707*. Oxford: Oxford University Press, 2008.

Shakespeare's Originality. Oxford: Oxford University Press, 2018.

Kewes, Paulina, Ian W. Archer and Felicity Heal, eds. *The Oxford Handbook of Holinshed's Chronicles*. Oxford: Oxford University Press, 2013.

Kidd, Colin. *Subverting Scotland's Past*. Cambridge: Cambridge University Press, 1993.

Kim, Jaecheol. 'The North-South Divide in *Gorboduc*: Fratricide Remembered and Forgotten', *SP*, vol. III, no. 4 (2014), 691–719.

Kim, Keechang. *Aliens in Medieval Law: The Origins of Modern Citizenship*. Cambridge: Cambridge University Press, 2000.

Klein, Bernhard. *Maps and the Writing of Space in Early Modern England and Ireland*. Basingstoke: Macmillan, 2001.

Knafla, Louis A. *Law and Politics in Jacobean England*. Cambridge: Cambridge University Press, 1977.

Knowles, Richard. 'Cordelia's Return', *SQ*, vol. 50, no. 1 (1999), 33–50.

Kott, Jan. *Shakespeare Our Contemporary*, trans. Boleslaw Taborski. Garden City, NY: Doubleday, 1966.

Le Goff, Jacques. *Time, Work and Culture in the Middle Ages*, trans. Arthur Goldhammer. Chicago, IL: University of Chicago Press, 1980.

Lee, Jr., Maurice. *John Maitland of Thirlestane and the Foundation of the Stuart Despotism in Scotland*. Princeton, NJ: Princeton University Press, 1959.

Lefebvre, Henri. *The Production of Space*, trans. Donald Nicholson-Smith. Oxford: Blackwell, 1991.

Levine, Mortimer. *The Early Elizabethan Succession Question, 1558–1568*. Stanford, CA: Stanford University Press, 1966.

Levy, F. R. 'The Making of Camden's *Britannia*', *Bibliothèque d'Humanisme et Renaissance*, vol. 26, no. 1 (1964), 70–97.

Tudor Historical Thought. San Marino, CA: Huntington Library, 1967.

Lewis, C. S. *English Literature in the Sixteenth Century, Excluding Drama*. Oxford: Oxford University Press, 1954.

Lidster, Amy. 'Challenging Monarchical Legacies in *Edward III* and *Henry V*', *English*, vol. 68, no. 2 (2019), 126–42.

Loomba, Ania and Jonathan Burton. 'Introduction', in *Race in Early Modern England: A Documentary Companion*. Basingstoke: Palgrave, 2007. 1–36.

Loughlin, Mark. 'The Career of Maitland of Lethington, c. 1526–1573'. Unpublished PhD thesis, University of Edinburgh, 1991.

'"The Dialogue of the Twa Wyfeis": Maitland, Machiavelli and the Propaganda of the Scottish Civil War', in *The Renaissance in Scotland: Studies in Literature,*

Religion, History, and Culture Offered to John Durkan, eds. A. A. MacDonald, Michael Lynch and Ian B. Cowan. Leiden: E. J. Brill, 1994. 226–45.

Lucas, Scott C. *A Mirror for Magistrates and the Politics of the English Reformation*. Amherst, MA: University of Massachusetts Press, 2009.

Lynch, Michael. 'Queen Mary's Triumph: The Baptismal Celebrations at Stirling in December 1566', *SHR*, vol. 69, no. 187 (1990), 1–21.

Lythe, S. G. *The Economy of Scotland in Its European Setting 1550–1625*. London: Oliver and Boyd, 1960.

MacColl, Alan. 'The Construction of England as a Protestant "British" Nation in the Sixteenth Century', *Renaissance Studies*, vol. 18, no. 4 (2004), 582–608.

Mack, Peter. *Elizabethan Rhetoric: Theory and Practice*. Cambridge: Cambridge University Press, 2002.

MacQueen, Jack. 'From Rome to Ruddiman: The Scoto-Latin Tradition', in *The Edinburgh History of Scottish Literature, Vol. I: From Columba to the Union*, eds. Thomas Owen Clancy and Murray Pittock. Edinburgh: Edinburgh University Press, 2007. 184–208.

Major, John Russell. 'Bastard Feudalism and the Kiss: Changing Social Mores in Late Medieval and Early Modern France', *The Journal of Interdisciplinary History*, vol. 17, no. 3 (1987), 509–35.

Maley, Willy. '"This Sceptred Isle": Shakespeare and the British Problem', in *Shakespeare and National Culture*, ed. John Joughin. Manchester: Manchester University Press, 1997. 83–108.

Salvaging Spenser: Colonialism, Culture and Identity. Basingstoke: Macmillan, 1997.

Maley, Willy and Andrew Murphy, eds. *Shakespeare and Scotland*. Manchester: Manchester University Press, 2004.

Mapstone, Sally, ed. *William Dunbar, 'The Nobill Poyet': Essays in Honour of Priscilla Bawcutt*. East Linton: Tuckwell Press, 2001.

Mapstone, Sally and Juliette Wood, eds. *The Rose and the Thistle: Essays on the Culture of Late Medieval and Renaissance Scotland*. East Linton: Tuckwell Press, 1998.

Martin, Ian C. 'The Manuscript and Editorial Tradition of William Thomas's *The Pilgrim* or *Il Pellegrino Inglese*'. Unpublished PhD thesis, University of Toronto, 1999.

Martin, Joanna. 'The Border, England and the English in Some Older Scots Lyric and Occasional Poems', in *The Anglo-Scottish Border and the Shaping of Identity, 1300–1600*, eds. Mark P. Bruce and Katherine Terrell. New York, NY: Palgrave Macmillan, 2010. 87–102.

'The Maitland Quarto Manuscript and the Literary Culture of the Reign of James VI', in *James VI and I, Literature and Scotland: Tides of Change, 1567–1625*, ed. David J. Parkinson. Leuven: Peeters, 2013. 65–81.

Martiz, Jessie and J. A. Maritz. 'The Classical Image of Africa: The Evidence from Claudian', *Acta Classica*, vol. 43 (2000), 81–99.

Mason, Roger A., ed. *Scotland and England, 1286–1815*. Edinburgh: John Donald, 1986.

Mason, Roger A. *Kingship and the Commonweal: Political Thought in Renaissance and Reformation Scotland*. East Linton: Tuckwell Press, 1998.

'Scotland, Elizabethan England and the Idea of Britain', *Transactions of the Royal Historical Society*, vol. 14 (2004), 279–93.

'From Buchanan to Blaeu: The Politics of Scottish Chorography, 1582-1654', in *George Buchanan: Political Thought in Early Modern Britain and Europe*, eds. Caroline Erskine and Roger A. Mason. Farnham: Ashgate, 2012. 13–47.

'1603: Multiple Monarchy and Scottish Succession', *History*, vol. 105 (2020), 402–21.

'Dame Scotia and the Commonweal: Vernacular Humanism in *The Complaynt of Scotland* (1550)', *The Mediaeval Journal*, vol. 10, no. 1 (2020), 129–50.

Mattox, John Mark. '*Henry V*: Shakespeare's Just Warrior', *War, Literature and the Arts*, vol. 12, no. 1 (2000), 30–53.

McCabe, Richard. 'The Masks of Duessa: Mary Queen of Scots and James VI', *ELR*, vol. 17, no. 2 (1987), 224–42.

The Pillars of Eternity: Time and Providence in The Faerie Queene. Dublin: Irish Academic Press, 1989.

Spenser's Monstrous Regiment: Elizabethan Ireland and the Poetics of Difference. Oxford: Oxford University Press, 2002.

McEachern, Claire. *The Poetics of English Nationhood: 1590–1612*. Cambridge: Cambridge University Press, 1996.

McElroy, Tricia A. 'Executing Mary Queen of Scots: Strategies of Representation in Early Modern Scotland'. Unpublished DPhil thesis, University of Oxford, 2004.

'Imagining the "Scottis Natioun": Populism and Propaganda in Scottish Satirical Broadsides', *Texas Studies in Literature and Language*, vol. 49, no. 4 (2007), 319–39.

'A "Quarrell sett out in metre": Towards a New Edition of Scottish Reformation Satirical Literature', *Studies in Scottish Literature*, vol. 39, no. 1 (2013), 22–30.

'The Uses of Genre and Gender in "The Dialogue of the Twa Wyfeis"', in *Premodern Scotland: Literature and Governance 1420–1587*, eds. Joanna Martin and Emily Wingfield. Oxford: Oxford University Press, 2017. 199–210

McInerney, Jeremy. 'Nereids, Colonies and the Origins of *Isegoria*', in *Free Speech in Classical Antiquity*, eds. Ineke Sluiter and Ralph Rosen. Leiden: Brill, 2004. 21–40.

McKechnie, William S. 'Thomas Maitland', *SHR*, vol. 4, no. 15 (1907), 274–93.

McLaren, Anne. 'Gender, Religion and Early Modern Nationalism: Elizabeth I, Mary Queen of Scots and the Genesis of English Anti-Catholicism', *The American Historical Review*, vol. 107, no. 3 (2002), 739–67.

McMahon, Jonathan. 'The Humanism of Sir Thomas Smith'. Unpublished MA thesis, College of William and Mary, 1999.

McMullan, Gordon. 'The Colonization of Early Britain on the Jacobean Stage', in *Reading the Medieval in Early Modern England*, eds. Gordon McMullan and David Matthews. Cambridge: Cambridge University Press, 2007. 119–42.

McPherson, David. 'Ben Jonson's Library and Marginalia', *SP*, vol. 71, no. 5 (1974), 1–106.

McRae, Andrew. 'Fluvial Nation: Rivers, Mobility and Poetry in Early Modern England', *ELR*, vol. 38, no. 3 (2008), 506–34.

Mentz, Steve. 'Strange Weather in *King Lear*', *Shakespeare*, vol. 6, no. 2 (2010), 139–52.

Meron, Theodor. *Henry's Wars and Shakespeare's Laws*. Oxford: Clarendon, 1993.

Merriman, Marcus. 'The Platte of Castlemilk, 1547', *Transactions of the Dumfriesshire and Galloway Natural History and Antiquarian Society*, vol. 44 (1967), 175–81.

'The Assured Scots: Scottish Collaborators with England during the Rough Wooings', *SHR*, vol. 47, no. 143 (1968), 10–34.

The Rough Wooings: Mary Queen of Scots 1542–1551. East Linton: Tuckwell Press, 2000.

Mill, Anna Jean. *Medieval Plays in Scotland*. Edinburgh, Blackwood, 1927.

Millican, Charles Bowie. *Spenser and the Table Round: A Study in the Contemporaneous Background for Spenser's Use of the Arthurian Legend*. Cambridge, MA: Harvard University Press, 1932.

Moir, D. G. *The Early Maps of Scotland to 1850*. Edinburgh: Royal Scottish Geographical Society, 1973.

Montrose, Louis. 'The Elizabethan Subject and the Spenserian Text', in *Literary Theory/ Renaissance Texts*, eds. Patricia Parker and David Quint. Baltimore, MD: Johns Hopkins University Press, 1986. 303–430.

The Subject of Elizabeth: Authority, Gender, and Representation. Chicago, IL: University of Chicago Press, 2006.

Morrison, Toni. *Playing in the Dark*. New York, NY: Random House, Vintage Books, 1992.

Moshenska, Joe. *Iconoclasm as Child's Play*. Stanford, CA: Stanford University Press, 2019.

Moul, Victoria. 'England's Stilicho: Claudian's Political Poetry in Early Modern England', *International Journal of the Classical Tradition*, vol. 28, no. 1 (2021), 23–50: https://link.springer.com/article/10.1007/s12138-019-00529-z.

Mullaney, Steven. *The Place of the Stage: License, Play and Power in Renaissance England*. Chicago, IL: University of Chicago Press, 1988.

Murphy, Andrew. '"Tish ill done": *Henry the Fift* and the Politics of Editing', in *Shakespeare and Ireland: History, Politics, Culture*, eds. Mark Thornton Burnett and Ramona Wray. Basingstoke: Macmillan, 1997. 213–29.

But the Irish Sea Betwixt Us: Ireland, Colonialism, and Renaissance Literature. Lexington, KY: University Press of Kentucky, 1999.

Neely, Carol Thomas. '*King Lear* and Incest, 1969–2016: *In Media Res*', *Borrowers and Lenders*, vol. 13, no. 1 (2020), 1–22.

Newlyn, Evelyn S. 'A Methodology for Reading Against the Culture: Anonymous, Women Poets and the Maitland Quarto Manuscript (c.1586)', in *Women and the Feminine in Medieval and Early Modern Scottish Writing*, eds. Sarah

M. Dunnigan, C. Marie Harker and Evelyn S. Newlyn. Basingstoke: Palgrave, 2004. 89–103.

Nicholson, Ranald. *Scotland: The Later Middle Ages*. Edinburgh: Mercat Press, 1974.

Onians, R. B. *The Origins of European Thought*. Cambridge: Cambridge University Press, 1951.

Orgel, Stephen. *The Illusion of Power*. Berkeley, CA: University of California Press, 1975.

Orr, David G. 'Roman Domestic Religion: The Evidence of Household Shrines', in *Aufstieg und Niedergang der römischen Welt*, ed. Wolfgang Haase. Berlin: De Gruyter, 1978. 1559–91.

Oruch, Jack B. 'Spenser, Camden, and the Poetic Marriage of Rivers', *SP*, vol. 64, no. 4 (1967), 606–24.

Osgood, Charles. *Spenser's English Rivers*. New Haven, CT: Connecticut Academy of Arts and Sciences, 1920.

Palfrey, Simon. *Poor Tom: Living 'King Lear'*. Chicago, IL: University of Chicago Press, 2015.

Parker, Patricia. 'The Metaphorical Plot', in *Literary Fat Ladies: Rhetoric, Gender, Property*, ed. Patricia Parker. London: Methuen, 1987. 36–53.

Parminter, Geoffrey de. C. 'Edmund Plowden as Advocate for Mary Queen of Scots: Some Remarks Upon Certain Elizabethan Succession Tracts', *Innes Review*, vol. 30 (1979), 35–53.

Parry, Glyn. 'William Harrison and Holinshed's *Chronicles*', *HJ*, vol. 27, no. 4 (1984), 789–810.

'John Dee and the Elizabethan British Empire in Its European Context', *HJ*, vol. 49, no. 3 (2006), 643–75.

Patterson, Annabel. *Shakespeare and the Popular Voice*. Oxford: Blackwell, 1989.

Pearlman, E. '*Edward III* in *Henry V*', in *Criticism*, vol. 37, no. 4 (1995), 519–36.

Perry, Curtis. 'British Empire on the Eve of the Armada: Revisiting *The Misfortunes of Arthur*', *SP*, vol. 108, no. 4 (2011), 508–37.

Shakespeare and Senecan Tragedy. Cambridge: Cambridge University Press, 2021.

Peyré, Yves. 'Eclecticism and Syncretism in Gascoigne and Kinwelmarsh's *Jocasta*', *Translation and Literature*, vol. 29 (2020), 45–58.

Phillips, Gervase. *The Anglo-Scots Wars, 1513–1550*. Woodbridge: Boydell, 1999.

Phillips, James Emerson. *Images of a Queen: Mary Stuart in Sixteenth-Century Literature*. Berkeley, CA: University of California Press, 1964.

Philo, John-Mark. *An Ocean Untouched and Untried: The Tudor Translations of Livy*. Oxford: Oxford University Press, 2020.

Pincombe, Mike. 'Dream and Mystery in Sir Thomas Wyatt's "Tagus Farewell"', *Studia Neophilologica*, vol. 87, no. 1 (2015), 36–47.

Pocock, J. G. A. 'British History: A Plea for a New Subject', *The Journal of Modern History*, vol. 47, no. 4 (1975) 601–21.

The Ancient Constitution and the Feudal Law: A Study of English Historical Thought in the Seventeenth Century. Cambridge: Cambridge University Press, 1987.

Pollock, F. and F. W. Maitland. *The History of English Law Before the Time of Edward I*. [1898]. Indianapolis, IN: Liberty Fund, 2010.

Pollitt, Ronald. 'The Defeat of the Northern Rebellion and the Shaping of Anglo-Scottish Relations', *SHR*, vol. 64 (1985), 1–21.

Prestwich, Michael. *Edward I*. New Haven, CT: Yale University Press, 1997.

Prior, Roger. 'Was *The Raigne of King Edward III* a Compliment to Lord Hunsdon?', *Connotations*, vol. 3, no. 3 (1993–4), 243–64.

Quint, David. '"Alexander the Pig": Shakespeare on History and Poetry', *Boundary 2*, vol. 10, no. 3 (1982), 49–67.

Rabkin, Norman. 'Rabbits, Ducks and Henry V', *SQ*, vol. 28, no. 3 (1977), 279–96.

Rancière, Jacques. *The Politics of Aesthetics*, trans. Gabriel Rockhill. London: Bloomsbury, 2004.

Reichberg, Gregory M., Henrik Syse and Endre Begby, eds. *The Ethics of War: Classic and Contemporary Readings*. Oxford: Blackwell, 2006.

Reid, Steven J. 'Classical Reception and Erotic Latin Poetry in Sixteenth-Century Scotland: The Case of Thomas Maitland (ca.1548–1572)', in *The Impact of Latin Culture on Medieval and Early Modern Scottish Writing*, eds. Alessandra Petrina and Ian Johnson. Kalzamazoo, MI: Medieval Institute Publications, 2018. 3–39.

'A Disciple of Buchanan in the Marian Civil War: Thomas Maitland's "The Consecration of James VI, King of Scots" (Jacobi VI, Scotorum Regis Inauguratio)', in Steven J. Reid (ed.), *Re-thinking the Renaissance and Reformation in Scotland: Essays in Honour of Roger A. Mason* (Boydell: St Andrews Studies in Scottish History, 2023).

Reynolds, Susan. *Fiefs and Vassals: The Medieval Evidence Reinterpreted*. Oxford: Oxford University Press, 1994.

'Fiefs and Vassals in Scotland: A View from Outside', *SHR*, vol. 82 (2003), 176–93.

Rhys, Gusto. 'Approaching the Pictish Language: Historiography, Early Evidence and the Question of Pritenic'. Unpublished PhD thesis, University of Glasgow, 2015.

Ribner, Irving. *The English History Play in the Age of Shakespeare*. London: Routledge, 2005.

Roche, Thomas P. *The Kindly Flame: A Study of the Third and Fourth Books of Spenser's Faerie Queene*. Princeton, NJ: Princeton University Press, 1964.

Rockett, William. 'The Structural Plan of Camden's *Britannia*', *Sixteenth Century Journal*, vol. 26, no. 4 (1995), 829–41.

Royan, Nicola. 'Hector Boece and the Question of Veremund', *Innes Review*, vol. 52, no. 1 (2001), 42–62.

Russell, Conrad. *King James VI/ I and His English Parliaments*, eds. Richard Cust and Andrew Thrush. Oxford: Oxford University Press, 2011.

Ryrie, Alec. *The Origins of the Scottish Reformation*. Manchester: Manchester University Press, 2006.

Sanderson, Margaret H. B. *A Kindly Place? Living in Sixteenth-Century Scotland.* East Linton: Tuckwell Press, 2002.

Schwyzer, Philip. *Literature, Nationalism and Memory in Early Modern England and Wales.* Cambridge: Cambridge University Press, 2004.

'The Jacobean Union Controversy and *King Lear*', in *The Accession of James I: Historical and Cultural Consequences*, eds. Glenn Burgess, Rowland Wymer and Jason Lawrence. New York, NY: Palgrave Macmillan, 2006. 34–44.

Schwyzer, Philip, and David Mealor, eds., *Archipelagic Identities: Literature and History in the Atlantic Archipelago.* Aldershot: Ashgate, 2004.

Scribner, Robert. *Popular Culture and Popular Movements in Reformation Germany.* London: Hambledon, 1987.

Sherman, William H. *John Dee: The Politics of Reading and Writing in the English Renaissance.* Amherst, MA: University Massachusetts Press, 1995.

'Putting British Seas on the Map: John Dee's Imperial Cartography', *Cartographica*, vol. 35, nos. 3–4 (1998), 1–10.

Shrank, Cathy. *Writing the Nation in Reformation England: 1530–1580.* Oxford: Oxford University Press, 2004.

'Manuscript, Authenticity and "Evident Proofs" Against the Scottish Queen', in *English Manuscript Studies 1100–1700, Volume 15: Tudor Manuscripts, 1485–1603*, ed. A. S. G. Edwards. London: British Library, 2010, 198–217.

Skelton, R. A. and J. Summerson. *A Description of Maps and Architectural Drawings in the Collection Made by William Cecil, First Baron Burghley, Now at Hatfield House.* Oxford: Roxburghe Club, 1971.

Skinner, Quentin. *The Foundations of Modern Political Thought.* 2 volumes. Cambridge: Cambridge University Press, 1978.

Skura, Meredith. 'Dragon Fathers and Unnatural Children: Warring Generations in *King Lear* and its Sources', *Comparative Drama*, vol. 42, no. 2 (2008), 121–48.

Slights, Camille Wells. 'The Conscience of the King: *Henry V* and the Reformed Conscience', *Philological Quarterly*, vol. 80, no. 1 (2001), 37–55.

Sloan, Kim. *A New World: England's First View of America.* London: British Museum Press, 2007.

Small, John. 'Queen Mary at Jedburgh in 1566', *Proceedings of the Society of Antiquaries of Scotland*, vol. 3 (1881), 210–39.

Smith, Rosalind. 'Reading Mary Stuart's Casket Sonnets: Reception, Authorship and Early Modern Women's Writing', *Parergon*, vol. 29, no. 2 (2012), 149–73.

Sobecki, Sebastian I. 'Introduction: Edgar's Archipelago', in *The Sea and Englishness in the Middle Ages: Maritime Narratives, Identity and Culture*, ed. Sebastian I. Sobecki. Cambridge: D. S. Brewer, 2011. 1–30.

Spencer, Janet M. 'Princes, Pirates and Pigs: Criminalizing Wars of Conquest in *Henry V*', *SQ*, vol. 47, no. 2 (1996), 160–77.

Stevens, Andrea. *Inventions of the Skin: The Painted Body in Early English Drama, 1400–1642.* Edinburgh: Edinburgh University Press, 2013.

Stewart, Alan. *The Cradle King: A Life of James VI and I*. London: Chatto and Windus, 2003.

Strong, Roy. *Hans Eworth: A Tudor Artist and His Circle*. Leicester: Museums and Art Gallery, 1966.

Gloriana: The Portraits of Queen Elizabeth I. London: Thames and Hudson, 1987.

Sullivan, Garrett. *The Drama of Landscape: Land, Property, and Social Relations on the Early Modern Stage*. Stanford, CA: Stanford University Press, 1998.

Summerson, Henry. 'Tudor Antiquaries and the *Vita Ædwardi* Regis', *Anglo-Saxon England*, vol. 38 (2009), 157–84.

Sumption, Jonathan. *The Hundred Years War, Volume I, Trial by Battle*. 4 volumes. London: Faber and Faber, 1990.

Taylor, A. B. *Alexander Lindsay: A Rutter of the Scottish Seas Circa 1540*. London: National Maritime Museum, 1980.

Taylor, E. G. R. 'A Letter Dated 1577 from Mercator to John Dee', *Imago Mundi*, vol. 13, no. 1 (1956), 56–68.

Taylor, Gary. 'Monopolies, Show Trials, Disaster and Invasion', in *The Division of the Kingdoms: Shakespeare's Two Versions of King Lear*, eds. Gary Taylor and Michael Warren. Oxford: Clarendon Press, 1983. 75–119.

Thirsk, Joan. *Economic Policy and Projects: The Development of a Consumer Society in Early Modern England*. Oxford: Clarendon Press, 1978.

Thompson, Katherine P. 'All Things to All Men: Mary Queen of Scots and the Scottish Civil Wars 1568-73', *Journal of the Sydney Society for Scottish History*, vol. 9 (2001), 1–74.

Thornton, David E. 'Edgar and the Eight Kings, AD 973: *textus et dramatis personae*', *Early Medieval Europe*, vol. 10, no. 1 (2001), 49–79.

Trevor-Roper, Hugh. *The Invention of Scotland: Myth and History*. New Haven and London: Yale University Press, 2008.

Tyacke, Sarah and John Huddy. *Christopher Saxton and Tudor Map-Making*. London: British Library, 1980.

Van Es, Bart. *Spenser's Forms of History*. Oxford: Clarendon Press, 2002.

Verweij, Sebastiaan. *The Literary Culture of Early Modern Scotland: Manuscript Production and Transmission, 1560–1625*. Oxford: Oxford University Press, 2016.

Vine, Angus. *In Defiance of Time: Antiquarian Writing in Early Modern England*. Oxford: Oxford University Press, 2010.

'Copiousness, Conjecture and Collaboration in William Camden's *Britannia*', *Renaissance Studies*, vol. 28, no. 2 (2014), 225–41.

Warren, Christopher N. *Literature and the Law of Nations, 1580–1680*. Oxford: Oxford University Press, 2015.

Webb, Claire. 'The "Gude Regent"? A Diplomatic Perspective upon the Earl of Moray, Mary, Queen of Scots and the Scottish Regency, 1567–1570'. Unpublished PhD thesis, University of St. Andrews, 2008.

Whittington, Leah. *Renaissance Suppliants: Poetry, Antiquity, Reconciliation*. Oxford: Oxford University Press, 2016.

Whyte, Christopher. 'Bakhtin at Christ's Kirk: Carnival and the Scottish Renaissance', *Studies in Scottish Literature*, vol. 28, no. 1 (1993), 178–203.

Williamson, Arthur. *Scottish National Consciousness in the Age of James VI: The Apocalypse, the Union and the Shaping of Scotland's Public Culture.* Edinburgh: John Donald Publishers, 1979.

'Scotland, Antichrist and the Invention of Great Britain', in *New Perspectives on the Politics and Culture of Early Modern England*, eds. John Dwyer, Roger Mason and Alexander Murdoch. Edinburgh: John Donald, 1982. 34–58.

'The Edwardian Moment', in Williamson, *'The Nation Epidemicall': Scotland and the Rise of Social Theory*, forthcoming.

Willson, David Harris. *King James VI and I*. London: Jonathan Cape, 1956.

Wingfield, Emily. *The Trojan Legend in Medieval Scottish Literature*. Cambridge: D. S. Brewer, 2014.

Winston, Jessica. 'Expanding the Political Nation: *Gorboduc* at the Inns of Court and Succession Revisited', *Early Theatre*, vol. 8, no. 1 (2005), 11–34.

Womack, Peter. 'Imagining Communities: Theatres and the English Nation in the Sixteenth Century', in *Culture and History, 1350–1600: Essays on English Communities, Identities and Writing*. London: Harvester, 1992. 91–145.

Woolf, Alex. *From Pictland to Alba, 789–1070*. Edinburgh: Edinburgh University Press, 2007.

Wormald, Jenny. *Mary Queen of Scots: A Study in Failure*. London: George Phillip, 1988.

Yates, Frances A. *Ideas and Ideals in the North European Renaissance, Volume III of Collected Essays*, eds. J. N. Hillgarth and J. B. Trapp. London: Routledge, 1984.

Zurcher, Andrew. *Spenser's Legal Language: Law and Poetry in Early Modern England*. Woodbridge: D. S. Brewer, 2007.

Index

Aethelstan, 37
Africa, 221, 243
  in Claudian's poetry, 241
Agincourt, 192, 193, 198, 218
Albanact, 15, 35, 113, 156, 163, 164, 248, 253
Albania. *See* Albany
Albany (Scotland), 15, 227, 229, 245, 248, 251, 253,
  258, 270
Albany, Robert duke of, 199
Alexander III of Scotland, 15, 38
Algonquian peoples, 237
Anglo-Saxon scholarship, 72, 74, 85
ante-nati, 158
Argyll, earl of, 65, 119, 131, 137
  defects to Mary, 141
Ariosto, Ludovico, 79

Bacon, Francis, 260
Bakhtin, Mikhail, 274, 275
Bale, John, 84
Balliol, John, 198
Bannockburn, Battle of, 87, 198, 211, 212
Barbour, John
  Bruce, 120
Beaton, Cardinal David, 32, 48
Bede, 224, 234
Bellenden, John
  translator of Hector Boece, 284
  translator of Livy, 285
Berwick, 50, 52, 58, 60, 137, 140, 197, 203
black masquerade, 221
Blind Harry
  Wallace, 120
Blyth, Lauderdale
  spoiled by English forces, 146
Boece, Hector, 237, 239
  claims for antiquity of Picts and Scots, 19, 229
  on Macbeth, 285
  Scotorum Historia, 18, 93, 201, 263, 284, 285
Boiastuau, Pierre
  Histoires Tragiques, 213

Bothwell, James Hepburn, earl of, 138
  Lieutenant Warden of the Borders, 149
Boulogne, Treaty of (1550), 63, 67
Bower, Walter, 19
  Scotichronicon, 18, 201
Brende, Sir John, 8, 27, 50, 52, 89
  Late Expedition in Scotlande, 20
Brexit, 188
Britannia, 17, 220, 221, 242, 243, 244
  image of, 183
  in Claudian's poetry, 241
British history, neo-Galfridian, 14–21, 24, 73, 154,
  161, 174, 185, 238, 248
Britishness
  anachronistic use of, 155
Britons, 232, 233, 241, 242
  as Gauls, 232, 233
  distinguished from Picts by Buchanan, 242
  identified with Picts by Camden, 227, 233, 234,
    238, 242, 243
Broughty Craig, 8, 10, 47, 58, 59, 64, 65, 66,
  67
Brunaburgh, Battle of (937), 38
Brutus, 6, 15, 16, 17, 24, 31, 41, 68, 70, 71, 72,
  73, 77, 85, 96, 98, 101, 134, 154, 222,
  224, 226, 230, 231, 238, 239, 250, 251,
  253, 270
  as divider of Britain, 16, 36, 161, 223, 229,
    238, 248
  as founder of Britain, 3, 14, 37, 71, 156, 239
Buchanan, George, 91, 121, 143, 181, 237
  chorography of Scotland, 231
  Detectio (Detectioun), 135, 149–51, 152
  Dialogue On the Law of Kingship among the
    Scots (*De iure regni apud Scotos Dialogos*),
    4, 116–17, 125, 135
  Genethliacon, 128
  History of Scotland (*Rerum Scoticarum
    Historia*), 124, 223, 230–3
  linguistic ethnography of Britain, 232–3
  writing contrasted with Maitlands', 122

Caesar, Julius, 231, 232
Calvin's Case, 175, 186
Camber, 15, 113, 248
Cambria (Wales), 15, 229
Camden, William, 91, 237
  Britannia, 4, 7, 12, 72, 100, 221, 222, 223, 224, 226, 236, 242
  follows Buchanan, 230, 233–5
  discredits Buchanan, 233
  Marriage of Thame and Isis (*De Connubio Tamae et Isis*), 78, 100–1, 108, 239
Carey, Henry, Lord Hunsdon, 203
  annotates Froissart, 197
  governor of Berwick, 197
  invasion of Scotland, 119, 145, 197
  Shakespeare's patron, 119, 197
cartography
  in literary criticism, 75, 246, 268–71
Castile
  union with Portugal, 179
Cecil, William, Lord Burghley, 10, 43, 77, 119, 216
  anti-Marian propaganda, 137, 138–41, 143
  belief in English title to Scotland, 85, 121, 124, 136, 154, 166, 281
  involvement in 1540s war, 11, 45, 50
  policy of coastal security, 11, 84–5, 89, 239
  uses Nowell's maps, 86
Chaloner, Thomas, 45, 51
Charles I, 154
Chartier, Alain
  Quadrilogue Invectif, 193
chorography, 72, 73, 76, 77, 91, 239
Christis Kirk on the Grene, 133
Cicero, Marcus Tullius, 18
Claudian, 235
  De bello Getico, 236
  panegyric of Honorius, 236
  annotated by Jonson, 241
Clinton, Admiral, 64, 65
Clyde, river, 79, 113, 114, 231, 232
Confederate Lords, 118, 138, 141
Congregation, Lords of, 132, 133
Cope, Anthony, 29
Cousin, Jean the Elder, 106
Craig, Sir Thomas, 71, 115, 157, 165, 278, 291
  A Treatise on the Union of the Kingdoms of Britain (*De unione regum Britanniae*), 69–71
Cromwell, Thomas, 29

Darnley, Henry, Lord, 119, 150
  murder of, 116, 135, 137
David II of Scotland, 198, 207
de Bry, Theodore, 237
De natis ultra mare, statute (1351), 160, 167

Dee, John, 21, 72, 74, 89, 96, 104, 109, 156, 181, 239, 262, 269, 277
  advocate of English sea empire, 89–90, 92–5
  Limits of the British Empire (*Brytanici Imperii Limites*), 74, 92
  Memorials pertayning to . . . Navigation, 92, 107
  praises King Edgar, 182
  THALATTOKRATIA BRETTANIKI, 92
Delaune, Étienne, 106
Delitiae Poetarum Scotorum, 125
Denmark
  Scotland's trade with, 28
  Scotland's ally, 26
Digges, Thomas, 96, 110
Discourse of Naturalisation, 159, 179, 180, 184
Diurnall of Occurents, 131, 137
division of Britain, legend of, 5, 14, 15, 249, 252, 267
Dolce, Lodovico
  Giocasta, 258, 260
Douglas, Archibald, earl of, 199
Drayton, Michael, 77, 98
  Poly-Olbion, 76, 155
Drummond, William, 240
Drury, Sir William
  governor of Berwick, 137, 140
Dudley, John, earl of Warwick, 59, 67, 88
Dudley, Sir Andrew, 59
Dunbar, burning of (1544), 8, 28
Dunbar, William
  in Maitland Folio, 133
Dundee, 8, 10, 60, 64, 65

East Indies, 179
Edinburgh, 49, 59, 60, 86, 147
  Castle, 27
  sack of, 26
Edward I, 15, 17, 18, 38, 87, 90, 93, 120, 154, 163, 164, 198, 211
  invasion of Scotland, 6
  rewrites Geoffrey of Monmouth, 15
Edward II, 42, 198, 211
Edward III, 42, 160, 163, 197, 206–8
Edward the Confessor, 181, 283
  reign compared with Macbeth's, 284
  symbol of ancient constitution, 283, 290
Edward VI, 20, 26, 43, 63, 177, 178, 238, 248
  invasion of Scotland, 6
Elder, John, 28, 31, 39
Elizabeth I, 74
  Ditchley portrait, 1–2, 75
  refuses audience with Mary, 142
Empson, William
  ambiguity in *Macbeth*, 281
England as island, 74–6

Epitome, An (1548), 21, 99, 165, 191, 200, 248, 249, 283
Euripides, 251
  Medea, 48
  Phoenissae, 258, 260, 273

Famous Victories of Henry the Fifth, 196, 208
Ferrars, George, 45, 51
Ferrerio, Giovanni, 88
Flanders
  Scotland's trade with, 28
Fordun, John of
  Chronicle of the Scottish Nation, 17, 18, 287–8, 290
foreign birth, disability of, 160, 174
Forth, river, 59, 60, 64, 65, 79, 113, 114, 141, 231, 232
Fowler, William, 133
France
  Scotland's trade with, 28
  Scots liberties in, 176, 178, 179, 180
Franco-Scots alliance, 26, 145, 189, 191, 193, 195, 196, 201, 202, 204, 218
Freiris of Berwick, The, 133
Froissart, Jean, 197, 207
Fulbecke, William, 260

Gaius
  Institutes, 141
Gamboa, Sir Pedro de, 50
Gascoigne, George
  Jocasta, 250, 255, 258–60, 273, 274
  Supposes, 259
Gathelus
  legendary Greek prince, 18, 222, 230, 231
Gaythelos. *See* Gathelus
Geoffrey of Monmouth, 20, 90, 178, 226, 228, 231, 249, 262, 276
  History of the Kings of Britain (*Historia Regum Britanniae*), 6, 13, 14, 17, 253
Gheeraerts, Marcus, the Younger, 1, 2
Gonson, William, 62
Gorboduc, 6, 248, 249, 254, 255
  tragedy of, 249, 250, 251, 256–8, 272, 274
Grafton, Richard, 21, 45, 50, 198
Great Britain, empire of, 43, 57, 70, 156, 238, 248
Greene, Robert
  Friar Bacon and Friar Bungay, 196, 208–10, 218

Haddington, 10, 67
  siege of, 130–1
Hakluyt, Richard, 74, 269
  praises King Edgar, 182
  Principal Navigations, 72, 156
Hales, John, 167, 173

Hall, Edmund
  Chronicle, 20, 194, 197, 198, 202
Hamilton, James, earl of Arran, 29, 44, 88
Hardyng, John
  Chronicle, 16, 21, 90, 165, 250
  forged homages, 16, 38, 42, 164
Harriot, Thomas
  Briefe and True Report of . . . Virginia, 235, 237
Harrison, William, 72, 91, 223, 230, 239
  Historical Description of the Iland of Britaine, 21, 78, 92, 95–9, 228, 230
Henri II of France, 10, 63
  winning of Calais, 132
Henrisoun, James, 39, 44–5, 290
  Exhortation to the Scotts, 45, 49
Henry IV, 134
  takes James I prisoner, 200
Henry V, 163, 191, 203
Henry VI, 35
Henry VIII, 43, 73, 195
  conduct of war, 26–9
  Declaration, 16, 26, 30, 34, 49, 90, 93, 165, 195, 198, 248
  invasion of Scotland, 6
Hesiod, 112
Highlanders, 131
Holinshed, Raphael, 78
  Chronicles, 7, 20, 21, 54, 69, 95, 156, 194, 197, 229, 239, 247, 250, 283, 285
  on Henry V, 197–203
  on Edward the Confessor, 284
  on Macbeth, 284
Holyrood, Palace of, 28
homage
  ceremony of, 164, 172
  constitutional allegory of, 172–4
  English manipulation of, 164–5
  performed by Scottish kings for English lands, 283
Hotspur (Henry Percy), 199
Hoveden, Roger, 164
Hughes, Thomas, 260
Hundred Years War, the, 190, 197, 215, 279
Huntly, George Gordon, earl of, 56, 119, 137

Inchcolm, 8, 58, 59, 64, 65, 66, 67
invention, rhetorical
  circumstances, 149
  incrementum, 256, 257
  metalepsis, 47, 280
  metaphor, 46–7
  metaphorical plot, 196
  prosopopoeia, 289
Isadore of Seville
  Etymology, 236

James I of Scotland, 35, 191
  prisoner to Henry V, 192
James IV of Scotland, 221
James Stewart, earl of Moray, 118, 138, 141
  assassination of, 119
  English support of, 119
James V of Scotland, 29, 41, 88, 285
James VI and I, 190, 191, 197, 226, 240, 279
  accession to English throne, 1, 11, 69, 155
  baptism at Stirling, 128
  coronation as James VI, 141
Jedburgh, 29, 149
Jonson, Ben
  annotated Claudian, 240
  owned Buchanan's *Rerum Scoticarum
    Historia*, 240
  The Devil Is an Ass, 188
  The Masque of Blackness, 4, 221, 222, 225–6, 240
Justinian
  Digest, 141

Kantorowicz, Ernst, 154, 162
Kelso Abbey
  destruction of, 28
Kenneth McAlpin (Cinaed mac Alpín), 224
King Arthur, 6, 14, 17, 24, 71, 72, 73, 93, 94, 101,
    164, 224, 239, 250, 253
  Caerleon coronation, 17
  proof of English sea empire, 73–4
  subdues Scots and Picts, 17, 93, 228, 262
King Edgar, 178, 283
  icon of English sea-sovereignty over Scotland,
    181–4, 277
King John, 164
King's Evil, the, 284
King's Men, the
  English playing company, 247, 251
King's Party, the, 118, 138, 141, 146, 152
King's Two Bodies, doctrine of, 4, 7, 154, 155, 159,
    161, 162, 170, 173, 175, 185
Kinwelmarsh, Francis
  Jocasta, 250, 258, 273
knees
  associated with potency, 172
Knox, John, 126

Lamb, William
  Ane Resonyng, 38–43, 195
Lambarde, William, 72, 74, 85
Lauder, George, 143
law of nations, *ius gentium*, 39
  just war, 193, 194
  as nation-defining, 195
law of persons, free and unfree, 141, 159
  subject and alien, 159

Le Moyne, Jacques, 237
Lebor Gabála Érenn (Book of the Takings of
    Ireland), 17
Lee, Sir Richard, 50
Leir, 6, 248, 249, 250, 253
Leith, 26, 59, 65
Lekpreuik, Robert, 121, 140
Leland, John, 16, 22, 24, 62, 72, 223, 239
  Assertio inclytissimi Arturi Regis Britanniae, 73
  Cygnea Cantio, 20, 28, 54, 61, 78, 83–4, 85, 239
  early river poetry, 100
  Genethliacon, 20, 85
Lennox, earl of, 145, 147
Lethington House
  Maitland family house
    confiscation of, 147
Lhoegria. *See* Logres (England)
Lily, George
  map of Scotland, 114
Lindsay, David, 32, 48
  Tragedie of the Cardinall, 32–4
Livy, 231
Livy (Titus Livius), 18, 29
  on Tarquin the Proud, 285
Llwyd, Humphrey, 72, 223, 226, 229, 230, 232,
    233, 239
  The Breviary of Britain (*Commentarioli
    Britannicae descriptionis fragmentum*),
    228, 229, 230
Locrine, 15, 113, 156, 163, 164, 239, 248
  as overlord of Albany, 16, 37, 163, 248
Logres (England), 15, 229, 248
Luttrell, Sir John, 59–68
  Eworth portrait, 63–4
Lyndsay, Alexander
  rutter, 87, 88

Maccabeus. *See* Macbeth, 285
Magna Carta, 160, 161, 186, 187
Mair, John
  History of Greater Britain (*Historia Maioris
    Britannia*), 93, 201
Maitland family, of Lethington, 117
Maitland Folio, 121, 132, 133–4
Maitland Quarto, 121, 123, 132–3, 144–8
Maitland, John
  Lord Chancellor of Scotland, 143
  poems celebrating release from prison,
    133
  poetry, 152
  secretary to James VI, 125, 133
Maitland, Marie
  mother of poet George Lauder, 143
  poet, 133
  scribe of Maitland Quarto, 132

Maitland, Sir Richard, 290
  collector of Scots poetry, 121
  Justice Clerk for the Borders, 152
  poetry of, 4, 121, 144–8, 291
  Practiques, 147
Maitland, Thomas, 117, 123, 125–32, 143
  deposer then supporter of Mary Queen of
    Scots, 126
  early death of, 127
  Lethington House (*Domus Ledingtona*), 129–31
  pasquinade attributed to, 126
  The Coronation of James VI, King of Scots
    (*Jacobi VI, Scotorum Regis Inauguratio*),
    126, 128
Maitland, William, 123, 138, 141, 145
  deposer then supporter of Mary Queen of
    Scots, 123–4
  secretary to Mary of Guise, 125
  secretary to Mary Queen of Scots, 125, 149
Malory, Thomas, 79, 261
Margaret Tudor, 221
Marie de France
  Lanval, 228
Marlowe, Christopher, 198
  Edward II, 211
Mary of Guise, 66, 88, 119, 132, 133, 149, 203
Mary Queen of Scots, 26, 29, 160, 167, 174, 203
  arrival in Scotland, 132
  deposition of, 118, 129
  imprisonment in Lochleven, 140
  marriage to Bothwell, 140
  marriage to Dauphin, 10, 68, 132, 148
  royal entry into Edinburgh, 221
  trial of, 119
Melun, siege of, 201
Mercator, Gerard, 94
Minos, legendary king of Crete, 104
Mirror for Magistrates, The, 33, 250
Misfortunes of Arthur, The, 250, 251, 255, 260–5,
  267, 274
Modred, 254, 263
  variant genealogies of, 261–3
Montgomerie, Alexander, 133
More, Elen, 221
myth of English indifference to Scotland, 2, 4,
  12, 281

national consciousness, English, 76
national consciousness, Scottish, 42, 121, 124
navy, English, 61
Nedham, Marchamont, 183
Neville's Cross, Battle of (1346), 207
Nicolay, Nicolas de
  map of Scotland, 87–9
Northampton, Treaty of (1328), 37, 42

Northern Rising, the, 119, 132, 145
Norton, Thomas, 249
Nowell, Laurence, 72, 85, 239
  founder of Anglo-Saxon studies, 85
  friendship with Lambarde, 85
  map of Scotland, 86, 89
  reading Leland, 85

Otterburn, Adam, Provost of Edinburgh, 27,
  44, 49
Ovid
  Metamorphoses, 225

Paget, William, 9, 28, 67
Painter, William
  Palace of Pleasure, 213
Paris, Matthew, 163
Patten, William, 45
  The Expedition into Scotland, 50, 52–3, 59
Peblis to the Play, 133
Peele, George
  Arraygnement of Paris, 74
Perth (St John's Town), 60, 65
Philip II of Spain, 179
Philip VI of France, 207
Picts, 7, 18, 222, 235, 236, 237
  as Gauls, 232
  identified with Britons, 223, 224, 227
  Scythian origin in Bede, 234
  shared history with Scots, 19, 99, 227, 228, 229,
    230, 253
Piggott, Sir Christopher, 291
Pinkie, Battle of (1547), 8, 48, 50, 53, 59, 64,
  193
  English atrocity, 54–6
plat, 24–5, 34, 46, 269
Plowden, Edmund, 4, 7, 154, 175, 238
  Reports, 162, 169
  Sir John Constable's Case, 110
  Treatise on the Succession (1567), 159, 161–74
Pope Boniface VIII, 15, 17, 90, 93
post-nati, 158, 175
propaganda, English anti-Marian, 121
Protector Somerset, 9, 42, 66, 67, 131, 177, 181,
  198, 248, *See* also Seymour, Edward Earl
  of Hertford
  amphibious war strategy, 46, 58–61
  Epistle, 20
  Proclamation, 49

Queen Anne, 222, 243
Queen's Party, the
  supporters of Mary Queen of Scots, 118
Queen's Men, the
  English playing company, 208

Reformation, Scottish, 9
'Ring of the Roy Robert, The', 134
river poetry, 77, 83, 91
Robert III of Scotland, 199
    death on news of son's capture, 200
    defiance of Henry IV, 134, 200
Robert the Bruce, 198, 202

Sackville, Thomas, 249
Sandys, Sir Edwin, 186, 187
Savile, Sir Henry, 157, 159
    Historical Collections (1604), 175, 178
Savile, Thomas
    letter to Camden, 233
Saxton, Christopher, 76
    county maps, 1, 77, 85, 86, 270
    county maps of, 270
Scone, stone of, 18
Scot
    metonomy for Scotland, king of Scots, 195,
        204–5, 216–18, 279
Scota
    legendary Egyptian princess, 18, 230
Scots
    as Gauls, 232
Scott, Sir Walter
    source of name 'Rough Wooings', 53
Scottish borders, devastation of (1545), 8, 22–4
Scottish-Dutch trade, 40
Scythians
    Scots as, 98, 99, 113
sea sovereignty, English claims, 72, 89, 178
Selden, John
    Mare Clausum, 183
Selve, Odet de, 45, 57
Sempill, Robert, 121, 140
Seneca, Lucius Annaeus
    Apocolocyntosis, 233
    Oedipus, 266
    Phoenissae/Thebais, 256, 257, 258, 261, 266, 272,
        273, 275
Seymour, Edward, earl of Hertford, 24, 25, 43, 54,
        60, *See* also Protector Somerset
Shakespeare, William
    1 Henry IV, 196, 199
    2 Henry IV, 196
    Cymbeline, 247
    Henry V, 6, 48, 188, 196, 197
        four captains scene, 189–90
        imagining nationhood in, 192–3
        lessons learned from *Edward III*, 212–19
    King Lear, 4, 5, 7, 19, 245–7, 254–5,
        266–7
        Oedipal Senecanism of, 271–5
    Macbeth, 4, 19, 59, 279–90

Richard II, 75
The Taming of the Shrew, 259
skin, painted or tattooed, 234–6
Smith, Sir Thomas, 10, 43, 67, 77
    *Discourse of the Commonweal of This Realm of
        England*, 9
    distributes anti-Marian propaganda in
        France, 143
    involvement in 1540s war, 11, 45
Solway Moss, Battle of, 29
Sophocles, 251
Speed, John
    Theatre of the Empire of Great Britaine, 237
Spelman, Sir Henry, 158, 177, 187, 252, 277, 283
    Of the Union (1604), 175, 178, 180, 278
Spenser, Edmund, 21, 91
    A View of the Present State of Ireland, 91, 92, 98
    Epithalamion Thamesis, 78, 95, 100
    Faerie Queene, The, 4, 6, 71–2, 156, 250, 262
        legend of Chastity, 72, 78, 79–82, 103–8
        Thames and Medway marriage, 78, 102,
            107–9, 113–14
    law of shipwreck, 109
    letter to Harvey, 78, 95
    nations of Britain, 91–2
St Andrews, 18, 27, 89
St Brendan, 17
St Congal, 17
Stewart, James, earl of Moray, 119, 127, 136,
        137, 140
Stow, John
    Annals, 284
sub-nationhood, Scottish, 186, 191
Sussex, earl of, 145, 197

Tacitus, 18, 232, 235
    Agricola, 231
Tay, 60, 65, 66
Tay, river, 47, 59, 60, 64, 65, 66, 79, 113,
        114
Thomas, William, 36
Thucydides, 104
Timuca peoples, 237
trade, anti-Scots English arguments, 179–81
tragedy, Senecan, 247, 252, 255, 256, 264, 266
    British history as, 250, 252
Treaty of Greenwich, 29
trivialisation strategies, 52, 221
Troynovant, 18, 61, 83, 250
True Chronicle Historie of King Leir, The, 267
Tunstall, Cuthbert, 36, 42

Ulster, colonisation of, 190
Union debate, 155, 158, 247, 249, 276, 278
    role in English literary criticism, 155

Vairement, Richard (Veremundus), 17, 18
Virgil
   Aeneid, 112, 178
   Ciris, 103–5
Vergil, Polydore, 42, 163

Walsingham, Thomas, 163
war of Anglo-Scots historiography, 6, 18
Warner, William
   Albion's England, 250
Watson, Christopher
   Hystories of Polybius, 203
Wedderburn, Robert, 290
   Complaynt of Scotland, 193

West Indies, 179
White, John, 237
whiteness
   literary, 244
Wilford, Sir James, 131
William the Lion, king of Scotland, 164
Wilson, Thomas, 136, 142
Wolfe, Reginald, 20, 21
world upside-down, 27, 51
Wyatt, Thomas, 62
Wyndham, Thomas, 64
Wyntoun, Andrew of, 18, 134

Yelverton, Christopher, 260